BAR BRITISH SERIES 677, 2022
ARCHAEOLOGY OF ROMAN BRITAIN
VOLUME 9

FACING THE ENEMY?

A GIS Study of 1st Century Roman Fortifications in the Scottish Landscape

Andrew Tibbs

Published in 2022 by
BAR Publishing, Oxford, UK

BAR British Series 677

Archaeology of Roman Britain, volume 9
Facing the Enemy?

ISBN 978 1 4073 6015 7 paperback
ISBN 978 1 4073 6016 4 e-format

DOI https://doi.org/10.30861/9781407360157
A catalogue record for this book is available from the British Library

© Andrew Tibbs 2022

COVER IMAGE *LiDAR image of Inchtuthil Legionary fortress, Perthshire.*

The Author's moral rights under the 1988 UK Copyright,
Designs and Patents Act are hereby expressly asserted.

All rights reserved. No part of this work may be copied, reproduced, stored, sold, distributed, scanned, saved in any form of digital format or transmitted in any form digitally, without the written permission of the Publisher.

Links to third party websites are provided by BAR Publishing in good faith and for information only. BAR Publishing disclaims any responsibility for the materials contained in any third party website referenced in this work.

BAR titles are available from:

BAR Publishing
122 Banbury Rd, Oxford, OX2 7BP, UK
info@barpublishing.com
www.barpublishing.com

ARCHAEOLOGY OF ROMAN BRITAIN
A specialist sub-series of the BAR British Series

SERIES EDITORS
Edward Biddulph (Oxford Archaeology),

Martin Pitts (Exeter University)

Roman Britain presents a dynamic and exciting field of study, with an abundance of data amenable to multi-disciplinary approaches, 'big data' studies, the application of theoretical approaches, and a variety of visually stimulating artefacts and reconstructions that speak to our own age in a remarkably direct way. This series promotes research relating to the Roman province of Britannia, spanning a broad period from the late Iron Age to post-Roman Britain (roughly from the 1st century BC to the 5th century AD), as well as encompassing studies that examine the interaction between the British Isles, the nearby Continent, and other parts of the connected Roman empire.

If you would like to submit a proposal for the Archaeology of Roman Britain series, please contact editor@barpublishing.com

EDITORIAL ADVISORY BOARD

Rob Collins, Newcastle University

Andrew Gardner, University College London

James Gerrard, Newcastle University

Rebecca Gowland, Durham University

Birgitta Hoffmann, Independent Researcher

John Pearce, King's College London

Alex Smith, Headland Archaeology

Stephen Rippon, Exeter University

Fiona Seeley, MOLA

Ellen Swift, Kent University

Lacey Wallace, Lincoln University

Philippa Walton, University of Reading

Sadie Watson, MOLA

Jake Weekes, Canterbury Archaeological Trust

TITLES IN THE ARCHAEOLOGY OF ROMAN BRITAIN SUBSERIES

The Clayton Collection
An archaeological appraisal of a 19th century collection of Roman artefacts from Hadrian's Wall
Frances McIntosh
BAR British Series 646 | 2019   Volume 1

Worcester Magistrates Court
Excavation of Romano-British homes and industry at Castle Street
Andy Boucher
BAR British Series 658 | 2020   Volume 2

London's Roman Tools
Craft, agriculture and experience in an ancient city
Owen Humphreys
BAR British Series 663 | 2021   Volume 3

Belonging and Belongings
Portable artefacts and identity in the civitas of the Iceni
Natasha Harlow
BAR British Series 664 | 2021   Volume 4

On the Edge of Empire
Society in the south-west of England during the first century BC to fifth century AD
Siân Alyce Thomas
BAR British Series 667 | 2021   Volume 5

Roman Rural Settlement in Wales and the Marches
Approaches to settlement and material culture through big data
Leah Reynolds
BAR British Series 670 | 2022   Volume 6

Dying Young
A Bioarchaeological Analysis of Child Health in Roman Britain
Anna Rohnbogner
BAR British Series 673 | 2022   Volume 7

The Rise and Decline of Druce Farm Roman Villa (60-650 CE)
Excavations 2012-2018
Lilian Ladle
BAR British Series 675 | 2022   Volume 8

Facing the Enemy?
A GIS Study of 1st Century Roman Fortifications in the Scottish Landscape
Andrew Tibbs
BAR British Series 676 | 2022   Volume 9

For more information, or to purchase these titles, please visit **www.barpublishing.com**

OF RELATED INTEREST

Visitor Experiences and Audiences for the Roman Frontiers
Developing good practice in presenting World Heritage
Edited by Nigel Mills
BAR International Series 3066 | 2021

Ad Vallum: Papers on the Roman Army and Frontiers in Celebration of Dr Brian Dobson
Edited by Adam Parker
BAR British Series 631 | 2017

Further Discoveries about the Surveying and Planning of Roman Roads in Northern Britain
A sequel to BAR 492
John Poulter
BAR British Series 598 | 2014

Roman and Native in the Central Scottish Borders
Allan Wilson
BAR British Series 519 | 2010

Surveying Roman Military Landscapes across Northern Britain
The planning of Roman Dere Street, Hadrian's Wall and the Vallum, and the Antonine Wall in Scotland
John Poulter with a supplementary report on the mapping of the Antonine Wall by Peter McKeague
BAR British Series 492 | 2009

Roman Military Objectives in Britain under the Flavian Emperors
Alison E. Grant
BAR British Series 440 | 2007

The Roman Frontier on the Gask Ridge: Perth and Kinross
An interim report on the Roman Gask Project 1995-2000
D.J. Woolliscroft with contributions from A.T. Croom, M.H. Davies, A.C. Finnegan, M.A. Hall, K.F. Hartley, B. Hoffmann, A.J. Hughes, N.J. Lockett and S. Ramsay
BAR British Series 335 | 2002

The Forts on Hadrian's Wall
David J. A. Taylor
BAR British Series 305 | 2000

For more information, or to purchase these titles, please visit **www.barpublishing.com**

To my parents, Mike and Sheana.
Thank you for the opportunities.

Acknowledgements

This monograph began as a PhD thesis, undertaken at Durham University, and there have been various people who have provided support and advice throughout its production. In particular, I would like to thank my supervisors, Professor Richard Hingley, and Dr Rob Witcher, along with my examiners Dr David Petts and Dr Rob Collins. Several academic, and Roman frontier colleagues have been supportive throughout this process, generously sharing their knowledge, and helping to inform and shape this research. My thanks go to Professor David Breeze, Erik Graafstal, Dr Rebecca Jones, and the late Professor C. Sebastian Sommer. A special thanks to Dr David Woolliscroft and Dr Birgitta Hoffmann who encouraged my research interests at the outset. I would also like to acknowledge the positive feedback from the Reviewers, as well as the advice and support from the team at British Archaeological Reports. In 2018, I was invited to the home of Janet Davies, widow of the late Roy Davies. Roy died over 40 years ago, at the age of 35, but had published several papers on the Roman army. Due to circumstances, Janet was giving away their extensive collection of books, and I was one beneficiary of this. Many of these have proved invaluable in this research. I am incredibly grateful to Janet for sharing this unique collection with me, and to my colleague Martha Stewart for introducing us.

I would also like to thank the following organisations who have provided financial support towards the costs of undertaking this research; The Robert Kiln Charitable Trust, the Tameia Trust, and the Gibson Graham Charitable Trust. I am also grateful to Professor Tim Burt and Professor Anne MacLarnon, both of Hatfield College, who, along with the Hatfield College Trust, gave additional financial assistance to undertake fieldwork opportunities which helped to inform the direction and findings of this research.

Finally, I have had encouragement and support from friends and family in pursuing this research. I would like to thank my parents for their support, along with that of my husband, Dr Paul Bennett whose patience and support has been unwavering, while his editorial and proofreading skills have been invaluable, and without whom, I could not have made this journey.

Table of Contents

List of figures xi

List of tables xv

Editorial Note xvii

Abbreviations xviii

Abstract xix

1. **Introduction** 1
   1.1. Aims and Objectives 3
   1.2. Method and Approach 4
   1.3. Research Limitations and Implications 5
   1.4. Summary 8

2. **Romans and Scottish Landscapes** 9
   2.1. An Early Frontier Zone? 10
   2.2. Historical Background 12
   2.3. Interpretation Influences 14
      2.3.1. Tacitus 14
      2.3.2. Richard of Cirencester 15
   2.4. Native and Roman Interaction 15
   2.5. Roman Military Infrastructure 17
      2.5.1. Other Structures 18
      2.5.2. Legionary Fortress 18
      2.5.3. Camps 19
      2.5.4. Forts 19
      2.5.5. Fortlets 20
      2.5.6. Towers 21
      2.5.7. Coastal Sites 21
      2.5.8. Road Networks 21
      2.5.9. Coastal and River Networks 25
   2.6. Interpretation Challenges 27
      2.6.1. Fortification Sequencing 28
      2.6.2. Fortification Dating 31
   2.7. Natural Environment 33
      2.7.1. Water 35
   2.8. Summary 36

3. **Data and Methods** 39
   3.1. Data Collection and Sources 39
      3.1.1. Roman Literary Texts 39
      3.1.2. Legacy and Site Data 40
      3.1.3. Mapping Data 40
   3.2. Analytical Methods 41
      3.2.1. Positioning: Defensive and Elevation 42
      3.2.2. Intervisibility: Viewpoints, Binary Viewsheds and Lines-Of-Sight 43
      3.2.3. Orientation 45
      3.2.4. Interconnectivity 47

4. **Location and Positioning** 51
   4.1. Classical Texts: Positioning 51

	4.2.	Positioning: Spatial Analysis	52
	4.3.	Analysis: Defensive Topography	53
	4.4.	Analysis: Site Elevation	57
	4.5.	Analysis: Binary Viewsheds	57
	4.6.	Summary	59

5. Intervisibility 63
    5.1. Roman Signalling 63
    5.2. Analysis: Line-Of-Sight (Signalling) 65
        5.2.1. Towers on the Gask Ridge 67
        5.2.2. Towers in Southern Scotland 74
    5.3. Summary 76

6. Orientation 79
    6.1. Classical Texts: Orientation 79
    6.2. Orientation: Recent Studies 82
    6.3. Analysis: Fortification Orientation 82
    6.4. Analysis: Directions that Fortifications Face 93
    6.5. Summary 100

7. Interconnectivity 103
    7.1. Road Networks 103
    7.2. River Networks 105
    7.3. Classical Texts: Waterways 106
    7.4. The Antiquarian Account 106
    7.5. Analysis: Fortifications and Roads 106
    7.6. Analysis: Coastal and River Networks 107
    7.7. Analysis: River Crossings 108
    7.8. Scotland's River Networks 108
        7.8.1. River Tweed 108
        7.8.2. Firth of Forth 110
        7.8.3. Firth of Tay 113
        7.8.4. Northeast and Moray Firth 116
        7.8.5. Firth of Clyde 118
        7.8.6. Southwest and Solway Firth 120
    7.9. Summary 122

8. Discussion 127
    8.1. Roman Control of Scottish Landscapes 128
    8.2. Role of 'Temporary Encampments' 128
    8.3. Intervisibility And Signalling: Testing a Methodology 130
    8.4. Profiling Fortification Sites 130
    8.5. Roman Military Strategies in Scotland 132
    8.6. Profiling Fortifications Beyond Flavian Scotland 133
    8.7. Research Opportunities 134
        8.7.1. Fortifications Dating and Sequencing 134
        8.7.2. The Indigenous Population 134
        8.7.3. Signalling 135
        8.7.4. Road Network 135
        8.7.5. Water Levels 135

9. Conclusion 137

Bibliography 139
Appendix One: Flavian Sites 153
Appendix Two: Site Data 157
Index of Main Sites 163

List of figures

Figure 1.1. Flavian fortification sites covered in the text 6

Figure 2.1. Roman sites (multiple periods) on the coast or within tidal ranges on firths and rivers 22

Figure 2.2. Roman roads in Scotland 24

Figure 2.3. Possible Roman road, Cauldhame Wood, Kirriemuir (September 2019) 24

Figure 2.4. Main firths and rivers around Scotland highlighted in the text 25

Figure 2.5. Unconfirmed and undated fortifications in Scotland. Data from Canmore 29

Figure 2.6. Methods used to assign a date to Flavian fortifications 32

Figure 2.7. Different camp gates/entrances found in Scotland 32

Figure 2.8. LiDAR image of Inchtuthil legionary showing existing rivers and possible channels 36

Figure 3.1. Outline of defences and principia of Inchtuthil legionary fortress showing direction of orientation 42

Figure 3.2. Defensive topography of Inchtuthil legionary fortress with viewpoints 43

Figure 3.3. Elevation analysis of the landscape surrounding Barochan fort 44

Figure 3.4. Single viewpoint where only one corner of the defences is known 45

Figure 3.5. Model of how viewpoints for viewshed analysis are used 46

Figure 3.6. Extent of binary viewshed analysis (shaded area) from Inchtuthil legionary fortress 46

Figure 3.7. Line of sight analysis from Inchtuthil legionary fortress to nearby fortifications 47

Figure 3.8. Layout of a typical Roman fort in Northern Britain 48

Figure 3.9. Orientation of Flavian fortifications centred on Inchtuthil legionary 48

Figure 3.10. Degree range for each cardinal point 49

Figure 4.1. Topographical areas where Flavian fortifications are located 54

Figure 4.2. The camp at Carlops Spittal positioned against steep hills 54

Figure 4.3. Example of a camp (Muiryfold) located on a slope 55

Figure 4.4. Example of a fort (Fendoch) located on a hill 56

Figure 4.5. Binary viewshed (shaded area) from Glenlochar fort 58

Figure 4.6. Binary viewshed (shaded area) from Ardoch fort 58

Figure 4.7. Binary viewshed (shaded area) from Gatehouse of Fleet fortlet 59

Figure 4.8. Binary viewshed (shaded area) from Abernethy camp 60

Figure 4.9. Binary viewshed (shaded area) from Normandykes camp 60

Figure 5.1. Line of sight analysis from Dunning camp to nearby Gask Ridge towers 65

Figure 5.2. Binary viewshed (shaded area) from Dunning camp 66

Figure 5.3. Line of sight between the camps of Muiryfold and Auchinhove 67

Figure 5.4. Line of sight between Castledykes fort, Bankhead fortlet and Bankhead II camp 68

Figure 5.5. Line of sight between Castledykes camp and Bankhead II camp 68

Figure 5.6. Line of sight between the various Dalswinton sites and the camp at Fourmerkland 69

Figure 5.7. Elevation analysis of fortifications on the Gask Ridge 69

Figure 5.8. Signalling capacity on the southern section of the Gask Ridge 70

Figure 5.9. Signalling capacity on the western section of the Gask Ridge... 70

Figure 5.10. Signalling capacity on the central section of the Gask Ridge 71

Figure 5.11. Signalling capacity on the eastern section of the Gask Ridge 71

Figure 5.12. Line of site between Bertha fort and Woodhead tower 72

Figure 5.13. Line of site between Bertha and Woodhead via Grassy Walls camp.. 72

Figure 5.14. Line of site analysis between the camps at Hillside and the fort at Doune 73

Figure 5.15. Overview of Line of site analysis of sites on and around the Gask Ridge 74

Figure 5.16. Network diagram of signalling between the Gask Ridge fortifications. Red boxes indicate the quickest signalling route 75

Figure 5.17. Line of sight analysis between Newstead fort and Eildon Hill North tower 76

Figure 5.18. Line of sight analysis between Oakwood camp and Eildon Hill North tower 77

Figure 6.1. Polybian Camp with front entrance at the bottom (After Johnson 1983)....................................... 80

Figure 6.2. Hyginian Camp. The porta decumana is at the top (After Johnson 1983) 81

Figure 6.3. Cardinal Direction of Flavian Fortifications... 83

Figure 6.4. Orientation of forts A-C... 84

Figure 6.5. Orientation of forts D-M 85

Figure 6.6. Orientation of forts M-S 86

Figure 6.7. Orientation of camps A-B... 87

Figure 6.8. Orientation of camps C-D 88

Figure 6.9. Orientation of camps D-G 89

Figure 6.10. Orientation of camps G-L... 90

Figure 6.11. Orientation of camps L-R 91

Figure 6.12. Orientation of camps S-W 92

Figure 6.13. Orientation of fortlets 92

Figure 6.14. Orientation of Gatehouse of Fleet fortlet.. 93

Figure 6.15. Total number of fortifications facing east, northeast or southeast by period............................... 94

Figure 6.16. Orientation of Antonine Wall forts 95

Figure 6.17. Orientation of the Stanegate forts... 96

Figure 6.18. Orientation of Cumbrian coastal forts 97

Figure 6.19. Orientation of Hadrian's Wall forts 98

Figure 6.20. Percentage of fortifications facing presumed direction of advance.. 99

Figure 6.21. Visibility (shaded area) and orientation from Crawford fort 100

Figure 7.1. Fortifications on the River Tweed 108

Figure 7.2. Fortifications and possible sites on the Firth, River Forth and tributaries................................... 110

Figure 7.3. Binary viewshed (shaded areas) from the Firth of Forth sites detailed by Sibbald........................111

List of figures

Figure 7.4. Fortifications and possible sites on the Firth, River Tay and tributaries 114

Figure 7.5. Possible ford/crossing point over the River Tay by Bertha fort 115

Figure 7.6. Satellite image of Derder's Ford by Bertha fort. (Source: Google Earth June 2018; accessed 10 July 2022) 116

Figure 7.7. Fortifications, possible and unconfirmed sites in the north east, Moray Firth and tributaries 117

Figure 7.8. Fortifications, possible and unconfirmed sites on the Firth, River Clyde and tributaries 119

Figure 7.9. Cleared area (circled) at Brigurd Point, creating an 'n' shape. (Google Earth April 2021; accessed 10 July 2022) 119

Figure 7.10. Fortifications in the south-west, Solway Firth and tributaries.. 121

Figure 7.11. Binary viewshed (shaded area) from Ward Law camp.. 123

Figure 7.12. Binary viewshed (shaded area) from Lantonside fortlet 123

List of tables

Table 1. Abbreviations used in the text xviii

Table 2. Summary of the relevant ScARF: Roman Landscape Research Recommendations 2

Table 3. Number of sites facing east, northeast or southeast. Total number of sites examined is in brackets 94

Table 4. Breakdown of Flavian fortifications which are facing waterways 99

Table 5. Breakdown of Flavian fortifications which are constructed near water 107

Table 6. Site details for fortifications on the River Tweed 109

Table 7. Details of the possible sites around the Firth of Tay 113

Table 8. Set of criteria for profiling potential fortification sites in Flavian Scotland 131

Table 9. Details of the Flavian Fortress in Scotland 153

Table 10. Details of Flavian Forts in Scotland 153

Table 11. Details of Flavian Camps in Scotland 154

Table 12. Details of Flavian Fortlets in Scotland 155

Table 13. Details of Flavian (Gask Ridge) Towers in Scotland 156

Table 14. Summary of site data for the Flavian fortress 157

Table 15. Summary of site data for the Flavian forts A-D 157

Table 16. Summary of site data for the Flavian forts E-S 158

Table 17. Summary of site data for the Flavian fortlets 158

Table 18. Summary of site data for the Flavian camps A-C 159

Table 19. Summary of site data for the Flavian camps D-G 160

Table 20. Summary of site data for the Flavian camps G-M 161

Table 21. Summary of site data for the Flavian camps M-W 161

Editorial Note

All the images within this book are copyright and credited to the author, unless otherwise stated. The maps, and any LiDAR images, have been compiled and processed, where relevant, by the author and contain OS data © Crown copyright, Database Right (2020, 2021, 2022), and OS Terrain 5, OS Terrain 50, OS OpenMap – Local & Strategi right (2020, 2021) unless otherwise stated. The main chronological period for the research covered in this monograph is the Common Era (CE).

Some site data, particularly grid references and classifications, have been extracted from Canmore, the National Record of the Historic Environment in Scotland. The data relating to Roman roads has also been extracted from Canmore. The fort plans and some camp outlines have been drawn from various sources, including excavation reports, aerial photography, and LiDAR imaging by the author. The remaining camp outlines have been adapted from previous research undertaken by Dr Rebecca Jones, for which I am grateful. Some images in the text, particularly relating to the Line of Site analysis, have been adapted from the original GIS results to make visual interpretation simpler, and where relevant, this is noted in the text.

Abbreviations

The following abbreviations are used in this monograph:

Table 1. Abbreviations used in the text.

BCE	Before the Common Era (previously referred to as BC)
CE	Common Era (previously referred to as AD)
DEM	Digital Elevation Model
DTM	Digital Terrain Model
GIS	Geographical Information Systems
HER	Historic Environment Record
JRS	Journal of Roman Studies
LIA	Late Iron Age
LiDAR	Light Detection And Ranging
NGR	National Grid Reference
NSA	*New Statistical Account of Scotland or The Report Of The Committee Of The Society For The Sons And Daughters Of The Clergy Superintending The New Statistical Account Of Scotland, To The General Assembly Of The Church Of Scotland*
OS	Ordnance Survey
OSA	*Old Statistical Account of Scotland Drawn from the Communications of the Ministers of the Different Parishes*
RCAHMS	Royal Commission on the Ancient and Historic Monuments of Scotland
ScARF	Scottish Archaeological Research Framework

Abstract

Scotland is one of the few areas of the ancient world which was never completely occupied by the Roman army, and despite numerous attempts, it was never fully assimilated into the Empire. Arguably, it was during the 1st century that the Imperial Army made the most successful inroads into the lands beyond the province of *Britannia*, reaching as far as the shores of the Moray Firth. However, the full length and extent of Roman occupation in this period remains debated by scholars.

In this period, Roman military engineers took several factors into consideration when selecting a site for a fortification. This often included the defensive capacity of the surrounding topography, intervisibility between sites, proximity to transport networks (roads and rivers), and to a lesser extent, how close indigenous settlements were. Primarily focussing on those sites established during the 1st century Flavian campaigns, this study combines remote sensing techniques with archaeological and historical legacy data, and topographical information in a GIS. It undertakes computational analysis to explore the relationship between early Roman military structures in Northern Britain, and the landscape in which these are located. This is the first time that a 'big data' GIS-based study has been undertaken into the location and positioning of early Roman sites, in Scotland, and their relationship with the landscape surrounding them.

By exploring the positioning and location of early Roman fortifications in the Scottish landscape, this study concludes that the military strategy in the 1st century was not to control the wider landscape, as has been argued, but to manage the main corridors of movement around the fortifications. This enabled the army to exert visual control and authority over the indigenous population, and negate the need to manage the entirety of the landscape.

1

Introduction

Forts are usually located on communication routes, though the road lines are not always known and rarely independently dated. Often forts are found at river crossings. They are generally about one day's march apart (15-20 miles), though distances vary. There has, however, been no systematic study of the location of forts in terms of their relationship with roads/rivers, orientation, tactical considerations, articulation with other installations, or relations to indigenous settlement patterns or landscape features.

ScARF 2012a:32-33

Spatial analysis, through the combining of archaeological and mapping data in a Geographical Information System (GIS) database, is a computational technique increasingly being applied to the study of archaeological features in the landscape, mainly due to an increase in the availability and accessibility of information, technologies and datasets gathered from LiDAR, satellite imagery, GIS, and remote sensing. Spatial analysis has the potential to indicate possible reasons for locating a fortification in a certain position in the landscape, why it is facing in a particular direction, and its relationship with other features or sites in the area. In recent years, there has been an increase in the application of spatial analysis, through GIS, to the study of fortifications in the landscape in various parts of the Roman Empire, such as the Dutch *limes* and the Southern Arabian Petraea, as well as in Roman Spain. The general conclusions, drawn from such analyses is that fortifications are placed in locations which allow them to control the immediate landscape, often with visible command of resources or movement routes, such as mountain passes or roads.

Studies of Roman fortifications have frequently focussed on physical structures rather than the wider topographical setting, although this is beginning to change, but as Costa-García writes, "... in order to understand the impact of the Roman military... it is necessary to better understand the surrounding archaeological landscapes through comprehensive, interdisciplinary studies" (2018: 993). This has also been observed by Graafstal in relation to the Antonine Wall, who notes, "it is striking to see how subordinate the place of terrain and topography has been in most discussions whether on a site or systematic level" (2020:143). This not only applies to the Antonine Wall, but can be seen in many studies of fortifications from other periods and geographical areas. GIS spatial analysis which has been undertaken in Scotland has mainly been restricted to the Antonine Wall, with the conclusions relating to the positioning of those fortifications have broadly been the same as those from elsewhere in the Empire; that the forts (on the Wall) are constructed to control the immediate landscape; this can be defined as fortifications located in positions which either give them a good view of the landscape, enabling them to react to any approaching threats, or help them to protect assets or resources. In some instances, the fortifications were positioned on corridors or movement routes which were used by the indigenous population to move from one location to another, enabling the military to keep an eye on local traffic. A similar observation was made early in the 20th century by Abercromby (1902:196) who was the first to note that a number of forts, along the edge of the Scottish Highlands seemed to be deliberately positioned to block movement between Roman territory and the lands beyond. One of the most recent, comprehensive and systematic study of a group of fortifications in the Scottish landscape was undertaken by Woolliscroft and Hoffmann (2006), and who focus on 1st century sites north of the Forth-Clyde isthmus, although their work does not utilise GIS spatial analysis. More recently, Graafstal (2020) has undertaken a study of the spatial analysis of the Antonine Wall forts, demonstrating that each of these fortifications are intervisible with their adjacent neighbour; some also appear to be located at the entrances to valleys, suggesting that these are positioned in such locations as to oversee movement along these.

The research undertaken in *Facing the Enemy* contributes to the wider archaeological research agenda for Scotland. *ScARF: The Roman Presence* (2012) gives a comprehensive summary of the current knowledge of Roman activity in Scotland, covering the interaction with the indigenous population, supplying and resourcing the army, and looking at the wider impact of the Romans on the landscape, and remains relevant over a decade after its publication. While *Facing the Enemy* is not a direct response to the ScARF report, important areas of those research recommendations inform and influence the aims and objectives of this publication, and a summary of these are in Table 2 (ScARF 2012:IV). In Scotland, there has been limited application of GIS spatial analysis of Roman fortifications in their immediate and wider landscapes, something which has been recognised in *ScARF: The Roman Presence*.

Focussing on the areas outlined by ScARF, this monograph is an exploration of the relationship between Roman military structures in Scotland, and the landscape in which they are located. It primarily focusses on those fortifications dating to the Flavian period, defined as the

Facing the Enemy?

Table 2. Summary of the relevant ScARF: Roman Landscape Research Recommendations.

ScARF: Roman Presence Research Recommendation	
3.8	A systematic overview of the road network in Scotland, considering all lines claimed as Roman, from aerial and ground survey and excavation evidence, is required.
	The Gask Ridge road requires further assessment – can the current known road be dated? If it is 2nd century in date, there is still likely to have been a road between the 1st century fortifications and, as these have their entrances oriented on the known line, this may prove to overlie a Flavian predecessor.
3.11	An understanding of the fortress of Inchtuthil in its wider landscape would be of broad and substantial benefit to international scholars of Roman frontiers.
	Knowledge of the road network is very poor. Critical appraisal and targeted fieldwork are needed to clarify it.
	Any chance to investigate the maritime context, especially in terms of wrecks or water-front structures, should be seized.
4.2	The systematic study of forts within their wider landscapes should be encouraged.
4.7	The need to look beyond the fort for other aspects of its landscape…

period CE 77-86/90 (ScARF 2012a). This period has been selected for three reasons:

- The classical literary text, *Agricola*, gives a historical account of Roman activity and the strategy of the army in the period and geographic location covered by *Facing the Enemy*;
- With the most extensive period of military activity in Scotland dating to the 1st century, there is a large evidence base of around 120 different fortifications from across Scotland, many of which have not subsequently been altered or destroyed by later Roman activity. Therefore, there are enough early sites to include in a spatial analysis, and to be able to identify any trends in the positioning, intervisibility, orientation, and interconnectivity of fortifications in this territory and in this period;
- This period represents the earliest large-scale and organised incursion into Scotland, with the army positioning fortifications in locations for the first time which allows us to draw conclusions regarding their approach and strategy; during later invasions, the army tend to reoccupy earlier sites, making it less clear to discern if they have their own strategy for fortification positioning, or are following that of the 1st century military.

Facing the Enemy therefore focuses on the positioning, the intervisibility, the orientation, and the interconnectivity of fortifications which are dated to, or likely to have been established in the 1st century. For clarity, these four elements can be defined as follows:

- Positioning - the immediate location in the landscape where a fortification has been constructed. Fortifications in Scotland, are usually located on a plain, a slope or on a hill to give them a strategic advantage;
- Intervisibility - the ability to see and/or signal from one fortification to another;
- Orientation - the direction which a fortification is facing;
- Interconnectivity - the physical link (through road and/or coastal and river networks) between a series of fortification sites.

In this investigation, I refer to fortifications as being linked through interconnected networks, defined as multiple points (the fortifications) linked together by pathways (roads or coastal and inland waterways). Using terminology such as connectivity, suggests that two points are connected by a single pathway, but this does not reflect our knowledge of these networks in Flavian Scotland; it is not always clear if pathways are linking just two sites, or even if these are contemporaneous with the fortifications which they are alleged to connect; the term interconnectivity may better represent those fortifications which are linked by being located on the coast and on rivers because of the extensive network of waterways as most fortifications are on the major rivers, or tributaries of these.

Scotland was chosen as the main geographic focus for this research because of its almost unique position in the Roman world as a territory which was never fully or permanently occupied on a long-term basis in any period. As Roman fortifications have not been found in all geographic areas of Scotland, the area covered by this research can further be defined as being bordered by the Solway Firth and the River Tweed in the south, and the Highland Faultline in the north. References to Northern Scotland, generally refer to the area north of the Forth-Clyde isthmus, or what becomes the line of the Antonine Wall; the term Northern Britain refers to the territories above the Stanegate/Tyne-Solway area (which itself becomes the location of Hadrian's Wall in the 2nd century). There are a significant number of fortifications in Scotland which originate in the 1st century, many of which have not shown evidence of reoccupation in a later period; for those which were used again, the original orientation of the site is clear. Where this is not clear, this has been noted in the text. As a general rule, sites in Northern England have not been included here as the chronology of these fortifications is often less clear, making it more challenging to draw conclusions about the Flavian military strategies in these areas. As will be shown, the Antonine military strategy in Scotland has many similarities to the 1st century approach, and could be applicable to sites of other periods in Northern Britain.

First century Flavian fortifications are found in southern, central and northern Scotland, except for the Scottish Islands, Argyll and Bute, and the Highlands. Despite three major invasions, and potentially some additional incursions, the north of Britain was never fully integrated into the Roman Empire, while arguably, it was during the 1st century that the Roman military made the most successful inroads into Northern Britain, with the army reaching Aberdeenshire as confirmed through radiocarbon dating at the camps of Kintore and Milltimber (Cook and Dunbar 2008; Cook, Dunbar, and Heawood 2009; Cook 2018; Dingwall and Shepherd 2018); the assumption is that most of the camps in the northeast and Moray coast have their foundation in this period. There are even some indications that the army in the 1st century went beyond the Moray coast (e.g. Tibbs 2019:193), although the full extent of Roman activity in 1st century Scotland remains unknown. Towards the end of the 1st century, fortifications in Scotland appear to have been abandoned and most are not reoccupied in later periods; there are a small number of possible exceptions, including the forts at Ardoch (Breeze 1970), Birrens (Robertson 1975), Strageath (Frere and Wilkes 1989), Bertha (Woolliscroft and Hoffmann 2006), and Newstead (J. Curle 1911; Hunter 2015; Hanson 2015).

To date, there has been no systematic spatial analysis of 1st century fortifications from across Scotland using GIS, therefore *Facing the Enemy* explores the hypothesis that the positioning, intervisibility, orientation and interconnectivity of early Roman fortifications in the landscape was essential to secure and control the local environment, and asks if spatial analysis of the early sites can tell us anything about the approach of the Roman military in Scotland during the 1st century.

1.1. Aims and Objectives

By creating a comprehensive GIS database of early Roman fortifications in Scotland, and synthesising satellite and mapping data with additional layers of evidence, such as the findings of historical archaeological research, this investigation examines the strategic intentions of the military in the north in the Flavian period. It does this primarily through a quantitative investigation into spatial arrangements of fortifications in both their immediate setting, and the wider landscape to discern possible reasons for constructing military structures in particular locations. The spatial analysis of these sites focusses on the positioning, the intervisibility, the orientation, and the interconnectivity of these fortifications, comparing them with similar arrangements from elsewhere in the Roman Empire. Therefore, the overall research aim of this investigation seeks to profile fortification sites, and to understand the intentions of the army in selecting locations for military structures in the landscape. Additionally, *Facing the Enemy* aims to:

- Identify any trends in where fortifications are located in the landscape
  - Is there a strategic significance (if any) of the site chosen for early fortifications?
  - Is there a common pattern of topography which explain the locations selected to place a fortifications?
  - Are fortifications positioned with an offensive or defensive capability?
- Determine the extent to which military sites could exercise control of the local area through surveillance and visual communication
  - Were the fortifications able to control local settlements, movement routes or roads?
  - Is the function of a site discernable through its positioning and intervisibility?
- Examine the interconnectivity between Flavian sites, through the road and river networks
  - Are fortifications intervisible and is there a purpose to this?
  - Is the location of a fortification dependent on its proximity to the road, river crossings and/or watercourses?
  - What is the archaeological evidence for the use of waterways by the Flavian army?

In the process of examining the 1st century sites in Scotland, this research will also:

- Examine the dating evidence for Flavian fortifications, and the impact of this on interpreting such sites
  - How secure is the dating for individual sites labelled as 'Flavian'?
  - Are there any challenges in interpreting camp sequences?

Although there have been previous spatial studies of Roman sites in Northern Britain, only a few have used GIS modelling (studies include Hanson and Maxwell 1986; Hanson 1991; Breeze 1993; 2017; Breeze and Dobson 2000; Woolliscroft and Hoffmann 2006; Hannon 2018; Hannon, Wilson, and Rohl 2020; Murphy, Gittings, and Crow 2018; Symonds 2018; 2020; E. Graafstal 2020; 2021; Breeze 2011; E. Graafstal et al. 2015). These studies have shown that there can be differences between fortifications constructed on a road, such as the Stanegate and those on the Gask Ridge in Perthshire, and those built on a linear barrier such as the Antonine Wall, the latter developing after the 1st century (Symonds 2018:72). Recent work analysing the positioning of forts on the Antonine Wall, has indicated that intervisibility between each site was important, along with a requirement for the fort to have visual control of adjacent valleys, and for the site to be located on a plain where available. An objective of this research is to undertake a similar study of all of the known and likely Flavian fortifications, rather than just the forts, to see if they are located in similar positions, and additionally, to see if they are making use of the natural topography for defence. Furthermore, the outcomes of this research will test the argument by Abercromby regarding whether or not the forts on the Highland-line are deliberately positioned to block the glens.

As noted above, Graafstal recorded that intervisibility between sites on the Antonine Wall appears to have been a consideration when selecting where to build the forts. This has also been noted elsewhere in Britain, particularly by Woolliscroft who has analysed signalling (which requires an element of intervisibility) capabilities on various frontiers, including the Flavian sites in central Scotland (e.g. 1989; 1993; 1994; 1996; 2009; 2010; Woolliscroft and Hoffmann 2006; Woolliscroft, Swain, and Lockett 1992). Although Woolliscroft's signalling modelling considered the Flavian fortifications north of the Antonine Wall, his experiments involving replicating signalling between sites, did not include camps. There have been few attempts to examine the extent of visibility from 1st century sites in Scotland, and developing this type of analysis is another of the objectives of this work; to build on the original signalling work of Woolliscroft on the 1st century sites in Scotland by utilising GIS analysis to test and enhance his original approach and develop this through the inclusion of camps. Developing this methodology using GIS viewshed and line-of-sight modelling, has the potential to increase accuracy, extend the geographical coverage of the analysis, incorporate the camps into the modelling, and also enable variation of the different parameters used by Woolliscroft, to see if this makes a difference to the potential relationships which he previously identified; this is particularly important given that the original height of fortifications in Flavian Scotland remains speculative.

Roman literary sources state that there are certain directions in which fortifications should face, with the indication being that this is for both practical and symbolic purposes. While those sources are generally post-Flavian, little research has been undertaken exploring this aspect of fortification design, and how strategically important it was to orientate a site in a particular direction, although it does seem likely that if a fort had a front or main entrance, then there would have been some importance attached to the direction it faced. With the evidence from other frontiers suggesting that fortifications were positioned to control resources and the landscape, sites in Northern Britain may have been orientated to reflect this. *Facing the Enemy* investigates the orientation of fortifications in the landscape within the geographical and temporal scope of this work, but it will also look beyond Flavian Scotland for comparative insights.

While there have been significant amounts of research into military networks, particularly in the Roman period, there has been little analysis of this in the context of 1st century Scotland. The connectivity of sites through the road network is important, particularly as it enables movement of supplies and troops through the landscape, but knowledge of this in Scotland is fragmented and there is even some indication that some sites were not connected by roads (Maxwell 1989). The importance of river networks in the 1st century to move troops and scope enemy territories was noted by the Roman writer Tacitus, and given that a significant number of Flavian and post-Flavian sites were built next to bodies of water, such positioning had significant importance to the military. A systematic GIS analysis of the relationship between roads, coastal areas and waterways, and fortifications, in Scotland, has not previously been undertaken, and *Facing the Enemy* reappraises our knowledge of the river network using case studies, to see if we can postulate how these were used in the Roman period.

1.2. Method and Approach

At the core of this research is the analysis of legacy archaeological data through quantitative analysis. This data has initially been gathered from Canmore.org.uk, the national record of the historic environment in Scotland, and expanded upon using excavation reports, maps, site analyses by other authors, and aerial imagery. Mapping data was extracted from Edina Digimap (originating from Ordnance Survey) and processed in an extensive Geographic Information System database. As Jones and Leslie (2015) have stated, there is a need to integrate different data sets such as geophysical surveys, aerial photographs, laser scanning, and topographical data to achieve an integrated site profile, which would enable a better understanding of Roman frontiers, and a GIS database is the ideal vehicle to achieve this with. GIS has been successfully and extensively used in the analysis of the distribution of archaeological sites in the landscape, particularly in relation to Roman activity (Komoróczy and Vlach 2009; e.g. Chapman 2006; Verhagen 2010; Verhagen and Jeneson 2012; Verhagen et al. 2012; Foglia 2014; Hannon 2018; Bachagha, Wang, et al. 2020; Bachagha, Luo, et al. 2020; Hannon, Wilson, and Rohl 2020; J. Lewis 2020; Blanco et al. 2020)[1]. As noted previously, Graafstal argues, in relation to the Antonine Wall, that various factors such as planning order, alignment, spacing, operational requisites and intervisibility need to be considered together when undertaking analyses of frontiers, an approach described by the author as sequential stratigraphy (2020:143-144). There are some clear parallels with the approach adopted in *Facing the Enemy*. The application of such analyses, through a GIS, enables not only interpretation of the spatial (and where relevant, temporal) distribution of sites, but of their setting in the immediate topography of a location, as well as the wider landscape[2]. The application of a systematic approach to all of the 1st century fortifications in Scotland in their geographic setting has not previously been undertaken, yet this type of analysis is vital for identifying common patterns and trends in the data and drawing valid conclusions in respect of the research questions.

There are around 300 Roman fortifications in Scotland (Tibbs 2019), with a general consensus that most date to one of the three major invasions of North Britain;

---

[1] A similar approach has been undertaken using LiDAR to identify medieval sites in Italy (Lasaponara et al. 2010; Masini et al. 2018)
[2] A discussion of some of the criticisms and challenges relating to GIS-based viewshed analysis can be found in Chapter Three.

Flavian (c. CE 77-86/90), Antonine (c. 139-165), or Severan (c. 208-211). However, there are a substantial number of fortifications which remain undated, and the further possibility that some date to pre-Flavian or post-Severan periods of activity (ScARF 2012a:25). Despite this, there is no single list of fortifications and foundation dates which is commonly accepted, so for this research, I have compiled a list of Roman fortification which are either confirmed as dating to the 1st century through datable evidence, as well as those considered likely to originate in this period, but where there is a lack of datable evidence; approaches to the dating of Roman sites in Scotland is discussed in more depth later. The list of just under 130 fortifications are outlined in Appendix One, and includes five different types of military structures; a legionary fortress, camps, forts, fortlets and towers. Some of these sites consist of multiple fortifications of the same type constructed in close proximity, or on top of each other. In addition to these, there is also the road network, most of which remains undated and unconfirmed.

The list of sites comes with a caveat; much of the evidence used to assign an origin date to many of these is limited, but rather than limiting this study to the few sites with robust evidence supporting Flavian dating, I have widened the scope to include fortifications which are likely to date to the 1st century, despite dating evidence being inconclusive. I have also included some sites which may not be Flavian (such as the camps at Bankhead (Carnwath) II, Bellie, Lochlands, Logie Durno and Ythan Wells I). These locations have multiple fortifications overlaying each other, and as most remain unexcavated, it is difficult to discern which camp or fort was constructed first and when; however, as there is some indication of Flavian activity at each site, I have erred on the side of caution and included them in some of the analysis. Sites such as Bar Hill and Cramond have not been included because there has been no evidence of 1st century occupation, and they are not in close proximity to other fortifications of this period, and therefore early activity at these places remains speculative. The inclusion and exclusion of such sites is not a comment or judgement on the dating methods, excavation techniques, or subsequent analysis, but particular caution needs to be exercised in interpreting findings and attributing a date of origin to these sites, particularly when considering interrelationships between sites that are assumed to be contemporary.

The primary sources for compiling the list of sites examined in this research has primarily drawn on the data contained within Canmore.org.uk (the National Record of the Historic Environment in Scotland), as well as from *ScARF: The Roman Presence* (ScARF 2012a), *Roman Camps in Scotland* (R. H. Jones 2011), and *Rome's First Frontier* (Woolliscroft and Hoffmann 2006). The list of Flavian sites analysed in this research can be seen in Figure 1.1.

1.3. Research Limitations and Implications

To date, there has been very few wide-ranging and systematic investigation of Flavian fortifications in Scotland, and none which have simultaneously considered the location, positioning and orientation of fortifications, intervisibility between these, interconnectivity with roads and rivers, and the relationship with the indigenous population. Those studies that exist have focused on one or two, or occasionally, a group of fortifications focussed around a limited geographical area. There are a small but increasing number of studies, most of which focus on frontiers beyond Scotland and northern England, which utilise modern analytical techniques, involving the application of GIS to examining fortifications in a landscape setting, as well as in the wider context of a frontier.

There are several limitations which have the potential to affect some of the findings and results within *Facing the Enemy*. This includes the quality and accuracy of the data[3], much of which is legacy, and therefore lacking in the essential detail to confirm various characteristics of the sites, such as the extent of the fortification defences, internal structures, or even the orientation. The dating, or establishment of fortifications in Scotland is significantly limited, with a relatively small number of sites subjected to scientific dating. Most are dated through morphology as well as sequencing, but as I have indicated, this is often flawed because we do not know enough about the sequencing of such locations; dating of sites from artefacts is often reliant on small fragments of pottery uncovered on sites, often from fieldwalking or from trial trenching of ditches. Not that we should entirely dismiss the dating framework for Roman Scotland, but we must be much more cautious and prioritise revision of this to ensure more accuracy when determining chronology. Concerns over the reliability of dating has meant I have had to be particularly cautious when drawing conclusions about the relationships between sites as intervisibility and interconnectivity between these is not possible if they are not contemporary.

When analysing Roman fortifications, either individually, part of a system, or even focussing on them as a product of one period, we must consider all elements, the fortress, forts, camps, fortlets, and towers, together to make sense of their overall and co-dependent functions. For too long fortifications have been examined individually on their own, and discussed as separate and independent entities. The evidence presented here indicates that we should also think of the fortifications as having an interconnected relationship within a wider landscape system. If some camps are fortifying the landscape (as opposed to being temporarily occupied), then they are working in partnership with other fortifications, and this can be missed if these sites are not considered in a wider, militarised setting.

---
[3] Limitations relating to the GIS processing and modelling, as well as the site data, are outlined in Chapter Three.

Facing the Enemy?

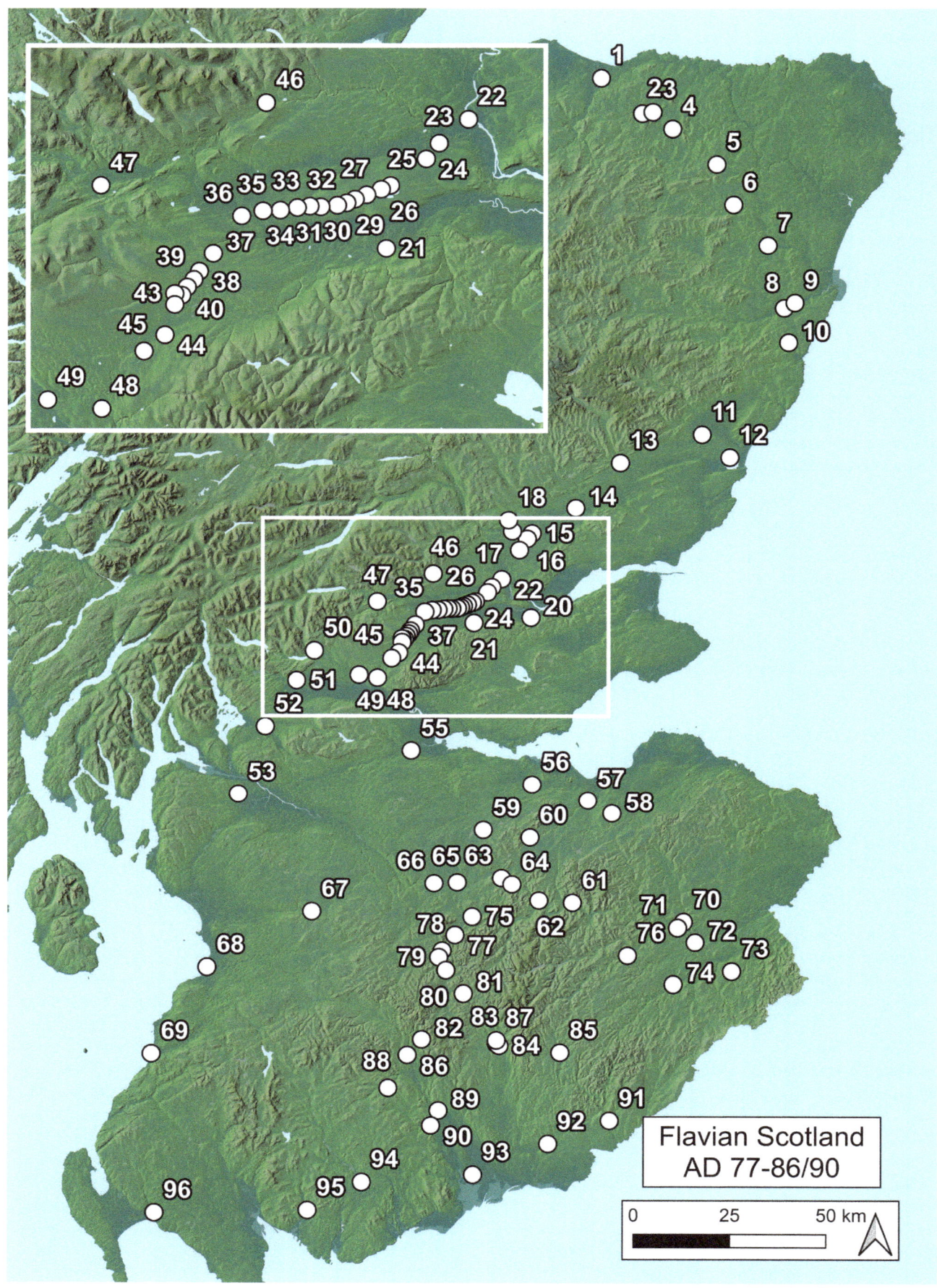

Figure 1.1. Flavian fortification sites covered in the text.

Introduction

Key to sites in Figure 1.1

1	Bellie (Camp)	49	Doune (Fort)
2	Auchinhove (Camp)	50	Bochastle (Fort, Camp)
3	Muiryfold (Camp)	51	Malling (Fort, Camps)
4	Burnfield (Camp)	52	Drumquhassle (Fort)
5	Glenmailen (Ythan Wells) (Camps)	53	Barochan Hill (Fort)
6	Logie Durno (Camp)	54	Lochlands (Camps)
7	Kintore (Camp)	55	Camelon (Forts)
8	Normandykes (Camp)	56	Gogar Green (Camp)
9	Milltimber (Camp)	57	Elginhaugh (Fort)
10	Raedykes (Camp)	58	Woodhead (Camp)
11	Stracathro (Fort, Camp)	59	Castle Greg (Fortlet)
12	Dun (Camp)	60	Carlops Spittal (Camp)
13	Inverquharity (Camp, Fortlet)	61	Eshiels (Camp)
14	Cardean (Fort)	62	Easter Happrew (Fort)
15	Black Hill (Tower)	63	Kirkhouse (Camp)
16	Cargill (Fort, Fortlet)	64	Castlecraig (Camp)
17	Inchtuthil (Fortress, Camps)	65	Bankhead (Camp, Fortlet)
18	Gourdie, Steeds Stalls (Camp)	66	Castledykes (Fort, Camps)
19	Woodhead (Tower)	67	Loudoun Hill (Fort)
20	Abernethy (Carey) (Camp)	68	Ayr (Camp)
21	Dunning (Camp)	69	Girvan Mains (Camps)
22	Bertha (Fort)	70	Newstead (Fort, Camps)
23	West Mains of Huntingtower (Tower)	71	Eildon Hill North (Tower)
24	Peel (Tower)	72	Hiltonshill (Camp)
25	Westmuir (Tower)	73	Cappuck (Fort)
26	Thorny Hill (Tower)	74	Denholm (Eastcote) (Camp)
27	Moss Side (Tower)	75	Cornhill (Camp)
28	Witch Knowe (Tower)	76	Oakwood (Fort & Camp)
29	Gask House (Tower)	77	Lamington (Camp)
30	Muir O' Fauld (Tower)	78	Wandel (Camp)
31	Kirkhill (Tower)	79	Cold Chapel (Camp)
32	Roundlaw (Tower)	80	Crawford (Fort)
33	Ardunie (Tower)	81	Beattock Summit (Tower)
34	Raith (Tower)	82	Durisdeer (Camp)
35	Parkneuk (Tower)	83	Beattock: Barnhill (Fortlet), Bankend (Camp)
36	Strageath (Fort)	84	Milton (Fort, Camp)
37	Westerton (Tower)	85	Raeburnfoot (Camp)
38	Kaims Castle (Fortlet)	86	Drumlanrig (Fort), Islafoot (Camp)
39	Shielhill North (Tower)	87	Beattock, Barnhill (Fortlet)
40	Shielhill South (Tower)	88	Kirkland (Fortlet)
41	Black Hill (Tower)	89	Dalswinton: Bankhead (Fort), Bankfoot (Fort, Camps)
42	Ardoch II & V (Camps)	90	Fourmerkland (Camp)
43	Ardoch (Fort)	91	Broomholm (Fort)
44	Woodlea (Greenloaning) (Tower)	92	Birrens (Fort, Camp)
45	Glenbank (Fortlet)	93	Ward Law (Fort)
46	Fendoch (Fort)	94	Glenlochar (Fort, Camp)
47	Dalginross (Fort, Camp)	95	Gatehouse of Fleet (Fortlet)
48	Hillside, Dunblane (Camps)	96	Glenluce (Camp)

Determining the interconnectivity of sites has been limited by our partial understandings of the road network, as well as coastal sites and near-coastal riverside sites. *Facing the Enemy* has not set out to study the entire road network in Scotland, but it has led to a series of questions about what this looked like, how far it extended, whether there is evidence of pre-Roman routes and, if so, when these got 'upgraded' to Roman roads, and how much more confident can we become in dating the network? We also need to consider the limitation of our knowledge surrounding the coastal and river networks, including the archaeological evidence. As I demonstrate in this investigation, these networks are more complex than we currently assume, but again, we are limited by a lack of confirmation for some sites, as well as little or no chronological referencing for many of these, making it much more difficult to place some fortifications into the wider military strategy for each period.

A final key area where our knowledge is limited and which impacts on this study, is the relationship between the Romans and the indigenous population. A lack of Late Iron Age population centres, and insignificantly small promontory and hillforts, make it difficult to establish who the 'enemy' was, and the threat they posed to the army, while some evidence suggests a symbiotic relationship between the Romans and the indigenous population. However, Tacitus indicates that it was not an entirely peaceful relationship, with several attacks on the army, as well as the battle at *Mons Graupius*. Despite recent work, there is still a gap in our knowledge of Late Iron Age (LIA) sites and their relationship to Roman fortifications, and further research may alter our limited understanding and the interpretation of the relationship between the indigenous population and the army.

1.4. Summary

This research investigates the statement outlined at the beginning of the chapter, by *ScARF: The Roman Presence*, that forts are located on communication routes and at river crossings. *Facing the Enemy* is a systematic study, the like of which has not previously been undertaken, into fortification locations and their relationship with roads and rivers, but also expands this to incorporate all types of Flavian military structures found across Scotland. It demonstrates that these fortifications are, like sites on other frontiers, located in strategic positions with the overall purpose of controlling movement through the immediate landscape. It also demonstrates that most fortifications are located next to, and often facing water, and argues that this was deliberate, and an attempt to secure these routes and possibly river crossings. The investigation also argues that some camps are also located in strategic positions, essentially copying the role of forts, which suggests that these do not fit in with the typology of camps outlined above; furthermore, some camps are located on the coast, suggesting that they are securing both coastal routes, as well as the entrances to rivers, with fortifications often positioned further upstream of these. It goes on to conclude that based on the findings presented in this investigation, it is possible to create a set of criteria for fortification positioning which could be used to identify additional sites.

2

Romans and Scottish Landscapes

The application of modern analytical techniques, such as spatial analysis, to archaeological sites has expanded our knowledge of Roman frontiers, including their role and function. It has also facilitated better comparative analysis between the frontiers from across the Empire. Landscape and spatial studies of Roman frontiers has continued to increase in recent years, not just through publication of Limes Congress proceedings, but with the accessibility and affordability of new technologies and datasets such as GIS and LiDAR. These techniques are increasingly being used in the study of Roman frontiers, although less attention has been given to those in Britain predating the Walls of Hadrian and Antoninus Pius. Recent work in Wales has made some use of remote sensing and analytical techniques (Burnham and Davies 2010), while Woolliscroft and Hoffmann (2006) have undertaken limited analysis of this type in northern Scotland, albeit before the widespread availability of GIS, mapping and terrain datasets. This approach to spatial analysis has been more wholeheartedly embraced by researchers focussing on frontiers beyond Britain (e.g. Verhagen 2010; Verhagen and Jeneson 2012; Groenhuijzen and Verhagen 2015; Costa-Garcia 2018; Franconi and Green 2019; Verhagen, Joyce, and Groenhuijzen 2019). As mentioned, there are limited applications of GIS spatial analysis to the study of Roman activity in Scotland, and in *Facing the Enemy*, I attempt to readdress this with the intention of enhancing our understanding of the approach of the military in Northern Britain during the Flavian period.

As well as empirical studies, there are also a range of theoretical approaches to the study of Roman frontiers. Breeze (2018) has attempted to synthesise frontier theory in his article for the Theoretical Roman Archaeology Journal, where he records at least 21 different theoretical approaches to the study of Roman frontiers. As Breeze states, the views and approaches taken by individuals changes, influenced by what is going on in the world and by their own backgrounds, and this finds itself reflected in their theoretical approach; such approaches to the study of frontiers have been undertaken by scholars (e.g. Dyčka 2018; Marcu et al. 2018; Pažout 2018; Teodor 2018; E. Graafstal 2020; Hannon, Wilson, and Rohl 2020). My focus, however, is on spatial analysis of empirical data, and while this should never be assumed to be theory neutral; this study is not situated within the tradition of theoretical Roman archaeology.

Our archaeological knowledge of Scotland in the 1st century is mixed. We know a considerable amount about some sites and about Roman activity in certain geographic areas, but for others we know very little. Most of the forts and fortlets, along with the fortress at Inchtuthil, have been subjected to various degrees of exploration. Most camps remain undated and other than limited trial trenching to confirm their Roman origins, have not been fully explored, though there a small number of exceptions. The organised exploration of Roman sites begins to emerge in Britain in the middle of the 19th century, although it is not until the end of that period that systematic excavations take place in Scotland. These become more limited as the 20th century progresses, and the large-scale fort excavations of the 1900s are rarely replicated with a few exceptions, including Birrens (Robertson 1964; 1975), Inchtuthil (Pitts and St Joseph 1985), and Strageath (Frere and Wilkes 1989). In recent years, a small number of sites have been uncovered which have been subjected to more rigorous and advanced techniques and analyses than were available earlier in the 20th century, including the 1st century camps at Ayr (Arabaolaza 2019), Milltimber (Dingwall and Shepherd 2018) and Kintore (Cook and Dunbar 2008; Cook, Dunbar, and Heawood 2009), along with the fort at Elginhaugh (Hanson 2007a; 2007b). The excavations at these four sites uncovered large sections of the fortifications, providing a good picture of their origins and usage; the evidence from Kintore suggests possible long-term occupation of the camp, long after the Flavian withdrawal.

Data relating to the environment in the Roman period in Northern Britain is also fragmentary, particularly during the 1st century. We know very little about the conditions which may have affected the placement of fortifications in the landscape, locally available resources, and how environmental factors have affected the sites since their abandonment. There is a growing body of data focussing on the Antonine period and the area around the Wall, and while it is possible to extrapolate this for the rest of Scotland, these findings needs to be considered with caution. Most excavations in the late 19th and early 20th century did not collect environmental samples, although there were exceptions such as the work at Newstead, where plant remains were recorded and analysed (Tagg 1911). Environmental analysis becomes more common from the latter half of the 20th century onwards, with sampling undertaken at Inveresk (Bishop 2004), Elginhaugh (Hanson 2007a), and Bearsden (Breeze 2016), but these only give a snapshot of the immediate area around a site and from a particular period; in the case of these three sites, they are post-Flavian.

This chapter begins by setting the research in the context of wider frontier studies and details the key findings resulting from spatial analysis of Roman fortifications from across the Empire as a comparator with the situation in the north. The chapter contextualises the Flavian period in Scotland, which it does by giving an overview of the historical background of the 1st century invasion, before focussing on two texts which have unduly influenced the interpretation of Roman sites in Northern Britain. It then seeks to summarise the main areas of thought relating to the relationship between the indigenous population and the invading army. The second half sets out an understanding of the military fortifications and related infrastructure originating in the Flavian period in Scotland. I provide an overview of the archaeology of the types of fortifications found in the research area, including the legionary fortress, camps, forts, fortlets and towers, and detail our knowledge of the road, coastal and river networks, with the latter section also looking at the archaeological evidence for use of these. Dating is critical to defining the set of relevant fortifications for inclusion in the analysis, so I cover the sequencing of camps and set out the different approaches and evidence which has been used to date Flavian sites. As this study examines the relationship of fortifications and the wider landscape, the last section summarises the evidence about the natural environment and availability of resources, including water, in Roman times, as well as landscape changes since, such as flood risks, erosion and channel movements which may significantly affect interpretation of fortifications in the landscape.

2.1. An Early Frontier Zone?

Before seeking to compare Roman activity in Scotland with that occurring elsewhere in the Empire, it is helpful to define what a frontier is, and how this relates to 1st century sites in North Britain. It is challenging to define what a Roman frontier is, and what this means; is it a series of fortifications constructed alongside a linear barrier such as a road; is it a group of fortifications positioned at regular intervals; or is it something less tangible? In this context, 1st century Scotland was certainly the northernmost area which the army reached, and the construction of forts and a legionary fortress located on the edge of the Highland massif, indicates an intention to secure the lowland areas on a long-term basis.

Frontier design and type varies from location to location. Natural topographical features were often utilised as formal boundaries for the Empire, although these were not necessarily perceived as the outer limits of interest, activity, and power; the army would cross the boundary when required, so military frontiers should not simply be perceived as either a "line on a map" or a legal boundary (Breeze 2011:5; see also Whittaker 1997:95). Thorne (2007) describes frontiers as being artificial and arising from establishing infrastructures, ultimately designed to support the army in undertaking security work at the edge of the Empire. Graafstal (2020:147) offers an alternative description of frontiers as, "highly complex systems combining functions related to the control of movement, observation, alarm and military response. They, the Romans, typically used running barriers, cordons of observation facilities, garrisons attuned to the local security situation, and frontier roads for lateral communication and scaling up response".

In some areas, frontiers are based on natural boundaries such as rivers or mountains, whereas in other locations the arrangements are based on creating military fortifications. Visy (2015) notes that the Romans preferred water borders (such as rivers, coasts, and seas) because it created a visual boundary, and potentially because these were easy to define. The benefits of a river frontier included visibility of the waterway making it easier to delimitate the border, as well as the ability to slow down attackers seeking to cross these. Rivers also act as good communication conduits, enabling the quick transfer of messages, as well as goods and troops. In more mountainous or hilly territory, the army sought to control passes on the frontiers (e.g. Breeze 2011:133).

Regarding Scotland, Whittaker (1997:45) describes the Forth-Clyde isthmus as a scientific frontier. Some are a combination of both such as on the River Rhine which was a natural frontier with military installations on both embankments, one side formally in Roman territory, and the fortifications on the opposite shore formally outside. The lands outside the frontier were referred to as barbaric according to the 5th century *Notitia Dignitatum* (Breeze 2011). It was also easier to move goods and people along rivers because they provided natural routes to the interior of a territory, and could often be quicker than roads in some areas. Wells (1972) argues that rivers do not make good frontiers, an argument counteracted by both Nicasie (1997) and Rankov (2005) who claim Wells has underestimated the defensive capabilities of wide watercourses (Himmler 2009). Rivers of all sizes have a natural in-built defensive capability, slowing down enemies seeking to cross the waterway.

Waterways have undoubtedly played a significant and strategic role in expansion of the Roman Empire, something seen in various parts of the Empire, such as the *limes* in Germany (e.g. Sommer 2009) which makes use of rivers including the Donau, Iller, and Rhine. Analysis of the Dutch river frontier, has also been extensive, as there the River Rhine has a network of large tributaries making it the easiest way to navigate around the country. Analysis of this includes examination of pre-Flavian supply networks (e.g. Kooistra, Rijn, and Lange 2018), shipping (e.g. Jansma and Morel 2007), harbours (e.g. Polak and Wynia 1991; Driessen 2009), as well as interregional transport (e.g. Domínguez-Delmás et al. 2014; Groenhuijzen and Verhagen 2015). But it is Verhagen et al. (2019:6) who suggests that the construction of an early Roman-period canal demonstrates the importance of the river networks in the Netherlands by essentially establishing the rivers as a transportation network. This is supported by Graafstal who has examined towers on the south bank of the Oude-Rijn river, at Utrecht, concluding that these were established to create and protect supply lines, a similar arrangement to sites on the Upper Danube and the Iron Gate. Essentially, Graafstal argues that like the Upper Danube, and the Lower Rhine, the Oude-Rijn is a fortified transport corridor, something he notes is similar to the arrangement with the Gask Ridge fortifications. Similar analysis by Evans et al. (2010) summarises the evidence for coastal and river activity in Wales, concluding that there is little firm evidence of shipping routes. Burnham and Davies (2010) in the same volume, argue that there was a need to transport goods via rivers, which explains why Chester and Caerleon legionary fortresses are on navigable rivers, and why the fort at Hindwell Farm is overlooking the Walton Basin (Evans et al. 2010). Scotland may not have substantial waterways like in Germany or the Netherlands, but it does have an extensive network of rivers, and it would be effective to use these, via the coast, to aid movement through the landscape, and to reach the interior.

Scotland, in the 1st century, shares many of the components of frontiers found elsewhere in the Empire, but the frontier status of this territory, or at least parts of it, is contested; was it a frontier or not? For example, Woolliscroft and Hoffmann (2006) argue that the concentration of fortifications on the Gask Ridge comprise the oldest land frontier in the Empire, although others disagree (e.g. ScARF 2012a). Certainly, Scotland can be considered as being a military fringe, that is, the army was engaged in fortifying an area being their main base of operations, that being the legionary fortress at York and the Stanegate. Isaac (1988) argues that the term *limes*, which is now often used to refer to Roman frontiers comprised of fortifications and related infrastructure, was originally used in the 1st century CE to refer to military roads which were seen as the borders of the Empire, and which supports the assertion by Woolliscroft and Hoffmann in relation to the Gask Ridge, something echoed by Hanson (2007a:22-24), although he argues against the early Flavian foundation of fortifications beyond the Forth-Clyde isthmus. In this period, the concept of linear frontiers, or areas divided by a barrier is only beginning to form (e.g. Luttwack 1976), and while topographical features (such as rivers) were used to mark the edge of the Empire, it is not after the Flavian period that substantial barriers (such as walls) are constructed to mark frontiers (Breeze 2011). Whittaker (1997:56) takes a different approach in his study of frontiers, looking at these from the perspective of social and economic functions. Whittaker argues that frontiers were rarely static, particularly in the periods before linear barriers were established, and notes that in the Flavian period, there is often evidence of activity beyond the main area of military operations. Whittaker concludes that frontiers are as much a product of the socio-economic environment as they are for defence, the latter being more important in post-Flavian Britain. The economic need for new resources, and even taxation, is what leads to the establishment of frontiers, with this being formalised in the construction of Hadrian's Wall and the Antonine Wall. In 1st century Scotland, Whittaker's interpretation would indicate that there was not a frontier in this period because the limits of the Empire were still being explored and expanded.

While Scotland certainly had a fortified road along the Gask Ridge, and which meets the criteria of a *limes* as noted by Isaac, the arrangement of fortifications beyond the Forth-Clyde isthmus is more complex than a road and fort arrangement. It is perhaps most helpful to think of this part of Scotland, and potentially the area north of the Stanegate as being a frontier zone, defined by Breeze (2011:15) as "an area in which the Romans and the indigenous population, both within and without the Empire, and which was complicit in maintaining life in the frontier region". Fortifications in this area appear to be formed of two groups; one which run alongside the edge of the Highland mastiff and are known as glen-blocking (or Highland-Line) forts because they are located at the entrances to the glens running into the Highlands. The second group are generally located by the natural corridor between the edge of the Highlands and the coast heading from the Forth-Clyde region to the fertile lands of Angus, Aberdeenshire and Moray. Woolliscroft and Hoffmann (2006) have argued that these fortifications may have made up an inner and outer *limes*, a term which suggests that the forts may have been established and functioned as two separate groups. A lack of precise dating for these sites, as well as a limited analysis of the purpose of these sites limits what can be concluded about the function of these fortifications as a group. Beyond the Gask Ridge area, it is less clear as to what the frontier status of north Scotland was. The classical sources only suggest that the intention was to occupy North Britain indicating that the coastline would be the edge of Roman territory. However, this did not happen and the most northerly Roman fortifications are a series of camps ending on the banks of the River Spey in Moray. This indicates that military campaigning was interrupted, and territorial gains were not secured by the establishment of forts a road infrastructure. The lack of the latter means the north of Scotland appears to fall out with of Issacs's *limes* definition, but perhaps this is not surprising given that road construction would not have been the main priority when moving into new areas. Although the area north of the Gask Ridge was on the edge of the Empire, it was never intended to be a frontier because campaigning was actively ongoing until it abruptly stopped. There are some similarities in other parts of the Empire, with 1st century forts along the Rhine frontier being located in territory beyond the river and Roman area, while Breeze has noted that some forts are located in the desert but on traditional movement routes; as discussed later in this monograph, this also appears to be happening in 1st century Scotland.

As Breeze (2011:42) notes, fortifications can, "form part of a wide military zone and also that… frontier works did not necessarily constitute the boundary of the empire." While Woolliscroft and Hoffmann argue that the Gask Ridge fortifications formed a frontier, Whittaker's analysis suggests that the area is not quite one as the boundaries and limits are continuing to expand before being settled on. Certainly, the archaeological evidence, and the text from Tacitus indicates that natural topography played an essential role in the establishment of a frontier, taking the form of an isthmus with fortifications between the Tyne and Solway (the Stanegate) suggesting a linear arrangement, although the geography of the Forth-Clyde isthmus naturally lends itself better to such arrangements although there is little archaeological evidence of such arrangements.

At the beginning of this section, I asked the question, what is a frontier? Could it be a series of fortifications which are built next to a road, such as on the Gask Ridge, or could a frontier be described as a group of sites which are positioned at regular intervals such as the Highland line forts or the camps located north of Stracathro? In relation to Flavian Scotland, the answer is probably neither; it remains on the military fringes of the Empire. It seems probable that the Stanegate area between the Solway and Tyne rivers was secured by the Romans with a series of fortifications, from which they then progressed into Scotland; there is no comparable east-west chain of fortifications beyond this to the north; progress into Scotland appears to have been in two north-south columns, one in the east and one in the west until the Forth-Clyde isthmus, where the army progresses more or less along the Highland Fault Line, with one set of fortifications closer to the Highlands than the other. From the legionary fortress at Inchtuthil, this then becomes a single line of fortifications to the Moray coast. None of these fit the various definitions of a frontier, with the possible exception of the Gask Ridge sites, but this line seems too small and easily circumvented to have formed a secure *limes* in its own right. Instead, I would argue that the frontier status of North Britain is constantly evolving; it starts out beyond the Empire, before the lowlands are secured, but campaigning is ongoing as are the efforts to secure the territory particularly beyond central Scotland. Southern Scotland could be classed as the frontier, the edge of the Empire which is being occupied, but the north is much more of a frontier zone; an area in the process of being absorbed into the Empire, but one where the job is never fully completed.

2.2. Historical Background

For the time being, this book, intended to honour Agricola, my father-in-law, will be commended, or at least executed as a tribute of dutiful affection.
Tacitus *Agricola* 3

Scotland, in the Flavian period, has traditionally been interpreted in the context of a single, Roman-period text, the *Agricola*, which describes, in some detail, campaigning in the north of Britain in the 1st century, under the then governor, Julius Gnaeus Agricola. The text has extensively influenced interpretation of many Roman sites in Scotland, particularly in the absence of datable archaeological evidence. It is therefore pertinent to understand the portrayal of Northern Britain in the *Agricola*, and how this has impacted and influenced the interpretation of Roman sites in Scotland, the latter being expanded upon in the next chapter. Written by Agricola's son-in-law, Tacitus, the *Agricola*[4] was probably published around CE 98, after Agricola's death (Hanson 1991), and makes bold claims about his achievements including that he was the first to invade North Britain. Some of these claims are being questioned because of more recent archaeological discoveries. Therefore it is always pertinent to take a cautious approach when interpreting classical texts (Breeze 2009:1; Hoffmann 2013:174). It is helpful to always keep in mind that Tacitus wrote the *Agricola* as a eulogy to his father-in-law; it cannot be relied on as a neutral, unbiased or unembellished account. Another claim, made by Tacitus and which we have to regard with caution, is that Agricola personally selected the individual location for fortifications founded during his campaigns (*Agricola* 20), something which would have probably been highly impractical, particularly when considering that there were dedicated soldiers (*agrimensores*) for such tasks (Dilke 1971). This sort of claim has led to the *Agricola* text being relied on to underpin the interpretation of many northern sites, as well as influencing early scholarship on Roman Scotland. This has particularly been to the detriment of the other classical texts which allude to pre-Agricolan activity in North Britain.

It was not until the 20th century that there were challenges, based on archaeological evidence, to the notion that Agricolan army was the first to enter Scotland[5]. J.P. Bushe-Fox (1913) hypothesised that Roman construction at Carlisle began before Agricola arrived in Northern Britain. This remained unconfirmed until the late 20th century when dendrochronological analysis of timbers from the fort showed they were felled by CE 72, prior to Agricola becoming Governor (Shotter 2001; 2004; Zant 2009:413). This dating is consistent with artefactual evidence from forts in the north of England at Ribchester, Lancaster, and Low Borrow Bridge which show occupation at this time, while some coins from Newstead, Cramond, Castledykes and Camelon forts, share the same dating as the fort at Carlisle (Shotter 2009). Woolliscroft and Hoffmann (2006) suggest that a Neronian coin found at Strageath is the earliest evidence of Roman occupation from Gask Ridge; they argue that this indicates campaigning in the area from the CE 70s, although this could also be evidence of early trading or bribery on the part of Rome, something seen elsewhere in Scotland in later periods. A possible foundation hoard of early coins were recovered from beneath the fort at Elginhaugh and indicates a *terminus ante quem* of CE 77-78 for the construction of the site showing that the army had reached Midlothian early on in Agricola's governorship (Hanson 2007a; 2007b). Shotter supports the idea of pre-Agricolan activity north of the Forth-Clyde isthmus, citing early coins found at Forteviot (Hall 2002; Shotter 1996; 2009). However, Hanson (2009:49) argues that some evidence suggests a post-Agricolan date of construction. While the evidence for an early foundation of these fortifications is not always clear, there are nonetheless indications of possible early activity in this part of Scotland, and which is supported by the evidence from Carlisle that the army was already in

---
[4] The edition of *Agricola* which will be used for quotations in this research is the translation by Anthony Birley (2010). An alternative translation has been made by Woodman and Kraus (2014), which does, to some extent provide a different meaning for certain sections of the translation of the classical texts and is referenced where relevant.

[5] For a summary of knowledge relating to possible pre-Agricolan incursions into Northern Britain, see *First Contact* (2009) and the ScARF Roman Report.

the north before the arrival of Agricola. As the Elginhaugh coins are the only pieces of evidence to have been recovered *in situ*, (the other coins are surface finds), a cautious approach needs to be taken when interpreting these finds in the context of pre-Flavian activity. The subject of pre-Flavian activity in Scotland was the focus of a Tayside and Fife Archaeological Committee Conference in 2008 (Breeze et al. 2009), and the conclusion which can be drawn from the papers presented there is that while there is some limited evidence of pre-Flavian activity relating to Scotland, there is not enough to suggest a substantial military presence was creating frontiers or establishing permanent fortifications in the north, before Agricola took command.

The geographic location of territory invaded by Agricola remains unclear, with Tacitus giving few specific clues. In Agricola's third year of campaigning we are told that the army headed north, reaching the *Taum* (*Taus* in the Birley translation) (*Agricola* 22). Often identified as the Firth of Tay, given the Romans' predilection to name estuaries, the *Taum* has been interpreted by some academics as the River Tyne (Woodman and Kraus 2014:207-208) although others disagree (Birley 2010:85; Hind 2013:4). As Woodman & Kraus note, *Taum* is one of the few geographical place names which occur in the *Agricola,* and which is usually interpreted as an estuary. However, they argue this could be a mistranslation, and possibly refers to a river. This has a wider impact on identification of other estuaries which appear later in the text, and the translation of this section affects our interpretation of where Agricola was campaigning in the north, and therefore also interpretation of those sites ascribed an Agricolan foundation date. Woodman suggests the possibility that rather than campaigning on and beyond the Forth-Clyde isthmus, Agricola's early activities actually take place north of the Solway Firth – River Tyne line.

The fourth season of campaigning saw Agricola secure the territories which he had previously invaded, creating a new frontier between the *Bodotria* and *Clota* (*Agricola* 23). Again, the assumption has always been that the *Bodotria* and *Clota* refer to the Forth and Clyde as these are two estuaries creating a narrow neck of land or isthmus between them. There may be little foundation for this; Rivet and Smith (1981:269-271. 309-310) analyse both words, and attempt to match them with the Forth and Clyde, but do not have enough evidence from the etymology of the original Latin to match these up to the actual estuaries, as they state under the entry for the *Bodotria*, "In the absence of firm forms, this variety of speculation is the best that can be offered." (1981:271). Tacitus notes that by fortifying the *Bodotria* and *Clota* isthmus line, the indigenous population are pushed into the northern land, as if it was a different island. This seems possibly to be a reference to the perceived narrow stretch of land between the two Firths. Two seasons later, Agricola enveloped tribal areas beyond the *Clota*, while undertaking reconnaissance of local harbours with the Roman fleet. It is here that Tacitus is explicit in claiming that Agricola made use of the navy in the invasion by "…pushing forwards simultaneously by land and sea" (*Agricola* 24). Tacitus says that once the local population had seen that the Romans were invading from the sea, they turned to armed struggle and attacked some sites. Under Agricola, the fleet circumnavigated Britain and but also attempted to "…find the furthest limit to Britain at last." (*Agricola* 27). As the book heads towards its climax, Agricola makes further use of the fleet, sending it to plunder and attack the local population (*Agricola* 29). This is followed by Agricola's confrontation with indigenous tribes at *Mons Graupius*, where he faced 30,000 tribesmen and won with minimal loses. Tacitus writes that the battle took place after the end of summer, causing Agricola to postpone his conquest, although the weather was not so bad that it prevented him instructing the fleet to sail around *Britannia*.

At the same time the fleet, with a favourable wind and reputation behind it, occupied the Trucculensian harbour, from which it has set out to coast along the adjacent shore of Britain, and to which it had now returned intact.
Tacitus *Agricola* 38

The site of the Trucculensian harbour is unknown, although there is some suggestion by Ogilvie and Richmond (1967:283) that the site could be Richborough, later home to the *Classis Britannica*, although this is dismissed by Woodman & Kraus (2014).

During his time in the north, Tacitus intimates that fortifications established by Agricola were secure until the army withdrew from Scotland, and implies that the army continually occupied fortifications because they had enough supplies to see themselves through the winter, and so prevent fortifications being occupied or razed by the enemy.

There was even time to spare for establishing castellum [camps or forts]. Experts commented that no other general selected suitable sites more wisely. No fort established by Agricola was ever taken by the enemy by storm or abandoned either by capitulation or by flight. In fact, they could make frequent sallies, for they were assured against long sieges by supplies to last for a year. Hence winter there had no terrors; the garrisons were self-sufficient.
Tacitus *Agricola* 22

At the end of the third year of campaigning, Tacitus notes,

The enemy were baffled and in despair, because they had been used to making good the summer's loses by successes in winter, and now they were under pressure in summer and winter alike.
Tacitus *Agricola* 22

It is not, however, clear if Tacitus is referring to permanent or temporary fortifications, but this ability to occupy northern fortifications through the winter is further demonstrated after the battle of Mons Graupius, as Tacitus states,

> *As the summer was already over and the war could not be extended further, he led the army down into the territory of the Boresti[6]... He himself, marching unhurriedly... settled the infantry and cavalry in winter quarters.*
>
> **Tacitus *Agricola* 38**

Hingley has commented that some units may have remained in the north, while others travelled back to fortifications in the south for the winter. The evidence for this flexibility comes from the Vindolanda tablets, which although dating to the CE 90s and early CE 100s, are probably reliable in relation to Agricola's activities (Bowman 1994:24, Hingley pers. comm.). By placing the army on the edge of Caledonia, or within in it at the fortress at Inchtuthil, the army was well-placed to monitor the indigenous population. Tacitus, through his description of Mons Graupius, portrays the local populations in the north of Britain as a significant threat, but this is not necessarily represented in the archaeological evidence. A lack of population centres and the concept put forward by Hingley of tribes consisting of a loose confederation of families, argues against the threatening portrayal of those in the north by Tacitus. It should be noted that there has been limited large-scale excavation of fortifications in the north of Scotland to conclude whether or not these had ever been attacked by the indigenous population.

It is unclear how long the Flavian sites were occupied for, with the general consensus being that the 1st century occupation of the north lasted around seven years (e.g. ScARF 2012a), although Woolliscroft and Hoffman (2006) argue that it may have been as long as 20 years. Tacitus stated in *Histories* (1, 2) that Britain, having been conquered was immediately let go. This could be a reference to the withdrawal from northern Scotland which is likely to have resulted from serious trouble having emerged with the kingdom of Dacia creating a need to find soldiers to fight there. Hobley (1989) suggests that the Roman coin supply at the northern forts dried up in CE 86-7, which forms the basis of the concept of this being the date of withdrawal. However, the same caveat as noted above applies here; so few northern Roman sites have been excavated, and in the absence of any further datable evidence, caution must be applied when making such a widespread assumption about the date of withdrawal. Hobley also studied coins from north of the Cheviots, noting that coins of CE 86, but not of 87 are found, which supports the argument of abandonment of Northern Britain around 86-88, with complete withdrawal by CE 90. If confirmed, this would suggest that north of the Forth-Clyde isthmus was only occupied for around 9-10 years.

There are a number of points which can be taken from the *Agricola*, albeit with some caution, and which impact on this research;

[6] Woodman notes the arguments for an alternative translation of *Boresti* as northern territories (2014:283).

- Agricola was the first Roman governor to lead an invasion of North Britain;
- Geographic locations and references (such as *Taum*) cannot necessarily be matched up with modern place names and locations in Scotland;
- Naval forces has a role in reconnaissance of the coast, inlets and possible firths;
- Naval forces also partook in harassment and attacks against the enemy;
- The Roman army was operating in a hostile environment, culminating in the battle at *Mons Graupius;*
- The occupation of North Britain was brief (based on Tacitus and limited archaeological evidence) and ended abruptly;
- Some fortifications had the potential to be occupied in the winter. It is not clear if these were forts or camps;
- The above point suggests that supply lines were capable of transporting large quantities of food and equipment to sustain each fortification. The fortifications had potential space to store a year's supply of foods on-site.

For this study, there are two conclusions which can be drawn from the *Agricola*; that naval forces had a role in the invasion and occupation of Northern Britain, and that fortifications were not necessarily only occupied during the summer campaigning season.

2.3. Interpretation Influences

Before the establishment of scientific dating methods, it was challenging to establish a date of origin for the majority of Roman sites in Scotland. Many sites, particularly those away from the Antonine Wall, were assumed to date to the 1st century invasion of Scotland because of the influence of the *Agricola*, and another, post-Roman text, *de situ Britanniae*. The latter, originating in the 18th century, was claimed to be Roman in origin and which details various locations as being originating in the Roman period. In some instances, these texts have led to the false attribution of an origin date to some sites, and therefore some caution needs to be exercised when dating sites in the absence of datable artefacts and materials. Although the influence of these texts does not affect the general findings of this study, it is necessary to recognise that re-appraisal of the datable evidence from various fortifications could see an increase or decrease in those sites attributed to the 1st century.

2.3.1. Tacitus

Not only has our knowledge of 1st century activity in Scotland been enhanced by the archaeological evidence, but more significantly by the rediscovery of a Roman period text, *Agricola*, a quasi-biographical and historical text detailing the 1st century military intervention into north *Britannia*. It is this account which has had an unduly influential impact on the modern understanding and interpretation of Roman activity in Scotland.

Rediscovered in the 15th century, it influenced early scholars who were beginning to explore Roman remains, especially as Tacitus claimed that Agricola personally selected the site of every fortification the army constructed during his governorship (*Agricola* 20). Many of the early antiquarians and archaeologists took the *Agricola* at face value, and assumed that most fortifications were therefore founded in this period (e.g. Roy 1793; Macdonald 1934:237), purely because Tacitus places Agricola in North Britain, although this is never defined as a more specific geographical area. When examining the various fortification sites in Scotland, it is notable that it is this influence which often underpins the dating of the sites where no artefacts or environmental remains have been located and which would potentially offer firmer dating. Has been outlined, there is some limited archaeological evidence to suggest pre-Agricolan activity in Scotland which itself suggests some embellishment of Agricola's achievements by Tacitus.

2.3.2. Richard of Cirencester

In 1747, a Copenhagen based professor, Charles Bertram, published Richardi Corinensis monachi Westmonasteriensis de situ Britanniae libri duo. E. Codici MS. descripsit, Notisque et Indice adornavit Carolus Bertram, otherwise known as de situ Britanniae. Bertram promoted this as a hitherto unseen work, allegedly written by Richard of Cirencester, a monk who lived around 1335-1401, and produced at least one other, genuine historical work, Speculum Historiale de Gestis Regum Angliae. Little notice was given to de situ Britanniae until William Stukeley (1756) argued that it was genuine, publishing it as *An Account of Richard of Cirencester, Monk of Westminster, and of his Works: With his Ancient Map of Roman Britain*; and the Itinerary Thereof. Stukeley was no stranger to Roman antiquities, having written such volumes as *An Account of a Roman Temple, and other Antiquities, near Graham's Dike in Scotland, and Palaeographia Britannica: Or Discourses on Antiquities in Britain* (1720). Stukeley's belief that Bertram's volume was genuine, led to its acceptance by antiquarians and scholars, and it was not until the 19th century when questions arose about its validity, because Bertram had never released the original document, only facsimiles. Wex (1846) was the first person to publish a treatise doubting the authenticity of Bertram's work. Bertram's forgery arguably had the most impact on interpreting Roman Scotland since the rediscovery of Tacitus' work, Agricola. Bertram's forgery influences works produced after the mid-18th century as seen in the maps and accounts in various volumes (e.g. Maitland 1757; Pennant 1790; Chalmers 1807; J. Stuart 1822; Small 1823). Such works detail various places and claiming these were the location of Roman fortifications taken from maps in Bertram's account. These maps also detail sections of Roman road, including in the northeast of Scotland where no Roman roads are confirmed. There are even mentions in the Aberdeenshire Historic Environment Record (HER) of roads suspected of being Roman in origin, and the original sources seem to have been influenced by Bertram.

Like *Agricola*, the work of Bertram does not directly affect the findings of this research, but there are a number of sites listed in his work as being Roman in origin, but which remain unconfirmed, such as Dundee and Stranraer. Some of these locations are mentioned by the 18th century antiquarian, Sir Robert Sibbald (1707) as having Roman origins, some of which crossover with *de Situ Britanniae*, and it is fair to speculate that both Bertram and Sibbald may have had access to a separate text which formed the basis for some of their speculations. Jones (2011) lists a number of unconfirmed camp sites, some of which may owe their Roman attribution to Bertram. Therefore, there should be some scepticism when sites are attributed a Flavian origin date without secure datable evidence, particularly when in older volumes which may have been influenced by Bertram and which may not have Roman origins.

2.4. Native and Roman Interaction

There is still disagreement about the nature of the Roman occupation of southern Scotland (and northern England) and whether it was opposed by the local population to the extent of stimulating an uprising or the need to impose a special control.

(ScARF 2012a:16)

As demonstrated later, fortifications were located in positions which allowed them to control aspects of the landscape, and this suggests some sort of relationship with the indigenous population, although whether or not this was one of convenience or hostility is not clear. Knowledge of the LIA has increased in recent years, with evidence indicating a coexistence in the Roman period which may have been because the army required local goods and resources. There are few large Iron Age settlements near Flavian sites, but there is evidence at several Roman forts of roundhouses at the same location, such as at Cargill, Bertha, and Cardean (Woolliscroft and Hoffmann 2006; Hoffmann 2009). Recent archaeological investigations at sites such as Tap O' Noth and Dunnicaer show thriving communities existed in Scotland before the Romans and continued after their departure, although the evidence from these sites suggest they were not occupied during the 1st century (Noble and MacIver 2016; 2017; Noble et al. 2018; 2019). Hingley (2014) argues, in relation to settlements on the Northumberland coastal plain, that the Roman army was probably reluctant to disrupt agricultural systems because they could benefit from these, something reflected in work by Mercer (2018), discussed in more depth later. A more recent study of LIA Scotland, focussing on the changing interpretation of regionalism, has shown an abundance of Iron Age activity in Northern Britain, although there remains a lack of more specific dating of most of these sites, and it is unclear which were occupied at the time of the Roman invasion (Toolis 2021:248, 250-251). The publication of the *Atlas of the Hillforts of Britain and Ireland* (G. R. Lock and Ralston 2022) has yet further indicated the complexities and lack of in-depth knowledge we have about the vast majority of Iron Age settlements in Britain. Putting aside the issues of dating, it is apparent that there were clusters of occupied sites in Northern Britain at the time of the initial Roman incursions. Further work is required to uncover more about these sites, and it is indicative than many which are located near Roman fortifications may have been occupied at the time of the initial invasion, and the during the subsequent occupation of Northern Britain. Until there is formal scientific dating of these sites, caution must be taken when drawing conclusions on the relationship between the indigenous population and the Roman military.

Limited excavations have taken place on LIA sites, and those that have taken place have not been on a large scale; many of these remain unpublished (Hingley 1992:26). This limits our ability to draw conclusions from the site occupants and their interactions with the invading forces. In many cases, datable evidence, such as materials and artefacts are lacking (ScARF 2012b:119) or simply do not survive. Site dating can also be hampered by poor excavations in previous years, and the ongoing issue with classifying indigenous fortifications as hillforts (Harding 2017:6-9). But as the SCARF report on the Iron Age notes,

> *" A problem for the detailed reconstructions of Iron Age life advocated in this report is that it is difficult to narrow down the occupation of sites to the extent that contemporaneity can be confirmed. While many sites may have been occupied over a period of decades, if not hundreds of years... have misled archaeologists into expectations of longevity for later prehistoric sites in general."*
> **ScARF Report on Iron Age Scotland 2012:119**

In the 21st century, scientific dating of Iron Age sites has become more commonplace and has enabled us to develop a more thorough idea of occupation periods. For example, radiocarbon dating and environmental analysis of Traprain Law (D. Hamilton and Haselgrove 2009) has helped to build up a chronological profile of occupation of a site which covered 4,000 years+, while targeting specific sites for analysis is an approach which is actively promoted and has been successful (ScARF 2012b; Cook 2010). Other types of scientific analysis are increasingly being applied to Iron Age materials, but a lack of some types of artefacts, hampers the establishment of wider dating frameworks (e.g. ScARF 2012b). Attempts at establishing pottery typologies has had some limited success, but needs further development, and more finds to be excavated in context. Instead, most fortifications remain undated, and it is difficult to allocate an occupation period to most sites when many may have been occupied for generations, and because sites can be much more complex than they initially appear, as has been noted in relation to settlement activity near Traprain Law (ScARF 2012b:10, 118). Without significant development of dating frameworks, which will rely upon targeted sampling and more excavations, along with reassessment of existing datable artefacts, it will be challenging to assign a secure, or even approximate occupation date to the majority of LIA sites.

One of the most used sources for dating of sites is when Roman material culture has been found on indigenous sites, although ScARF (2012b:121) notes that the challenge with this type of dating is that it can lead to, "a misleadingly short and late chronology". There is also the possibility that Roman artefacts were in use long after the military had departed North Britain. There have been few studies of the interaction between Romans and the indigenous population in Scotland. Harding (2012; 2017) provides one of the most recent and up-to-date synthesis of the pre-Roman period in Scotland, although he generally takes a maximalist approach to sites in Scotland because of the limited work which has taken places on these sites. Harding writes that the general trend, north of the Scottish Borders, is for Iron Age settlements to either be individual homesteads or village communities, and while earthworks enclose some of these, the large hillforts found in southern England are a rarity in the north (2017:356). Evidence from northern England shows these societies were based on dispersed rural settlements with occasional hillforts although Toolis (2021) warns of the bias of taking a sweeping, regionalist approach to sites in this period. Harding (2017:199) states that In southwest Scotland many settlements continue in the Roman period, but not as extensively as in other areas, such as the Scottish Borders, although this is speculative given that the occupation dates of most of the sites in the area are unknown, the exception being the sites discussed by Mercer and Harding below, and Burnswark.

In order to understand what the Romans would have found when arriving in the north, the possible impacts of this on locational decisions, and patterns in the archaeological record today, it is helpful to understand Iron Age social and economic structures. Hingley puts forward a household model for Iron Age populations defined as, "a group of people who reside in a single dwelling or in a loosely related series of dwellings" (1992:26). He acknowledges that some social links may have brought local social groups together and this may explain settlement patterns, and why there appears to be a lack of trading between these communities. As noted previously, little archaeological investigation has taken place into most of these sites. Most items found on Iron Age sites are for domestic use, with more sporadic finds of Roman materials on larger sites. Harding (2017:357) speculates that some Roman finds from indigenous sites in the northeast of Scotland may be because of attempts to quell local unrest, although it should be remembered that this conclusion is extrapolated from a statistically small number of finds, some of which may have been in use after the Roman army had left the area. As Hingley notes, there needs to be further work analysing finds from these sites. Harding suggests that the local tribe possibly located around the area which becomes Scottish/English border, the *Brigantes*, were possibly part of an alliance of agricultural communities, but Hingley concludes that there is not even any convincing evidence for large, centralised political groups such as tribes. He says that is therefore unlikely that these household groups or communities could band together against the Romans. It could therefore be argued that Hingley's research suggests that the tribes in North Britain rarely banded together, with *Mons Graupius* being a possible exception, while this lack of threat, could explain the apparent lack of defences surrounding some camps such as at Ayr and Milltimber.

The LIA economy in North Britain combines pastoralism with agriculture, supported by local resources, with Jobey (1966:6) speculating that the analysis of organic evidence indicates that there was a zone, up to 30 miles north of Hadrian's Wall, where indigenous settlements were put under Imperial control, presumably for agricultural purposes. This idea is discussed further in Mercer's (2018) study of Iron Age activity in the southwest of Scotland, which focuses on several sites in Eskdale; Castle O'er and Ballieshill, both of which are near the Roman sites of Birrens. Harding (2017:231) argues that both sites could continue to exist by the Romans, because they could have supplied cattle to the army. It is possible that the indigenous tribes in this part of the country had long-term exposure to the Romans given that Carlisle was occupied in the early 70s CE, and this may have enabled them to establish and develop good relations with the army, but equally, we must be aware that this is one small area of Scotland and it may not represent the situation further away from the established Stanegate fortifications. With Roman forts constructed in fertile areas, it would have been necessary for the army to acquire local resources to build these, and easier to gain them from the tribes; this may explain why some hillforts and settlements co-existed with the military, but this also needs to be seen considering the Roman siege works at Burnswark. As well as cattle, Mercer suggests Iron Age households/communities may have supplied army's need for horses, as described by Caesar in southern England. In Scotland, evidence of chariots, from the burial at Newbridge near Edinburgh, albeit dating to the pre-Roman period (Carter, Hunter, and Smith 2010), and a wheel from the ditch at Raedykes (NSA 1845: xi, Kincardine, 249–50) has shown there would have been a need for horses in the north, although this is not necessarily reflected in the numbers of remains found on other Roman and indigenous sites.

Although there is a lack of archaeological evidence to suggest that there was a substantial indigenous threat to the Roman army in the north, the circumstantial evidence is indicative that the Roman army was reacting to some sort of security risk. The evidence indicates a larger Iron Age population than previously thought, albeit spread across the landscape. In the Hadrianic period, there was enough of a threat to warrant the construction of a series of coastal fortifications on the Cumbrian coast, and although it is unclear where the threat was coming from, there are a significant number of promontory fortifications and smaller hillforts on the Solway coast, opposite the Hadrianic sites, to suggest that these may have been a threat or the cause of construction of this section of the Wall and coastal defences (Toolis 2003; 2015; 2021). It seems unlikely that this threat only emerged in the Hadrianic period, a mere 50 years or so after the Flavian withdrawal from Scotland, particularly given that Tacitus records the Agricola harried indigenous coastal settlements (*Agricola* 22). Elsewhere in Scotland there are larger hillfort examples, such as at Traprain Law and Burnswark. Evidence from the latter site indicates Roman activity around the base of the hill in the form of two camps, with the most recent evidence dating this to the Flavian period. There is no datable evidence of occupation from the settlement on top of Burnswark, and no evidence from the immediate area of Flavian activity; the nearest fort, Birrens, which is a couple of miles to the south has yielded firm Hadrianic and Antonine evidence, with only a slight implication of earlier activity in the form of a ditch underneath the fort which Robertson (Robertson 1975) speculated was Flavian. That is not to say that the indigenous population was not problematic to the Romans, and perhaps attacks as that described by Agricola on a camp by the natives (*Agricola* 26) occurred frequently enough to warrant further military action. However, we do need to be cautious that we do not unreservedly project the findings from a small number of sites or region onto sites in the rest of the region. As will be demonstrated later few Roman forts are constructed near indigenous sites, and when they are, the native forts are usually quite small and could easily have been taken out by the Roman army if there was a need to; these may have posed less of a threat than portrayed by Tacitus.

2.5. Roman Military Infrastructure

The systematic study of forts within their wider landscapes should be encouraged...
ScARF 2012:35

As noted earlier, I have identified around 130 fortifications, which originate, or are likely to have originated in the 1st century. This section introduces the various different types of military fortifications and related infrastructure which have been identified in Flavian Scotland, and the archaeological evidence for these structures. Roman fortifications in Scotland primarily consist of five different types of structure:

- Legionary fortress – the largest type of Flavian-period fortification found in Scotland. Described as the winter quarters for a legion (Bishop 2013:1), the fortress would have acted as the regional command centre for troops in the area;
- Camps – Tented cities surrounded by (usually) a single turf rampart and ditch, leaving little trace in the archaeological record, and are traditionally assumed to have been occupied on a temporary basis;
- Forts – Permanent installations constructed from turf and timber (in Flavian Scotland), with more complex defences than camps;
- Fortlets – Small structures with simple rampart and ditch defences, often located in strategic positions in the landscapes, such as on roads or at river crossings;
- Towers – Wooden structures with simple defensive arrangements, and which may have acted as early warning posts, signal relay stations, or both.

A second type of fortress, the vexillation fortress, has been identified at Carpow in Perthshire, which is assumed to date to the 3rd century Severan, although Warry (2006:65-69) argues that Carpow has a Commodian foundation based on a fragmentary inscription. These fortifications are larger than auxiliary forts and smaller than legionary fortresses, and housed both auxiliaries and legionaries. Bidwell and Hodgson (2009:26), cite the example of Longthorpe, in England which could have accommodated 1,440-1,760 legionaries and around 1,000 auxiliaries, including cavalry. There are no examples of such fortifications from Flavian Scotland.

2.5.1. Other Structures

Before considering the evidence for the standard types of fortification previously outlined, there are a number of additional structures which have traditionally been associated with the Roman military, although these sites tend to lack archaeological evidence proving Roman origins. These structures include the alleged burial mound of a sailor (Tibbs 2019:113), the possible building known as Arthur's O'on (Tibbs 2019:57-58), and the possible harbour at Brigurd, Ayrshire (Newall and Lonie 1972); I discuss the latter site later in this chapter. A series of ditches have been recorded during excavations, as lying underneath the forts at Birrens (Robertson 1975), Cramond (N. Holmes 2003), and Bar Hill (Macdonald and Park 1906); however, there has only been evidence for 1st century activity found at Birrens. Jones (2020) has published a paper which argues that the ditches at Bar Hill fort may belong to a construction camp for the fort. This is an argument that might apply to the Birrens and Cramond as well, although all three sites have other space nearby which could have accommodated a separate construction camp. Further investigation of these features is needed to confirm this, potentially through geophysical survey. Until there is further evidence, we should not rule out either possibility, that these ditches either belong to an earlier fortification or a construction camp.

Woolliscroft et al (2002), and with Hoffmann (2006:109-111), have put forward an interesting proposal which suggests that some small Romano-British enclosures may have a Roman military purpose. This was based on their excavation of an open-ended enclosure on the line of the Gask Ridge, located next to the Roman road as it approaches the fort at Strageath. Although they summarise that the evidence is too inconclusive to definitively prove that this was a Flavian military structure, it is reminiscent of several small camps, such as Gourdie, which share some similarities with enclosures; this is an area which would benefit from further study.

Acknowledgement of the sites discussed in this section is relevant because they indicate that the military occupation of Scotland is complex, and may extend beyond that the main military structures. The enclosure excavated by Woolliscroft and Hoffmann is particularly relevant because if such enclosures are built by the Roman army, it would suggest a whole new classification of camp which would potentially alter our understanding of military occupation of Scotland in the Roman period.

2.5.2. Legionary Fortress

There is one 1st century fortress in Scotland, at Inchtuthil, and which covers an area of 21.5 hectares. It is located on a raised plateau, shared with at least two Roman camps and one indigenous site, carved out by the River Tay; the fortress and camps at Inchtuthil are well-protected from potential attackers. The River Tay runs around the eastern and southern sides of the peninsula, although there is some sign that it has changed its course and may have originally run to the north of the fortress, eroding the peninsula and defences (Woolliscroft and Hoffmann 2006). The fortress would have controlled Roman activity in the area, and possibly for most of Scotland given that its next nearest fortress was at York, 250 miles to the south. Inchtuthil is the same size and has a similar layout to the 1st century fortification at Caerleon, occupied by the *Legio II Augusta* around CE 74 (Bishop 2013:61). The fortress at Inchtuthil is 21.5 hectares, 0.5 hectares more than the fortification at York, occupied by the *Legio IX Hispana* from CE 81 to possibly around CE 106 (ibid:118), and originally constructed in turf and timber, occupied by the *Legio II Adiutrix* from CE 78-88, and then rebuilt in stone with the *Legio XX Valeria* occupying the site from about CE 89 onwards (ibid:64). No epigraphic material or literary references have been recovered from Inchtuthil, so there is no confirmation of which legion occupied the site, or even the Roman name for the fortress.

Inchtuthil legionary fortress would have been an integral part of the Roman occupation of the north, although there is evidence that the fortress was incomplete at the time of its abandonment; the wooden *principia* was much smaller than the space allocated for it in the centre of the fortress, and Pitts and St Joseph (1985) speculated this was because it was due to be reconstructed in stone. Curiously, the wooden *principia* is positioned at a slightly different angle to the *via praetoria* and the *porta praetoria* which either suggests that it was constructed before the rest of the site is laid out, or that it belongs to a fortification on a slightly different alignment.

The earliest reference to Inchtuthil dates to 1526 when Hector Boece (1527) refers to the site as a Pictish town in his *Scotorum Historiae*. Most of the early antiquarians mention the site, including Roy (1793), Maitland (1757), and Pennant (1790). The first detailed plan of the site was drawn by Roy in 1755, although the site was altered by agriculture only a few years later. In 1901, John Abercromby (1902) undertook an excavation of parts of the fortress on behalf of the Society of Antiquaries of Scotland, including the *via principalis* and several features outside of the fortress including the so-called redoubt or eastern compound. More extensive excavations took place between 1952 and 1965, with Richmond and St Joseph (1985) uncovering evidence of internal buildings such as the *principia*, the *praetorium*, granaries, and barracks. They found that some of the buildings had not yet been built as there were gaps where there should have been structures. Richmond and St Joseph concluded that the fortress was deliberately dismantled before construction of the interior was completed. Although they extensively excavated the site, they did not uncover all of it; their plan of the fortress is a composite, showing the foundations of the building based on their knowledge of other sites, rather than only what they excavated. Between 2009 and 2011, Woolliscroft and Hoffmann of The Roman Gask Project, undertook magnetic and resistance surveys of the fortress and some of the surrounding features. The results confirmed Richmond and St Joseph's plan of the site, and also revealed evidence of a potential smaller camp at the southwestern end of the peninsula. Early datable artefact evidence for the legionary fortress at Inchtuthil was uncovered by Richmond (1952) during his early excavations and published by Pitts and St Joseph. The pottery found indicates a Flavian date (specified as Agricolan CE 83-85).

2.5.3. Camps

The most common type of fortification found in Roman Scotland are camps, with in excess of 150 examples known, while there are numerous unconfirmed and possible camp sites (R. H. Jones 2011); of these, there are 65 likely to originate in the 1st century. In-depth analysis of camps in England has been undertaken by Leslie (1995), Welfare & Swann (1995), and Jones (2012). An extensive survey of camps in Scotland has been undertaken by Jones, so I do not propose to repeat this type of analysis here, while the layout of a camp, from the classical texts, is discussed as part of the orientation of fortifications, later in this monograph.

Camps are interpreted as temporary structures, constructed quickly and occupied briefly, perhaps only overnight or for a few days as the army moved from one place to another, but as part of this research, I argue that the terminology which refers to this type of fortification as a temporary encampment, is misleading. Tacitus implies that camps may have been occupied through the winter months,

> *No castellum [camp or fort] of his was ever stormed or ever abandoned through surrender or flight. In fact, the men made frequent sallies, for they were protected against long siege by supplies to last a year. Thus winter in these castellum was free from fear, and each could take care of itself.*
> **Tacitus *Agricola* 22**

As will be shown later, some encampments are positioned in locations similar to those of forts indicating that they potentially fulfilling the same role; controlling routes of movement through the landscape. It therefore would make sense that these types of camps were occupied on a longer-term basis, something which may be seen in the archaeological record from Kintore camp, where dating evidence from the ovens indicate an occupation of longer than a few days (R. H. Jones 2011:192; Cook and Dunbar 2008; Cook, Dunbar, and Heawood 2009).

> *There are potentially three sorts of fortification defined for a camp. The first is for the passage of one night or for brief occupation on a march. The raised turves are laid out in line, forming a rampart...*
>
> *But a stationary camp is fortified with greater care and effort, whether in summer or winter, when the enemy is near... The men distribute their shields and packs in a circle around their own standards and, armed only with a sword, open a fosse 9-foot-wide... or if a major hostile force is feared 17 foot... The rampart is then raised between lines of revetments or barriers of logs and branches, interposed to stop the earth easily falling away. Above it a system of battlements and turrets is constructed like a wall.*[7]
> **Vegetius *Epitoma* III:8**

Vegetius discusses three types of military camp, although he is writing 300 years after the Flavian period, and military techniques may have changed between the 1st and 4th centuries. Richmond (1955:300-304) develops the concept of the four types of Roman camp, which is further refined by Lepper and Frere (1988:260), and re-analysed by Jones (2011:7). Essentially camps in Scotland can be divided into four categories (R. H. Jones 2011:7):

- Marching camps: temporary bases of a tented army on campaign or manoeuvres away from their base.
- Practice camps: small camps which often cluster together indicating the exercise grounds and training regimes of the soldiers, including construction of ramparts, ditches and gates.
- Siege camps: enclosures constructed to house troops besieging a nearby site.
- Construction camps: temporary enclosures housing soldiers involved in construction of a nearby fort or frontier.

The majority of camps fall into the first category, while clusters such as those at Dalswinton and Lochlands are assumed to have been built as practice sites for the soldiers. The only identified siege camps can be found at Burnswark, while most of those classified as construction have been labelled as such because of their proximity to the Antonine Wall. Later, I argue for a further type of camp, one which is replicating the role of a fort in that it is positioned to control movement through the immediate landscape, and which may not have been occupied on a temporary basis.

2.5.4. Forts

While camps are portrayed as temporary structures, forts are interpreted as the opposite; permanent installations,

---
[7] Vegetius does not note what the third type of camp is.

built from turf with timber super-structures (in 1st century Scotland), but with more extensive rampart and ditch defensive arrangements. Forts functioned as local base for soldiers, while also fulfilling administrative, religious, financial functions, along with accommodation and food storage, but had a broadly similar layout to camps. A fuller description of the origins, functions and history of Roman forts in Britain can be found in Bidwell (2013).

Thirty-three forts originating in the Flavian period have been identified in Scotland, primarily dated using artefactual or scientific methods. The forts are found across most of the country, with the majority in the Lowlands, and the most northerly known site at Stracathro in Angus; beyond this, only camps have been identified. This seems an unusual place to end the chain of permanent fortifications as it leaves open the possibility that those outside the military zone could travel to the east of Stracathro fort and enter Roman territory without detection. This either indicates an as yet unidentified Roman site near Stonehaven, or that the military strategy was not to control the wider landscape through the positioning of forts. The latter reason may also explain why there are a lack of Flavian fortifications identified on the Forth-Clyde isthmus. Tacitus writes the following, which has been interpreted by most scholars as referring to this isthmus,

> *The fourth summer is spent securing the districts already overrun... For the Clota [Firth of Clyde] and Bodotria [Firth of Forth], carried far back inland by the tides of opposite seas, are separated by only a narrow neck of land. This neck was now secured by garrisons, and the whole sweep of land to the south was safe in our hands.*
> **Tacitus *Agricola* 23**

Despite attempts to locate Flavian forts on the isthmus Scotland (e.g. Hanson and Maxwell 1986; Hanson 1991), there are relatively few confirmed sites, although there is a concentration of sites in the east where the River Caron meets the Forth around Camelon. These are the Lochlands series of camps, the Camelon forts, and the probable Roman structure Arthur's O'on. The fort of Mollins (Hanson and Maxwell 1980) is centrally located on the Fort-Clyde isthmus, while the next Flavian site further west is the fort at Barochan Hill. Further north of the central isthmus, camps are located to the south and east of the Highland Fault Line, with a concentration of encampments and forts at Ardoch. It is therefore unclear if Tacitus was mistaken with his information regrding the construction of fortifications in this area, or there are still 1st century fortifications awaiting discovery on the isthmus. An alternative explanation presents itself in light of my research; that the chain of fortifications refered to by Tactitus not only consisted of forts, but also of camps fulfilling the role of their permanent counterparts.

2.5.5. *Fortlets*

A fortlet was a small fortification, often unfavourably compared to forts, despite the difference in internal layout, structures and size. Where we know the internal layout of such sites in Scotland, they follow the same pattern: an internal space containing buildings (probably barracks) and storage space, separated by a small road. A rampart and ditch surrounded the internal structures, over which there was a causewayed road. Some fortlets are surrounded by several ditches, and some may have had an annexe attached to them. While there are examples constructed from stone, those in Scotland are usually constructed out of turf and timber. Fortlets are generally positioned between the forts, or used to guard areas of strategic importance, such as river crossings or road junctions (Symonds 2018; 2020)

Nine fortlets have been identified in Scotland as originating during the 1st century, with the dating evidence from each site varying. Sites which are dated using finds include the fortlet at Gatehouse of Fleet which was first recorded by St Joseph (1951:51), who subsequently excavated it over two years (1960:29; 1961a:35). St Joseph noted that the pottery finds from the site indicated a Flavian date of occupation (See also Hartley 1972:11). Excavating at Milton in the 1940s and 1950s, Clarke uncovered a fortlet dated to the Antonine period, although Clarke (1947; 1948; 1949; 1950:200; 1951; 1952) speculated it was established in the late Flavian era while noting that some of the pottery may have been late Hadrianic. The fortlet at Cargill was excavated by St Joseph (1965), although the results remain unpublished (Woolliscroft and Hoffmann 2006:151), and the site assumed to be Flavian (RCAHMS 1994:77). Dating was finally confirmed by Woolliscroft and Hoffmann (2003), who discovered shards of late 1st century glass during field walking of the site. Castle Greg was first recorded in the OSA, and subject to archaeological explorations in the middle of the 19th century (M'Call 1894:9-12) revealing pottery and coins, the latter having a range of dates including Vespasian, Hadrian, and Antoninus Pius. The fortlet also has a Stracathro-type style gate indicating a 1st century date of origin.

Other fortlets have been given a date due to their proximity to other sites, and their chronology is less certain, such as the fortlet at Bankhead (Carnwath) which was discovered from the air by Maxwell and has been partially destroyed by quarrying (Frere, Hassall, and Tomlin 1985:265). The fortlet was excavated by Maxwell and Wilson (1987) who assumed it had a Flavian date because of its dimensions and triple ditch, similar to the fortlet at Castle Greg. We have recovered no datable evidence from Glenbank fortlet, however, it is assumed it is Flavian based on the dating of similar structures in the area (Woolliscroft and Hoffmann 2009a). Another site assumed to date to the Flavian period is the fortlet at Kirkland, also identified by Maxwell during aerial reconnaissance and subsequently excavated by him and St Joseph (Frere, Tomlin, and Hassall 1990:312). The fortlet had one period of occupation and was subsequently demolished with the supposition being that the site originated in the Flavian period (Burnham et al. 1993:281).

Another fortlet site which has vague dating is at Inverquharity, where no datable evidence has been recovered, but is assumed to be of Flavian date due to the similarities and proximity to a camp, also assumed to be Flavian (Frere, Tomlin, and Hassall 1984). As Steer (1964) notes, there is a lack of datable evidence for the fortlet at Kaims Castle, but its proximity to Ardoch and its similarities to sites at Old Burrow and Martinhoe in Devon, suggest it is probable it is Flavian, though may have been re-occupied in the Antonine period. The possible fortlet at Beattock Barnhill is another example of this, first identified from the air in 1977 (Maxwell and Wilson 1987:31) as an enclosure within the northwest corner of the camp. Trenching in 1984 indicates that it is earlier than the camp, the latter dating to the Flavian period suggesting that the fortlet is also from the 1st century.

2.5.6. Towers

Towers are found on many frontiers from across the Empire, and in Scotland are primarily concentrated around the Gask Ridge in Perthshire where they are positioned on alternate sides of a Roman road, creating a secure route. Additional towers are located on various hills in southern Scotland and also appear to have formed part of a separate signalling network. Capacity to signal effectively between these sites was more limited because of the large distances between each one. There are some other probable tower sites, most of which are unconfirmed as being Roman and are undated, and these have not been included here. Datable evidence for the tower sites is lacking, but the assumption is that the towers in Scotland belong to the 1st century, usually because of their proximity to Flavian forts such as Ardoch, Strageath, Bertha and Newstead; the dating for these sites is an assumption.

The purpose of the chain of fortifications along the Gask Ridge remains unclear; Woolliscroft (2002), and with Hoffmann (2006) argue it is a secure frontier with towers acting as both signal stations and observation posts, with the latter being the primary function, while Dobat (2009) proposes that it is a protected supply line for Inchtuthil legionary fortress. Hanson and Maxwell (1986:157) go further, arguing that the system was set up to protect indigenous tribes in Fife from attack from those living in the Highlands. All three proposals could be possible; the former is confirmed by signalling modelling, although I discuss this in further detail later. The absence of a large supply base on the coast suggests an overland supply route, but given the positioning of a number of camps on the coast, making them suitable for landing sea-borne supplies indicates that a supply base has not yet been identified. The concept that the Gask Ridge line is a protective barrier for friendly tribes, is an interesting idea, but could be easily circumvented by land or sea rendering it ineffective, plus such a concentration of fortifications would be resource intensive if fully manned. Graafstal has noticed similarities between this arrangement in central Scotland, and a series of towers recently discovered on the Oude-Rijn river in Utrecht, part of the Dutch frontier, and discussed earlier in this chapter. Graafstal (2020:188) argues that these sites make up a fortified transport corridor, with the fortifications providing continuous surveillance and protection of supply lines, in this instance, they may have formed part of the supply infrastructure for the planned advance into *Britannia* by Caligula. While this hypothesis could explain the purpose of the fortifications along the Gask Ridge, more work needs to be undertaken into the sites in southern Scotland to clarify if these were capable to signalling between each other.

2.5.7. Coastal Sites

Given the discussion, later in this monograph about the relationship between fortifications and waterways, it is worth briefly considering those sites located on the coast. Circumstantial evidence, which will be discussed in more detail later, may support the assertion the Romans invaded North Britain, depending heavily on the sea, and using rivers and their valleys to reach the interior. The transportation of supplies and small groups of soldiers (to secure an area and establish fortifications), as part of an invading force, could potentially be achieved much more efficiently and quickly via the sea and inland waterways, rather than attempting to move them over unfamiliar and possibly dangerous terrain, particularly before establishment of a formalised road network. The role of coastal sites is worth exploring further and may help to challenge assumptions previously held about Roman fortifications and their location. For example, Dobat (2009) has suggested that the Gask Ridge chain of fortifications created a protected supply line for the fortress at Inchtuthil. Such a route originating in southern or central Scotland, leading to Inchtuthil, is not the most efficient or quickest path imaginable; landing supplies at a coastal camp (the nearest being Dun on the Montrose Basin), or shipping them directly to the fortress on the River Tay would be more efficient.

As part of this research, around 50 Roman sites (Figure 2.1) have been examined. These sites inlcude 7 Flavian camps are located either directly on the coast, or just inside the river mouths, with a small number further inland on the Firths (e.g. Bertha and Camelon) which are at the extent of the tidal limits. Also examined are a number of undated and possible fortification sites, along with a number identified as having Roman origins as noted by Sir Robert Sibbald in the 17th century (see Chapter 7.4). This may suggest that Flavian sites are on the whole avoiding coastal positioning, while those in later periods are not, although there are a number of unconfirmed and undated fortifications on the coast. By locating fortifications at the mouths of rivers, it could represent an attempt to control both movement along the coast, and access to the inland waterways, as well as also acting as landing points for supplies to be shipped upriver.

2.5.8. Road Networks

The Roman road network in Scotland is much more complex than frequently portrayed in the literature. Despite how the network appears in Figure 2.2, most sections of road remain unconfirmed and undated, while

Facing the Enemy?

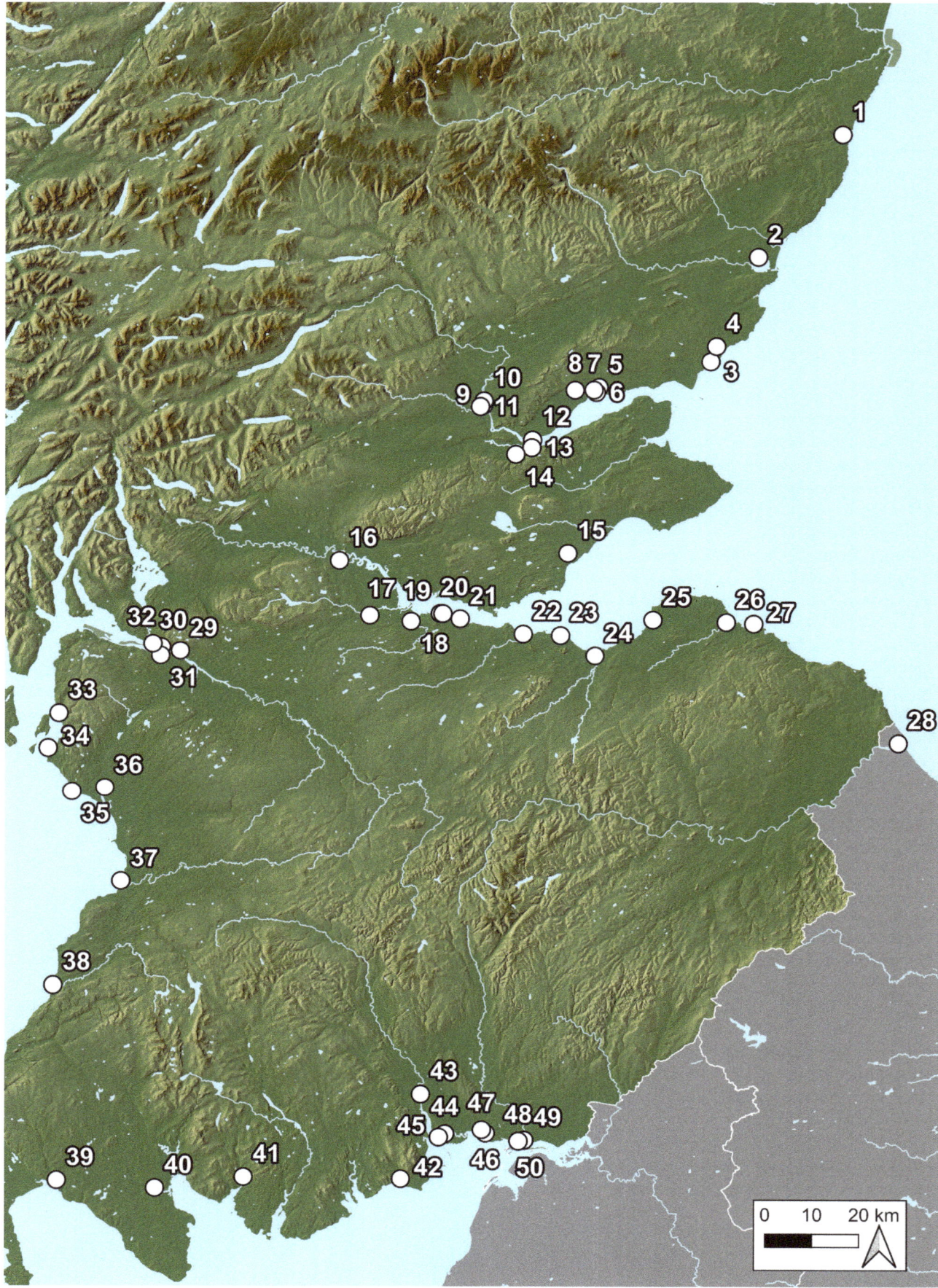

Figure 2.1. Roman sites (multiple periods) on the coast or within tidal ranges on firths and rivers.

Key to Figure 2.1:

#	Site	#	Site
1	Stonehaven (Camp - Possible)	26	Tyninghame (Sibbald Site)
2	Dun (Camp)	27	Dunbar (Sibbald Site)
3	Scryne Smithy (Camp - Possible)	28	Berwick (Sibbald Site)
4	Grahamston Cottages (Camp - Possible)	29	Old Kilpatrick (Fort)
5	Bullion (Camp - Possible)	30	Dumbuck Hill (Sibbald Site)
6	Invergowrie (Camp)	31	Bishopton, Whitemoss (Fort)
7	Mylnefield (Fort - Possible)	32	Dumbarton (Sibbald Site)
8	Longforgan (Camp)	33	Largs (Camp - Possible)
9	Scone Park (Camp)	34	Brigurd (Harbour - Possible)
10	Grassy Walls (Camp)	35	Ardrossan (Camp - Possible)
11	Bertha (Fort)	36	Irvine - Kilwinning (Camp - Possible)
12	St Madoes (Camp)	37	Ayr (Camp, Sibbald Site)
13	Carpow (Fort, Camps)	38	Girvan Mains (Camps)
14	Abernethy (Carey) (Camp)	39	Glenluce (Camp)
15	Carberry (Camp - Possible)	40	Bladnoch (Fortlet)
16	Stirling (Sibbald Site)	41	Gatehouse of Fleet (Fortlet)
17	Camelon (Forts, Sibbald Sites)	42	Mains of Southwick (Camp - Possible)
18	Inveravon (Fort, Camps, Sibbald Site)	43	Dumfries (Sibbald Site)
19	Bridgeness (Sibbald Site)	44	Ward Law (Fort, Camp)
20	Carriden (Sibbald Site)	45	Lantonside (Fortlet)
21	Blackness (Sibbald Site)	46	Summerfield (Camp - Possible)
22	Cramond (Fort, Sibbald Site)	47	Ruthwell (Camp)
23	Leith (Sibbald Site)	48	Hayknowes (Camp - Possible)
24	Inveresk (Fort, Sibbald Site)	49	Hillside (Camp)
25	Aberlady (Sibbald Site)	50	Annanfoot (Camp)

the legacy of *de situ Britanniae* (Stukeley 1756; Bertram 1809) can be seen on various entries in Canmore and in the regional HERs. The first significant attempt, in the 20th century, to understand the Roman road network in Scotland, was started by Crawford (1949) who identified roads through aerial photographic surveys in the north, beyond the Antonine Wall. Both he and St Joseph (amongst others) were active aerial surveyors in Scotland around this time, and traced extensive road sections. St Joseph covered larger parts of Scotland and, for example, produced several reports in *The Roman Occupation of South Western Scotland* (Miller 1952), tracing many of the routes through the Clyde valley, as well as the road westwards through Dumfries & Galloway. Many other reports have been produced which trace sections of road, such as Maxwell and Hanson (1986) who attempt to locate sections of road in the southeast of Scotland. Next to St Joseph, Maxwell (e.g. 1983; 2015; and with Hanson and Maxwell 1986; Maxwell and Wilson 1987) is probably the most significant contributor to knowledge of Roman roads in Scotland, mainly resulting from his aerial photography programme with RCAHMS. While this work has provided a useful basis for our knowledge of the road network, most of these routes have not been excavated or confirmed as being Roman, and there is a risk that these are medieval or later drove or military roads. Maxwell (1980) even postulates that as roads have not been located at some sites, then it is possible that these were constructed and then abandoned before they could be joined to the network. This could lend credence to the argument, proposed later in the monograph, that some sites were initially connected via the river networks before the establishment of formalised roads.

Two of the only studies to utilise GIS and spatial analysis in the analysis of Roman Scotland have been undertaken by Hannon (2018) and Graafstal (2020:153). Hannon processes various types of mapping and laser scanning data in his analysis of the Antonine Wall, while Graafstal also examines the Military Way on the Wall, noting that it was crucial for the transport of food supplies, resources, equipment and building materials. Through his analysis, Graafstal concludes that the road was constructed early in the building sequence of the Wall because of the positioning of the road in relation to the forts and Wall.

As mentioned, the road north of the Forth-Clyde isthmus was first traced from the air by Crawford, with much follow up work from St Joseph. More recent work on this has been undertaken by Woolliscroft and Hoffmann (2006), with both continuing to investigate the road after it crosses the River Tay at Bertha (Hoffmann pers. comm.). From this area, the road is increasingly difficult to trace although it appears to branch near Kirriemuir where one section heads towards the sites at Inverquharity, while the other section appears to head towards the next major fort, at Stracathro, although there is no trace of the road near the site; this is de. Our knowledge of the network in Scotland is limited, leading to much speculation. For example, Crawford (1949:61) assumed that an exposed section of road in Cauldhame Woods, by Kirriemuir was Roman, but further analysis in the 1950s disputed this because the

Figure 2.2. Roman roads in Scotland.

Figure 2.3. Possible Roman road, Cauldhame Wood, Kirriemuir (September 2019).

road lacked a metalled surface and had no camber (JRS 1958:219). However, during a visit to this section of road in 2019, I identified a camber and ditches along both sides, which can be seen in Figure 2.3. This demonstrates how fragmented our knowledge of this infrastructure is, and the benefits of an extensive re-appraisal of the various sections of road.

2.5.9. Coastal and River Networks

As detailed earlier, several sections of the *Agricola* mentions coastal and river activities, and the use of these to the advantage of the Roman army. Figure 2.4 details the major Scottish rivers and firths mentioned in *Facing the Enemy*. Tacitus states that Agricola (*Agricola* 25) was the first governor to bring the navy and the army together as part of an invasion force and shows that Agricola was using the fleet for intelligence gathering and reconnaissance by spying on enemy harbours. What is not clear from the text is whether this was limited to coastal sites in the open sea, or if the fleet was sailing up the Firths and rivers, a tactic which Tacitus (*Annals* 2:5) notes Germanicus deployed when invading Germany. While there is little evidence on the ground to support this, there are camps in some of these locations such as Dun on the Montrose Basin. Tacitus writes that Agricola made use of water and the fleet, using them as an advance guard and as a source of wonder and threat over the indigenous population in the run up to the final confrontation at *Mons Graupius*,

> *Accordingly, he sent the fleet ahead to plunder at various points in order to spread general panic and uncertainty. The army was marching light...*
>
> **Tacitus *Agricola* 29**

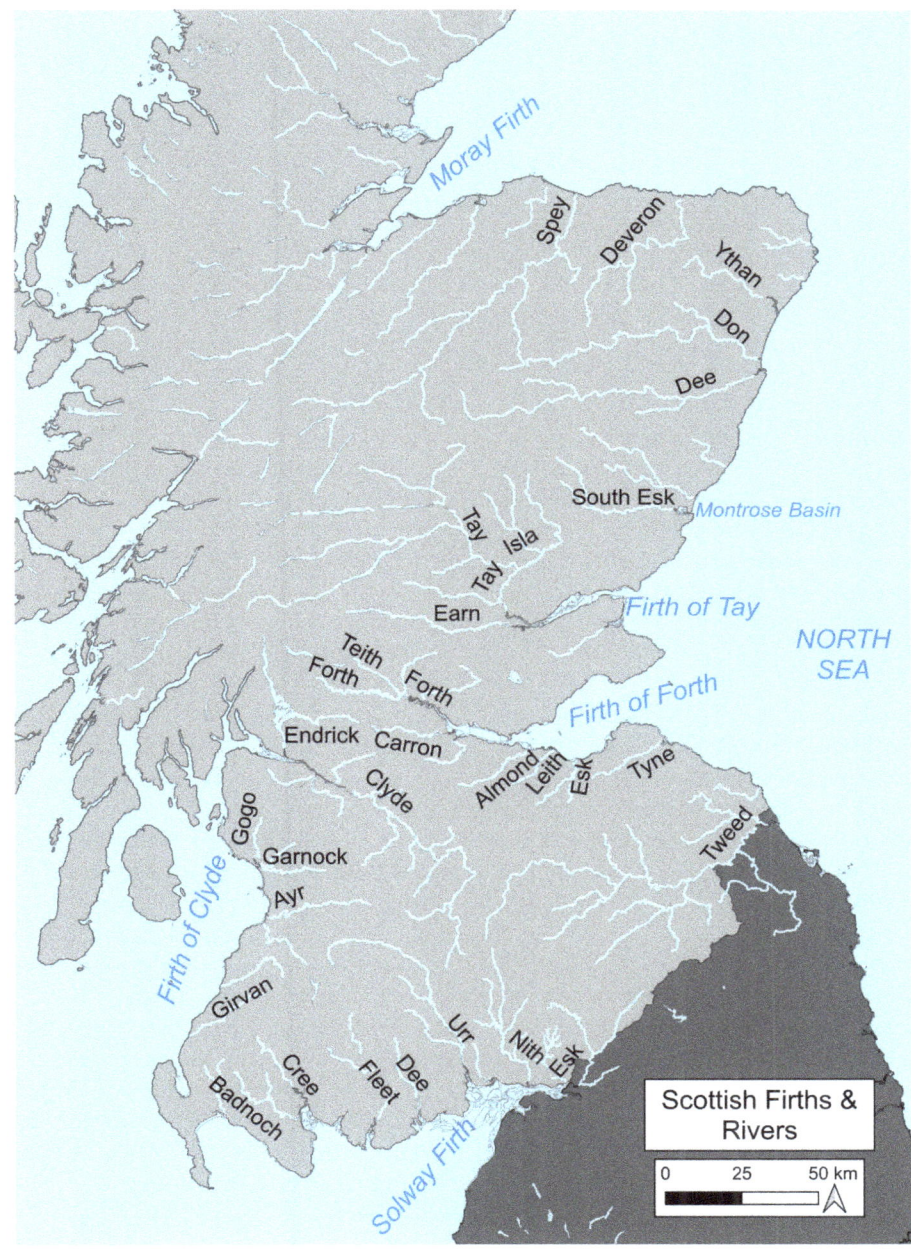

Figure 2.4. Main firths and rivers around Scotland highlighted in the text.

The location of the *Mons Graupius* battle site remains unlocated (e.g. Maxwell 1989; 1990; Hanson 1991; Breeze 1993; 2011; Keppie 1998), and although Tacitus notes there was an advance attack on coastal settlements, none of these have been identified in the archaeological record. This implies that there was an active fleet in the north of Britain, which must have had a base for repairs and supplies, but this remains unidentified. River fleets have been identified elsewhere in the Empire (Rankov 2009), and it is possible that there were similar arrangements for patrolling the coast and the Firths in Scotland; Tacitus (*Annals*) has recorded that troops and supplies were moved by water in Germany, and it seems probable this also happened in Scotland, but on the east coast, only two Flavian camps have been identified (although there are several undated sites), and similarly on the west coast, there are also a lack of 1st century fortifications, with a small number of exceptions.

While it would have been possible for ships to be beached when landing cargo, especially large and bulky items, this would have been impractical on a long-term basis given variances in weather, shoreline conditions and tides. For coastal sites, a beach may have sufficed, although mid-sized ships with a keel would have struggled to be beached. Given the Roman predilection for engineering, it is more than likely that some sort of harbour or docking infrastructure would be established. Further inland, away from tidal influences, there would have been less opportunity to beach boats and if supplies were being delivered to riverside fortifications, then a dock would have been necessary, particularly for fast-flowing rivers such as the Tay. There is the possibility that the fleet, or at least the smaller vessels, were servicing sites further inland but still had access to the sea. This is not accidental, and the ability to sail and navigate (by boat or on foot) inland along the river valleys, indicates that these structures may have been pivotal in the early invasion and subsequent consolidation of the territory before the road network is established and made fit for purpose.

Visy (2015:31) clarifies that water was an important element in the Roman strategy, and that the army aimed to reach river lines. The need of the army to secure this would also aid in the securing of natural resources and traffic routes. As Visy also notes, rivers change their courses and are ripe for later development making archaeological remains along wet areas much more difficult to identify. While there are very few Flavian sites identified or confirmed on the coast, the majority are located inland on the major rivers and the tributaries. Evidence of harbour or docking structures have been associated with three locations in Scotland. These are a 17th century account of part of a Roman harbour at Cramond, a stone harbour at Brigurd in Ayrshire, and the submerged remains of a wooden structure in the River Tay next to Bertha fort. These are discussed in more depth later.

Tacitus is also clear about the importance of using the sea to transport troops and equipment. Not only would this have been quick, but it would also have been the most economical method of moving goods and people over long distances (Green 1986). Using sea-going vessels, as part of the *Classis Britannica,* is extensively discussed by Martin (1992) and there is evidence that such vessels were widely used all over the Empire, as shown on Trajan's Column (L. Rossi 1971) and noted in Vegetius (*Epitoma* 31-36); Britain would not have been an exception. While there have been no discoveries of Roman wrecks in Scottish waters, examples have been recovered elsewhere in Britain: three wrecks from the Thames in London (Marsden 1994), one from Guernsey (Rule and Monaghan 1993), and another Gallo-Roman vessel from Wales (Nayling, Maynard, and McGrail 1994; Nayling and McGrail 2004). The five wrecks discovered in southern British waters date to the post-Flavian period, but give an insight into the vessels which may have been active in 1st century *Britannia*.

Other vessels on the continent have been found that may have been able to operate on Scottish rivers. Vessels with a flat-bottom would have been easier to navigate through shallow waters and could be easily beached. A series of six river vessels have been uncovered from the town of Zwammerdam on the Dutch frontier (J. du P. Taylor and Cleere 1978; Groenhuijzen and Verhagen 2015). These vessels range in size and date from 80-200 CE, were of a flat-bottomed design and used to transport goods and would have been able to navigate on some inland waterways. The vessels had a steering oar fitted to the side, similar in style to the type found at Newstead (see below and J. Curle 1911).

In Britain, there is little evidence of river fleets, and although several wrecks have been discovered on the River Thames and the Humber estuary, patrol vessels remain unidentified. Rankov (2005; 2009) attempts to investigate the role and function of river fleets on frontiers, but states that most previous analysis in this area has focussed on attributing fleets to one base. Instead, Rankov argues that fleets had a much wider role and function than is previously perceived, although he is not specifically discussing North Britain. Rummel (2009) has argued that the evidence from the continent supports the claim that fleets play a key role in the control of river frontiers, and suggests that there were provincial fleets. Himmler (2009) studied the operational tactics of late Roman river fleets, concluding that river patrols were frequent, with the vessels themselves being innovative and successful in this role; they extended the static fortifications which secured river frontiers. Mason (2003) has produced the most comprehensive study of the Roman navy in Britain, covering the origins and organisation of the fleets, as well as shipbuilding and establishment of the *Classis Britannica*. Mason does not cover Scotland to any great extent, probably because the archaeological evidence for maritime activities is lacking.

Mason does, however, detail several vessels which could have operated both at sea and on inland waterways to transport troops and goods, such as the Venetic vessel which is modified by Caesar to enable him to invade Britain (ibid:49). One of the smallest vessels in the Roman navy was discovered in 1981 at Mainz in Germany. The Mainz Type A was a long narrow boat, around 21 metres in length and 2.7 metres wide, and it is estimated that it would have taken 15 oarsmen, although is dated to the late 4th century CE (ibid:46). *Caudicaria* were a type of round-bottomed vessel used on the Tiber, but could also operate on the coast. These vessels tended to be towed, with a line running from the mast to a riverside path where it would be pulled along, or they could be winched at more challenging sections of the river (ibid:56). It seems unlikely that most vessels in Scottish inland waters would be towed, with no archaeological evidence of towpaths although this is not something which has been looked for in the archaeological record. Other small vessels, known from descriptions of the Mediterranean, are also used in harbours and for river transportation (Casson 1971), although the role that these had on a military frontier is unknown.

'In these straits, with all the routes blocked by Africanus and his men and no possibility of repairing the bridges, Caesar ordered his men to build boats of the type that his experience in Britain a few years before had taught him to make. The keels and ribs were made of light wood; the rest of the hulk was made of woven withies and covered with hides.

Caesar The Civil War 1:54

The implication from Caesar, writing around the middle of the 1st century BCE was that the Romans adopted local shipbuilding methods. In the incident described above, the boats were used to cross a river and were constructed on the spot, and there is no reason such a tactic could not have been used during the Flavian invasion of North Britain. As well as the coracle-style boats mentioned by Caesar, log boats were in use in Britain since the Bronze Age and continued in use until at least the 12th century in England. Mowat (1996:130) produced a dating table for log boats discovered across Europe, with only 4 examples (3 from Denmark and one from France) which could date to the 1st century CE. 150 examples of log boats have been found across Scotland, although only 28 survive (ibid:122). Constructed out of a hollowed tree trunk, these small boats vary in size, with the majority being between 3 and 8 metres in length (ibid:127). Some log boats are found by crannogs, indicating that the occupants were using them. Of particular note is the pre-Iron Age log boat discovered at Dumbuck on the River Clyde. The log boat itself was found in a wood-lined dock which opened up onto the Clyde. The dock was next to a crannog and the two are believed to be related. This log boat dates to before the arrival of the Romans, there is no reason to believe that the indigenous population during the Flavian period were not using similar vessels.

During the excavations at the Roman sites at Newstead on the River Tweed, a wooden object, measuring 1.65 metres, was recovered from a trench dug *'...on sloping ground at some considerable height above the Tweed.'* (J. Curle 1911:313). This was subsequently identified by Henry Balfour of the Pitt-Rivers Museum as a wooden oar (or rudder) for a '... *small low-freeboard boat.*' (ibid:313), similar to the vessels discovered at Zwammerdam. As there is no wear on the loom, McGrail (1987:244) has speculated that the object may have been a paddle rather than a rudder. While the oar itself is undated, it was found in a context which dates it to between CE 80 and 100. The evidence indicates watercraft were present at Newstead, some 36 miles from the mouth of the River Tweed. Another artefact recovered from the excavations at Newstead was a boathook (J. Curle 1911:288, Pl. lxvi 8), although this came from the ditch of the later, post-Flavian fort (Hunter and Painter 2013:117).

In summary, the literary evidence indicates that the army in the 1st century were using coastal and river networks to move soldiers and supplies, and although there is limited archaeological evidence to support this in Scotland, this is something which is happening on other frontiers in the Empire, including in the Lower Rhine *limes*. As has been demonstrated in Wales, coastal and river networks were an essential part of the Roman operation, with forts and fortresses positioned on coastal sites which enabled them to guard the entrances to rivers (Evans et al. 2010). The evidence from Wales also indicates that many roads were constructed along valleys (Silvester and Toller 2009), again supporting the notion of bringing soldiers and supplies inland from the river mouths, and which is also seen in recent analysis of the road network in the Netherlands, and its relationship to the coast and rivers on the frontier (Verhagen 2010; Verhagen and Jeneson 2012; Groenhuijzen and Verhagen 2015).

2.6. Interpretation Challenges

The evidence for the Flavian occupation of Scotland, is... complex. Tacitus provides a precise chronology for Agricola, but much depends on modern archaeological and historical interpretations and assumptions.
(R. H. Jones 2011:97)

Scotland may have an extensive history of exploration and research into Roman sites, but many studies remain unpublished, and the original records can be lacking in detail, inaccessible, and frequently missing (ScARF 2012a), making re-examination and re-interpretation of legacy data both challenging and complex. There are a number of examples which can be used to illustrate this. Jones (ibid:324-325) in her synthesis of Roman camps, attempted to locate the encampment at Bellie, originally discovered from the air by St Joseph and subsequently examined through trial trenching. Using St Joseph's records, Jones was unable to confirm the area excavated and ended up presenting three possible locations for the camp. This lack of accurate record keeping is typical of most archaeological explorations which took place prior to the latter part of the 20th century. This section therefore examines some of the challenges which face the interpretation of Roman sites in Scotland, and the issues with ascribing a date of origin to these. I then go on to critically analyse the methods of dating which have been used for assigning a date of origin to Flavian sites, and how this can affect the overall interpretation of fortifications.

Some 82% of the Roman sites known today have been discovered through aerial surveys, with another 11% identified by re-examination of such images (R. H. Jones 2011:1). This has been an invaluable tool for archaeological research, however, this does not necessarily mean that we know much about these sites. St Joseph, who spotted most of the sites during his aerial reconnaissance programme from around the middle of the 20th century onwards, would follow up the initial identification with a series of slot trenches usually placed through the defences to identify if there was a V-shaped ditch to confirm its Roman origins; occasionally, there was recovery of datable evidence, but this limited approach did not explore the stratigraphy of a site, making it difficult to establish a full chronology for the majority sites, with many remaining undated.

I have identified that there are in excess of 150 Roman sites (Figure 2.5) in Scotland which are undated and/or unconfirmed as being Roman in origin; most of the latter have either been identified as partial cropmarks, or related to antiquarian accounts and which have not subsequently been located. The map is intended to give an indication of how limited our existing knowledge is, and how the dating of these sites could influence the findings of future research.

This section is intended to show that a cautious approach needs to be taken when attempting to interpret Roman sites in Scotland, and assumptions should not be made about these as there is always the possibility that new information can radically alter our interpretation of Roman activity; this is demonstrated through the work by Hodgson (1995; 2009), who puts forward the case for a single period of occupation, rather than two, at most Antonine sites and argues that selective or fragmentary excavation of these sites has led to misidentification because only select parts of the fortification is seen. There are further factors which need to be considered when interpreting Flavian fortification sites:

- Some sites have shown limited evidence of possible activity before the arrival of Agricola, although this is not conclusive;
- Re-occupation and reconstruction of some fortifications in post-Flavian periods may have led to alterations of the original site, including repositioning and re-orientation of these;
- Datable evidence from these sites is limited, and with dating mostly based on theoretical approaches; Camps in particular are notoriously difficult to date, potentially because of their temporary nature and a lack of permanent structures and datable finds.

2.6.1. Fortification Sequencing

The evidence for fort 'types' and the character of garrisons should be reviewed...
(ScARF 2012a:35)

Before looking at dating methods, it is helpful to give a brief overview of attempts to group Scotland's 150+ Roman camps into a 'series' or sequence of encampments. This assumes that a group of such sites, sharing various features, were constructed in the same period, probably by the same group of soldiers (e.g. Hanson and Maxwell 1986; Maxwell 1990; R. H. Jones 2011). For example, all large sites of greater than 40 hectares are usually assumed to be Severan. Other examples include the camps at Abernethy, Dunning and Carpow which are similar in size, and the fortlets at Cappuck, Inverquharity and Mollins which, on excavation, have revealed similar floor plans. However, not all camps fit into such groupings. For example, the size of each site within such a grouping can differ by around a hectare, and some groups have gaps of more than a day's march between sites, indicating missing or incorrect dating of other camps in the sequence. By understanding the sequencing of camps, it may give an indication of the progress of the army through the landscape, as well as the reason for the positioning, intervisibility, orientation, and interconnectivity of these sites. To date, sequencing has only been undertaken for camps, but there is some indication that some forts could be grouped together; for example, the forts at Whitley Castle, Crawford and Loudon Hill are all trapezoidal in shape, with the former undated and the latter two originating in the Flavian period.

St Joseph (1973:229), in discussing comparisons between two groups of camps which shared similarities, warns that it is easy to see patterns where there may be none, something hampered by the lack of formal dating of most sites. This is a message which applies to the wider study of camps and, indeed, the wider spatial analysis undertaken in this study. Jones (2011) has summarised and re-analysed the evidence for the groupings, based on her examination of all the Roman camps in Scotland, and concludes that there does appear to be several series of camps, and that these could represent the route which the army took when campaigning in Scotland. Jones (2009a:875; 2011:107) further notes the picture is more complicated south of the Forth-Clyde isthmus where most camps are located and where sequencing is less clear. It is also worth remembering that while there is a tendency to attribute fortifications to the Flavian, Antonine or Severan periods, there are other, later and possibly earlier invasions of Scotland.

In the wider military landscape, there are distances of more than a day's march between many forts, and where there is a large gap, it is reasonable to suppose that soldiers moving between these sites would have had somewhere secure to shelter overnight, such as a camp or a smaller, more secure enclosure. If troop movements were happening regularly, then it is reasonable to suggest that such structures may not necessarily have

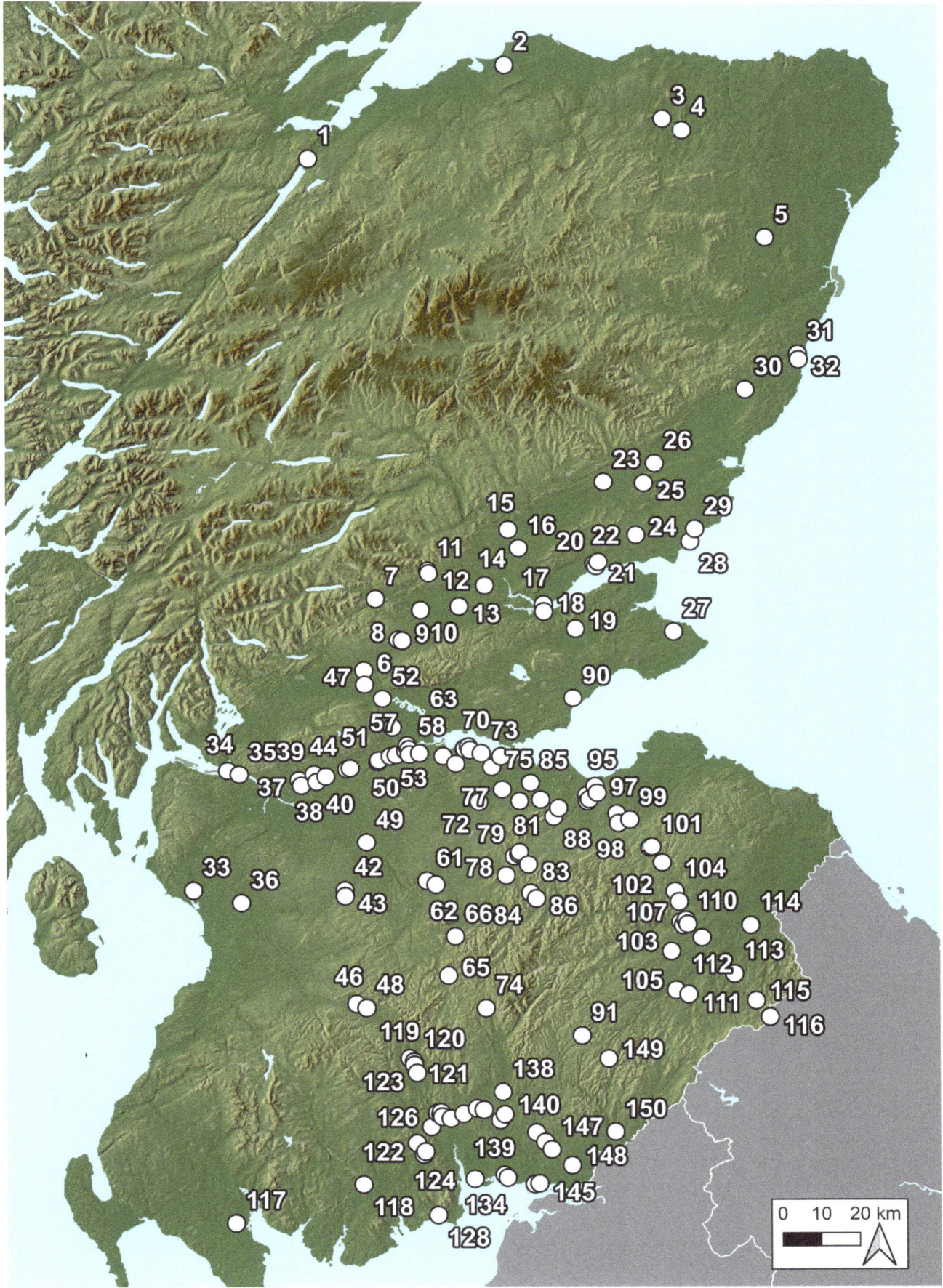

Figure 2.5. Unconfirmed and undated fortifications in Scotland. Data from Canmore.

Facing the Enemy?

Key to Figure 2.5:

1	Bona (Fort - Possible)		57	Lochlands (Camps)
2	Wester Alves (Camp - Possible)		58	Carmuirs (Camps - Possible)
3	Tarryblake Wood (Camp - Possible)		59	Tamfourhill (Camp)
4	Fourman Hill (Camp - Possible)		60	Falkirk (Fort - Possible)
5	Cairnhall (Camp - Possible)		61	Cleghorn (Camp)
6	Netherton (Camp - Possible)		62	Castledykes (Camps)
7	Dalginross (Camp - Possible)		63	Kincardine House (Fortlet - Possible)
8	Nether Braco (Camp - Possible)		64	Polmonthill (Camp)
9	Ardoch (Fort, Camps)		65	Crawford (Camps)
10	Strageath Cottage (Camp)		66	Lamington (Camp)
11	Sma' Glen (Tower - Possible)		67	Linlithgow (Fort - Possible)
12	Fendoch (Fortlet - Possible)		68	Kinglass (Fort - Possible)
13	Gask House (Camp)		69	Kinglass Park (Camp)
14	Easter Powside (Camp)		70	Bridgeness (Fort - Possible)
15	Inchtuthil (Camps)		71	Muirhouses (Camp)
16	Woodhead (Tower)		72	Kirkton (Fortlet - Possible)
17	St Madoes (Camp)		73	Burnshot (Tower - Possible)
18	Carpow (Camps)		74	White Type (Tower)
19	Newton (Fort - Possible)		75	The Den (Camp - Possible)
20	Mylnefield (Fort - Possible)		76	Windmill Knowe (Tower - Possible)
21	Invergowrie (Camp)		77	River Almond (Fort - Possible)
22	Bullion (Camp - Possible)		78	Carmaben Hill (Tower - Possible)
23	Westmuir (Tower - Possible)		79	North Slipperfield (Camp)
24	Gagie (Camp)		80	Tocherknowe (Fortlet)
25	Lunanhead (Camp)		81	Stonypath (Camp)
26	Finavon (Camp)		82	Ravelrig Hill (Towers - Possible)
27	Bonnytown (Camp - Possible)		83	Kaimhouse Lodge (Camp)
28	Scryne Smithy (Camp - Possible)		84	Wester Happrew (Camp)
29	Grahamston Cottages (Camp - Possible)		85	Millburn Tower (Camp - Possible)
30	Fordoun House (Camp - Possible)		86	Lyne (Fortlet)
31	Arduthie (Camp - Possible)		87	Warklaw Hill (Tower - Possible)
32	Stonehaven (Fort - Possible)		88	Glencorse Mains (Fortlet - Possible)
33	Irvine - Kilwinning (Camp - Possible)		89	Boghall (Camp - Possible)
34	Dumbarton (Fort - Possible)		90	Carberry (Camp - Possible)
35	Dumbuck Hill (Fort - Possible)		91	Craik Cross (Tower - Possible)
36	Kilmarnock (Camp - Possible)		92	Sheriffhall (Camp - Possible)
37	Summerston (Camp)		93	Eskbank (Camp)
38	Easter Balmuildy (Fortlet - Possible)		94	Lugton (Camp)
39	Torrance (Camp - Possible)		95	Monktonhall (Camp - Possible)
40	Bogton (Fortlet - Possible, Camp)		96	Dalkeith (Camp)
41	Easter Cadder (Camp)		97	Pathhead (Camps)
42	West Newton (Camp - Possible)		98	Crichton (Fort - Possible)
43	High Cauldcoats (Camp - Possible)		99	Fala Mill (Camp)
44	Twechar (Camp)		100	Channelkirk House (Camp - Possible)
45	Bar Hill (Camp)		101	Oxton - Channelkirk (Camp)
46	Knowe Cottages (Camp - Possible)		102	Blackchester (Camp - Possible)
47	Ochtertyre (Camp)		103	Milrighall (Camp)
48	Bankhead (Fortlet, Camp - Possible)		104	South Blainslie (Camp - Possible)
49	Motherwell (Camp - Possible)		105	Cavers Mains (Camp)
50	Tollpark (Camp)		106	Kedslie (Camp)
51	Garnhall (Camps)		107	Millmount (Camp - Possible)
52	Gowan Hill (Fort - Possible)		108	Newstead (Camps)
53	Dalnair (Camp)		109	Drygrange (Camp)
54	Greenhill (Tower - Possible)		110	Ravenswood (Camps)
55	Milnquarter (Camp)		111	Rubers Law Tower
56	Wester Carmuirs (Camp, Camp - Possible)		112	Maxton (Camp - Possible)

113	Cappuck (Camp)		132	Gallaberry (Camp)
114	Wooden Home Farm (Camp)		133	Amisfield Tower (Camp)
115	Pennymuir (Camps)		134	Ward Law (Camp, Tower - Possible)
116	Brownhart Law (Fortlet)		135	Murder Loch (Camp - Possible)
117	Bladnoch (Fortlet)		136	Trailflat (Camp)
118	Glenlochar (Camps)		137	Lochmaben (Camp)
119	Drumlanrig (Camp, Camp - Possible)		138	Hangingshaw (Camp)
120	Carronbridge (Camp)		139	Ruthwell (Camp)
121	Waterside Mains (Camp - Possible)		140	Applegarthtown (Camp - Possible)
122	Shawhead (Camps - Possible)		141	Summerfield (Camp - Possible)
123	Thornhill Tower		142	Hayknowes (Camp - Possible)
124	Lochrutton (Camp)		143	Annanfoot (Camp)
125	Moat Of Lochrutton (Fortlet - Possible)		144	Burnswark (Camps)
126	Fourmerkland (Camp - Possible)		145	Hillside (Camp)
127	Ellisland (Camps)		146	Middlebie Hill (Camps)
128	Mains Of Southwick (Camp - Possible)		147	Broadlea (Fortlet - Possible, Camps)
129	Dalswinton, Bankfoot (Camp - Possible)		148	Kirkpatrick-fleming (Fortlet - Possible)
130	Butterhole Brae, Dalswinton (Tower - Possible)		149	Ewes Doors (Tower)
131	Portrack House (Camp - Possible)		150	Gilnockie (Camp)

been temporary. This is why I have spent some time here critically evaluating the evidence around camps because, as I have noted previously, simply relying on the descriptive label ascribed to a site can affect interpretation of its purpose, how long it was occupied, and conclusions drawn about its interrelationships with the wider Roman military landscape. Without more accurate information on the dating and sequencing of camps, any suggestions or hypotheses relating to the movement of troops between fortifications in any period of the Roman occupation, will be speculative. A more in-depth analysis of camp sequencing can be found in Jones (2011:99-108).

2.6.2. Fortification Dating

The dating of Roman sites in Scotland is challenging, and even problematic due to a lack of datable finds such as pottery or organic materials, although this being said, dating for forts, which have seen more extensive archaeological explorations, tends to be more secure than the chronology of the other types of fortification. Where datable materials are not available, fortifications are dated based on morphology; a site is attributed a date because it shares similar features to another fortification which dates to the relevant period. As outlined earlier in this chapter, the primary source which has underpinned the chronological framework in Scotland is the *Agricola*. Until the advent of scientific analysis, most fortifications in Scotland which were discovered prior to the 20th century were given an Agricolan foundation by the antiquarians simply because of Tacitus. A majority of Roman sites in Scotland remain undated, and while classical literary texts may tell us more about these sites, Hoffmann (2013:174) points out that the reliability of these texts is always linked to the quality of the sources used by the original writers, their motives, and preconceptions.

For Flavian sites in Scotland, there are four broad methods used to ascribe a 1st century date to these fortifications: entrances, find, proximity (dating based on closeness to another site), morphology (sharing common features), and dating by scientific methods. Jones (2011) developed a similar list: historical - based on probability given the location of the site; association – a date is based on proximity to another Roman site; survey and excavation – used to identify phases of construction; and radiocarbon dating – from artefacts and stratigraphy.

Figure 2.6 summarises the methods used to date the Flavian fortifications covered in this study, although 22 of these sites were dated using two methods, which is reflected in the chart. As a general rule, the attempt to date forts is much more straightforward than confirming occupation periods for camps. Forts were typically more permanent structures, which may have been occupied on a longer basis than a camp (E.g. Agricola 22; Birley 2010:17). The longer a fortification was occupied, then the greater the opportunity for artefacts to have been lost or discarded by the occupiers, enabling archaeologists to assign a probable date to the site. The dating of Roman camps is notoriously difficult, with many finds being recovered outside of secure stratigraphic layers (R. H. Jones 2011), while some sites, such as Kintore, indicate multiple phases of occupation, sometimes from within the same period.

It is evident from many years of surveying, observations and aerial reconnaissance that Roman camps have a number of different entrance designs (i.e. parrot-beak, *titulus, claviculae*), and that these appear to represent different periods of activity (ibid:49), although as will be discussed, there are some sites where multiple gate-types are located which could indicate reoccupation of a site.

Flavian camps are assumed to have *claviculae*-style entrances, sometimes referred to as a parrot-beak or Stracathro-type gates (ibid:109). But there also some camps, such as Raedykes which are assumed to date to the

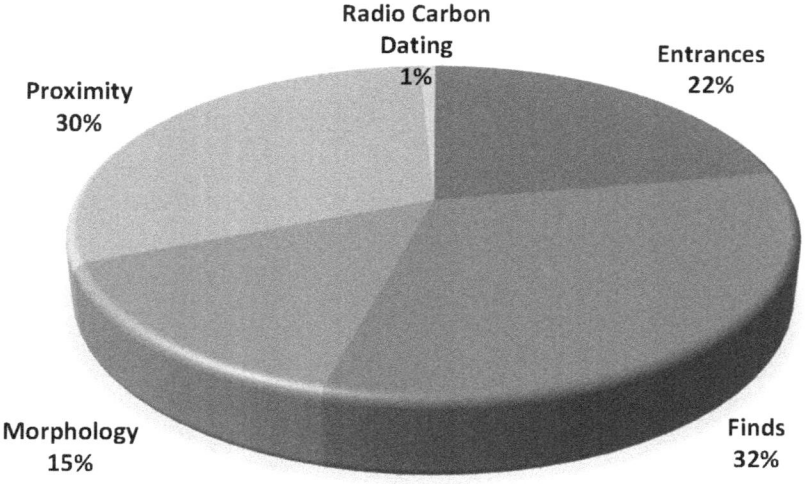

Figure 2.6. Methods used to assign a date to Flavian fortifications.

1st century but have traverse or *titulus* style entrances, a linear mound in front of an open entrance and is the most simplistic style; this type of gate is often found at camps associated with a later foundation date (see Figure 2.7 for the different types of gate). Stracathro gates are formed by two sections of bank and ditch at the gate, with one curving and one straight, extending outwards.

Using the types of entrances to the sites to date them is more prevalent with camps, although there are several forts which have distinctive entrances such as Dalginross, Dalswinton, Drumlanrig, Drumquhassle, and Easter Happrew, as well as fortlets such as Castle Greg, indicating that they may belong to the same period. For a more detailed account of dating using entrances, see Jones (2011).

Finds (such as coins, glass and pottery) are used to date a significant number of fortifications, although many sites, such as the Gask Ridge towers, have failed to yield such datable evidence (e.g. Woolliscroft & Hoffmann 2006:99). Pottery is the predominant type of find discovered on sites, with dates identified from potters stamps and typologies (e.g. Hartley 1972). These can help to attribute a date to the site, although this is rarely more specific than being able to attribute a 1st century occupation. However, at several sites such as Abernethy, Crawford and Elginhaugh, only single fragments of pottery have been recovered. At Mollins and Oakwood, there were limited pottery fragments recovered during excavation, and this is typical for such sites, with these finds forming the basis of the site chronology. The dating significance of some of these artefacts was

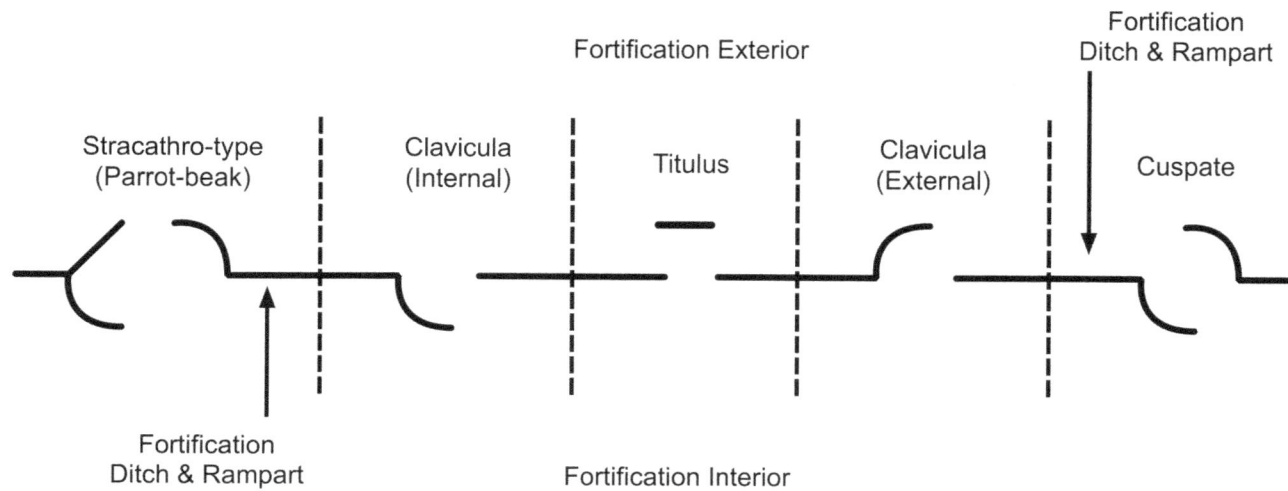

Figure 2.7. Different camp gates/entrances found in Scotland.

unrealised until the 1970s, when Hartley (1972) analysed many of the fragments, particularly from sites which had been excavated early in the 20th century, attributing likely occupation periods and revising site chronology for others. ScARF (2012a) suggests that such a reappraisal should again be undertaken for Roman sites in Scotland in light of advances in knowledge and understanding of the period. A stronger case for site chronology can be made if evidence can be corroborated, such as at Crawford where coins support and pottery the site being occupied in the 1st century. Coins have also been used to date Cargill (fort), Castle Greg, Crawford, Dalginross (fort), Easter Happrew, Elginhaugh, and Strageath. Glass has only been discovered and dated to the Flavian period on a handful of sites, including Cargill (fortlet), Girvan Mains West, and Strageath. There have been few excavations in recent years, and as a result, little organic material has been recovered from Roman sites, although there have been exceptions, such as at Elginhaugh, Normandykes, and the newly identified sites in Ayr and Milltimber. While datable evidence is scant at many of the sites (e.g. Burnfield, Castlecraig, Cold Chapel, Durisdeer, Glenluce), there is a body of circumstantial evidence surrounding these sites to indicate activity on-site during the Flavian period. As ever, more extensive and thorough excavation and analysis may reveal more reliable datable materials (e.g. through radiocarbon dating of organic matter). The sites covered here were occupied in the Flavian period, although many of the Lowland sites were reoccupied in later periods.

The proximity of one or more sites to each other, provides another method of dating. If a site confirmed as dating to a later period is fully or partially constructed on top of another, then the latter must be earlier. Examples of this are found with the series of camps at Ardoch and Lochlands, although dating these is further complicated by the numerous camps built on top of one another, making it difficult to discern which one was constructed first. This method can also be applied to sites which are constructed next to roads; where the road dates to the 1st century, the sites nearby can be dated, by proximity, to the same period or earlier. For example, Maxwell and Wilson (1987:32-33) noted that a number of camps running from the Upper Clyde valley to the Pentlands pre-dated Dere Street as the road cuts across the defences of several sites (Carlops, Kirkhouse and Wandel), indicating a likely Flavian date.

Morphology, which is essentially the same as camp sequencing which I have outlined above, but will briefly summarise here. This is where fortifications which share common features, usually size, are often assumed to be constructed at the same time or by the same soldiers, and in conjunction with additional evidence may deduced to be Flavian.

Only a handful of sites have been subject to rigorous scientific dating, such as the camps at Kintore (Alexander 1996; J. Hamilton and McGill 1997; Cook and Dunbar 2008; Cook, Dunbar, and Heawood 2009; Cook 2018), Milltimber (Dingwall and Shepherd 2018), and Ayr (Hunter 2018; Arabaolaza 2019), while more limited work has taken place outside of sites, such as at Newstead. The results of radiocarbon dating from these sites has indicated 1st century occupation. With 300 sites, most of which have not been dating using scientific methods, it is not always clear when sites were founded, occupied, or even re-occupied, and as Hodgson (1995) has argued regarding the periods Antonine I and II, occupation dating of sites is rarely straightforward. The camp at Innerpeffray East is another example of a site which was thought to be later, but subsequent excavation has indicated otherwise (Woolliscroft 2007; see also R. H. Jones 2011:230-231). The work on Elginhaugh, along with that of the Flavian camp at Kintore, has lent weight to the idea that the Roman military withdrew from much of Scotland by around CE 86-7.

The evidence for dating Roman sites in Scotland is, in many cases, limited; only a handful have been dated through scientific means. Most of the dating methods outlined above, have flaws and can be unreliable, particularly when the evidence for individual fortifications is in conflict (such as a site having two types of entrance, or two conflicting radiocarbon dates). Another issue with the dating of sites, particularly camps, is the length of occupation, with the traditional view being that they were occupied for brief periods, but with some indication that they were used for longer (e.g. R. H. Jones 2011:121-122; Cook and Dunbar 2008; Cook, Dunbar, and Heawood 2009). There is an insufficient body of evidence so it is not possible to attest to the length of occupation of an individual camp in the archaeological record, which means the role of a encampments in the wider military landscape is difficult to judge.

2.7. Natural Environment

Many excavations took place before the days of improved retrieval of environmental evidence, so there is a good chance that new excavations (at likely locations on the old sites) will produce significant material.
(ScARF 2012a:46)

To understand the relationship between fortifications and the landscape, it is helpful to have a good knowledge of the natural environment as it was during the Roman period. This is particularly the case when using GIS models that incorporate 21st century basemaps and environmental data, as a lack of awareness of environmental changes since the Roman period can result in errors of interpretation being made.

Knowledge of the natural environment in the north of Britain in the Late Iron Age and Roman periods is slowly growing, with several significant studies being published in recent years that utilise evidence from sites in Scotland, including Bearsden, Inveresk, and Kintore (Dickson and Dickson 2016; Máté and Bohncke 2016; Bishop 2004; Cook and Dunbar 2008; Cook, Dunbar, and Heawood 2009) There have been some attempts at synthesis studies of the environment in these periods including those by Armit and Ralston (2003),

Gwilt and Haselgrove (1997), Tipping (1997a; 1997b), and van der Veen (1992). Some studies cover the environment around Hadrian's Wall, such as Tipping and Tisdall (2005), while Davies (2020) undertakes a similar exercise on the Antonine Wall. This up-to-date summary of the natural environment in the Antonine period is the most useful source for my research, summarising environmental conditions 50 to 80 years after the Flavian period.

Various classical texts discuss resources in Britain, such as Pomponius Mela who states that Britain is a fertile land for cattle (*De Chorographia* III, 6, 50), breeding hunting dogs (*Cynegetica* I, 468-480, 225f), and even finding pearls (*Suetonius Julius* 47). The natural environment in Britain is also mentioned in classical sources, with Strabo writing that the Celti are not familiar with horticulture or agriculture, and that it is,

> *...flat and overgrown with forests, although many of its districts are hilly. It bears grain, cattle, gold, silver, and iron...*
>
> **Strabo IV, 5.2**

But it is Pliny the Elder, writing around CE 75, who gives a stronger description of Scotland,

> *Opposite to this region lies the island of Britain, famous in the Greek records and in our own... nearly thirty years ago, its exploration was carried by the armed forces of Rome to a point not beyond the neighbourhood of the Caledonian Forest.*
>
> **Pliny *Natural History* 16:4:102**

These accounts suggest that North Britain was a land covered by forests, but there is reasonable evidence to suggest that in some areas of Scotland, extensive forest clearance happened earlier, during the latter half of the first millennium BCE, with evidence from various sites (M. H. Davies 2020). Hanson and Macinnes (1980; and Hanson 1996) and Tipping (1997a) go further, suggesting that deforestation took place in the LIA, before the Romans arrive, although the sites examined by Hanson are from southern and central Scotland and show that clearances took place at different times in different locations. Van der Veen (1992:153)argues against this, suggesting the landscape was not cleared until the arrival of the Romans in the 1st century.

Dark and Dark (1998) attempt to summarise the environmental data on Roman Britain using readily available data from several sites, although their work is more focussed south of Hadrian's Wall, despite them processing data on sites in southern Scotland. While they conclude that there was pre-Roman land clearance in England, the same may not have been happening in Scotland. Although their sampling did not extend north of central Scotland, they concluded that,

> *Much of Roman Britain was already a predominantly agricultural landscape before the Roman conquest.*

> *In southern Britain, much woodland was removed in the Bronze Age. The late Iron Age seems to have seen the most significant increase in pre-Roman woodland clearance in the north of England, and the arrival of the Roman military at Hadrian's Wall led to further clearance.*
>
> **(Dark and Dark 1998:42)**

Without more comprehensive, widespread environmental data from the Flavian period, it is difficult to prove whether the Romans constructed sites in wooded or cleared areas, although a good supply of timber would be necessary for constructing fortifications. There has been much debate on the location of the Caledonian forest, and this study does not propose to revisit this as it is covered elsewhere (e.g. Hanson and Maxwell 1986; Maxwell 1990; Hanson 1991; Hanson 1996; Woolliscroft and Hoffmann 2006; Breeze 2008; M. H. Davies 2020).

From the evidence we have, agricultural practices in Scotland intensified from around 350 BCE onwards and contributing to deforestation (Tipping 1997b:41). Tagg (1911) undertook one of the earliest attempts at investigating land use, analysing soil samples retrieved during Curle's excavations at Newstead. This technique was rarely applied to Flavian sites in Scotland during the early excavations of the late 19th and early 20th centuries (the exception being Macdonald and Park 1906; and Miller 1922). Manning (1975) examined potential land use in the Highlands during the Roman period, focussing on cereals and the volume required to feed the invading army. Manning (ibid:115) focuses on the practicalities of grain supply, and hypothesises that each fort (when spaced out by around 10 miles) could draw on resources from around 100 square miles, although most of this would only be about 5 miles distance from each site. Manning does not consider if the same is true for camps, although storage of the grain on a temporary site for any length of time, would have been challenging. Boyd (1988) produced a catalogue of cereal fossils, some of which can be found on Roman sites (Birrens, Kintore and Newstead), although there are limitations in the data as they only sample three sites. Máté and Bohncke (2016:78) carried out an environmental analysis of samples taken from the excavations at the Antonine fort at Bearsden, finding that the area surrounding the site comprised 'wet meadows'. Such results are too localised to compare with the environment surrounding forts in other locations and periods.

Analysis of animal bones from later prehistoric sites in the Lowlands show that sheep, cattle and pig were being farmed (M. H. Davies 2020:42), with similar evidence from the Antonine period civilian settlement at Inveresk (Bishop 2004). Analysis of midden finds at Inveresk confirms woodland nearby, and a diet comprising shellfish, red and roe deer (ibid). Tipping & Tisdall (2005) have argued that not enough environmental sampling has taken place to clarify the extent of arable and pastoral land use. Burnham and Davies (2010:68) have identified that the

Romans constructed most forts in Wales, in fertile areas and river valleys, and despite the lack of data as outlined by Tipping, it appears anecdotally that something similar was happening in Scotland.

Most Roman fortifications are on land which is today classed as arable and improved grassland, used for grazing and crop growing. Since the Roman period, there have been significant changes and improvements in agricultural techniques and practices, most notably in the Middle Ages and then from the 18th century onwards, which have led to arable land expansion. We can see agricultural improvements at numerous Flavian sites, with streams canalised to facilitate drainage and field run off. Assertions of the suitability of areas for farming should be cautiously accepted until there is more environmental evidence confirming land use and vegetation cover around Roman fortifications.

Today, some of the most fertile areas of Scotland include Perthshire, Angus, Aberdeenshire and Moray, the same areas which has fortifications in the Flavian period. While this is probably not coincidental, there were a small number of forts and camps built in less arable areas, but this may have been out of necessity. Overall, from the forts which have been identified, all are located in fertile areas enabling the army to source sufficient food and other goods to sustain the military.

2.7.1. Water

Water was an essential resource which the classical sources state every site should have access to. As noted above, smaller burns and streams are frequently redirected and canalised because of agriculture with drainage and irrigation altering the water table. For most Roman sites, there would have been a need for sizeable amounts of water, not just for washing and drinking, but also for flushing latrines, industrial usage and animals. Most Roman sites in Scotland are near large rivers and lochs, so a ready supply of water was available, and even sites which are more remotely located such as Auchinhove, Muiryfold and Burnfield, are still next to minor watercourses.

There has been limited research into water levels in the Roman period, with the studies that have taken place focussing on sea-level changes. The studies usually begin their analysis with pre-Roman periods, such as Shennan et al. (2000; 2018), Gehrels (2010), and Kemp et al (2011). The consensus in these studies is that sea levels have increased. Post-glacial isostatic rebound will differ between Scotland and southern Britain as the north is rising, while the land in south is falling. If there were no changes to sea level over the past 2,000 years, then it would appear that Scotland had higher sea levels relative to the land in Roman times. A study by Lewis and Balchin (1940) examined sea levels at Dungeness in Kent, concluding that overall levels in the Roman period were around 1.5-1.6 metres lower than those in the 1940s, which is to be expected. Pirazzoli (1976) examined Roman remains in relation to the water levels in parts of the Mediterranean, and although it is not possible to draw conclusions with Northern Britain in the Roman period, Pirazzoli found there was an average rise in the sea's level by 7.5 centimetres every 100 years between 300 BCE and CE 150. He recorded that by 1 CE, the mean sea level was 0.5 metres lower than it is today; he further notes that tectonic activity would have affected the data. Pirazzoli concluded that the overall data from the region indicated that the water levels were lower in Roman times than they were in 1976. Work by Waddelove and Waddelove (1990) attempts to establish the high astronomical tide in certain locations in England during the Roman period, and while producing convincing results, their work does not cover sites further north than Merseyside. Analysis by Tipping and Tisdall (2005) focuses on the landscape context of the Antonine Wall and examines the sea levels of the area around this frontier. They conclude that river levels were likely to be around two meters higher in the Firths of Clyde and Forth in the Antonine period (ibid:446), while Smith et al. (2010) conclude that the tidal range was up to 6 metres higher than current levels at high water. Tipping and Tisdall (2005:445) and Smith et al., both suggest that this higher sea level could have been in retreat by the Iron Age. Most of this research focuses on the coast, or the Forth and Clyde estuaries (e.g. D. E. Smith et al. 2010; M. H. Davies 2020), and there has been no modelling of the levels of rivers further inland.

Sensibly, the advice from Vegetius and 'Pseudo' Hyginus was not to construct fortifications on land liable to flooding, although today, several of the fortification sites are prone to this, such as at Bochastle which is a low-lying site with two rivers on either side. The site could have flooded at certain times of the year, although this may not have been an issue if the camps were only occupied during campaigning in the summer.

Visible in the landscape modelling of several fortification sites is evidence of fluvial movement, river channels which have moved course over the past 2,000 years. One example can be seen with the course of the River Tay at Inchtuthil, which has moved course, with the paleochannels showing up in the LiDAR (Figure 2.8), and showing a much more complex pattern of fluvial movement in the past. The image indicates that at some point in the past, the course of the Tay has moved, creating the plateau that the fortress and camps sit on. While the current river runs to the south of the site, there is still a minor channel to the north, and it is on this side that there is evidence for erosion of the defences, as visible in the latter image, although it is not possible to say whether this occurred during Roman occupation or after. There is a similar situation at the site of Inverquharity where river erosion has affected the northern defences of the fortlet and camp in the past, while similar erosion has taken place on the northern defences of the fort at Stracathro.

GIS modelling using LiDAR and mapping data to identify flooding and erosion is not without its limitations; fluvial

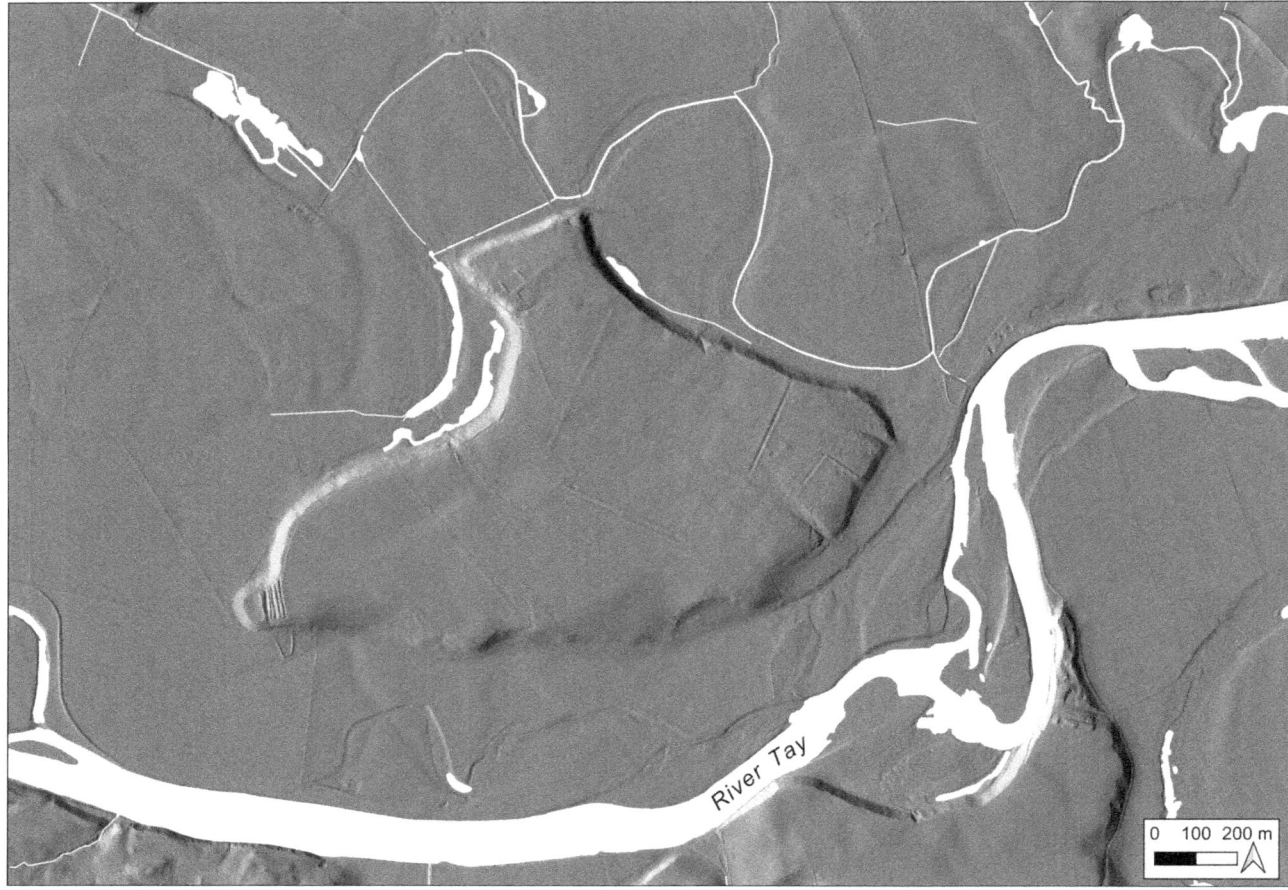

Figure 2.8. LiDAR image of Inchtuthil legionary showing existing rivers and possible channels.

movements at some sites are affected by agricultural improvements and industrial activity; at least 23% of the Flavian sites examined here may have been prone to flooding, but it is not possible to say if that risk was there during occupation of the sites. These sites include 24 out of 62 camps, 6 out of 33 forts and 1 out of 9 fortlets. The high number of camps which could flood is perhaps unsurprising, as these sites were possibly only occupied in summer when water levels are lower and flooding less likely. Camps usually take up more space than forts and in certain locations, such as at Dalswinton, occupying a large enough space without encroaching on the floodplain is not possible. Given that temporary encampments are only intended for limited occupation, the benefits would probably have outweighed the risks.

2.8. Summary

This chapter has provided a critical analysis of the current thinking on different aspects of Roman activity which can be related to the primary focus of this investigation. Scotland should be thought of as a frontier-zone; an area on the edge of the Empire which is not defined by a linear barrier like the Antonine Wall. There is a long tradition of research into Roman frontiers in Scotland, although until the 20th century, the *Agricola* and *de situ Britanniae* influenced most accounts. The impact of Tacitus in interpreting Roman archaeology in Scotland cannot be underestimated, and it is an influence which continues to be felt today. The evidence from Carlisle, and possibly southern Scotland, shows there may have been a pre-Agricolan incursion into North Britain. Shotter postulates that the Gask Ridge fortifications were constructed under Agricola's predecessor, Cerialis; the archaeological evidence to support or disprove this is lacking, but it remains an intriguing possibility and one which can be resolved through further dating and environmental analysis of key sites which show early occupation (such as Birrens). The archaeology of Roman Scotland is much more complicated than the antiquarians and early archaeologists imagined, and many sites remain undated; more work needs to be undertaken to confirm the origin of these, while new discoveries and re-interpretation of existing sites are likely to have a major impact on the dating and sequencing of fortifications, and thus potentially on attempts to understand the military strategy in North Britain, both in the 1st century, and in later periods.

This chapter has given an overview of the different types of fortifications that can be found in Scotland in the Flavian period, and has also looked at some of the challenges when attempting to interpret Roman activity in this period, such as the dating of these sites. The intention has been to show that these datasets are complex and often not entirely reliable; e.g. the dating is not as rigorous as it could be. This needs to be remembered when drawing conclusions, but that said, this should not limit the inclusion of this data when postulating the role and purpose of the fortifications in Scotland during the 1st century.

Our knowledge of the environment in the Late Iron Age and later Roman periods in Scotland is fragmented, making it more challenging to conclude why certain locations are selected for fortifications over others. Limited environmental sampling has been taken, but much more work, which takes a wider geographical approach and includes sampling from individual sites, needs undertaking; the lack of sampling from Flavian fortification sites does pose a challenge to interpreting the landscape in different parts of Scotland. Notwithstanding both natural and human-led environmental change over the past 2,000 years, analysis of modern land-use confirms that the army constructed fortifications in arable and grassland areas which could have supplied grain and crops to sustain the invading soldiers, as well as cattle and ponies; Burnham & Davies (2010) have made similar observations for Wales in this period. It is not possible to conclude whether or not there were enough local supplies (such as wood) to construct fortifications in the immediate landscape surrounding fortifications, although the army were not averse to shipping in timber as happened with the harbour at Voorburg-Arentsburg in the Netherlands where oak timbers were imported from south Germany (Domínguez-Delmás et al. 2014). Water levels in the Roman period were different to what they are today, and while there have been some attempts to model this for the Antonine period (e.g. Hannon 2018), there has been no equivalent analysis concerning these in the 1st century. Such analysis could lend weight to the argument, set out by Jones (2011) that some camps, particularly those on the coast (such as at Girvan, Ayr or Dun), may have been used by the military as supply bases, or locations where resources could be brought in by sea and moved further inland.

3

Data and Methods

So far, I have established the critical importance of understanding Roman fortifications in the wider landscape. Using a Geographical Information System (GIS), provides the methodological approach to investigating the fortifications and their topographical setting. GIS technology is software which captures, stores, analyses, manages and presents spatial and geographical data (Conolly 2006; Burrough, McDonnell, and Lloyd 2015). GIS has been used extensively to significant effect concerning spatial analysis of sites in archaeological landscapes (e.g. W. V. Lewis and Balchin 1940; Witcher 2000; Wheatley and Gillings 2002; Chapman 2006; Verhagen et al. 2012; Hannon 2018). While there has been only limited application of GIS to the Roman landscape in Scotland, an increasing number of studies are now being published that seek to redress this, although these mostly relate to sites on the Antonine Wall (Hannon 2018; Hannon, Wilson, and Rohl 2020; E. Graafstal 2020; 2021).

GIS has a functional application relating to landscape analysis, and through overlaying and the use of environmental and archaeological data, it can produce results useful for research. In the research for this study, it has been used to develop profiles of fortification sites, by examining the defensive topography around fortifications, elevation analysis of sites in the wider context, to undertake binary viewshed, and line-of-site analysis to see what could be viewed from the sites. The GIS database represents an original synthesis of a wide and diverse range of archaeological and geographical data, and has further been used to plot the orientation of fortifications in the landscape to see what, if anything, these fortifications were facing. It has further been used to provide maps of the road, coastal and river networks, to assess the interconnectivity between the Flavian sites. This chapter summarises the various sources of archaeological and topographical data analysed as part of this research, and details the approaches taken to analyse these datasets.

3.1. Data Collection and Sources

Accounts of Roman remains in Scotland stretch back as far as the 9th century, with Nennius recounting a stone building constructed on the banks of the River Caron reputed to have been brought to Scotland by the Emperor Carausius (Nennius 2000:31-32), while in the 16th century, Roman remains uncovered at Inveresk are recorded in a series of letters to the court of Elizabeth I of England (Moir 1860:4-5), and by the 17th century, the antiquarian rediscovery of the Antonine Wall was beginning (Keppie 2012). As noted previously, there is a sizable amount of information relating to the Roman occupation of Scotland, but this varies in quality and accuracy from site to site. Therefore, the data gathered relating to the sites covered in this research has come from a variety of sources, including antiquarian accounts of archaeological explorations, more recent excavation and survey reports and publications, national and regional HER, and classical texts such as the *Agricola*. Wherever possible, I have gone back to the original sources to establish the accuracy of the data, and where necessary, have taken new measurements.

There is strong topographic and terrain data available for Scotland from Ordnance Survey, but there has not been an extensive programme of LiDAR scanning as there is in England, and few 1st century sites are processed in this way; in undertaking this research, I have processed the available LiDAR data for a number of sites, including Inchtuthil legionary fortress, and the forts at Bertha and Dalginross, although only the former had significant results, detailed later in this chapter. LiDAR has the potential to reveal much about sites in Scotland, particularly the wider landscape, and has been used to significant effect on other Roman sites (e.g. Hannon 2018; Hannon, Wilson, and Rohl 2020; E. Graafstal 2020), and has the potential to reveal significant detail about fortifications and their environs, as identified in *ScARF: The Roman Presence* (2012a:43) which recommends an area of around 1 kilometre from forts is routinely investigated whenever development works near a site takes place; this is a pertinent approach to take to a wider analysis of such sites and their immediate landscape.

Besides the ScARF report on the Roman Presence in Scotland, there are several additional research documents which have informed this research, including the *ScARF Report on Iron Age Scotland* (ScARF 2012b), *The Antonine Wall Management Plan* (Scotland 2013), and a series of regionally focussed research frameworks currently being developed. A list of the main sites examined can be seen in Appendix One, with Appendix Two summarising the site data.

3.1.1. Roman Literary Texts

I have examined various classical literary texts, but in summary, the main sources have been 'Pseudo' Hyginus and Vegetius (Milner 2001), and who discuss various elements of construction of fortifications, as well as the *Agricola* which I discussed earlier. These texts were written at a particular time and for a particular audience; for example, Tacitus dedicates his text to his father-in-law, Agricola. Even the military manuals by 'Pseudo' Hyginus and Vegetius may not be directly relevant, given that the former was writing his book around 100 years after the Flavian period, while the latter was completed 300 years after the 1st century. The classical texts are not unadulterated factual accounts, and they may aid interpretation, but equally, modern research allows their once dominant claims about what is happening in the Roman period, to be contested.

3.1.2. Legacy and Site Data

The primary source of archaeological data used is Canmore (www.Canmore.org.uk), the national record of the historic environment in Scotland. Canmore is recognised as the standard resource on historic sites in Scotland, and the data extracted relating to archaeological sites include names, National Grid References (NGR), shapefiles, and a summary of archaeological activities where relevant. While Canmore is a useful resource and has relevant basic information about each site, it has some limitations, for example, the NGRs for each site give a general location and cannot be relied on to represent the centre of a fortifications, whereas I have required more accurate data, such as for creating viewpoints for viewshed analysis, so I consulted original data sources. GIS shapefiles were downloaded from Canmore and cover the known extent, and the scheduled areas of numerous Roman sites and road sections in Scotland. Where available, the data from Canmore has been cross-referenced with information from local HERs, where this was available.

Two significant sources which detail a number of Roman sites are *The Old Statistical Account of Scotland* (OSA), and *The New Statistical Account of Scotland* (NSA). These are collections of unique accounts of Scotland's history, geography and society, gathered from all the parishes across the land. The OSA was compiled between 1791 and 1799, and the NSA between 1834 and 1845. Both offer invaluable insights into the antiquities and historical artefacts, and contain many references to camps, forts and 'Roman stations'. Both have been extensively consulted in this investigation, particularly in relation to some of the more obscure sites, many of which remain unconfirmed as being Roman in origin. These texts are examined with caution because they were compiled by kirk ministers in each parish, so the quality and accuracy of the accounts can vary greatly.

> ...there are still the vestiges of a Roman camp. The wall and ditch, which surrounded the camp itself, are scarcely discernible in many places, having been taken into the adjacent corn -fields, but the wall and ditch which surrounded the praetorium are very distance, which shew it to have been an oblong square.
>
> **(OSA 1791-1799 4:498)**

The above quote is an example of this from the OSA and details a description of a Roman camp at Fordoun, but which has not been located since, if it ever existed (R. H. Jones 2011:336). The *praetorium* referred to in the quote is likely to be a moated medieval structure which still exists today (Canmore 36470),

Another key data source, which has some crossover with Canmore, is *Roman Camps in Scotland* by Rebecca Jones (2011). An in-depth study based on the author's PhD, the book contains information and site plans for the vast majority of temporary encampments in Scotland. The plans of camps included here draws on Jones' work and are credited where appropriate. There are further texts which have been invaluable while undertaking this research, in particular, *Rome's First Frontier: The Flavian Occupation of Northern Scotland* (2006) by David Woolliscroft and Birgitta Hoffmann, and who have surveyed and excavated many of the Flavian sites north of the Forth-Clyde isthmus, *The Antonine Wall* (Breeze 2006a; 2015), which includes an extensive analysis of Scotland's linear frontier, and *Roman Frontiers in Wales and the Marches* (Burnham and Davies 2010), which has been a useful comparative resource from a similar part of the Empire to Scotland. These sources have shaped the research questions underpinning this research, as well as my interpretation of the fortifications. Other sources used when comparing and discussing Flavian sites in Scotland, are detailed in the text, and I have also extracted additional information from *Scotland: The Roman Presence: ScARF Panel Report* (ScARF 2012a).

One of the most significant sources consulted here are the *Proceedings of the Congress of Roman Frontiers or Limes Congress*, produced after every gathering, dating back to the 1940s. Additional sources of archaeological data are found in the various journals and publications of the learned societies, such as the *Proceedings of the Society of Antiquaries of Scotland*, *Britannia*, the *Journal for Roman Studies* (JRS), and *Discovery and Excavation in Scotland*, while several regional societies also publish journals, such as *The Transactions of the Dumfries and Galloway Natural History and Archaeological Society*.

Archaeological data from non-Flavian sites, such as those dating to the Antonine and Severan fortifications, have been extracted from Canmore. This has also included many undated and some unconfirmed Roman sites. For example, I have taken a list of camps from Jones, including sites which may have possible and probable Roman origins (see R. H. Jones 2011:323-340). Where I have included some of the probable sites, I make it clear in the text. Data covering indigenous sites, including NGRs and the dating chronology, have also been extracted from Canmore.

3.1.3. Mapping Data

The functionality and effectiveness of GIS is reliant on good mapping data, and the most accurate dataset for North Britain is produced by Ordnance Survey. Whereas mapping use to be a manual process, these days this data is drawn from a range if sources, including satellite imagery. When attempting analysis such as viewsheds and line-of-sight, it is important to use the most accurate mapping data available, although the caveat is that this does not always highlight alterations in the landscape, such as quarrying, and does not necessarily reflect the area in the

Roman period. I downloaded the mapping data used in the GIS database from Edina Digimap, as well as *Ordnance Survey (OS) Open Data*; *OS Terrain 5 DTM (Digital Terrain Model)*, *OS Terrain 5 and 50 Contour*, along with height spots, *OS Basemap*, the *OS Water Network*, and *OS Open Rivers* data. The initial basemap is *OS Open Map - Local*, similar to the Landranger series of physical maps produced by OS. Although this mapping data does not appear in the outputs here, I have used it in the GIS database for identifying various archaeological features in the landscape, and which can be seen from LiDAR imaging or aerial photographs.

A Digital Elevation Model (DEM) is a data layer which displays a bare-earth raster grid, omitting modern features such as roads, power lines, buildings and vegetation, enabling an image of the surface of the land[8]. This topographical representation of the landscape gives a powerful impression of the area around each fortification, the site itself on occasions, and enables various features, such as hills, river valleys, and peninsulas to stand out. This is useful in when analysing the landscape around Roman fortifications, as these make use of the topography for defensive purposes. The landscape can also hinder the identification and analysis of sites, especially when natural events such as flooding and soil erosion have occurred since the Roman period. I processed DEM images in greyscale, with subsequent colourisation using the *Color Ramp Manager plugin > opt-city package > sd-a color ramp* applied.

I also undertook an alternative method of mapping the landscape using outputs from LiDAR scanning. This method captures the topography of the landscape by firing laser pulses at the ground, usually from an aircraft or drone. The results are then converted into a DEM. In Scotland, LiDAR scanning is undertaken at a resolution of 50 centimetres, 1 metre or 2 metres, and commissioned by the Scottish Environment Protection Agency and Scottish Water, focussing on areas prone to flooding, and often near the coast or low-lying land. Few Roman sites have been scanned using this technique, although the entire length of the Antonine Wall is LiDAR scanned, and recently been analysed by Hannon (2018:7) as part of the *Hidden Landscape of a Roman Frontier* project. As Hannon has shown, this scanning has supported some theoretical approaches to construction of the frontier, demonstrating the effectiveness of this technique in the analysis of archaeological sites, as well as Roman frontiers. Few Roman sites are scanned in this way, and where LiDAR data is available for 1st century fortifications, I have used this to examine the site and the surrounding landscape. LiDAR scans can enhance site images, although surviving features are not always visible. Once the image is hillshaded, features can become more visible.

---

[8] In the UK, the terms DEM and Digital Terrain Model (DTM) are interchangeable, both producing an elevation surface image which shows the bare earth. Some data sources (such as Ordnance Survey and Edina Digimap), use the term DTM rather than DEM, but for the purposes of this research, the latter will be used.

3.2. Analytical Methods

The benefits of GIS used as a tool for landscape analysis and archaeological analysis has been shown by various researchers including Wheatley (1995), Lock and Harris (1997), Lake et al. (1998), and Wheatley and Gillings (2002). Witcher (2000:18) notes that through landscape analysis, environmental factors can be used to generate maps with multivariate indicators which show areas that have varying degrees of attraction for settlement. These can explain spatial patterning in past settlements, something which is of direct value to addressing the research questions in this monograph. The advantages of GIS also include the capacity to analyse complex spatial phenomena, particularly when using the most recent topographical data such as LiDAR, which is much more accurate than previous terrain and mapping information provided by Ordnance Survey. For example, the OS height data used by Woolliscroft (1993; 2010) for measuring Roman signalling on the Gask Ridge fortifications, has now been superseded by more modern and accurate mapping technologies. As Wheatley (1996:90), Witcher (2000:14), and others note, we also need to be cautious when patterns of positioning and orientation are identifiable through GIS analytics. Patterns of association do not in themselves indicate a causal relationship but it is easy to draw this assumption, particularly where there are strongly held prior assumptions. Such presentations of the information can also be specific and not theory-neutral and can produce narrow interpretations of the past, something I have addressed within this research concerning the orientation of sites and what they are facing. As a research tool in archaeology, GIS needs to be used with care so that interpreting results is not too speculative, and that conclusions from the data are not abstract from the concepts, to the detriment of overall results (ibid:19). While GIS can be a useful tool in spatial analysis, it should not be the sole method of interpretation, and we should also consider other methods such as site analysis, excavation and remote sensing.

Before looking at the individual methodologies used in this study, it is worth commenting on some of the challenges which need to be considered when using GIS-based analyses, particularly when applying computation modelling to real-world situations; does the computer model accurately reflect what would have been visible on the ground, and has the landscape changed significantly over 2,000 years? Some of the more obvious challenges are changes in vegetation, including tree clearance which would affect visibility. As noted previously, it is not clear whether or not there had been large-scale deforestation in 1st century Scotland although there would have been a need for a substantial amount of wood for each Roman fortification. Another challenge comes from artificial changes in the landscape from activities such agricultural works, quarrying, road and rail construction. In some instances, the alterations are obvious, but more often, they are less clear. A prime example of this can be the altering and creation of watercourses as part of land drainage efforts. The date of such activities is less clear; are these changes pre or post-Roman, and in some instances they may have been undertaken by the Roman military. This itself poses an interesting question, particularly around those sites located on headlands or spurs such as Inchtuthil and Fendoch fort; are these naturally occurring or were they artificially created by the military to improve the overall defence of a location?

Criticisms have also been levelled at GIS visibility and viewshed analyses as an analytical tool, again due to the potential variations in computer modelling and the actualities on the ground. Visibility analysis relies on good quality ground surface data which forms the Digital Elevation Model (DEM), and for the purposes of this research, this has been extracted from data gathered by Ordnance Survey, and is subject to the resolution defined by them. This type of computational analysis also relies upon bare-earth models, where the landscape is stripped of all vegetation, and as noted in the previous paragraph, this also has the potential to give misleading results, although there needs to be some recognition that the Roman military would have stripped back the landscape both as part of a construction process, but also to facilitate communications and visibility between fortification sites. The tension between theoretical approaches and viewsheds 'on the ground' has been noted previously, although not necessarily as widely acknowledged (e.g. Gillings 2012 ; For further discussion on some of the challenges facing GIS analysis, see Leussen 1999; Chapman 2006; Polla and Verhagen 2014; Brughmans and Brandes 2017; Starek et al. 2020)

Nonetheless, used carefully and with an awareness of its limitations, GIS is an important tool to build up a profile of a site; to analyse the location, positioning, intervisibility, and orientation of Flavian fortifications in the landscape, and for analysing the wider interconnectivity and relationships between the sites in Scotland. GIS is also used to produce topographical analyses, viewsheds and landscape models of the fortifications and their environs. Creating and populating the GIS database has brought together an extensive dataset relating to Flavian Scotland, and is more comprehensive than any single database in the public domain. Bringing together this information, and the additional archaeological and topographical data outlined above, has facilitated a wide-ranging analysis of the spatial and temporal data concerning the Flavian invasion of Scotland. It has enabled analyses of various fortifications in their landscape position, most of which has not previously been undertaken on these sites.

3.2.1. Positioning: Defensive and Elevation

An important initial stage of the site profile analysis, was the creation of the GIS database, used to produce outputs that would show the positioning of sites in respect of their topography and elevation, and features vital to understanding the defensibility of the fortifications which would also help with subsequent analysis of viewsheds and lines-of-sight, which might facilitate both security and communication. Using the DEM as a base layer, I applied hillshading to create a 3D visual representation of the landscape, aiding visualisation of topographical features around the Roman sites. I did this in QGIS using *Raster > Analysis > Hillshade* and processed 5 times using various azimuth of light settings at 0°, 90°, 180°, 270°, and 315°; altering the direction which the light comes from often highlights distinct features in the landscape. Unless otherwise stated, all the images here, which are colourised or hillshaded, are produced with the azimuth of light set to 270°, as this has produced the best results for highlighting archaeological features on these sites. I added additional OS mapping data to the hillshaded base layer, including contours at 5 metres and 50 metres distances (*OS Terrain 5 and OS Terrain 50* respectively) to accentuate the landscape. Topographical data from *OS Strategi*, for the whole of Scotland, was added to QGIS, including the foreshore, tidal data, surface water and the overall water network (which includes rivers and streams).

To ensure positioning of the fortifications in the landscape was accurate, a range of data sources were consulted and where necessary uploaded into QGIS; the sources included excavation plans, aerial photographs, geophysical survey, and LiDAR imagery. I drew the outline of the fortification in the GIS database. For camps, I adapted the outline of the defences from those recorded by Jones (2011). The outline of these was extracted for the orientation analysis, as can be seen in Figure 3.1.

Figure 3.2 is an example of a topographical overview produced for each Flavian site covered in this study. The

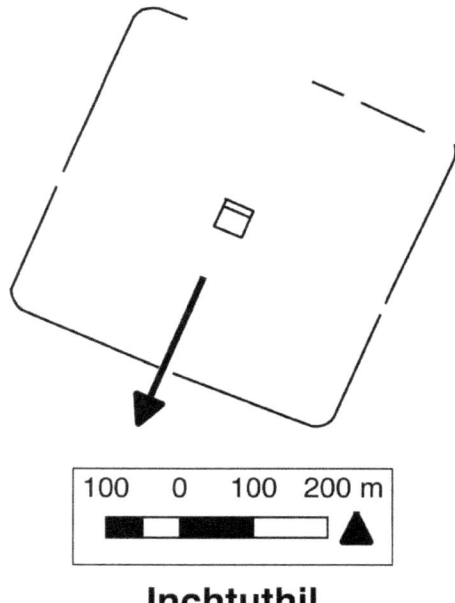

Figure 3.1. Outline of defences and principia of Inchtuthil legionary fortress showing direction of orientation.

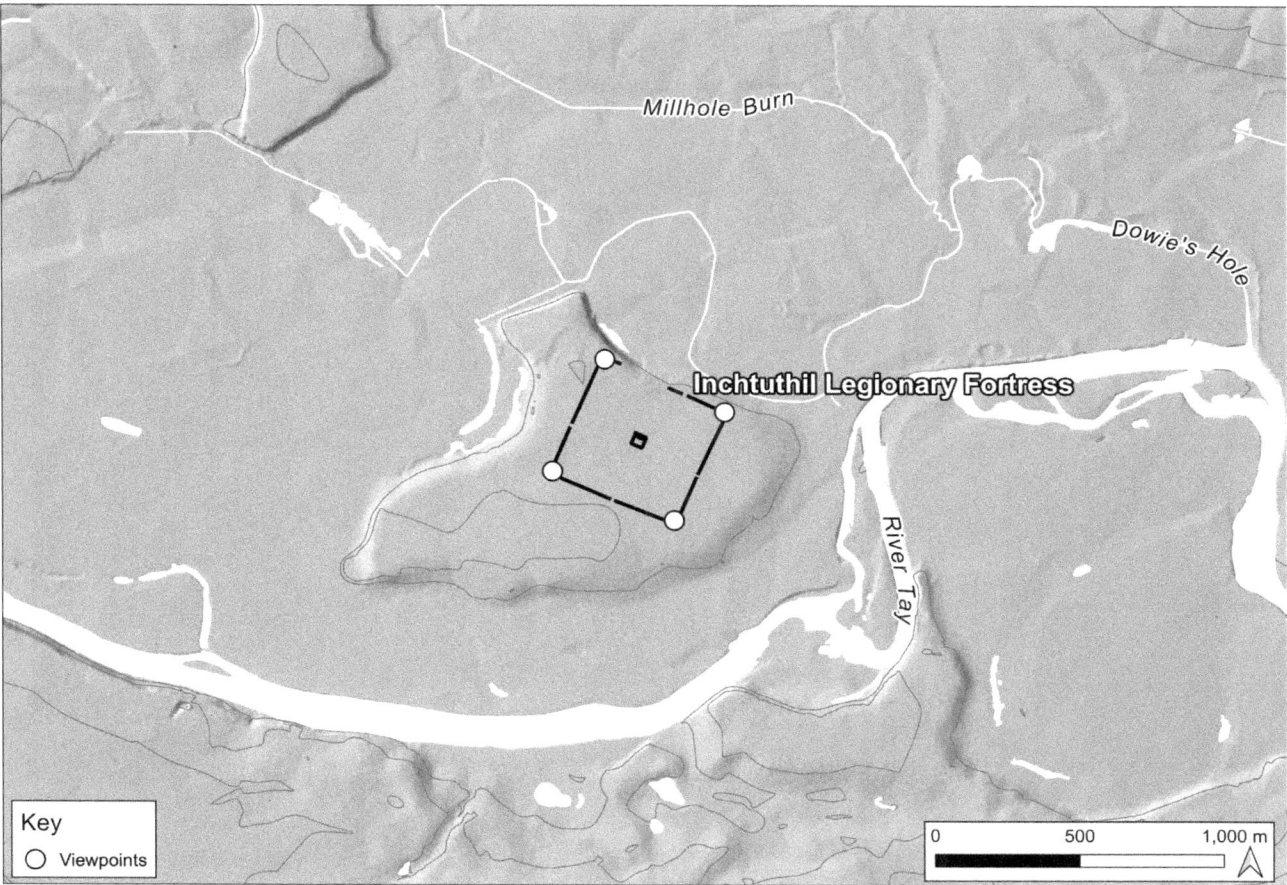

Figure 3.2. Defensive topography of Inchtuthil legionary fortress with viewpoints

inclusion of contours, 5 metres apart, helps to emphasise the defensive topography of the immediate area surrounding each fortification. The analysis also highlights key features in the landscape, such as the peninsula on which Inchtuthil is located, and the flatness of the plateau. We can see the River Tay to the south of the site, showing the steepness of the escarpment which is protecting the northern flank of the site.

Although similar to the analysis of the defensive topography, the elevation analysis, which shows the site in the surrounding landscape, with an emphasis on the elevation, is undertaken at a larger scale, and used for examining fort positioning relative to any key features in the wider landscape, such as river valleys and indigenous sites (E. Graafstal 2020:149-150). An example of an elevation analysis is shown in Figure 3.3, and was achieved in the same way as the defensive topography analysis but on a larger scale and using OS Contour 50 metre data.

Multiple fortifications are found on some sites, and for this analysis, each one is analysed separately. The exceptions to this are the camps at Ayr, Bellie, Bochastle I and II, Castledykes IA and B and Milltimber, where the defences are indistinguishable or unknown. The rest of this section summarises the methods used in the different type of analyses.

3.2.2. Intervisbility: Viewpoints, Binary Viewsheds and Lines-Of-Sight

Intervisibility analyses examine which parts of the landscape could be seen from a fortification using binary viewsheds and lines-of-site. As the elevation analysis above shows, a key benefit of GIS analysis is the ability to move beyond immediate site features and understand the relationship between these and the wider landscape such as with other fortifications. Moreover, GIS facilitates systematic analysis across large numbers of sites; this has not previously been undertaken in relation to 1st century fortifications in Scotland.

As noted earlier, fortifications appear positioned in certain locations to control the immediate landscape, and to investigate this I developed an analytical dataset focusing on landscape analysis through viewpoints, binary viewsheds, and lines-of-sight. A viewshed is defined as an area which visible from a specific location, and uses the elevation value of a cell within the DEM to determine the extent of visibility either from a single point (a binary viewshed), or between two points; an intervisibility or line-of-sight viewshed (Woolliscroft 2010:15-16). Although as Woolliscroft writes (pers. comm.), not all receiving sites would be visible from all observers' locations. To support this point, Woolliscroft et al (1992) cites one tower on

Facing the Enemy?

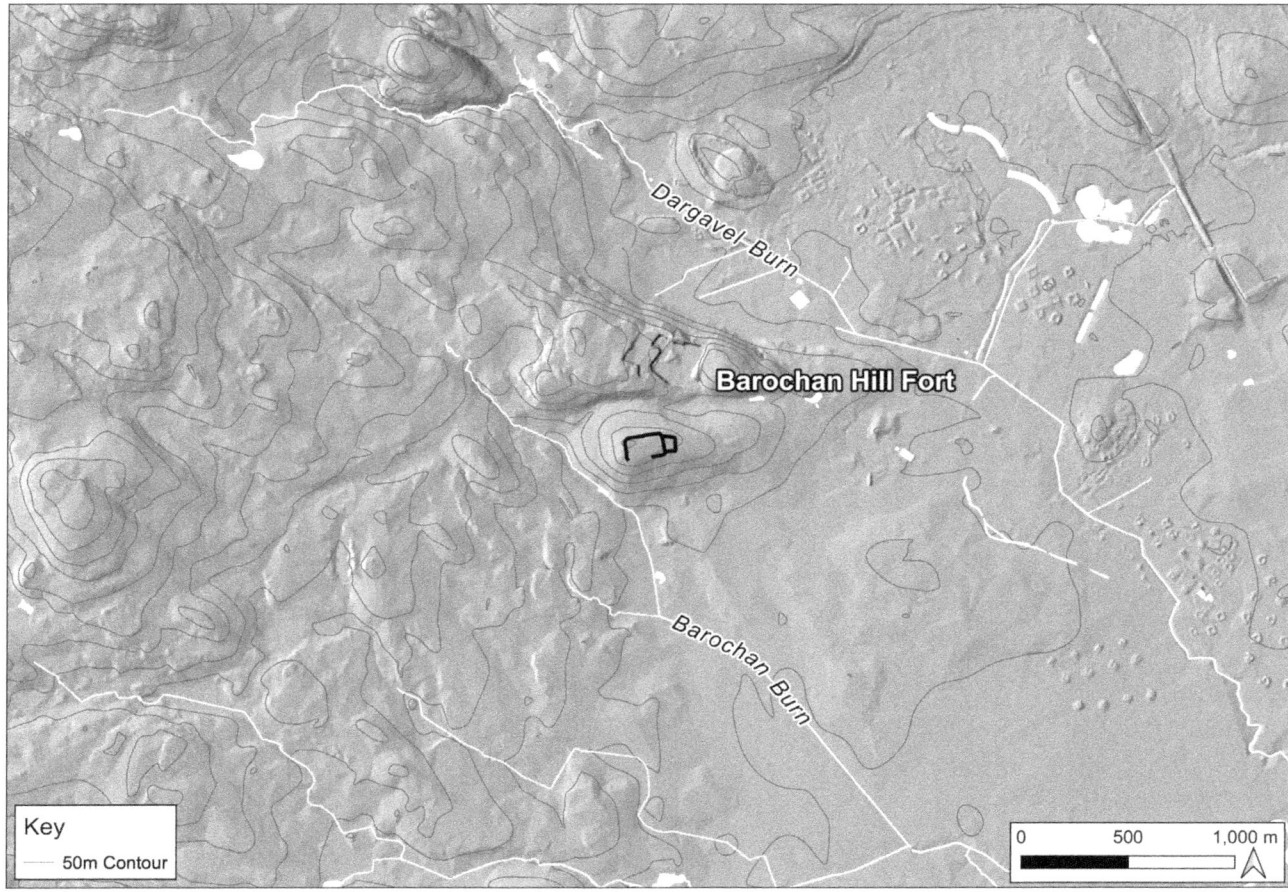

Figure 3.3. Elevation analysis of the landscape surrounding Barochan fort.

Hadrian's Wall, Barcombe B, which could signal to the northwest corner tower of Housesteads and possibly the west gate, but not to the other towers at Housesteads. The methodology regarding signalling, which is presented here, is based on the signalling experiments and work of Woolliscroft (Woolliscroft 2010:35, 48; Woolliscroft, Hughes, and Lockett 2002; Woolliscroft and Hoffmann 2006:29); this is the standard work in this area. The practical elements of Woolliscroft work have not subsequently been replicated, although such an exercise focussing on the tower sites in southern Scotland would help us to test the hypothesis that these were part of a network, as put forward by Murphy et al (2018).

For this research, the corners of each site (where known), have been plotted in QGIS (represented by white dots) as seen in the image of Inchtuthil legionary fortress (see Figure 3.2), and used as the observer's position, with similar points recorded at the site receiving the signal. It is unknown how many Flavian sites in Scotland had mid-towers, or where these are positioned in the ramparts, therefore these are not used for viewpoints and, in any case, focusing on the corner towers allows for the maximum intervisibility to be ascertained. For the sites where the signals originate, measurements (viewpoints) have been taken from each confirmed corner, except for fortlets and tower sites where a single, central site measurement is recorded. It is unclear if camps had corner towers, but to ascertain the maximum intervisibility, viewpoints have been recorded in the corner position of these sites. Where corners are unknown on a site, viewpoints were recorded at the known sections, and/or from a point where it is estimated that the missing corner would be (Figure 3.4). At the sites of Ardoch, Dalginross, and Dalswinton, which have multiple fortifications, viewpoints were taken from the larger forts. No measurements were taken from Ayr, Broomholm, Milltimber, Milton and parts of Mollins, as not enough of the defences are confirmed. Where the defences of the overall site were unknown, such as some of the Dalswinton fortifications, viewpoints were taken from the individual NGR co-ordinates for the sites, listed on Canmore, with a similar approach for the measurements from the fortlets and towers. It should be noted that using one viewpoint gives a limited viewshed of what is viewable from the site, and caution is needed when interpreting these fortifications.

The signalling methodology set out by Woolliscroft (e.g. 2010), remains essential to calibrating the newer technologies used in my research. Woolliscroft undertook practical experimentation of signalling which involved sending signals between two Roman fortifications on the Gask Ridge frontier, adjusting the height of the signalling equipment, and the distance for receiving it. This technique is detailed later in this monograph. Woolliscroft established that the maximum visibility range at which a signal could be seen,

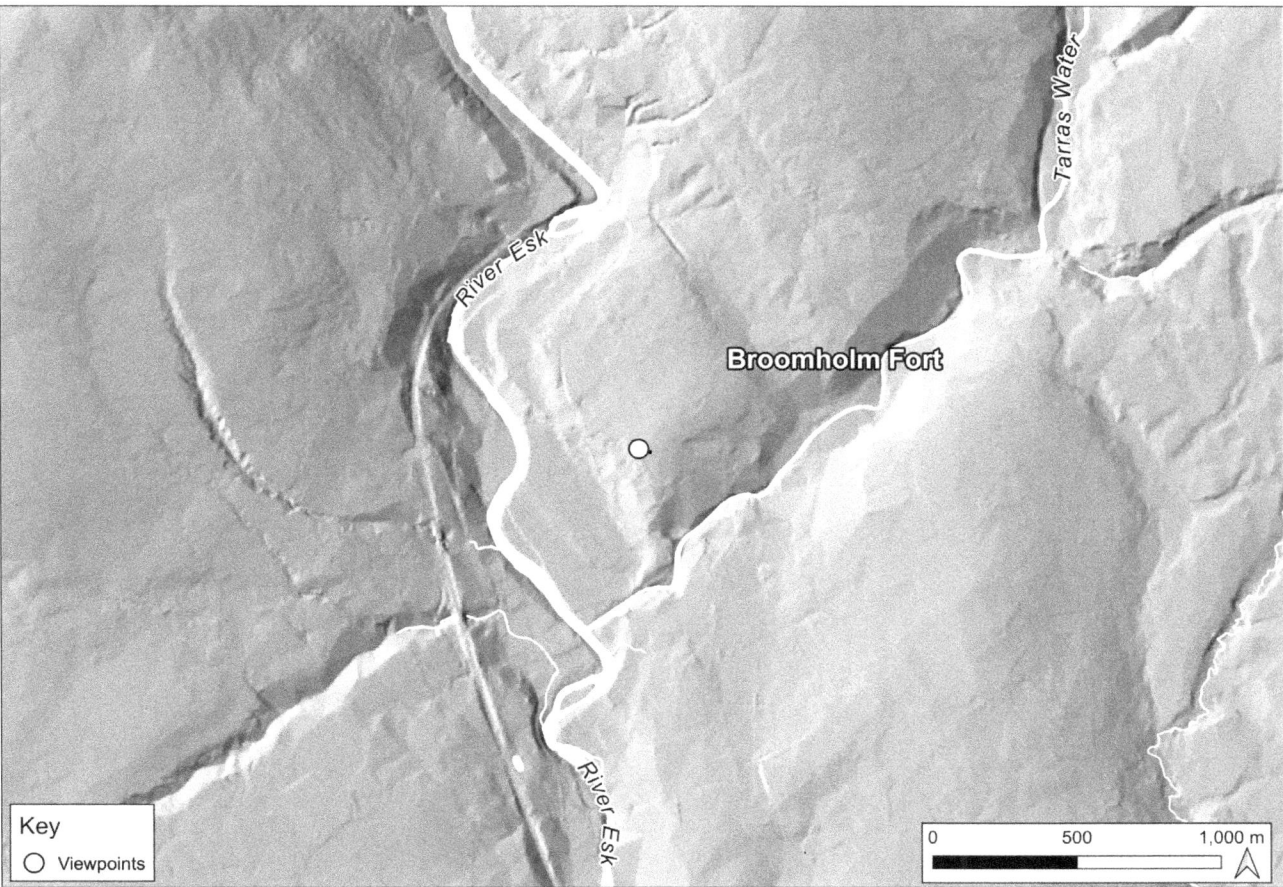

Figure 3.4. Single viewpoint where only one corner of the defences is known.

and the message interpreted, was 6 kilometres in daylight. When processing the binary and line-of-sight viewsheds, I have therefore used 6 kilometres as the limit of the radius for the analysis. Using Woolliscroft's methodology, along with additional analysis of archaeological remains, Shirley (Shirley 1996; 2001:45, 47) has estimated of the gate towers at Inchtuthil fortress as being 8.6 metres in height, and this is the height which I have used when undertaking viewshed analysis from the fortress, forts, and fortlets. The methodological approach taken by Shirley is reasonable, and there are broad similarities with the work by Johnson (1983) who undertook a comparative analysis of various fortifications, with a main focus on Inchtuthil. It is not possible to say how reliable these results are, but for the purposes of my modelling, Shirley's findings are adequate.

The height of the towers has been estimated by Woolliscroft and Hoffmann (2006:29) as being between 8 and 10 metres high, although Woolliscroft (2010:16) based his signalling experiments on towers being 10 metres in height, and this is the measurement used here. Camp ramparts have not survived in their original height, and it is not clear if these had signalling structures such as platforms or towers, so observer or signal receiver height for these is set at 1.7m, representing the height of a human. The receiver height for the binary viewshed has been set at 0 metres as the objective was to see what was visible at ground height, and the receiver in Woolliscroft's practical experiments was always at ground level, and not at the same height as the fortification or tower which was being targeted. A model of the role of viewpoints in a binary or intervisibility viewshed analysis is shown in Figure 3.5.

I undertake two types of viewshed analysis; a binary viewshed (Figure 3.6), and a line of sight analysis (Figure 3.7). Both require viewpoints taken from the observer (or signallers' location); this is the only measurement needed for a binary viewshed, but for a line-of-sight analysis, there needs to be a second set of viewpoints at the observer location. Woolliscroft concluded that 6 kilometres was the limit that signalling could be interpreted by those receiving the signal, and this is the distance which I have used for my computational models.

I processed both analyses in QGIS using the Viewshed Analysis tool, with the DEM used as the elevation raster. Signaller/observer and receiver/target viewpoints were plotted based on the type of fortification.

3.2.3. Orientation

Orientation of a fortification, or the direction which it faces, can be determined through identification of the *principia*, the central building in a fort or fortress or area in a camp, and Vegetius records that it is from here that the military surveyors laid out the camp (Dilke 1971; Johnson 1983;

Facing the Enemy?

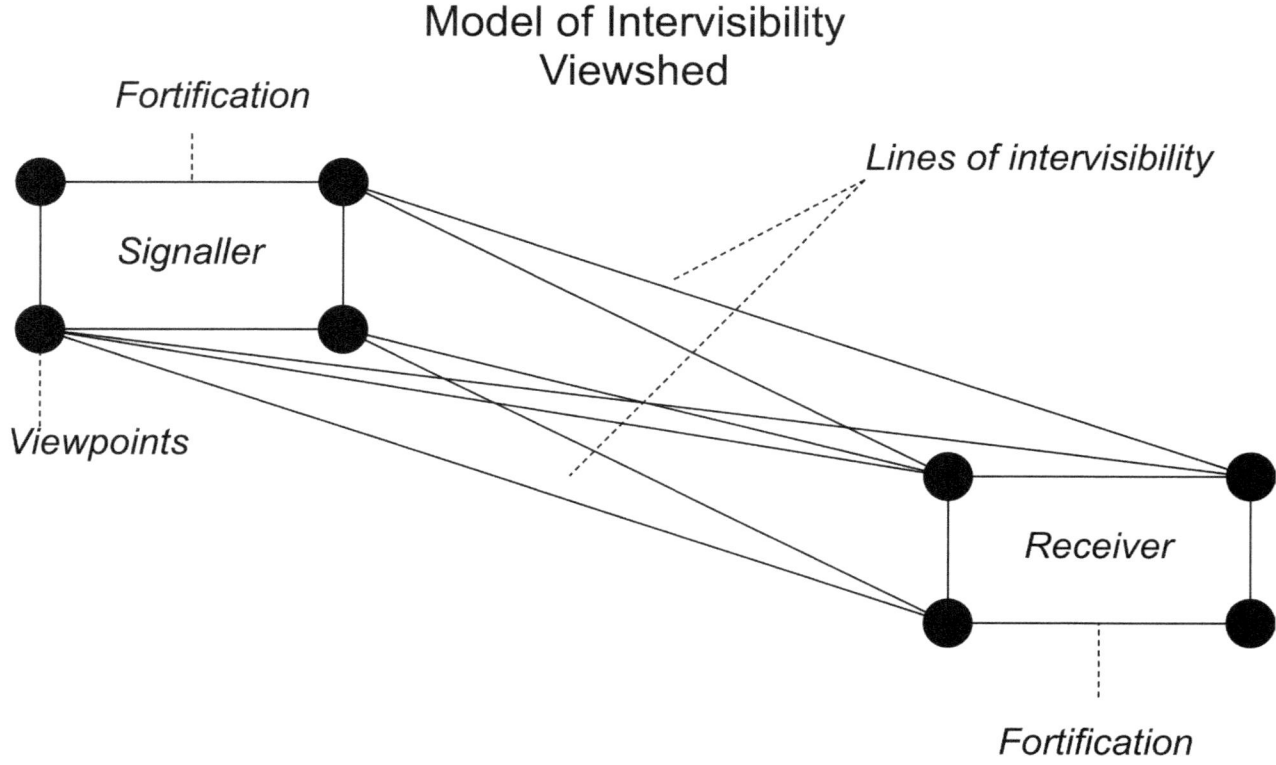

Figure 3.5. Model of how viewpoints for viewshed analysis are used.

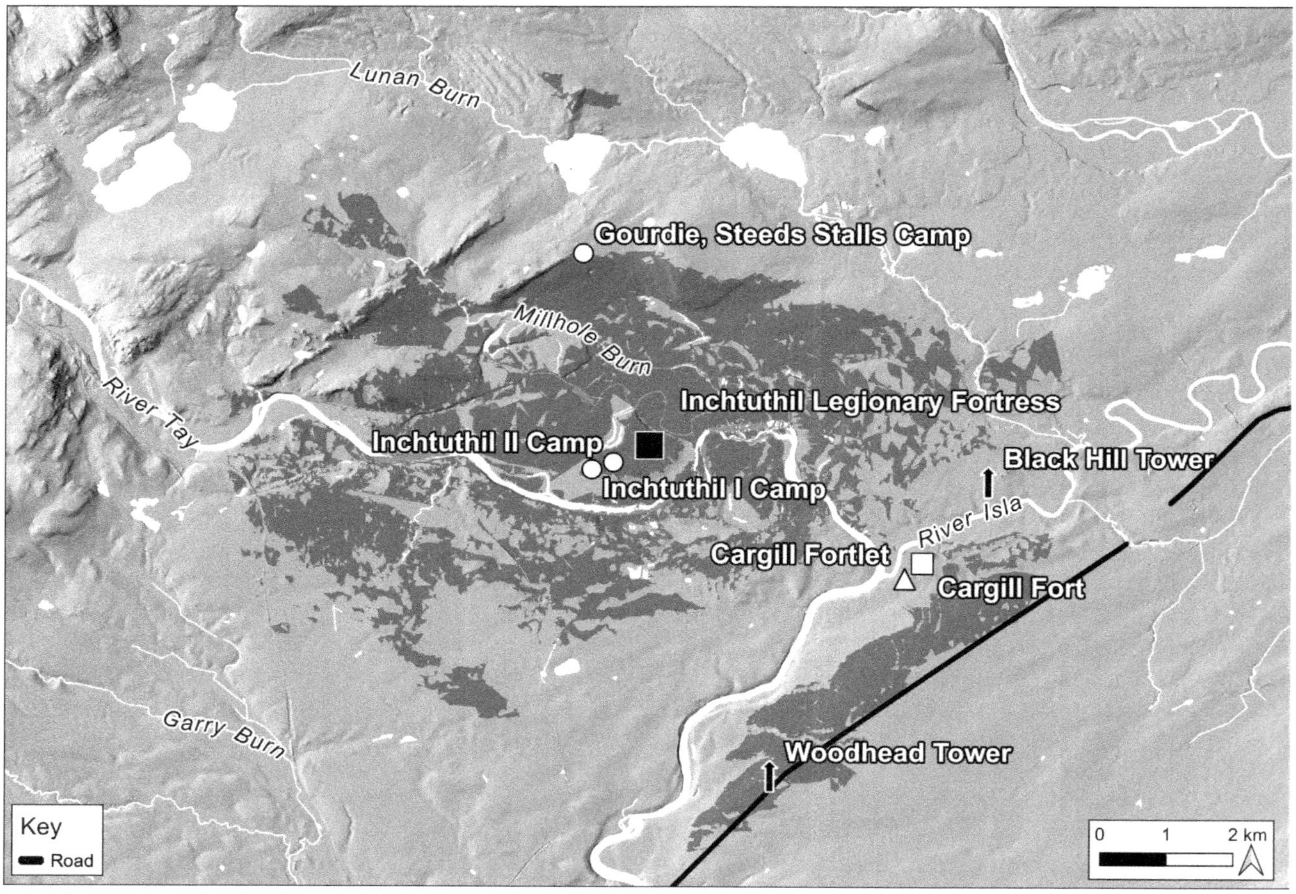

Figure 3.6. Extent of binary viewshed analysis (shaded area) from Inchtuthil legionary fortress.

Data and Methods

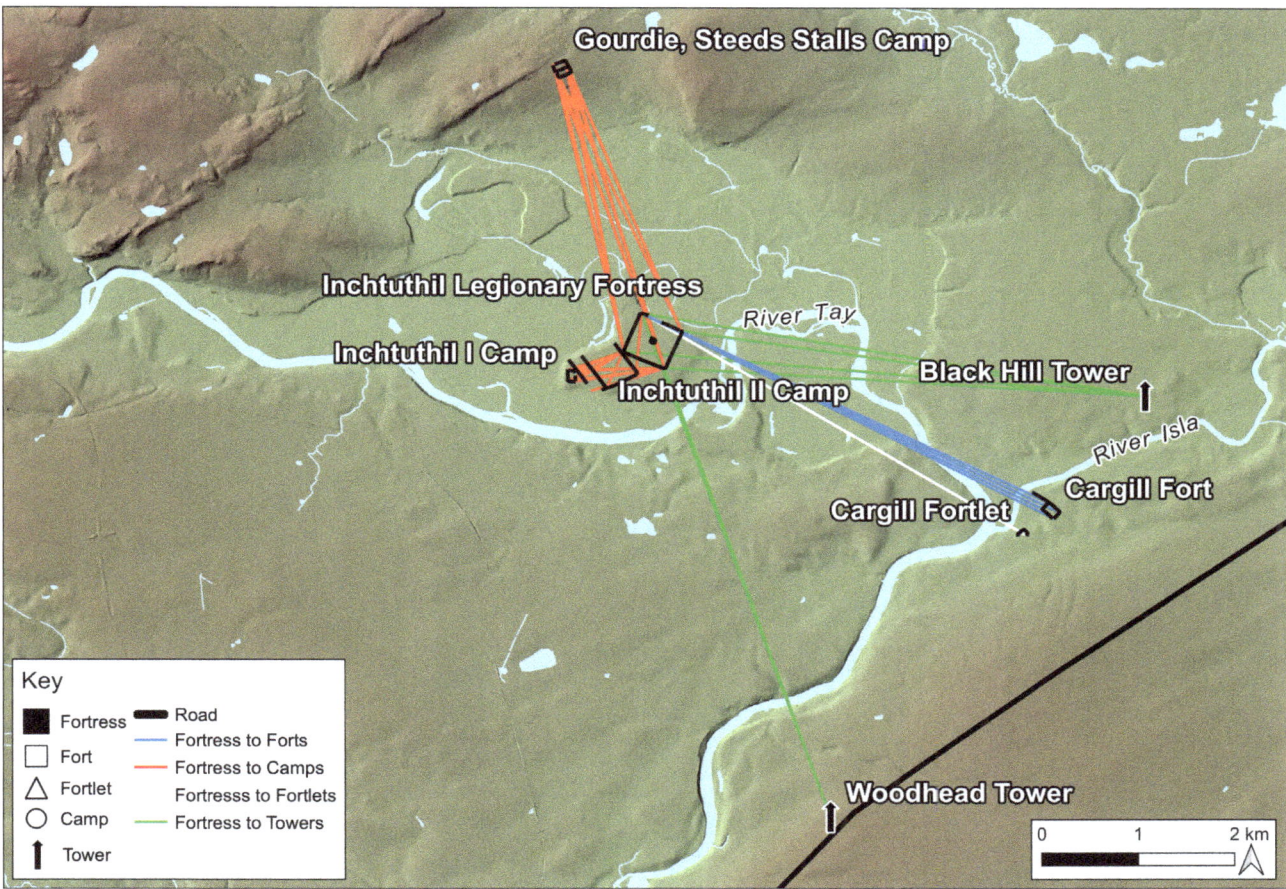

Figure 3.7. Line of sight analysis from Inchtuthil legionary fortress to nearby fortifications.

Shirley 1996; 2001; Bishop 2013). According to Polybius, it had a financial, religious, and administrative role; as the first building seen on entering a fort through the *porta praetoria*, the building has prominence. If the layout of the *principia* can be established then so can the orientation of the site. Towards the rear of the building are a series of rooms, with the central one (the *aedes* or *sacellum*) housing the regimental shrine and treasury. During the Flavian period, statues of the Imperial Cult were also housed here. This room is located at the very centre of the fort, and against the back wall of the *principia*, and 'looks along' the *via praetoria* and out of the *porta praetoria*. The orientation can also be determined if certain features, such as the long/short axis, the internal roads, and/or the gates are identifiable. To demonstrate the layout of a typical Roman fort, albeit in stone (Flavian sites in Scotland are turf and timber construction). Figure 3.8 gives an overview of the typical layout of a 1st century turf and timber fort in Scotland. The layout of a fort is similar to that of a camp, and it is from the classical texts that detail this that we get the information and names for the various elements.

The orientation of camps is usually less clear as they lack the structural remains of permanent buildings, and a tendency for the overall shape to not be rectangular, makes it difficult to discern which direction they face. Occasionally, the long/short axis or side gates are identifiable, indicating that a site faced in one of two directions. For this research, directional arrows have been placed over the sites in QGIS to indicate the orientation of a site, as exemplified in Figure 3.9. Individual site diagrams, also with directional arrows, have been created for the Flavian sites in Scotland, and sites from other frontiers.

Where the highest point of a site is identified, I have marked this as a spot on the individual site plans; this would, according to 'Pseudo' Hyginus (*De Munitionibus Castrorum* 56), show the highest gate of the site and the *porta decumana*. There are exceptions to this rule where other available evidence shows the *porta decumana* is not necessarily the highest point of the fortification. Although the *porta decumana* is recorded for many of sites covered here, caution needs to be exercised when using it as the only piece of evidence to indicate orientation.

Within QGIS, once the site is plotted and the direction it faces identified, the angle of the orientation of the site is calculated, using the long axis and its cardinal direction calculated as per Figure 3.10 For example, the fortress at Inchtuthil is orientated at 207°, which is categorised as 'south'.

3.2.4. Interconnectivity

To undertake an analysis of the interconnectivity of the Flavian fortifications, I used the basemaps outlined above,

Facing the Enemy?

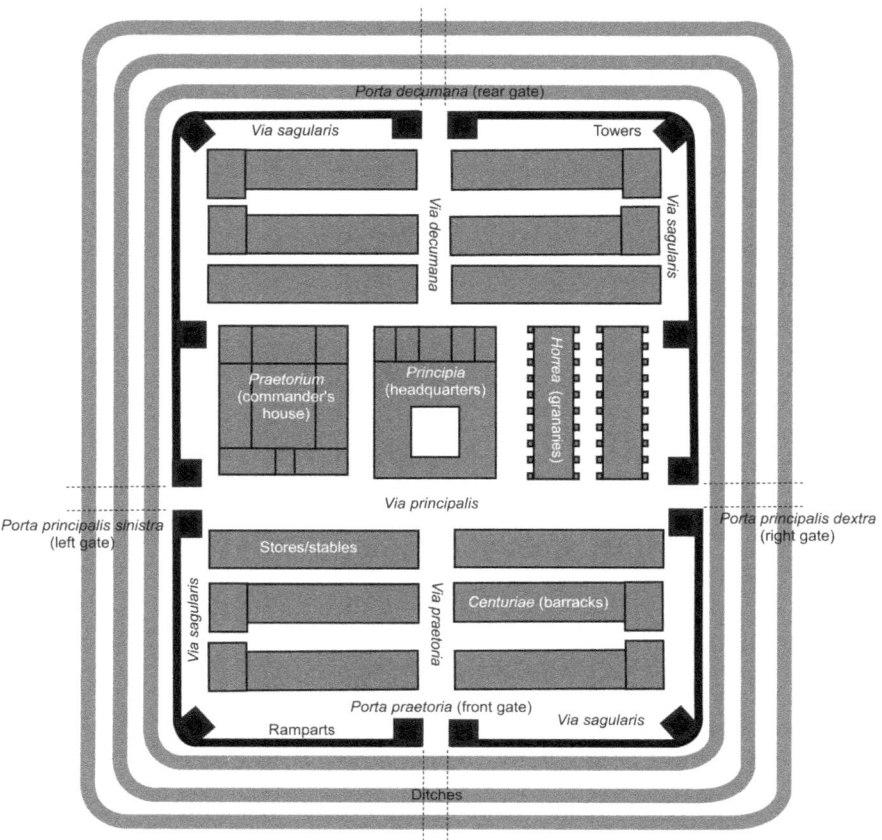

Figure 3.8. Layout of a typical Roman fort in Northern Britain.

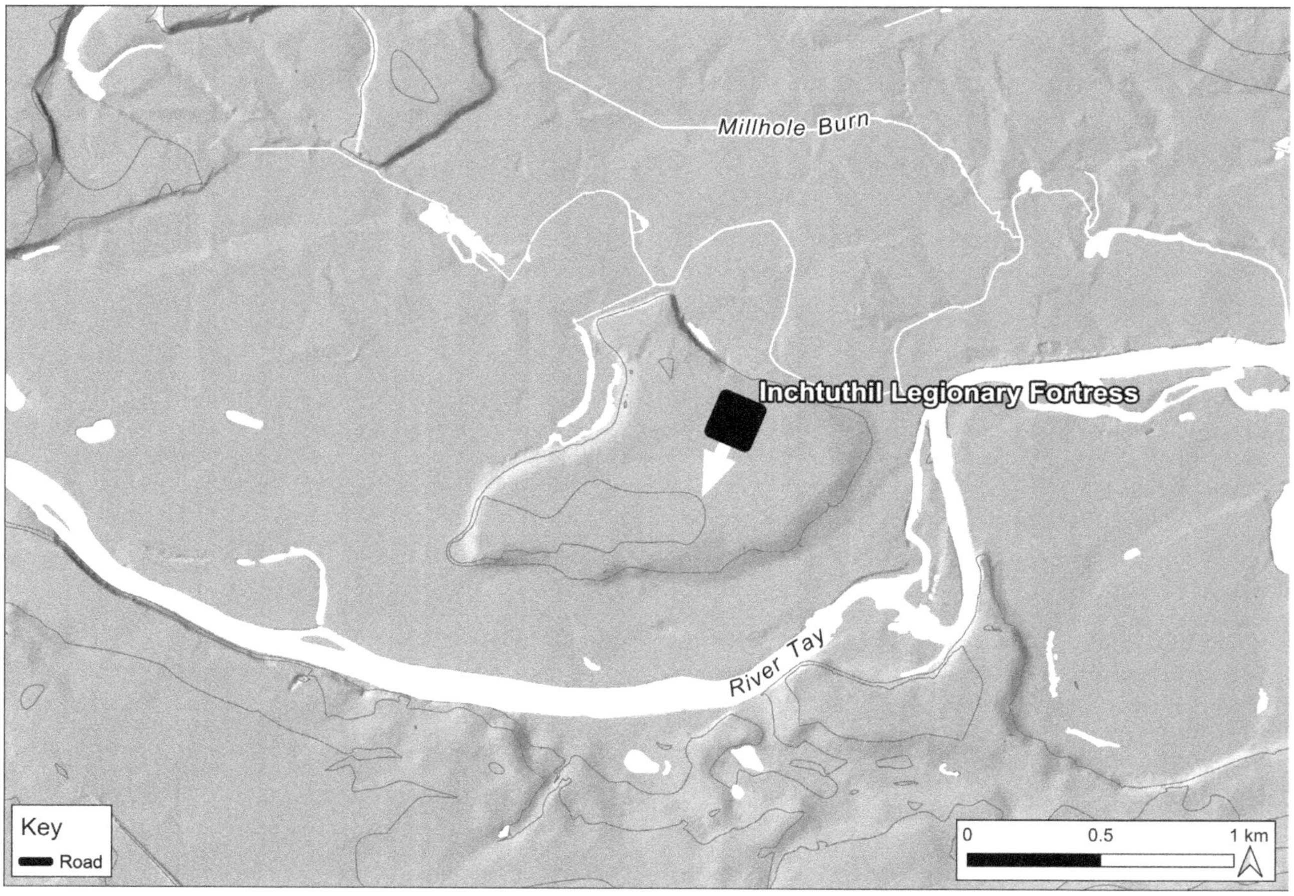

Figure 3.9. Orientation of Flavian fortifications centred on Inchtuthil legionary.

Data and Methods

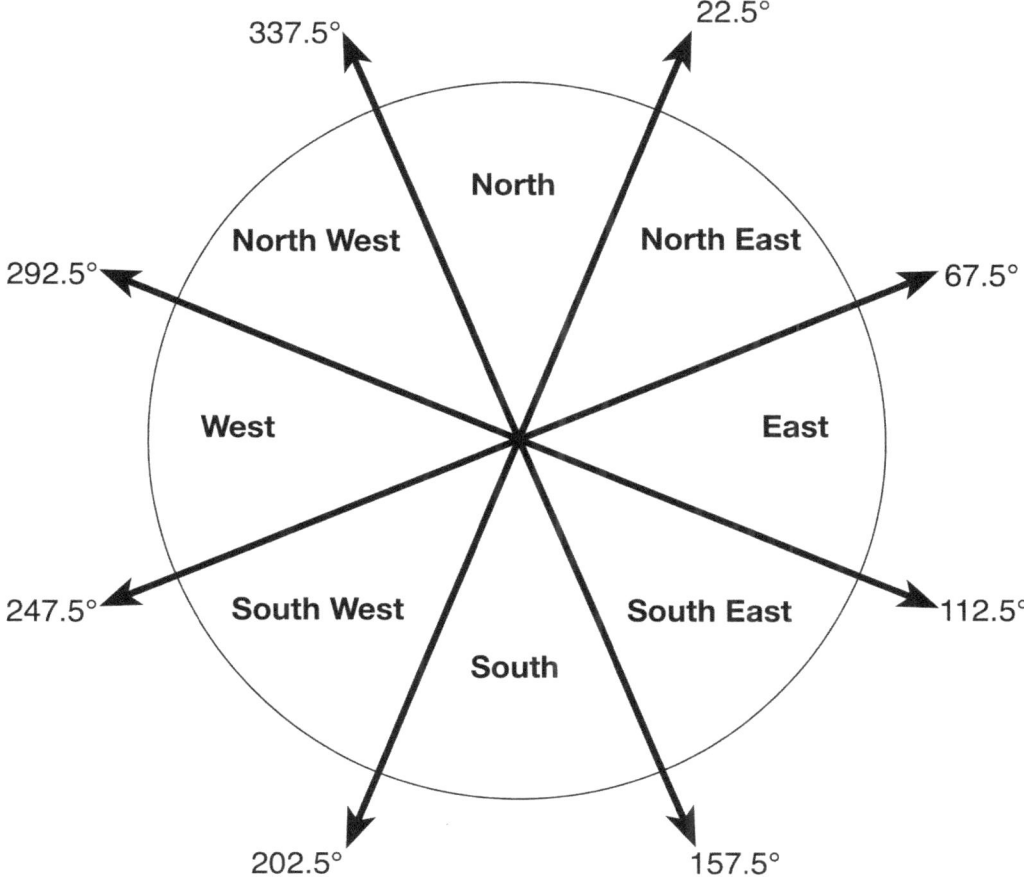

Figure 3.10. Degree range for each cardinal point.

with additional archaeological data from Canmore added. This includes sites classified as Iron Age and non-Roman forts in Canmore, as well as Antonine, Severan and undated Roman fortifications.

Additional mapping data was added to the GIS database, including shapefiles representing the Roman road network and river crossings/fords. While Canmore has some data on fords and river crossings, this is incomplete, and so forts and crossings (not including bridges) up to 5km from the sites were plotted in QGIS, using data from the 18th and 19th century OS maps from Edina Digimap. This analysis is intended to identify what, if anything the fortification is facing. In some areas such as Moray and Aberdeenshire, fewer fords were recorded, which may reflect differences in the resource which Ordnance Survey put into gathering this information rather than the actual prevalence of fords. This means the findings on fords in this chapter need to be interpreted cautiously. The data regarding the crossings has been added into the GIS and plotted on a base map using Ordnance Survey data.

The analysis undertaken through the GIS is integral to the research objectives of this work; it not only enables us to see the immediate topography around the fortification, but it also allows us to see each site in the wider landscape, and the relationship between the two, as well as any nearby archaeological features. It brings together the mapping and archaeological data in multiple dimensions, which can aid analysis and understanding of the strategy of the military in the 1st century landscape.

4

Location and Positioning

More work is ... required on temporary camps to provide for their independent dating... Continuing investigation and assessment of other northern forts is necessary in order to elucidate the possibility of the existence of later phases.

(ScARF 2012a:17)

The location selected for a fortification was important for several reasons; self-defence, for controlling an area or population, to secure a resource, and, in some instances, to enable intervisibility between two locations. Graafstal (2020:148) in his examination of the Antonine Wall fortifications concluded that several forts (Bearsden, Kirkintilloch, and Castlehill) are tilted to the south, so the opposite end appears elevated and stands out; this is something which 'Pseudo' Hyginus states forts should do, although this is less prevalent in the Flavian period. Permanent fortifications in Scotland were located in fertile areas, usually near to large rivers, and made use of the immediate topography for the defence of the site. Generally, camps are similarly located, although the need to establish a temporary site while passing through a landscape could restrict water supplies, and the use of the topography for defence.

Through landscape analysis of Roman sites in Spain, Costa-García (2018) has demonstrated that fortifications controlled mountain passes, hill ranges and access to camps, and that these rationales were prioritised over complete control of the surroundings. This reflects the evidence from other frontiers in the Empire; forts and fortlets needed to be located in positions which secured features in the local area, such as river crossings, valleys, and population centres. Many of the sites in Flavian Scotland command good views of river valleys, but less so of local roads, which could suggest that the fortifications were constructed before the road network. Wherever possible, Roman fortifications had to command good views, but also needed to be intervisible; this was an important factor in the positioning of the Gask Ridge fortifications which seem to have had a dual role, with Woolliscroft (1993; 2010) proposing a primary purpose of lookout posts, with a secondary one of signalling. Although the work of Woolliscroft (2010) considers the forts, fortlets and towers along the Gask Ridge, amongst other areas, his research in Scotland did not go beyond these types of fortifications, and he did not include camps in his modelling. Some tower sites in southern Scotland, may also have had a dual function. Murphy et al. (2018) has shown that some of these sites are intervisible at 30 kilometres, although as Woolliscroft found the effectiveness of signalling at this distance reduces significantly.

This chapter analyses the location and positioning of fortifications by examining the immediate and wider topographical landscapes surrounding a fortification. It summarises the results of my analyses of the location and positioning, and the intervisibility and signalling capacity of Flavian fortifications in Scotland. First, I summarise the previous research on fortification location and positioning, including spatial analyses, before I summarise some of the key studies into spatial analysis. I then analyse the locating of fortifications in the landscape, first looking at the immediate position of a site and the surrounding topography, and how this provides additional defensive support. Next, I look at the site in the wider landscape, and how the location of the site may impact on the fortification, i.e. are these located in positions which enable them control over the landscape. I then present the results of GIS intervisibility analysis, a binary viewshed showing what can be seen in an area.

4.1. Classical Texts: Positioning

Various Roman literary texts discuss the locating and positioning of fortifications in the landscape; *De Munitionibus Castrorum* ('Pseudo' Hyginus), *Epitoma De Re Militari* (Vegetius), *Bellum Iudaicum* (Josephus) and *Histories* (Polybius), although it is the first two which are most relevant to this research. Although 'Pseudo' Hyginus and Vegetius are writing after the 1st century, these texts furnish us with important claims about the design, layout, and to a lesser extent, positioning of camps. For example, Vegetius tells us there were three types of encampment: summer, winter and permanent; although none of these types are identifiable in the archaeological record (R. H. Jones 2011). Vegetius and 'Pseudo' Hyginus both give separate, but similar criteria for the best location for fortifications, designed to offer maximum protection to the inhabitants,

> *When surveying a camp, it is not sufficient to choose a good site unless it be so good that no other site better than it can be found. Otherwise a more advantageous site overlooked by us may then be occupied by the enemy, bringing danger. Also ensure that unhealthy water is not close by nor wholesome water too far away in summer, that there is no shortage of fodder and firewood in winter, that the site on which one is to camp is not liable to flooding after sudden rainstorms, that it is not in broken, remote country where the enemy may surround us and make it difficult to escape, and that missiles cannot be shot from higher ground by the enemy so as to reach it.*
> **Vegetius Epitoma De Re Militari III:8**

Vegetius writes that soldiers should construct the fortifications in a safe location with access to resources including water which should be nearby. If a long-term stay is planned, the site should be salubrious, not be overlooked by high ground or a mountain, as this would give the enemy an advantage. The camp also needs to be the right size for the number of soldiers, not too big or too small, and he states that it should be fortified by hand (i.e. ramparts and ditches) and nature, in other words using the natural topography for defence.

Concerning the choice of terrain for the establishment of the camp; first, they choose a site which rises above the plain, on a distinctive rise, and the porta decumana is set at the highest point so that the area is dominated by the camp. The porta praetoria should always look towards the enemy. The second place is on a flat plain, the third is on a hill, the fourth on a mountain, the fifth in whatever place is necessary, from which it is called an 'unavoidable camp'.

…Whatever the position of the camp, there should be a river or spring on one side or the other. Unfavourable positions, which were called mothers-in-law by our ancestors, should be avoided at all times: the camp should not be overlooked by a mountain from which the enemy could attack or see what is going on in the camp; there should be no forest nearby to conceal a hidden enemy, nor gulley's or valleys through which the enemy may secretly approach the camp; nor should the camp be near a fast-flowing river which might flood and overwhelm the camp in a sudden storm.

'Pseudo' Hyginus *De Munitionibus Castrorum* 56 and 57

Hyginus compiles a similar list of requirements to Vegetius, including that the encampment should ideally be located on a level or sloping site, with the next best location being a hill. Hyginus notes that the *porta praetoria* (the front gate) should always face the enemy, and that the *porta decumana* (the rear gate) should be sited on the highest point of the site wherever possible, as this makes the interior look more impressive to those viewing the fortification from a distance. These texts were not written in the 1st century, and that the intended audience was not the ordinary soldiery or their commanding officers (e.g. D. B. Campbell 2009), and therefore need to be considered with caution. It is likely that they reflect military practices which were popular at the time of their writing, and perhaps reflect the 'gold standard' in military planning and techniques. It is likely that soldiers out in the field would have needed to be much more adaptable to the terrain and local environment; this is what appears to be happening in Scotland. Fortifications are being constructed and adapted to best suit the local topography rather than being built in the locations prescribed by the classical authors.

One of the objectives of this study is to explore the topographical landscape of the immediate area around sites, as well as positioning in the wider surroundings, and the locating of a fortification would have required consideration of a number of different factors; it would not have been a case of placing it anywhere in the landscape. A significant amount of thought by the *prefect* or *tribune* went into selecting the right location, before it was laid out by the *agrimensores* (Dilke 1971). There were strategic needs to contemplate: a suitably large enough site; availability of resources and freshwater; the site had to be defendable; the role of intervisibility between Roman sites; a requirement to control certain features in the landscape; and the proximity of the local populations.

4.2. Positioning: Spatial Analysis

There are limited studies of spatial analysis which consider the location and positioning of fortifications. It is an area which is infrequently covered in studies of such sites, including Johnson (1983), Shirley (2001), and Bishop (2013), or groups of sites on frontiers, such as Richardson, Taylor (2000) and Bidwell and Hodgson (2009). There are some studies which examine location and positioning of forts and camps, albeit briefly, including Welfare & Swan (1995), Woolliscroft & Hoffmann (2006), and Jones (2011), and these usually discuss it in the context of the classical sources and the individual sites. Burnham and Davies (2010), in their edited volume on *Roman Frontiers in Wales and the Marches*, analyse the location of fortifications in the landscape and conclude that most early fortifications are in fertile areas, coastal tracts or river valleys. This level of spatial and GIS analysis has not been widely applied to early fortifications in Scotland, despite it having the potential to reveal additional information about these sites.

The main conclusions of those undertaking spatial analysis of frontiers has been that fortifications are located in positions which either allow them to control the local landscape or specific features and resources. Castro (2018) undertook spatial analysis of 624 sites, including 64 forts and fortlets, and 129 towers on the Southern Arabian Petraea. Castro concluded that the Roman fortifications had visual control of the local landscape, including settlements, water points, wadi passages (river valleys, usually without water in the dry seasons), and roads. A similar study was undertaken by Pažout (2018) in the frontier zone of Judea, looking at the visual control of the landscape from these sites, and the relationship between settlements. Pažout notes that the military sites were located close to the settlements and had good views of them. By modelling routes between sites, he showed that the military fortifications also have visual control of the roads. Costa-García (2018) looks at the visual control of the landscape around Roman sites of various dates in Spain, with his spatial analysis of these sites shows that they have control of mountain passes and hill ranges, but they prioritised access to Roman camps over complete control of the surroundings. He further observes that the priorities for locating a fortification include blocking mountain routes and ensuring access to water. He concludes that they placed fortifications in locations where good visual control over the immediate surroundings is ensured.

Graafstal (2020:142, 144) argues that considerations of the terrain, topography and location of fortifications on the Antonine Wall have been subordinate to discussions on construction of the frontier, and writes that the intervisibility of the fortifications are ignored in most previous studies. As noted earlier, he identifies the key components of fort locations on the Wall, finding that sites are located a level plateau with sloping edges or river valleys protecting one or more sides. Using contour analysis, Graafstal records that many forts are tilted to the south, so the north side would have appeared elevated and stand out, and by undertaking an elevation analysis, concludes that many sites in the west are located next to valleys which go into the hinterlands. I apply Graafstal's analysis of the defensive topography and elevation to Flavian fortification in Scotland later in this study.

4.3. Analysis: Defensive Topography

When selecting a site for a fortification, the classical texts state that various considerations had to be considered such as the topography, defensive capabilities, security, and availability of resources in the immediate location, although the prioritisation of these may have varied. On some frontiers, sites also had to be in a location which would support them controlling the landscape or a local population. Both 'Pseudo' Hyginus and Vegetius write that the ideal position for a fortification should be on a level site or one with a slight rise. If that was not available then a hill should be selected or, if that also wasn't possible, a mountain position. More used to the mountain ranges of the Alps and Pyrenees, it is reasonable to assume the Romans did not consider the hills of Scotland to be on the same scale, or at least not in the areas where they constructed fortifications. *Mons Graupius* is the exception, although Tacitus does not describe a mountain other than the occasional mention of the enemy being on the hilltops (*Agricola* 37).

Security of a location was important with the literary texts stating that fortifications should not be overlooked by the enemy, high ground, or mountains, limiting the opportunity for the missiles to be launched into the centre of the Roman site. 'Pseudo' Hyginus (*De Munitionibus Castrorum* 56) also states that the interior of a fortification should appear impressive to anyone overlooking it, and that the *porta decumana*, the rear entrance, should be located on the highest part of the site which enables anyone approaching to see inside. Although fortifications in Scotland are not overlooked by mountains, some have hills in close proximity, and sometimes indigenous hillforts are located on these. 57% of early fortifications examined for this study are overlooked by hills higher than the site location, although far fewer could have been fired upon, and there is no evidence that the indigenous population at this time would have had the technology to fire effective projectiles over the distances required[9]. It, therefore, seems unlikely that being overlooked would have been a significant factor in Scotland when the site is chosen by the army. For example, at Auchinhove and Bochastle, there is limited space on which to construct fortifications, so it is reasonable to assume the army prioritised finding the most suitable site over the risk that a site could be attacked. Many Roman sites are dominated by surrounding hills, there are few which have indigenous fortifications constructed on them. Those that do are undated and may not be contemporaneous with the Roman occupation, and thus would not have posed a threat. A summary of the site data can be found in Appendix Two.

One challenge when undertaking the analysis of the defensive topography of sites, has been the allocation of individual sites to the aforementioned landscape classification. While some sites are unequivocally on a plain or a hill, other sites are not so straight forward to classify. I have categorised fortifications as being on a plain if the height difference on the site does not differ by over 10 metres, which is a reasonable difference for a larger site such as a fort or camp, but would be very steep for a fortlet. The full extent of some sites remains unknown, and others appear to fall into one category when analysed through the GIS and mapping data, but after being visited on the ground, clearly fit another category. Where the difference in height is unknown at a site (usually because the full extent of the defences are unidentified), I have erred on the side of caution when categorising the fortification position. Another challenge, which has been alluded to in the previous chapter, is whether or not the slopes and hills on which some fortifications are constructed, have had their 'natural' defences improved by the military; slopes reshaped to become steep escarpments. Such analysis is beyond the remit of this study, but it is something which could affect the defensiveness of individual sites.

For the analysis of the defensive topography of sites, 105 sites were examined, and the results are shown in Figure 4.1. While the analysis confirms the preference for plains (although some of these are floodplains), fewer sites are positioned on slopes, compared to hills. Most Flavian fortifications in Scotland, are located next to the coast and waterways, and for the latter shows a reliance on this resource. But it may also indicate the need to control sections of the coast, entrances to rivers, and the river valleys, which would have been important if these were being used for navigation and to move troops and supplies. 62 of these sites are located adjacent to the confluence of two or more rivers; I discuss these later in this chapter.

Almost all fortifications make use of the topographic landscape for defence, whether they are located on a plain, slope, or hill. Topographic defence is facilitated by rivers and river valleys, or by constructing fortifications on hills and outcrops. In some areas, Scottish Borders, Moray, and some parts of rural Aberdeenshire, where the topography is less advantageous and there tend to be less rivers, fortifications are constructed adjacent to steep hills (e.g. the camp at Carlops Spittal in Figure 4.2), which would provide a more limited element of defence (assuming

---

[9] For the purposes of this analysis, for a hill or mountain to be considered as overlooking a Roman fortification, it had to be within 2 kilometres.

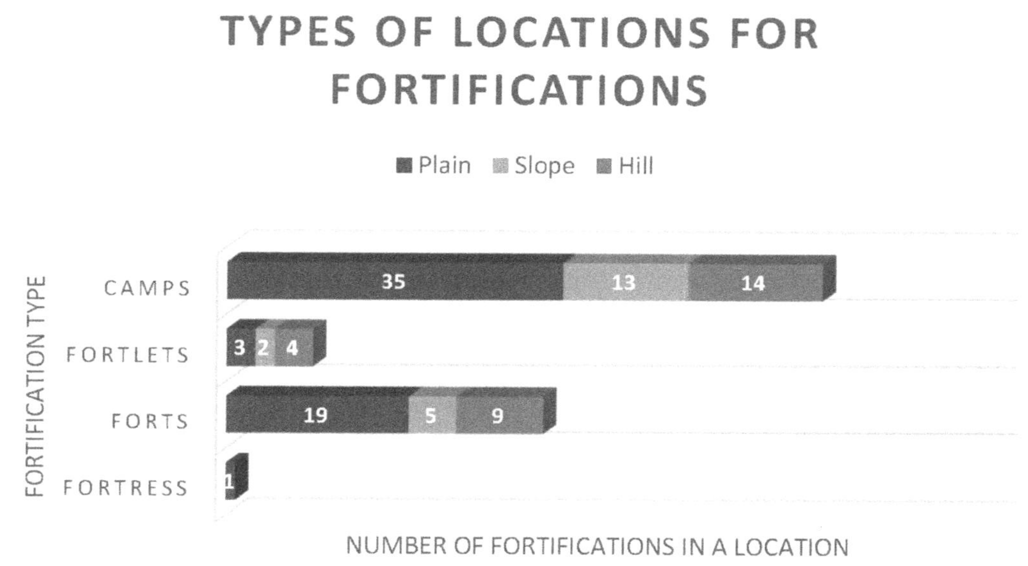

TYPES OF LOCATIONS FOR FORTIFICATIONS

■ Plain   ■ Slope   ■ Hill

FORTIFICATION TYPE

CAMPS: 35 | 13 | 14
FORTLETS: 3 | 2 | 4
FORTS: 19 | 5 | 9
FORTRESS: 1

NUMBER OF FORTIFICATIONS IN A LOCATION

Figure 4.1. Topographical areas where Flavian fortifications are located.

there are no hillforts on the summits). A lack of defensive topography, fertile lands and water resources may explain why there are less fortifications in these areas.

My analysis shows that most of the Flavian fortifications, the legionary fortress, 19 forts, 35 camps, and 3 fortlets are located on plains. The legionary fortress at Inchtuthil, along with at least two camps, is constructed on a raised, natural platform, making use of this for defence; there has been erosion to the northern side of the site affecting the defensive ditches, implying that this probably occurred after the Roman occupation. The location itself is a raised

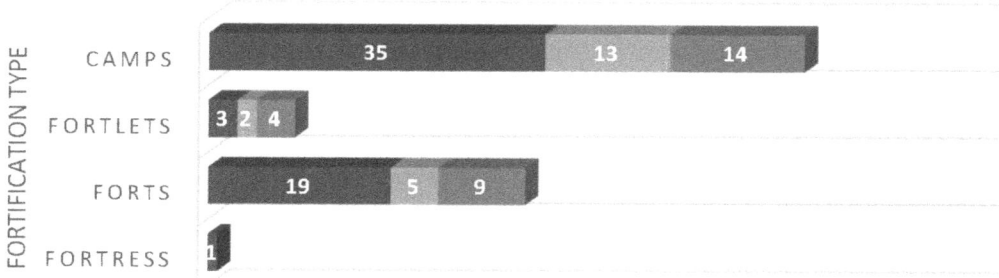

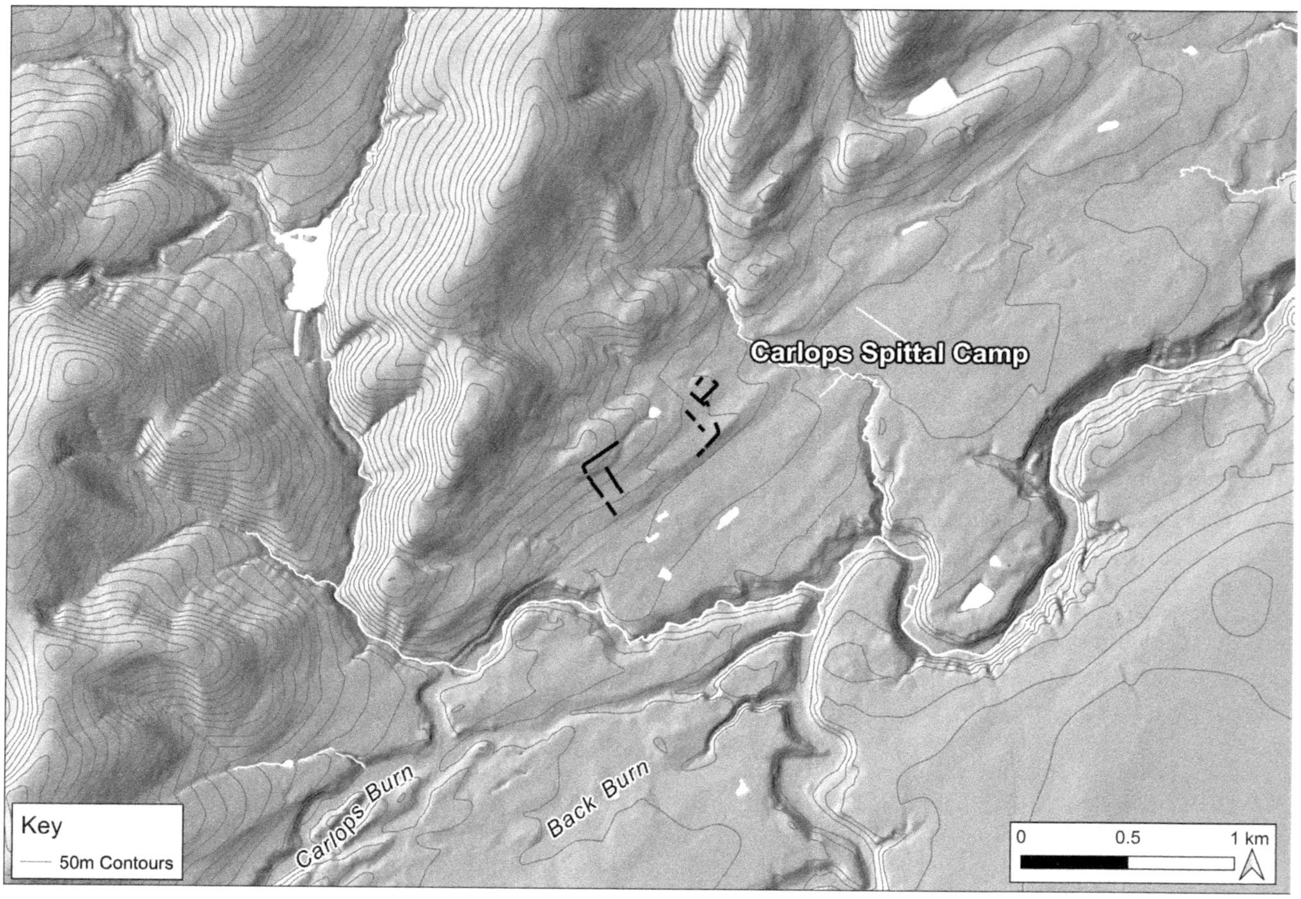

Figure 4.2. The camp at Carlops Spittal positioned against steep hills.

plateau, with the River Tay to the south, while to the north are several small waterways and to the west is Delvine Loch, possibly indicating a former course of the Tay.

Nineteen forts (including Camelon North and South as one) are located on plains. Most of these sites are located next to rivers, although these watercourses vary in size. Mollins is located next to the River Kelvin which is insubstantial at this location, however, the course and flow of the waterway have been affected by agricultural and development works such as construction of the adjacent motorway network and the Forth-Clyde canal, while Malling is the only site constructed next to a body of water, the Lake of Menteith. Woolliscroft and Hoffman (2006), through geophysical and aerial survey, have found evidence that the eastern defences of the fort may lie under the water, suggesting that the level has risen since the Roman period. While the other forts are constructed on plains, they make use of river valleys on at least one side to support the manmade defences, while some such as Bertha, Birrens, Bochastle, Cardean, Doune, Drumlanrig, and Stracathro all have watercourses on at least two sides. Several fortlets are located on plains, although Bankhead and Kaims Castle are located in a wider, hillier landscape. Kaims Castle is also the only site which does not make use of a river valley for defence. Located on the route from Ardoch fort to the Gask Ridge fortifications, it was probably constructed in this less-than-ideal location out of necessity, protecting the route and acting as a signal relay station between the sites. Of the 35 camps located on a plain, only part of the defences of some sites are identified, such as at Cold Chapel and Gogar Green. Like other fortifications, most of the camps are located near watercourses, although sometimes these are small streams, such as at Gogar Green; the landscape of the latter site has been heavily developed in recent years and cannot be assumed to be the same as it was in the Roman period. Most sites make use of the landscape for defence, usually using river valleys, except Dun, Gogar Green and Malling, the latter using the lake. Some sites are positioned close to steep hills, potentially offering additional protection such as at Cold Chapel, Denholm and Wandel. Some are surrounded by rivers on multiple sides, including Auchinhove and Cold Chapel.

Several fortifications are located on sites which slope: 5 forts (including the two Flavian period forts at Newstead), 13 camps and 2 fortlets. Muiryfold (Figure 4.3) is one example, while Milton fort occupies the top of a hill as well as the slope on eat least one side. The forts slope down to river valleys, except Loudon Hill, which is far from water; this site has been quarried and the original landscape has changed significantly in the past 70 years. The only fortlet which is located on a sloping site is at Glenbank, although it does not make use of the small river valley to the east for additional defensive support. 13 camps are located on sloping sites, and only a few of these make use of the

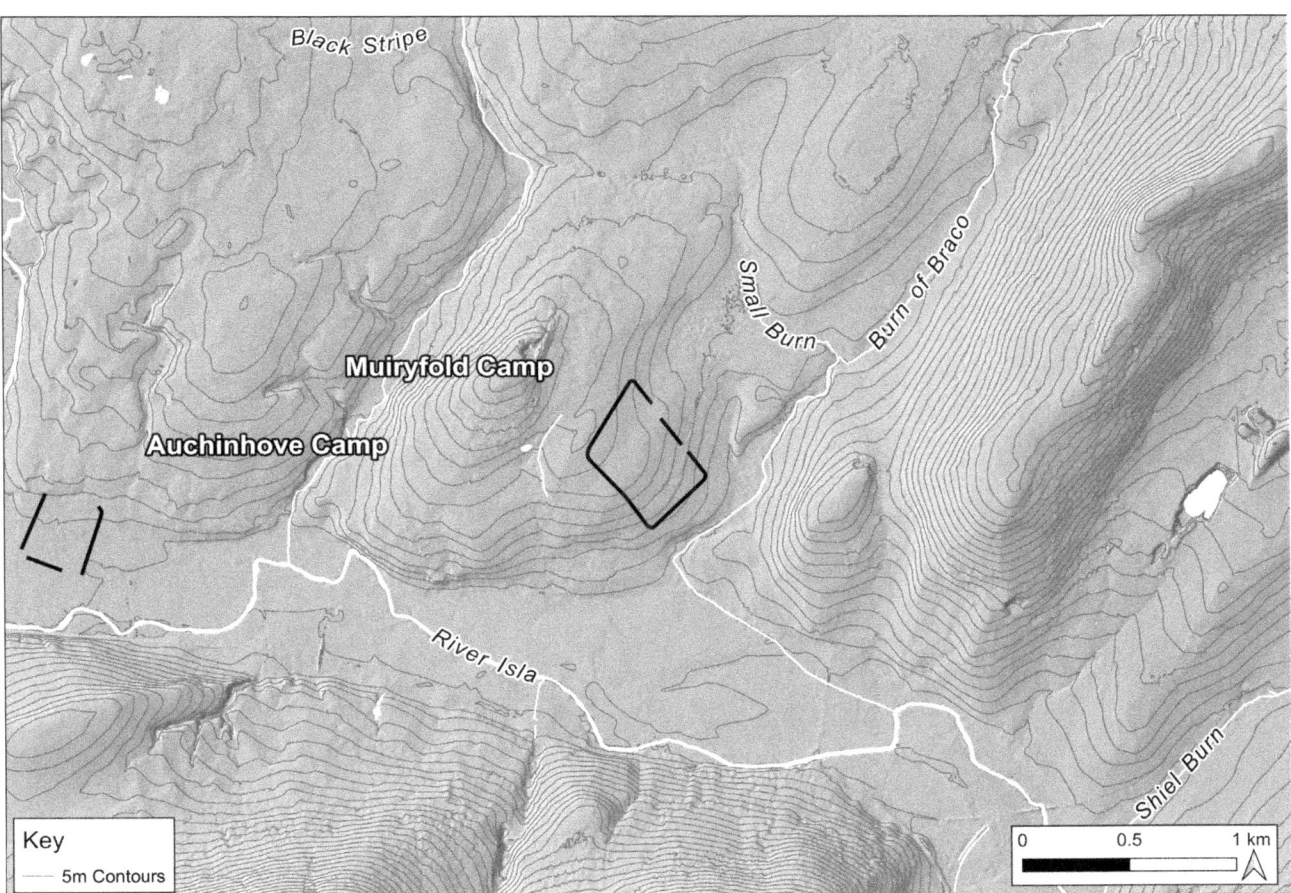

Figure 4.3. Example of a camp (Muiryfold) located on a slope.

landscape for defence, such as Cornhill and Durisdeer. These camps are larger than the other types of fortification, and the local landscape would have been restrictive for many of them. It would appear that there was no optimal space which is why these are constructed on sloping sites rather than plains; sites such as Kirkhouse and Raeburnfoot are steep, but the latter would have been in a good position to control movement along the river valley. Many of the towers are also located on sloping sites. This does not appear to have been necessarily for defensive purposes, although the tower at Beattock Summit is overlooking the valley below (Maxwell 1976). For most of the tower sites, especially those on the Gask Ridge, this is probably because these are in the best positions for one site to signal to another, with the slope providing additional height.

The army made more use of hills, with 9 forts (including Fendoch in Figure 4.4), 4 fortlets, and 14 camps located on hills. The classical texts state that this should only occur out of necessity, however, it adds an extra element of defence to a site and can enhance visibility. Graafstal (2020) notes that the fort at Bar Hill on the Antonine Wall is located on a 'whaleback' hill, and there are various Flavian fortifications which are similar, such as the fort at Barochan Hill (Figure 3.3). All the sites in this section are located entirely at the top of a hill, or have the summit within their boundaries. Some sites may not have originally been located on a hill, such as Dalswinton Bankhead fort and Inverquharity fortlet, where part of the slopes have been carved away by river erosion. Those forts located on hills, such as Barochan Hill, are on steeper hills than others and would have posed more of a challenge to an attacking enemy. Oakwood is unusual because it is not located on the highest hill in the area, while Castledykes is the only fort is on a hill with gradual slopes. The extent of Drumquhassle is unclear given the possible additional earthworks to the north of the site (Woolliscroft and Hoffmann 2006), while the extent of Broomholm is unknown, although it appears likely that it could cover the summit of the hill where it is located. Four fortlets are located on hills, although three of these (Cargill, Inverquharity and Kirkland) may have been accentuated by river erosion to the north of each site since they were constructed. Only the fortlet at Castle Greg is not located near a river. 14 camps are located on or near the summit of hills, while Raedykes has a hill within the defences of the camp, which would have given significant views of the surrounding landscape. The towers in southern Scotland are examined by Maxwell (1976) and Murphy et al. (2018), and as watchtowers or signal stations, they would have needed strong views of the surrounding landscape, so locating them on hills would have been ideal. While several potential towers are located in this part of Scotland, the examples here show the difference in the sites, and possibly their purpose. Eildon Hill North commands good views of the surrounding area, whereas Beattock appears better placed to secure a valley.

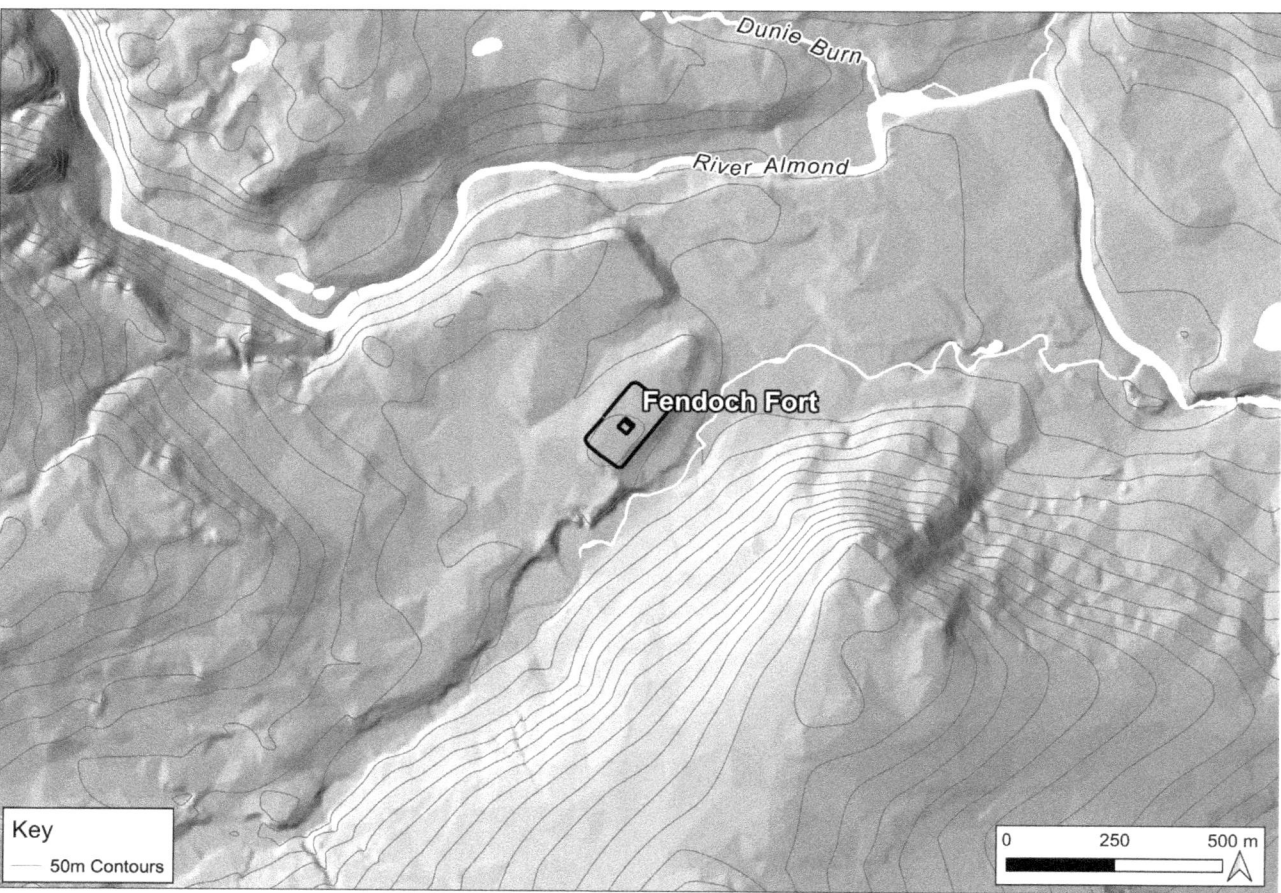

Figure 4.4. Example of a fort (Fendoch) located on a hill.

Out of 102 fortifications, 20 forts, 34 camps, and 8 fortlets are located within 2 kilometres of the confluence of at least two rivers. An additional five, not included in these figures, are located between 2 and 2.5km from a confluence. Most of these sites appear to have been located on ground slightly elevated from the confluence, presumably because of a risk of flooding to the sites. Cargill is constructed on a hillside near the confluence of the River Isla (which lies immediately to the north), and the River Tay, although the former may have moved. The site controls the two rivers, particularly as the Tay leads to Inchtuthil. The site may have protected roads and river crossings, although there is no evidence of these close to Cargill. The fort and camp at Stracathro, are located on flat ground, although the former is on a slight headland, and the north-eastern defences have been eroded by the river (which has since moved course). Here, the land drops away steeply, while to the south the ground slopes away, providing some defensive support. The fort is near the confluence of three watercourses, the one to the south is canalised for a medieval mill, and there is some evidence that the river to the north has eroded the fort defences on that side. The fort at Dalginross, which is adjacent to the camp, is located on a level plain, with low lying land to the southeast. The topography is not overly defensive, although it is adjacent to the river on the northwest side of the site, and it is curious why it doesn't make use of the confluence to the north, unless the river has moved since the Roman period.

By analysing the sites in a GIS, tabulating and comparing the results, it has been possible to identify trends in the different locations selected for each fortification. The analysis of the defensive topography for each of the Flavian fortifications, shows that more were constructed on plains than in other locations, but for camps this is most likely because of the size of area required for the encampment. Where available, natural topography is used to provide an additional layer of defence, such as a river valley or ravine on one side of the defences. Where the topography was more restrictive and such geographical features were not available, fortifications were located close to steep escarpments or hillslopes, which again would limit the ability of the enemy to encroach upon that side of the site.

4.4. Analysis: Site Elevation

Elevation analysis helps us to understand how and to what extent the fortification could exert visual control over a landscape. For example, elevation analysis can help reveal whether the Highland Line forts were located at the entrances of valleys to block or control movement along them. Costa-García (2018), Pažout (2018), and Graafstal (2020), have all observed that Roman fortifications are usually located in positions to control some aspect of the local area. Graafstal has demonstrated on the Antonine Wall that an elevation analysis of the landscape around a fortification can help to indicate its purpose, by showing the site in relation to its location in the wider landscape, i.e. was it at the entrance to a valley, on high ground, and so on.

The majority of Flavian fortifications are located in positions which give them control of rivers, river valleys, and routes through the landscape. Some sites appear to have been located in certain locations for convenience, particularly where temporary accommodation camps were constructed for the army moving through the landscape, but this does not appear to be the situation with all camps.

The two highest Flavian tower sites are the towers at Eildon Hill North at 405 metres, and Beattock Summit at 335 metres. Given that these sites were potentially used as a signalling relay network or early warning system, then the ability of the towers to command good views of the area would have been essential. Murphy et al. (2018) concludes that the sites were intervisible with Craik Cross being 445 metres high, and Ewes Door 340 metres above sea level. The latter two sites are undated but are at height levels similar to the two Flavian sites (both of which are unconfirmed as towers and may originate in the Flavian period because of their proximity to confirmed 1st century sites). A summary of the site data can be found in Appendix Two.

4.5. Analysis: Binary Viewsheds

By combining the results of the elevation analysis with binary viewshed analysis, it shows what could be seen from the fortifications. The analysis here shows that 55% of camps, 36% of forts, and 9% of fortlets are located either at the entrance to a valley, or where they converge into each other. The legionary fortress at Inchtuthil (Figure 3.6) is well placed to oversee traffic on the river as well as to the north of the site, assuming that the river was navigable at this point, which it may well have been if flat-bottomed vessels were used. The fortress appears to guard the route of the River Tay as it passes the site.

Some forts are located at the entrances to valleys, such as Bochastle, Crawford, Dalginross, Easter Happrew, Fendoch and Malling, although Fendoch is the only one which can see up the nearby valley, while the other sites have better views of the immediate area. The forts at Bertha, Cargill, Dalswinton, Doune, Drumquhassle, and Glenlochar (Figure 4.5) are all located overlooking river valleys, and have good views of these, although Bertha, Cargill, Glenlochar, and Newstead have poorer wide views, with their strength being the visibility of the immediate area, presumably over river crossings. Loudon Hill, Milton, and Oakwood have views along the river valleys. From this analysis, we can state that the forts in Flavian Scotland are located in one of three locations; at the entrance to valleys, where they converge, or overlooking them which gives them visual control over movement through these landscapes. Curiously, Ardoch (Figure 4.6) appears to be located at the entrance to a valley to the northwest, but the actual road and line of fortifications is to the north/northeast. Birrens is another site which is located on a route, and potentially guards a river crossing. The fort at Barochan Hill is not overlooking a valley, but there is a

Facing the Enemy?

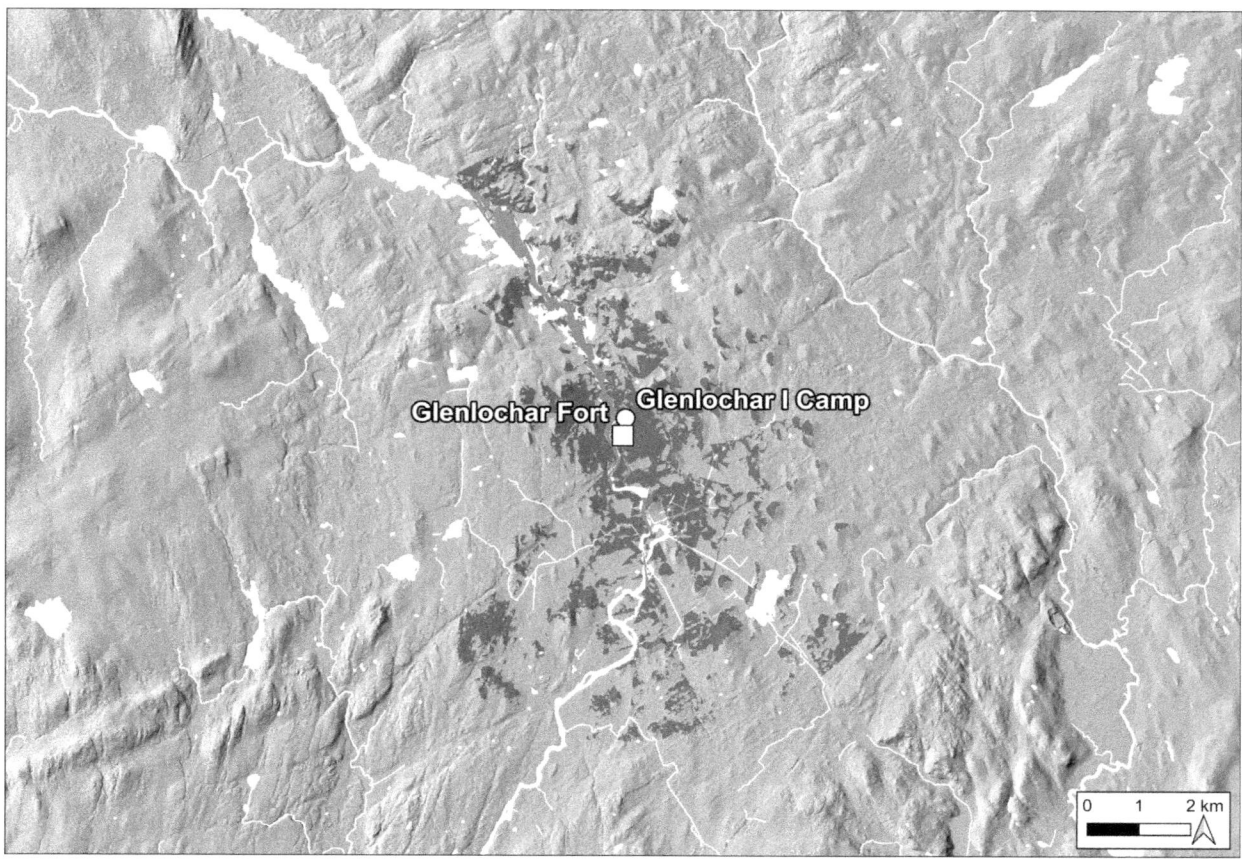

Figure 4.5. Binary viewshed (shaded area) from Glenlochar fort.

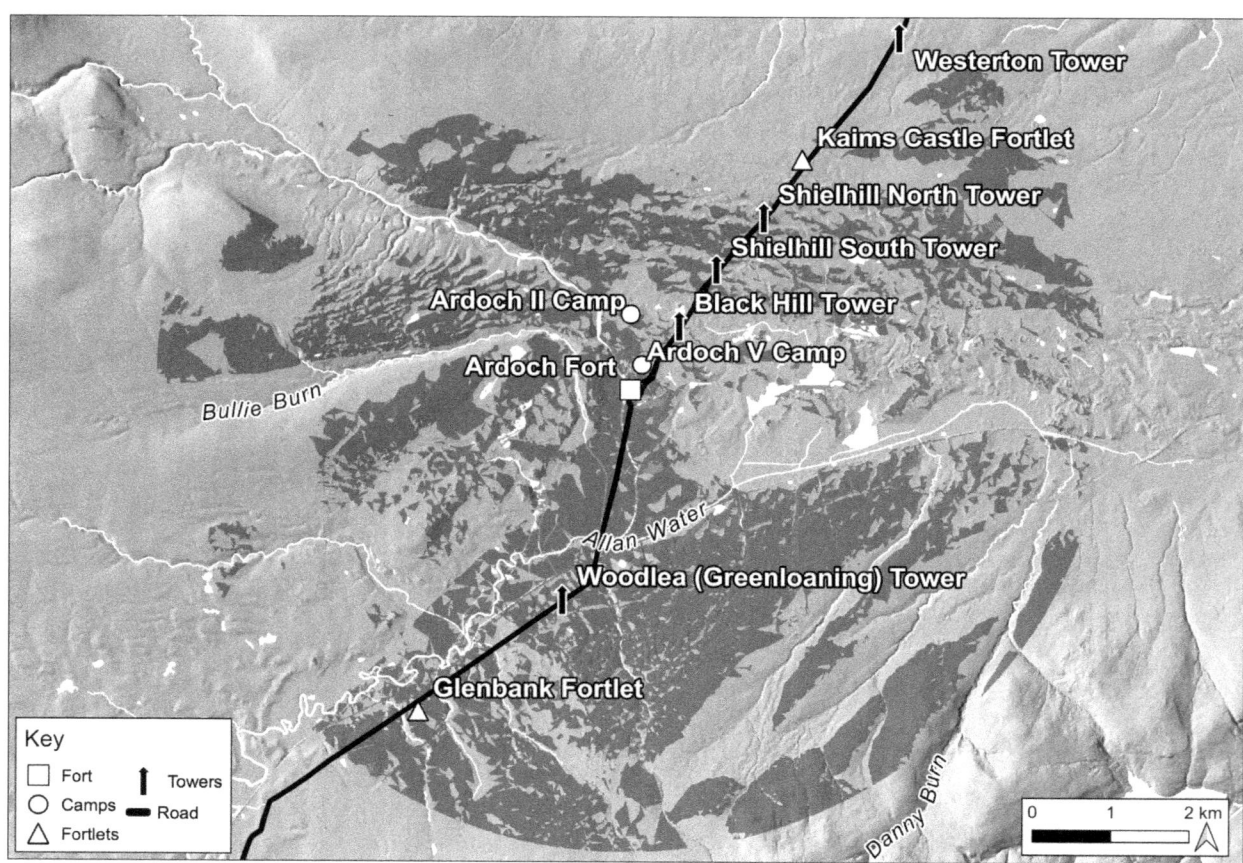

Figure 4.6. Binary viewshed (shaded area) from Ardoch fort.

large expanse of lower-lying ground to the southeast, and the site has good views of this.

The fortlets are located in a range of landscapes, with some such as Gatehouse of Fleet (Figure 4.7), Inverquharity, and Kirkland, locate at the entrance to valleys, with the former two containing larger rivers. Bankhead and Cargill are located at river confluences, although there are no distinct valleys in these areas. Cargill and Gatehouse have limited views of the wider area, which suggests they may have been guarding river crossings. Castle Greg, Glenbank, and Kaims Castle, are the three fortlets which are located on roads, with only the middle site being located on a river. Notably, these sites have the best views, and this may be because their role was to protect the road rather than to control the wider landscape.

Camps are found in a variety of landscapes, and the purpose of some is to have visual control wider landscapes, such as Abernethy (Figure 4.8), Carlops Spittal, Dun, Dunning, Glenluce, and Hillside, whereas others including Burnfield, Glenlochar, Normandykes (Figure 4.9), and Raeburnfoot had control of river valleys. Several camps are located on the coast or near to the coast, including Ayr, Dun, Girvan Mains, Glenluce, and Ward Law; most of these are in locations which may have accommodated seagoing vessels, with the exception being Ward Law which is located on a hill and may have acted as a lookout fort. The viewshed analysis shows that a large proportion of camps are constructed near, overlooking at the entrance to valleys, and essentially are undertaking the same role that forts are doing in this respect, although there is insufficient evidence to suggest if these were occupied on a temporary basis, or were constructed with the intention of being replaced by forts at a later date. An additional set of camps are located on the coast and have a dual role of overlooking their stretch of water, but these sites are protecting river entrances, often with a number of fortifications on the waterway but further upstream. It is possible that these camps also had a role in offloading/transporting supplies further inland, either on the river or on roads up these valleys. An additional set of sites can be classed as marching camps, in the traditional interpretation, encampments occupied on a temporary basis as soldiers moved through the landscape. These are fortifications which are part of a group which indicate the movement of soldiers through the landscape, and also do not seem to make limited use of the natural topography for defence, which may be something they were willing to sacrifice for a temporary stay.

4.6. Summary

Both Hyginus and Vegetius provide a detailed criteria to be taken into consideration when selecting a site for a fortification. The evidence presented here shows that the

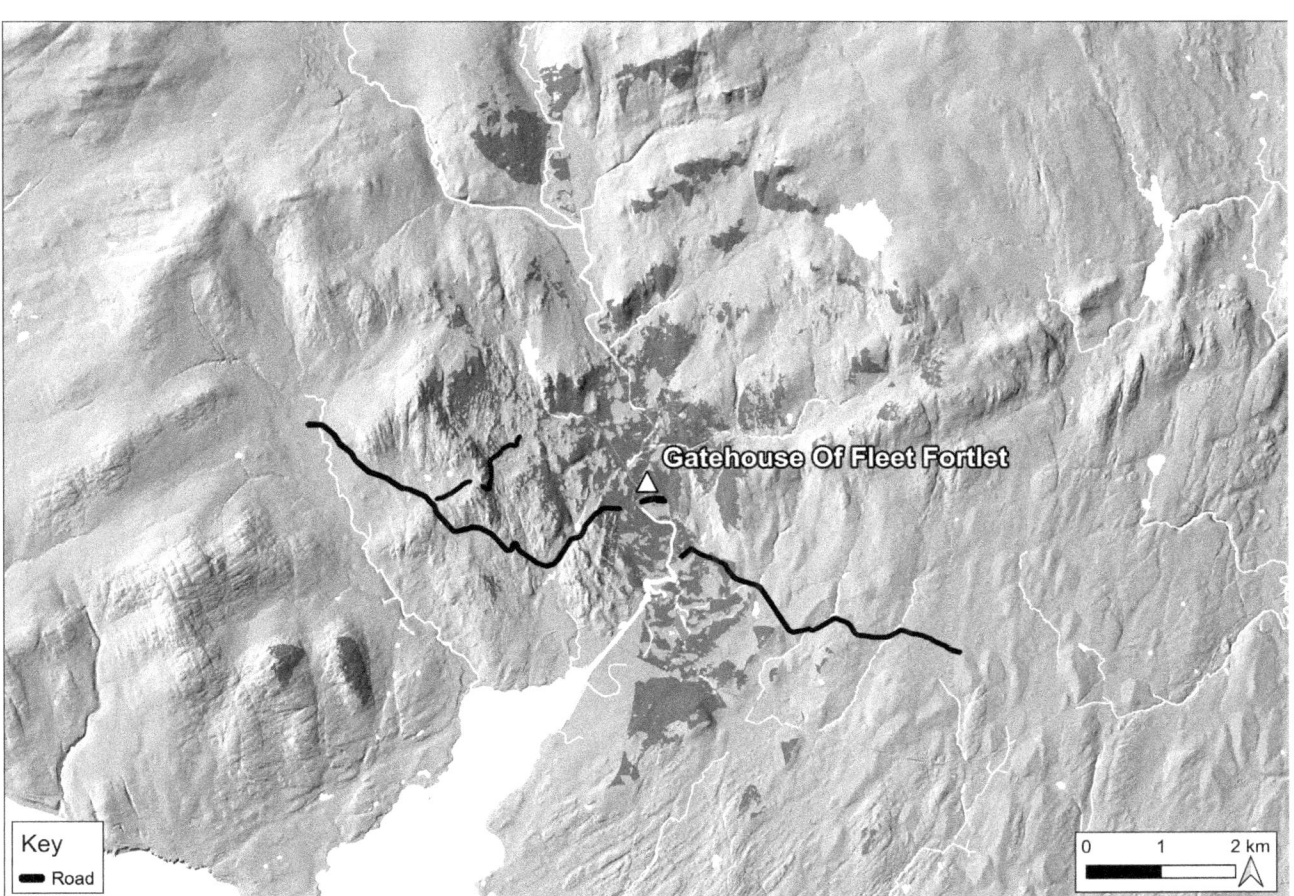

Figure 4.7. Binary viewshed (shaded area) from Gatehouse of Fleet fortlet.

Facing the Enemy?

Figure 4.8. Binary viewshed (shaded area) from Abernethy camp.

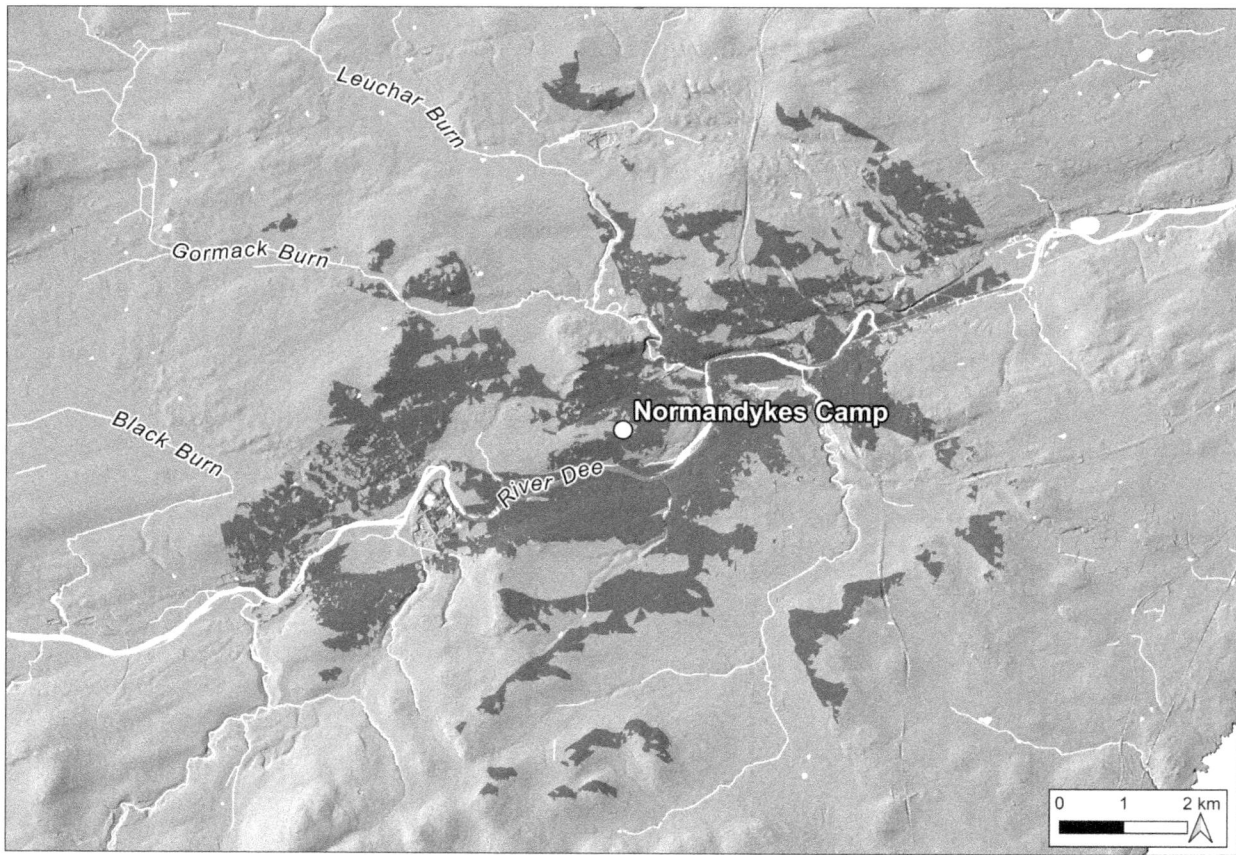

Figure 4.9. Binary viewshed (shaded area) from Normandykes camp.

criteria was followed to a limited extent, and there does not appear to have been a rigorous adherence to them when selecting the location; the army would select the most suitable position available within the desired locale. Occasionally, the site may not have been perfect, but was selected as it was the most suitable or largest available space in that particular area. Although no fortifications in Scotland are overlooked by mountains, I have found that over half of the forts were overseen by hills, although far fewer could have been fired on directly. There are a few hills surrounding fortifications which have indigenous fortifications such as hillforts or enclosed settlements constructed on them, although none that have been proven to be contemporaneous with the Flavian sites. It therefore seems unlikely that being overlooked was a significant consideration in site selection, it is reasonable to conclude that the army assessed the risk of being attacked in this way, as being minimal, and a lesser consideration than finding a suitably sized space for the encampment.

Wherever possible, the fortifications make use of the natural topography to support their defences; usually rivers and river valleys, but there are also instances of lakes and coastal areas being used. Fortifications are often placed near the confluence of rivers, sometimes using these to defend the site on two sides and perhaps because there can be a better view along the valleys. Sometimes this does not happen, such as at Cargill where the fortlet is on the opposite river bank to the confluence, which implies that its role was to control the confluence and traffic on the river. Most forts are constructed either at the entrance or convergence of valleys, or within them. There are some exceptions to this, such as at Ardoch and Birrens, where the forts are located on the route of Roman roads, and if these follow pre-existing trackways, then it would explain why the sites are located in these locations.

There are no confirmed 1st century forts on the Scottish coast, but several camps are located by the sea, and at the entrances to larger rivers or inlets leading to waterways, such as at Ayr and Girvan, most of which are large enough to have harbours in the modern era. Such locations appear to have been prioritised over headlands and outcrops, whereas indigenous forts favour promontory sites; such locations often offer more wider ranging views and natural defences than the mouths of rivers. Frequently, upstream on the major rivers, additional Roman fortifications can be found. For those sites where there are Roman encampments at the river mouths, it may suggest that camps are staging posts for supplies moved along the coast, the latter being an idea proposed by Jones (2018); for example, the site at Dun would be the nearest coastal site to the legionary fortress at Inchtuthil. Some coastal sites, such as Ward Law, may not have been accessible to sea-borne traffic given its position on a hill, but this would have been a good position for a camp acting as an outlook post. Forts were positioned to overlook and control river valleys, although a small number such as Bertha and Glenlochar have good views only of the immediate area, which may suggest they are protecting river crossings. Forts may be located at the entrances to glens, but there was often little visibility along the valley, although that would not necessarily have precluded them control of traffic moving through these.

Flavian fortifications in Scotland used the topographic landscape to their advantage when they can, with defensibility taking precedent over how level and accessible the site was; the exception to this is the locations where a fortification had to be constructed in a location, such as for temporary/overnight accommodation. Many fortifications are located in, or overlooking valleys, which indicates that they were placed there to control the immediate landscape. Visibility from these sites can be poor and not overly extensive, but would nonetheless have given the Roman army significant advantages in exerting surveillance and control over strategic points, and which suggests these fortifications have a role in managing movement through key areas, rather than one of defence; existing to prevent a hostile force attacking Roman territory. As outlined earlier, Harding (2017) has suggested that there are no large population centres, with the possible exception of Traprain Law, in Late Iron Age in North Britain, in the same way that there are hillforts in southern England. Hingley (1992) has also suggested that the indigenous population at this time were living in family groups, while Mercer (2018) argues that the evidence from several sites in Dumfriesshire indicates a coexistence between those living in Scotland and the Roman army, because the latter needed key supplies. These fit with my suggestion that the locating of Roman fortifications, was designed to control movement through the landscape. These fortifications were not intended to act as launchpads for further invasion, or to defend the Empire as they could be easily circumvented. Furthermore, it could be argued that this may have been because there was no significant threat to the army.

5

Intervisibility

Intervisibility, or the capacity to see one Roman site from another was, in some instances, an important factor to consider when locating fortifications as this would enable some frontiers to have a visual communication or signalling system. Such systems are often dependent on networks of towers linking in with forts and fortresses. A growing number of studies are looking at the intervisibility of Roman sites, aided by GIS modelling, and again, the Antonine Wall features strongly in these. Evidence from other Roman frontiers shows that intervisibility mattered when selecting many (but not all) sites, so that the army could exert control over an area. However, in Scotland intervisibility and line-of-sight between the Flavian fortifications was not necessarily a key factor for the army when selecting where to position the military structures, except for a handful of sites, including those on the Gask Ridge.

It is clear from various classical sources that passing a message between two or more locations (signalling) existed in various guises during different periods, and that it was a function which seems to have been in use in the Roman period. In Scotland, there is evidence of at least two signalling networks comprising of forts and towers; one in the Scottish Borders emanating from Newstead fort, and the second, a more complex chain running along the Gask Ridge in Perthshire. Both networks are discussed in more depth later. Intervisibility between fortifications would have been essential to the locating and positioning of fortifications, and there is some evidence that the fortlets at Glenbank and Kaims Castle were placed in their respective positions so that they could act as signal relay stations.

In this chapter, I summarise our current understanding of signalling in the Roman period, and the work undertaken by Woolliscroft (i.e. 2010), which forms the basis for this. I go on to present the results of GIS analysis of line-of-sight analyses between Flavian fortifications in Scotland, both testing the methodology presented by Woolliscroft, and altering the parameters of these to enhance our understanding of the different signalling networks in operation in 1st century Scotland.

5.1. Roman Signalling

A handful of papers have been published which examine signalling, including those by Webster (1985:254-256), Donaldson (1988), and Southern (1990); these papers do not attempt any modelling of signalling and contain little detail other than brief assessments of the literary evidence. The most in-depth studies have been produced by Woolliscroft (e.g. 1989; 1994; 1996; 2006; 2010), who has reviewed the classical literary sources and followed this up with practical experimentation (based on the literary evidence) to establish a signalling methodology, which he has physically tested on several frontiers and fortifications, including the Stanegate, the Gask Ridge, Hadrian's Wall, the Wetterau *limes*, the German/Raetian border and the Antonine Wall.

In his 2010 book, based on his PhD, Woolliscroft provides a thorough account of signalling in the classical period, bringing together a range of literary and epigraphic sources, such as Trajan's Column and the Aurelian Column upon which signalling is depicted. Woolliscroft (Woolliscroft 2010:22) writes that beacons and beacon chains are the most frequently mentioned method of signalling in the classical texts, both predating the Roman period, and continuing to be used as a method long after the fall of the Empire. He details US experiments at the end of the 19th century which show that a beacon can be seen 160-200 miles away, and examines signalling between Troy and Argos, which deployed chain of beacons around 520 kilometres long; the longest break between these beacons was 173 kilometres, although he discusses the difficulties in signalling at such lengths and ensuring that the correct message is passed-on. Woolliscroft suggests that signalling by fire was the most effective method, particularly for longer distances, although semaphore could have been used for closer sites, but again, the likelihood of misread signals was greater using this technique. Other techniques such as signalling by heliographs and carrier pigeons are mentioned in the classical texts, but there is no evidence for them in the archaeological record in Scotland, especially as the former relies on sunlight, something frequently in short supply on the northern frontiers. Furthermore, Southern, Donaldson, and Woolliscroft all have written about the limitations of signalling, including variables such as poor weather and the inability of the naked eye to make out signals at long distances.

Woolliscroft, who undertook his work before the widespread use of computer modelling, applied his knowledge of Roman signalling to practical experimentation, coming to a number of conclusions which have relevance here. Woolliscroft (1993; 2010:42) undertook practical experimentation at Roman sites on and around the Gask Ridge, where he would base himself at one tower site and have a colleague at another. Using a camera flash mounted on a long pole, the length of which was continually adjusted, they would flash at each other (during the day and at night) in an attempt to discern the best height for signalling, as well as the distance and extent to which signals could be seen. By experimenting between the Gask Ridge tower sites, Woolliscroft noted that the optimal height for sending a signal was between 8 and 10 metres, and he concluded that this would have been the height of a Roman tower, and he subsequently used these heights when modelling signalling on other frontiers. Excavation evidence from the Gask Ridge indicates that towers were wooden constructions with four corner posts to create a tower (Hanson and Friell 1995; Woolliscroft 1993; 2009; 2010; Woolliscroft and Hoffmann 2006). Woolliscroft & Hoffmann speculate that towers on the Gask Ridge may have been similar in design. A tower like this would require signal apparatus on multiple sides to be able to signal effectively, and a fire signal would have been hazardous to the structure. Thinking about the intervisibility from the site, and although the environmental evidence is limited, Woolliscroft's modelling does not consider the impact of the topographical or natural environment on the intervisibility between sites and how this would have affected signalling. If certain features blocked intervisibility, then towers would need to be moved, or relay stations installed, and if the landscape was wooded, then this would have caused additional problems by restricting views. Interestingly, this is an issue which can be seen today, with several of the Gask Ridge tower sites being surrounded by woodland. Many of these trees are in excess of 10 metres in height, and while these may not be the same species which would have been growing in this area 2,000 years ago, they do demonstrate an issue with Woolliscroft's theory, unless there had been extensive deforestation to enable intervisibility between the fortifications; this may have been undertaken by the Romans themselves when felling wood to build the forts and towers, but to see hostile forces approaching from routes beyond the Roman territory, would require the landscape to have been cleared of wood.

Furthermore, Woolliscroft's experimentation was based on the signal being sent at a height of 8-10 metres, but with the receiver standing at ground level; so, the signal is being received at person height (around 1.7 metres) rather than if the individual was standing at the top of the tower. Woolliscroft's experiments indicated that signal visibility was limited, and that the maximum distance at which a signal could both be seen and the meaning interpreted, was 6 kilometres in daylight; beyond this, the signal was too indistinguishable for the observer to make out the message. These experiments relied upon clear weather, with different conditions reducing the ability to see or interpret what was being sent. Woolliscroft also undertook experimentation at night, primarily using artificial light to signal, although he also used fire, with the conclusion being that in clear conditions, a signal could be seen up to 16 kilometres away, although at that distance there was difficulty in interpreting messages. If the towers were constructed to watch for an approaching enemy, then they would not have been effective at night, and even during the day, it is estimated at it is only when people get to a distance of around 6 kilometres away, that sufficient detail can be seen enabling identification of that person (Hannon 2018), which does bring in to question the purpose of these structures, although this is discussed later, but it does imply either a role in signalling or management of the road which runs between the Gask Ridge sites. Woolliscroft therefore concluded that for towers on the Gask Ridge, signals could be seen and received at a height of between 8 and 10 metres, and a distance of up to 6 kilometres. But, this is theoretical, and the height of such structures can only be postulated.

Woolliscroft applied his signalling methodology to the fortifications on Hadrian's Wall (1989), the Gask Ridge (1993) and the Antonine Wall (1996), with his work showing the importance of site positioning to enable them to signal to each other. Dyčka (2017; 2018) and Hannon (2018), to a lesser extent, replicated Woolliscroft's work on the Antonine Wall although this was not the primary focus of these papers. Murphy et al. (2018) have attempted to apply Woolliscroft's methodology to sites in southern Scotland, using computer analysis of the intervisibility between possible Roman tower sites, noting that while these sites along with forts, could form part of a signalling chain, the distance between each site is greater than 6km. This study uses Woolliscroft's methodology and attempts to replicate his modelling of signalling on the Gask Ridge sites, but using the latest mapping and topographic data, with processing in GIS software, rather than the manual approach undertaken by Woolliscroft, and also incorporates camps into the analysis. Woolliscroft's work and methodology was the first attempt to seriously study Roman signalling methods and remains the predominant approach for signalling. Woolliscroft's approach and experimentation has been invaluable, but further experimentation in the field, would help to confirm the likelihood that the Romans were using such signalling methods themselves. To date, no one has physically replicated the work of Woolliscroft, using similar equipment and signalling from site to site, although I have attempted to do this using computer modelling, and have experimented with different parameters including the height. I have included camps and extended the analysis to all fortifications in Scotland, not only in an attempt to replicate Woolliscroft's work, but to build on this.

Some recent studies have utilised GIS, spatial analysis, and Digital Terrain Models to examine intervisibility between Roman fortifications (Foglia 2014; Dyčka 2017; 2018; Hannon 2018; E. Graafstal 2020; Hannon, Wilson, and Rohl 2020), with most of these highlighting the apparent need for the sites to have visible command of the immediate surroundings. Essentially, there was a need for Roman fortifications to control the landscape which requires them to be intervisible both with other military sites, and with key features in the landscape; this is also demonstrated by Woolliscroft (2010), and on other frontiers. While Pažout (2018), in the frontier zone of Judea, has attempted to establish if there were any indications of a communications system between the sites, and concluded that there were two distinct military regions, each controlled differently. In the east and south, some fortifications were too far apart to communicate effectively, so Pažout ruled out a signalling network, but sites in the northwest were closer together and probably could communicate in this way.

But intervisibility is about more than two sites being able to see or signal to each other, it is also about the fortifications working together to secure and control an area. Hannon shows this in his analysis of the Antonine Wall LiDAR dataset that both the Antonine fort at Bishopton on the River Clyde and Lurg Moor fortlet have limited views of the landscape. But combined, they have significant visible command over this section of the River Clyde, providing security and oversight of the western flank of the Wall. Later in this monograph, I suggest a similar arrangement between the fortification at Ward Law, on the Solway coast, and the nearby fortlet at Lantonside on the River Annan.

Viewshed analysis of the Antonine Wall by Dyčka (Dyčka 2017; 2018) examines the immediate landscape surrounding the fortifications, asking if these sites are visible to any specific features. Dyčka concludes some fortifications were intervisible and could form part of a signalling chain, while sections of road were also visible in some places. Woolliscroft (2010) notes the limitations of using a single viewpoint in such analysis. During his signalling research, he discovered that Barcombe B Tower on Hadrian's Wall, which could only signal the northwest corner tower of Housesteads fort, and possibly the west gate (Woolliscroft, Swain, and Lockett 1992), demonstrating the need to undertake this type of analysis using multiple signal points. Graafstal, as part of his analysis of Antonine Wall and the phases of construction, looks at the intervisibility of the forts, using the north gate of each site as a point of reference; Graafstal suggests that the planners of the Antonine Wall intended to create an unbroken chain between the main fortifications, and concludes that the desire for optimum intervisibility may explain why the fort on Bar Hill is set back and not connected to the rampart of the Antonine Wall, giving it a better range of visual range.

5.2. Analysis: Line-Of-Sight (Signalling)

In his various studies, Woolliscroft did not include camps in his signalling experiments, and does not state why this is. There is evidence which may suggest that camps have a role in these systems, with the site at Dunning being able to see several of the towers on the Gask Ridge (Figures 5.1 and 5.2). There is a similar arrangement between the camp at Oakwood. But, if the chain has a role as an observation and look out system, the camp at Dunning does not add to this as the views at 6 kilometres are limited, although we only know the location of two corners of the defences from which to make this assessment. Had the camp had towers, similar in height to the structures on the Gask Ridge, then

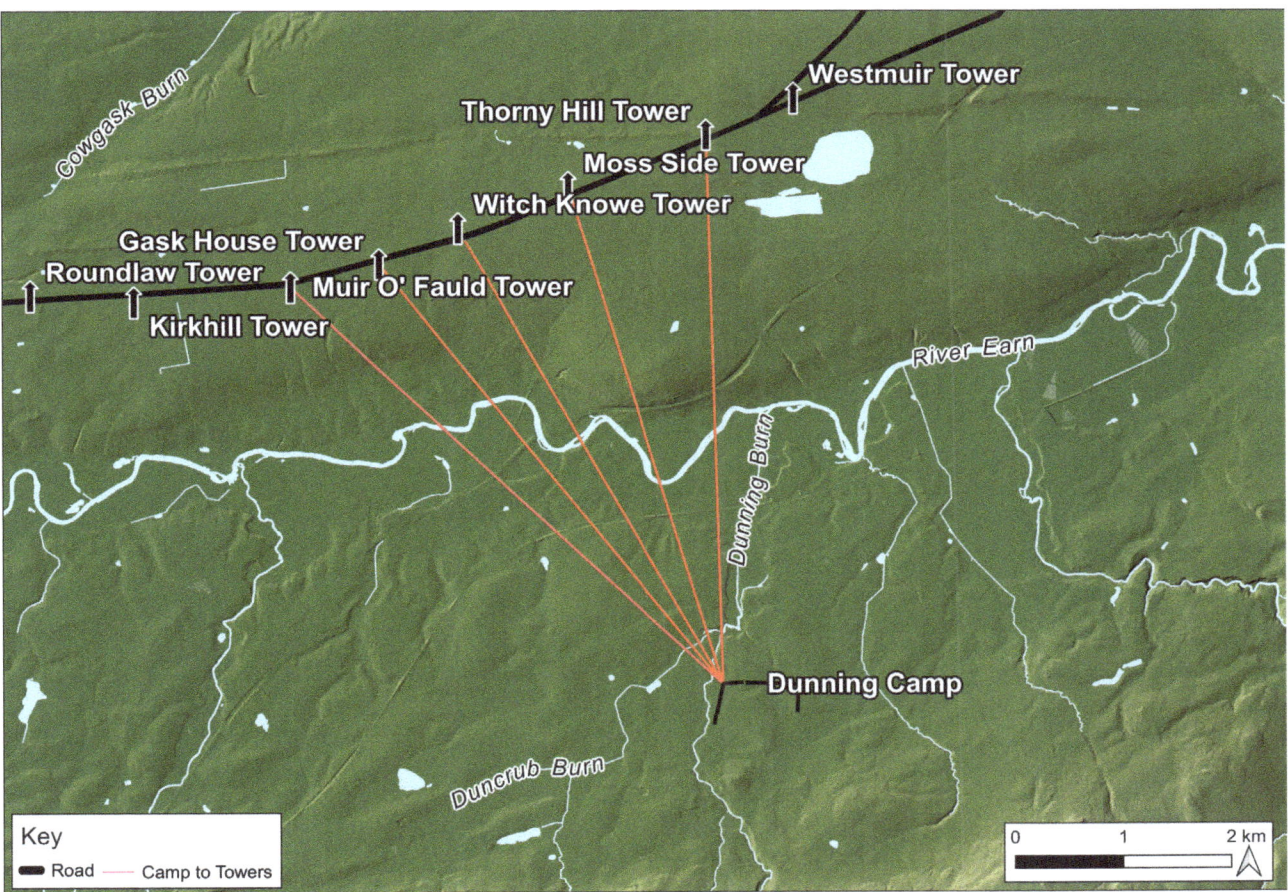

Figure 5.1. Line of sight analysis from Dunning camp to nearby Gask Ridge towers.

Facing the Enemy?

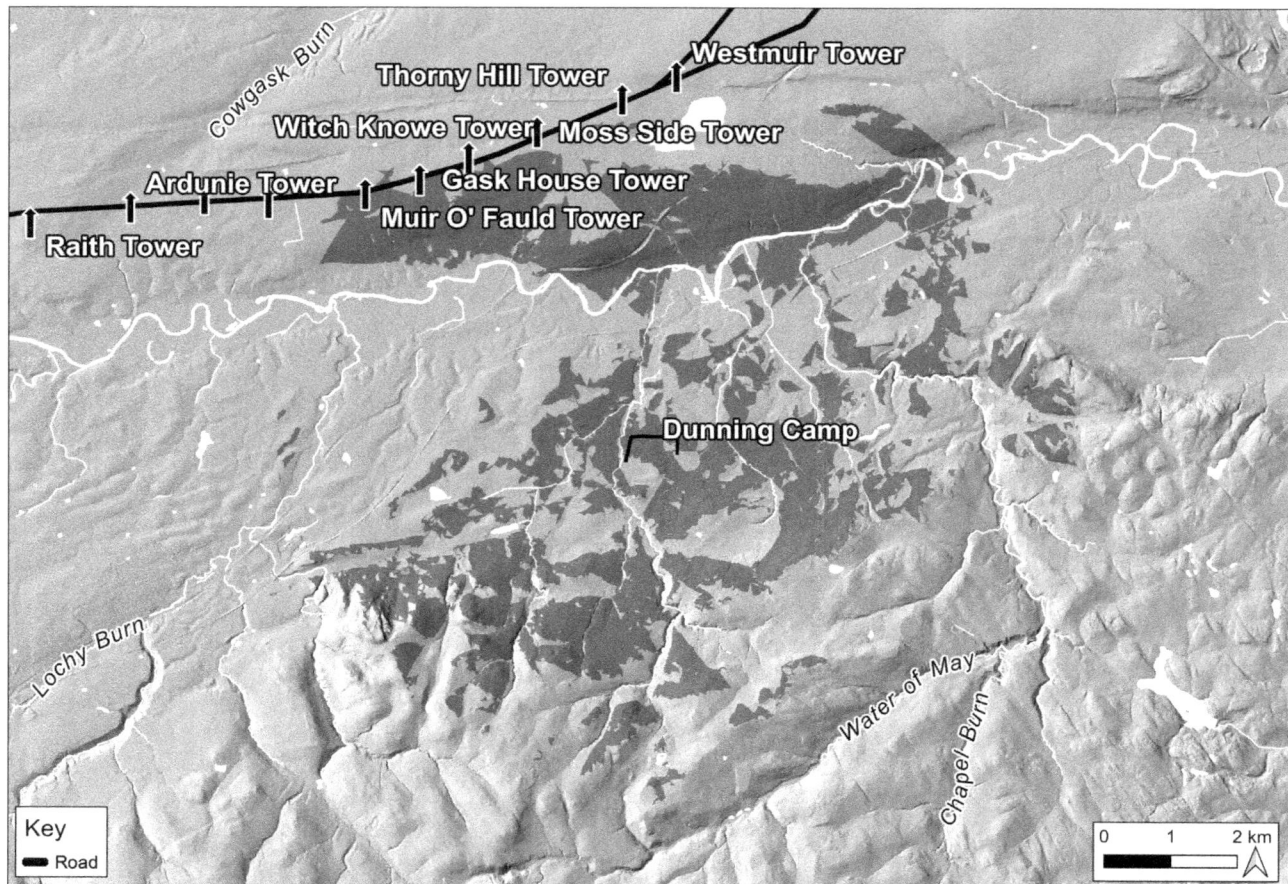

Figure 5.2. Binary viewshed (shaded area) from Dunning camp.

the views may have been more substantial. All of this could be coincidence and requires further investigation before we can draw any further conclusions.

There is no mention in the classical literary texts of the importance of locating sites in positions where they can signal to each other. But it is clear from the works by Woolliscroft that signalling between some sites was an important consideration. Towers frequently acted as relay stations between the forts, although this was not necessarily the case or even possible at every site. Such a system would enable the army to mobilise quickly if there was an oncoming threat. There are some indications that the arrangements for signalling are more complex than they initially appear, with some sites, particularly camps, potentially forming part of these networks.

My analysis not only tests the methodology of Woolliscroft, and confirms his findings, but it possibly also reveals new relationships. While Woolliscroft's methodology, and practical experimentation was undertaken over several years, computer modelling enables us to cover more sites, in less time, while utilising the latest archaeological and mapping data. It also enables us to experiment with line-of-sight analysis between different locations. While modelling in the GIS does not enable confirmation of new signalling networks, it reveals potential bilateral relationships between fortifications, which also enhance the analysis of individual for positioning, and which gives us a better understanding of the general importance, or not, of signalling to the whole network of Flavian fortifications.

Beyond enhancing our understanding of signalling on the Gask Ridge, my analysis has also found other Flavian sites which were intervisible and within signalling distance of each other. The two camps of Auchinhove and Muiryfold (Figure 5.3), are one example, located close to each other in Moray, and are believed to be contemporaneous. It is unusual for two camps to be located so close as to be entirely visible to the other and is the only time this occurs in the chain of camps running northwest from Raedykes. Given the local terrain, their positioning could be coincidental, and the fact they are intervisible does not mean that signalling actually occurred, and even less that it was one factor influencing positioning. Even so just knowing this, may aid future research and interpretations.

Figure 5.4 shows the intervisibility or capacity to signal between the fort at Castledykes and the fortlet at Bankhead, which could then relay a signal to Bankhead II camp (Figure 5.5). There are several fortifications at Dalswinton (Figure 5.6), including two forts and two camps, all of which are Flavian in date, and intervisible from each other, while the two forts are visible from Fourmerkland, as are the camps.

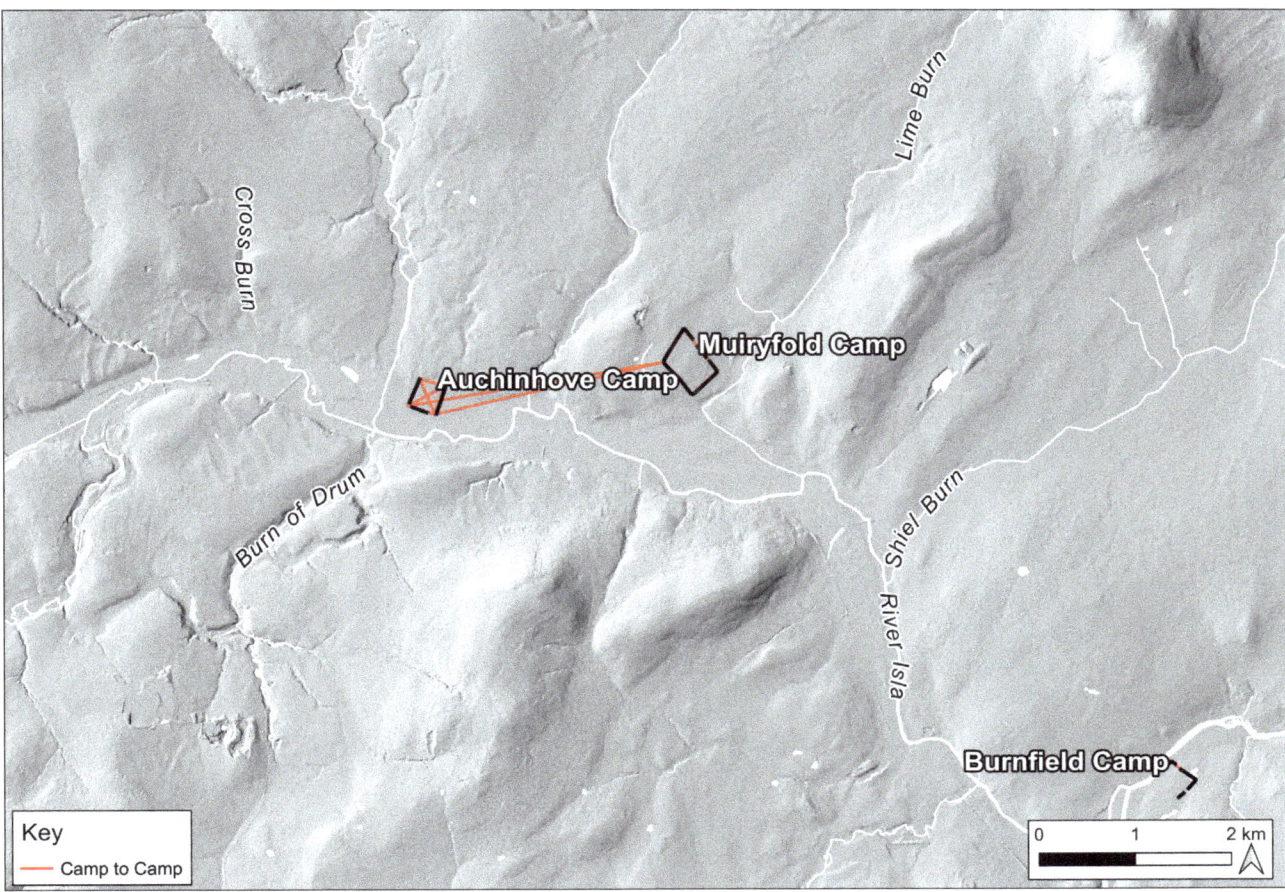

Figure 5.3. Line of sight between the camps of Muiryfold and Auchinhove.

I have undertaken this modelling using 8.6 metres for the height of the camp rather than the usual 1.7 metres, as this would be the height of an individual signalling from the top of a 5 metre high rampart. This demonstrates some of the complexities involved in signalling, which is reliant on estimating the height of fortification defences which have not survived in the archaeological record.

5.2.1. Towers on the Gask Ridge

Woolliscroft's signalling experiments on the Gask Ridge, confirmed that these fortifications formed a signalling network. An overview of the Gask Ridge fortifications can be seen in Figure 5.7. I have replicated Woolliscroft's work below, using the latest mapping data available from Ordnance Survey. The results of the GIS modelling can be seen in Figures 5.8-5.11, and which confirm Woolliscroft's findings. The GIS modelling also indicates that there is a possible gap between Westmuir and Peel, as per the Woolliscroft model. The results of my attempts align with Woolliscroft's results, demonstrating the viability of using computer modelling in line-of-sight analysis. It is not proposed to examine the Gask Ridge signalling system in any depth as this has previously been undertaken by Woolliscroft. It is relevant to note that there may be additional, unconfirmed tower sites to be added to the model, and possible dating issues with the road at the Strageath end of the chain. Additionally, there is a lack of secure dating for most of the towers. The aim here has been to test whether Woolliscroft's methodology is as effective using up-to-date data, which is confirmed.

At the northern end of the Gask Ridge chain is the fort at Bertha, while at the southern end of the Inchtuthil chain is the tower at Woodhead (Figures 5.12 and 5.13), with no known Flavian sites between them to link the chain. There is an additional camp between Bertha and Woodhead, at Grassy Walls, which is almost opposite the former. Bertha and Grassy Walls are intervisible, as are Grassy Walls and Woodhead tower, although this analysis is done over a distance of 8 kilometres rather than the ideal 5 kilometres, as noted by Woolliscroft. A similar analysis from the camp at Scone Park failed to find intervisibility between that site and Woodhead. The camps at Grassy Walls and Scone Park (see Canmore – Grassy Walls, Canmore – Scone Park 2018) are both believed to date to the Severan period, due to their size (Callander 1919), although a coin of Trajan origin was found at Grassy Walls (MacDonald 1918:232), which is unsurprising given that the Roman road passes through the site.

The GIS analysis of the area around Grassy Walls, indicates a probable location for a tower, although there is no current archaeological evidence to support this. To date such a structure has not been sought out and maybe

Facing the Enemy?

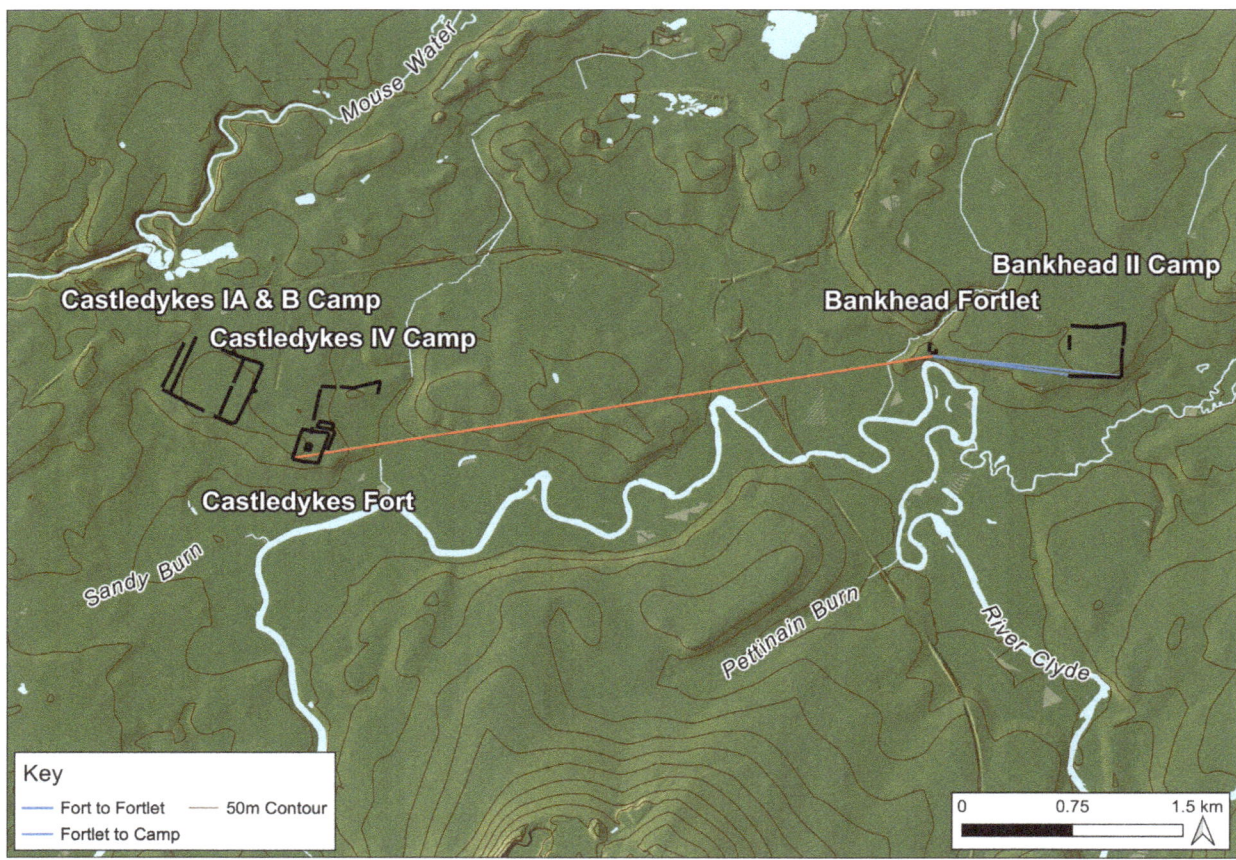

Figure 5.4. Line of sight between Castledykes fort, Bankhead fortlet and Bankhead II camp.

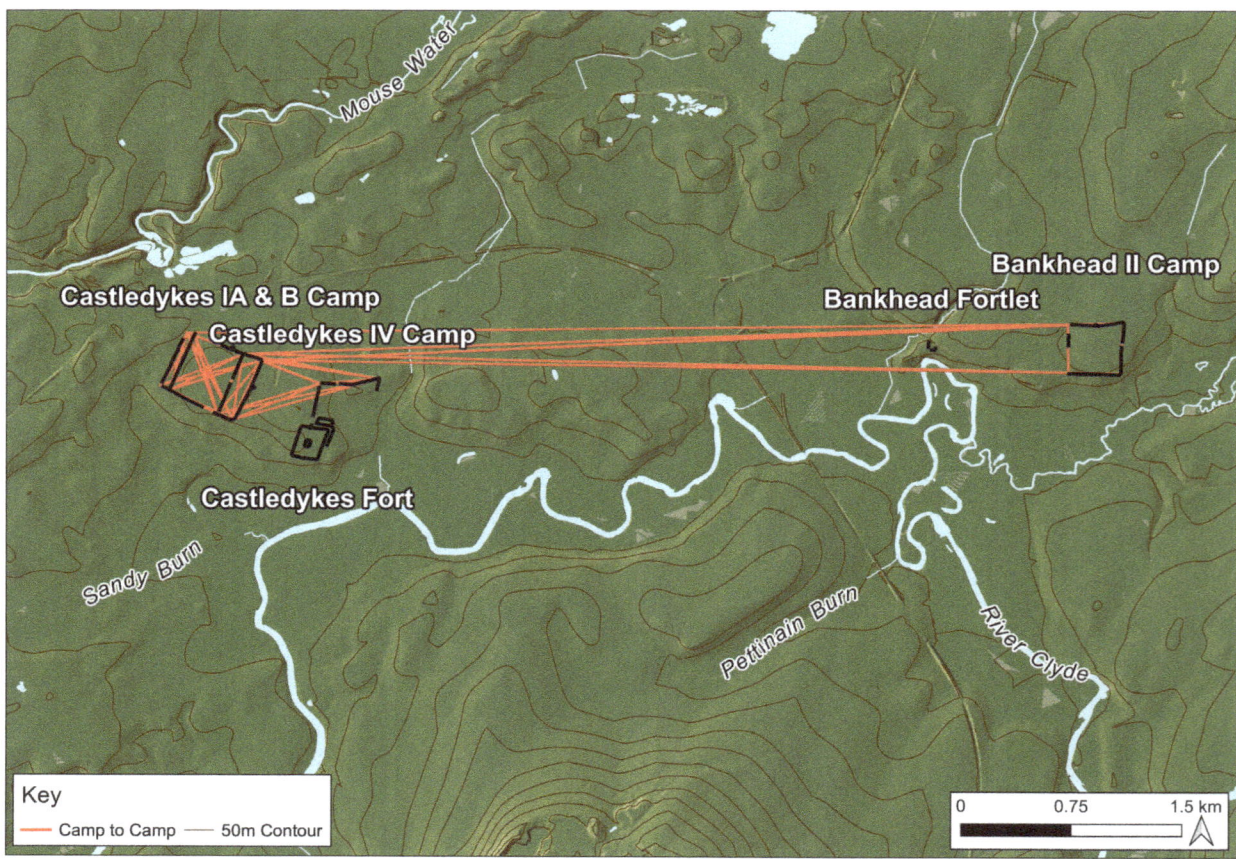

Figure 5.5. Line of sight between Castledykes camp and Bankhead II camp.

Intervisibility

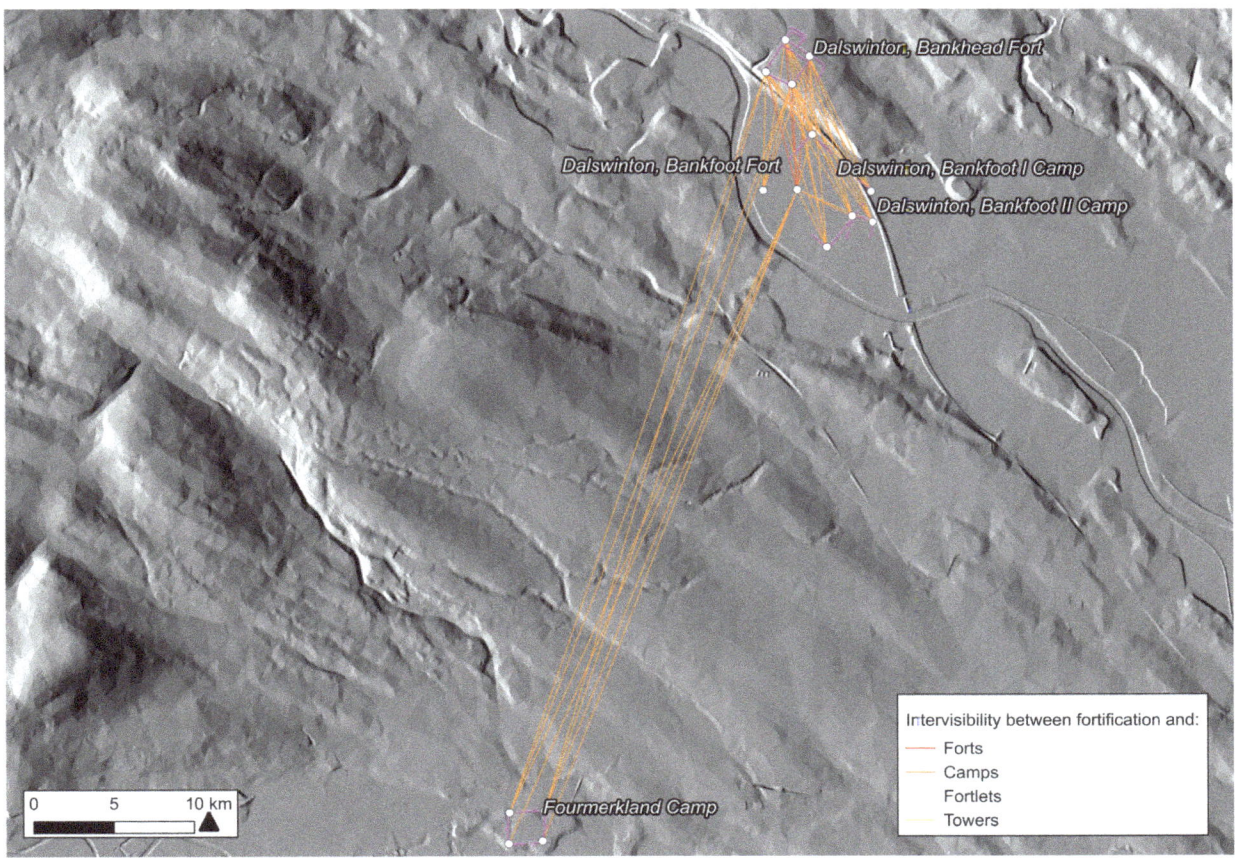

Figure 5.6. Line of sight between the various Dalswinton sites and the camp at Fourmerkland.

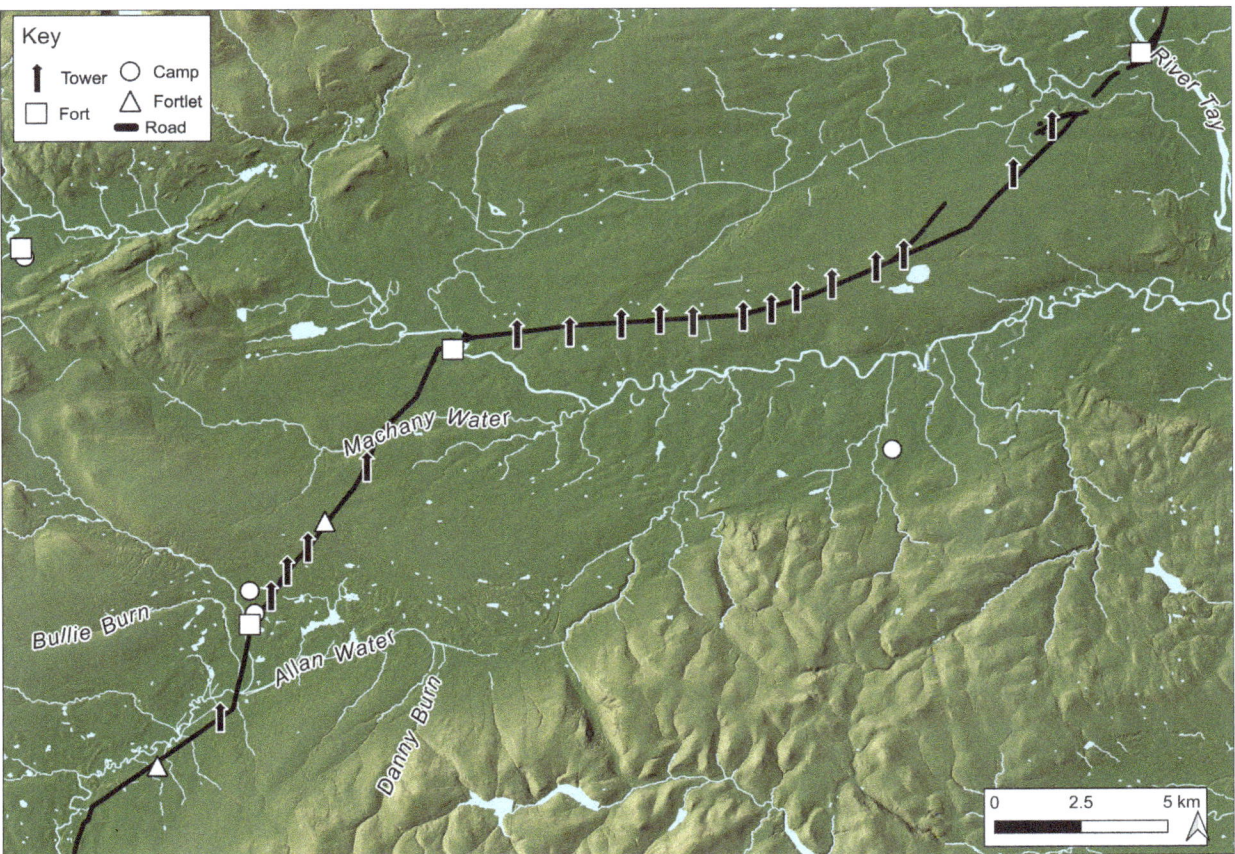

Figure 5.7. Elevation analysis of fortifications on the Gask Ridge.

Facing the Enemy?

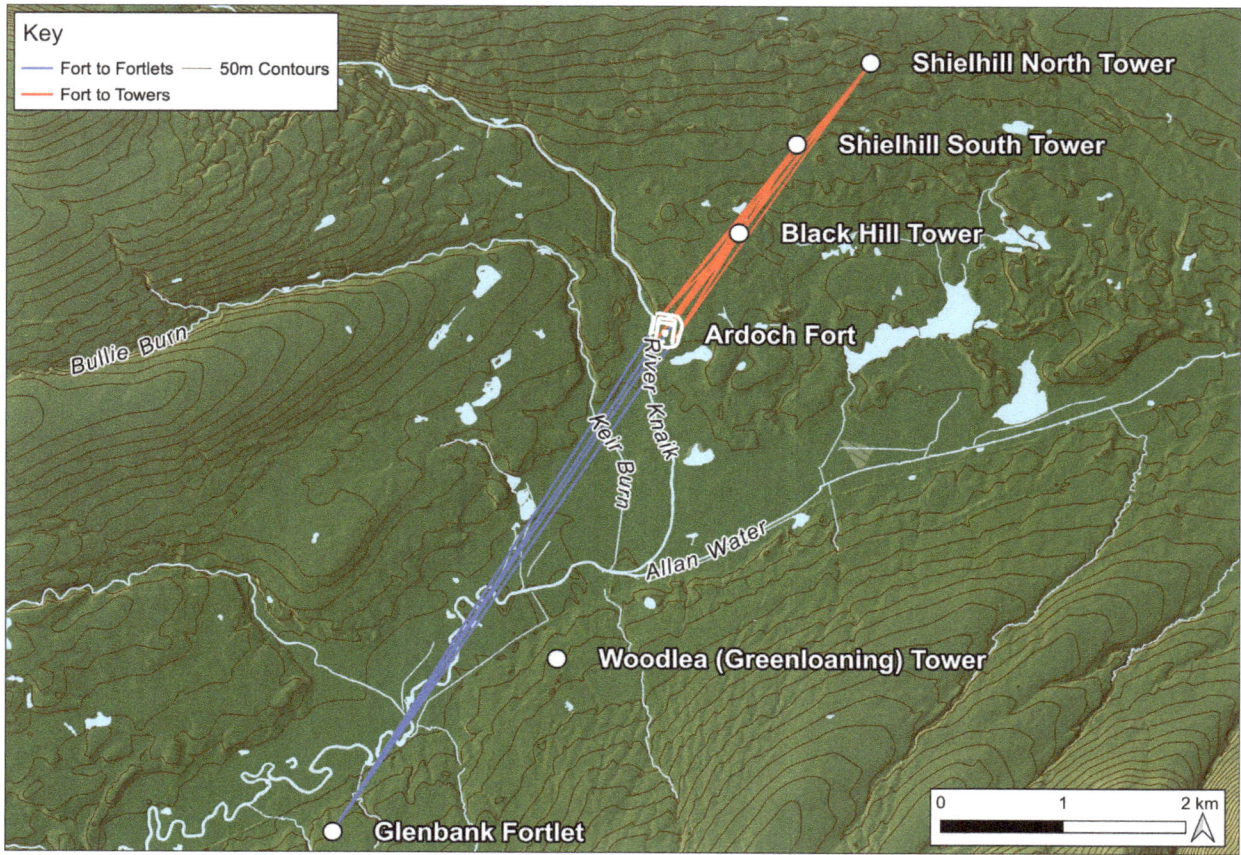

Figure 5.8. Signalling capacity on the southern section of the Gask Ridge.

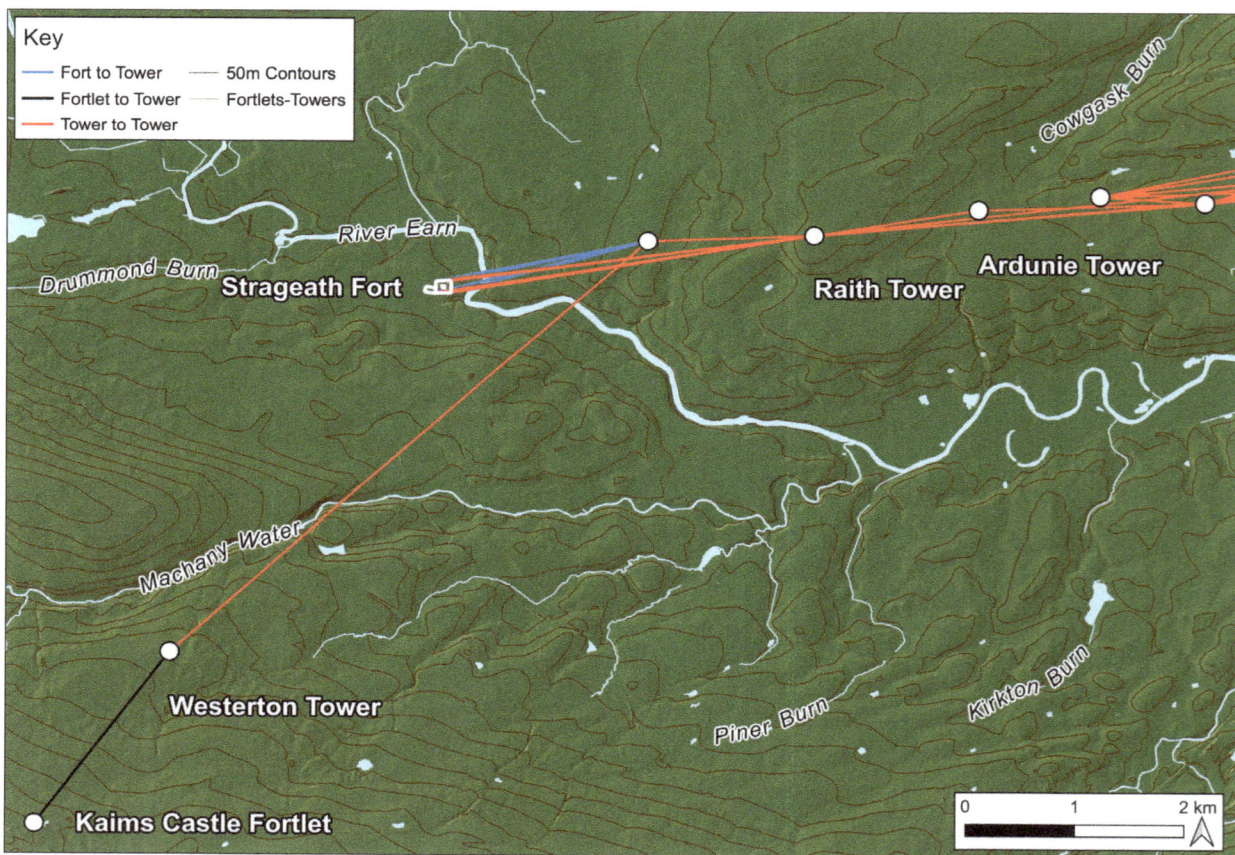

Figure 5.9. Signalling capacity on the western section of the Gask Ridge.

Intervisibility

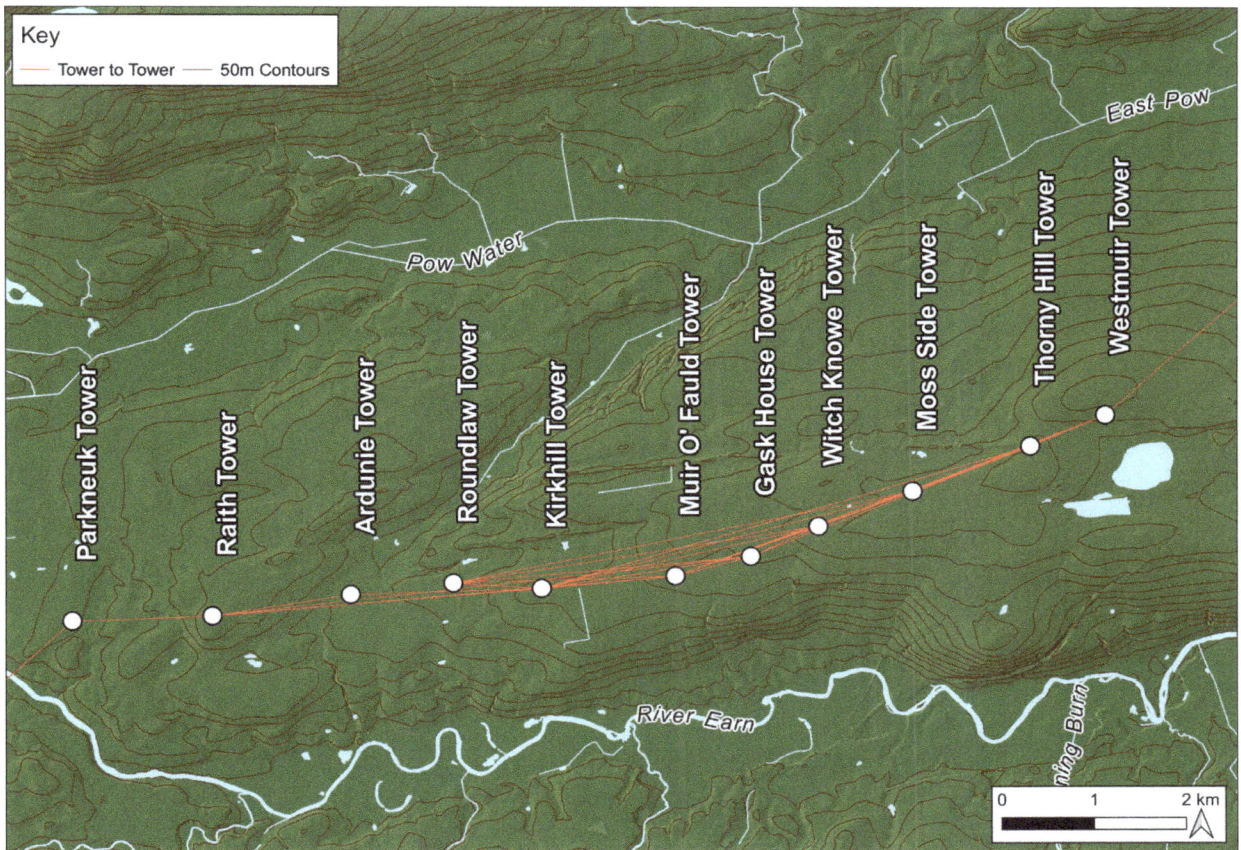

Figure 5.10. Signalling capacity on the central section of the Gask Ridge.

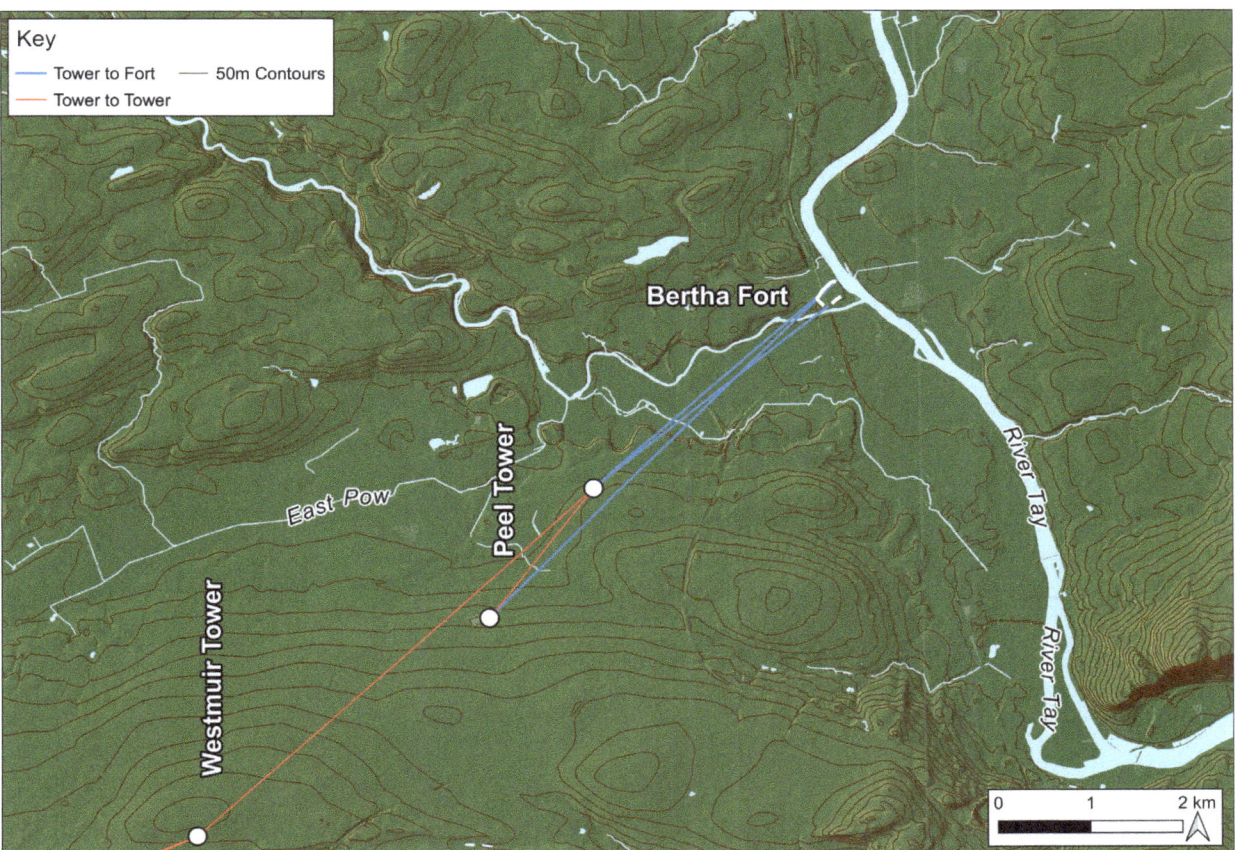

Figure 5.11. Signalling capacity on the eastern section of the Gask Ridge.

Facing the Enemy?

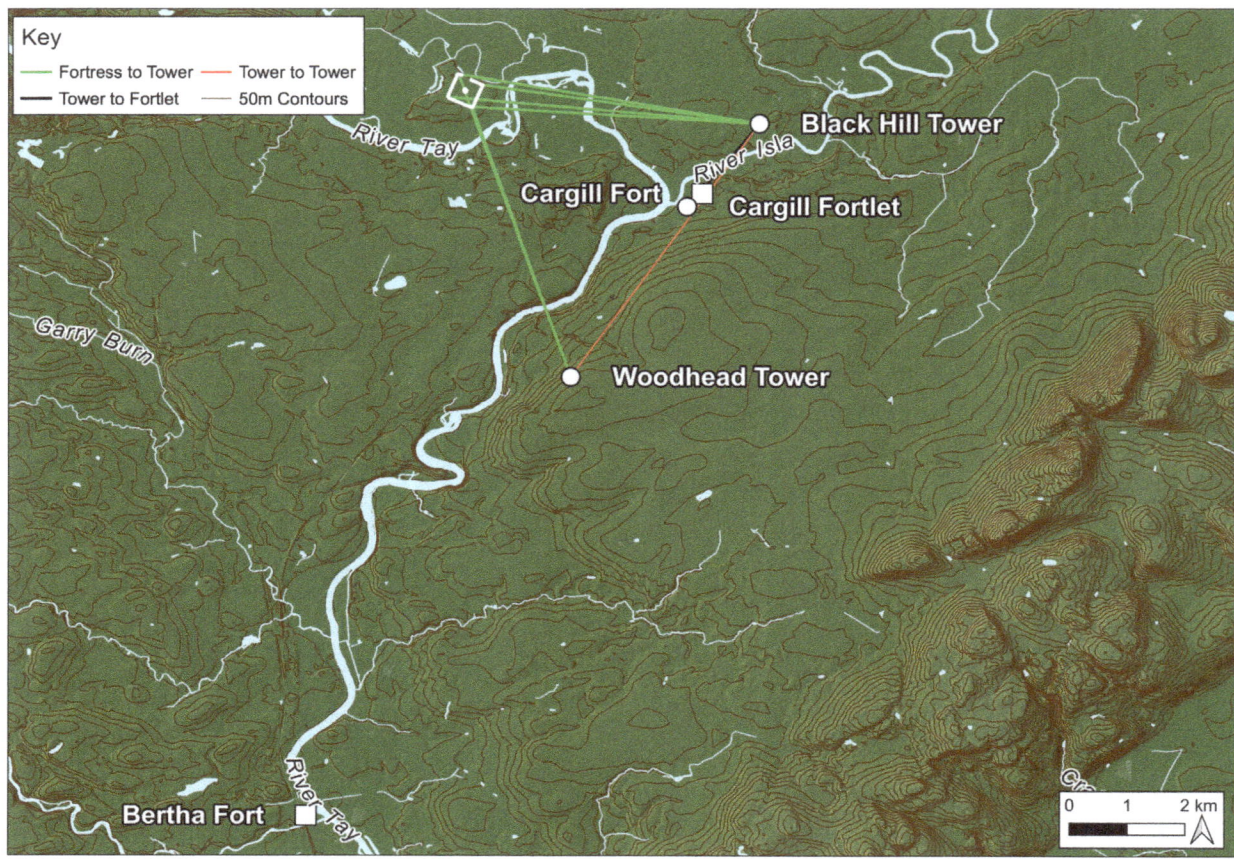

Figure 5.12. Line of site between Bertha fort and Woodhead tower.

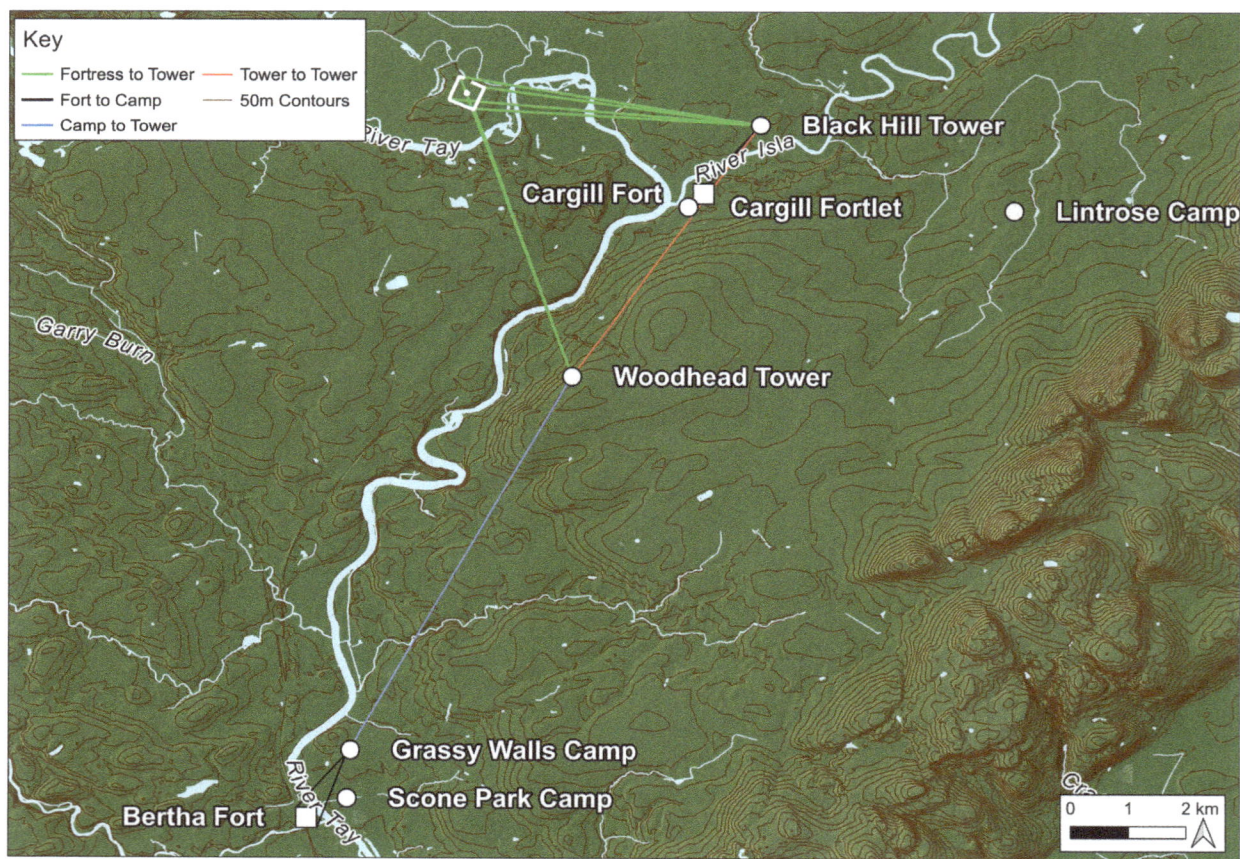

Figure 5.13. Line of site between Bertha and Woodhead via Grassy Walls camp.

awaits discovery, an assertion supported by Woolliscroft's signalling work which suggests that there are likely to be two towers between Bertha and Woodhead. Although it is not within the scope of this research to investigate potential tower sites, GIS modelling does enable us to pinpoint the most likely places for further investigation. As the plan by Crawford (1949:65) of Grassy Walls indicates some possible features worth investigating further in case there is a missing link in the signalling chain; this is seen in Figure 5.13.

Several sites are intervisible from, to, and around the legionary fortress at Inchtuthil (Figure 3.7), including the fort and fortlet at Cargill, as well as another tower named 'Black Hill'. This latter site is curious, as it can receive signals from both the fortress and Cargill fort and fortlet, these sites can also signal directly to one another, without relaying via the towers, which are also not visible from any of the camps. Given that Black Hill, Woodhead, and the Cargill sites, could signal to the legionary fortress, it implies these structures may all be contemporaneous. It is not clear why there are so many sites in close proximity to each other, or a double site at Cargill, but from the positioning of the latter, it appears that these may be guarding the approaching along the river to Inchtuthil. Woodhead may be a relay station from the Gask Ridge fortifications. Black Hill tower seems superfluous for this arrangement unless it is intended to either signal as part of a more northerly relay system, protects the minor confluence to the east, or acting as a look out post for anyone coming down the river valley from the north.

At the southern end of the Gask Ridge chain is the fort of Doune (Figure 5.14, adapted from the GIS results) which is intervisible with the camps at Dunblane. Note, however, I undertook this viewshed with the camp towers at a height of 8.6 metres rather than 1.7 metres, which alters what we can see, without adjusting the analysis, Doune is not otherwise visible from the Dunblane camps. The positioning of Doune is strategic, located next to the River Teith, while Dunblane is close to the Allan Water, suggesting a relationship between the two sites, with the possibility of signalling between Doune and Inchtuthil via Dunblane, although this would most likely require an additional tower to the north of Dunblane. The purpose of securing the area around Dunblane is not clear; it is possible that this was a part of the communications chain with the Gask Ridge sites, and that Dunblane or Doune played a pivotal role with this (as Strageath did), and that the signal was relayed from these fortifications via towers that await discovery. Doune, in a wider context, can be seen in Figure 5.15.

Figure 5.14. Line of site analysis between the camps at Hillside and the fort at Doune.

Facing the Enemy?

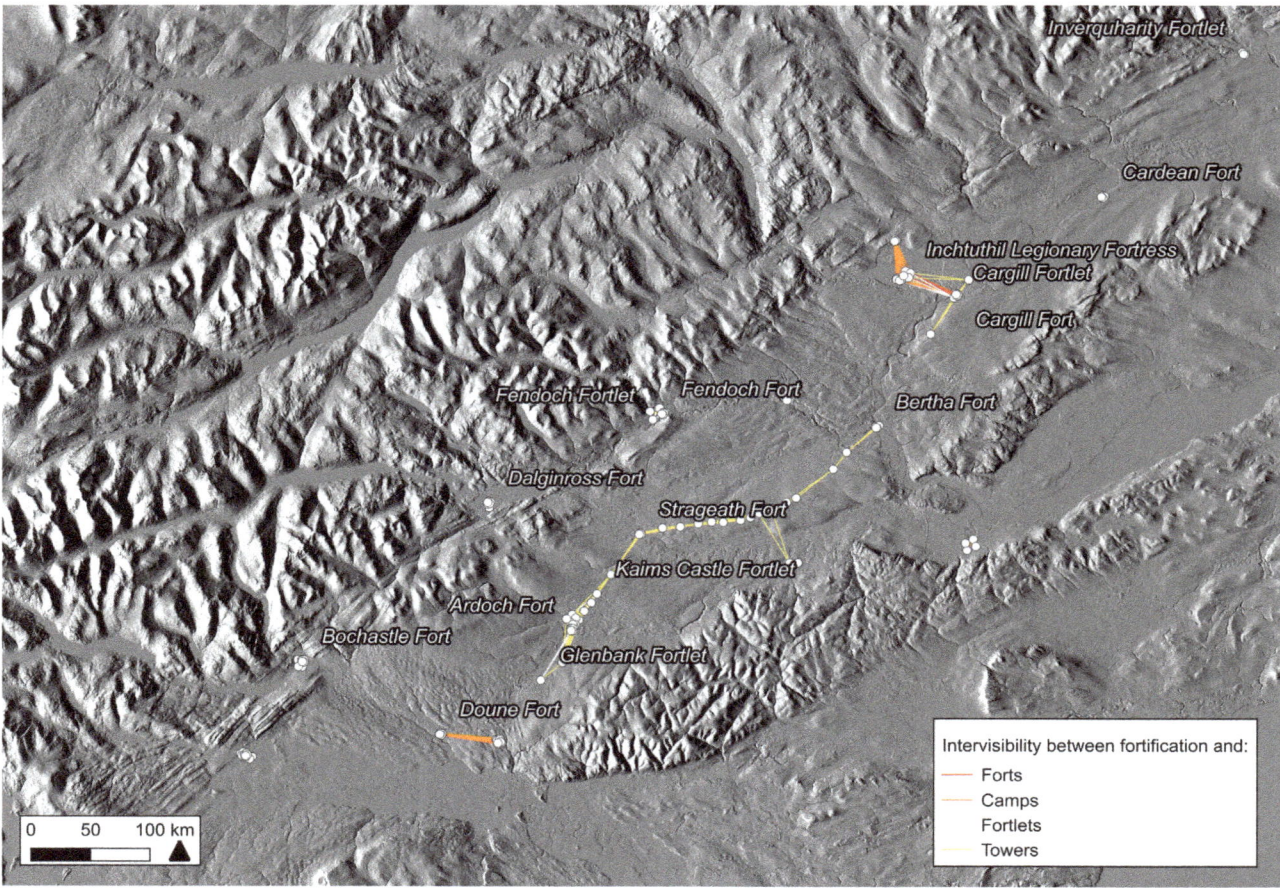

Figure 5.15. Overview of Line of site analysis of sites on and around the Gask Ridge.

Assuming that the Gask Ridge is part of a network which includes signalling capacity, the frequency of the towers seems unnecessary as the system could function with fewer such structures (Figure 5.16). As this diagram shows, a number of towers can be removed from the network and it would still function just as effectively. The sites in red show a signalling path using a minimal number of towers, rendering the remaining sites superfluous, which could indicate that not all the towers were in use at the same time. Two towers appear to be lynchpins, Gask House and Muir O'Fauld, with the chain fully capable of signalling with only one of these two sites. This leads to questions on why there are so many sites if the Gask Ridge is a signalling network. One explanation is that we are looking at two different signalling systems from different periods, although this does not explain the additional towers. Possibly, one set of installations were constructed then abandoned, and new towers built at a later date. Further research is required to explore this possibility, but given the evidence of Flavian and Antonine activity from the forts on the Gask Ridge, and the possible post-Flavian road near Innerpeffray West camp, it could be that the towers date to both the Flavian and Antonine periods. The diagram reflects the complexity of the Gask Ridge fortifications, and the requirement for further investigation into these.

Most of the fortifications which are interlinked are located on the Gask Ridge. As expected, the GIS analysis confirms the signalling findings of Woolliscroft, and this also provides confidence that the line-of-sight methodology that I have employed, is working accurately. I have been able to go further than Woolliscroft and included Gask Ridge camps in the analysis. This shows that from the northeast corner of the camp at Dunning, the Gask Ridge towers of Witch Knowe and Moss Side are visible. Given that the camp is on a rise, it could be that from the as yet unlocated southeast and southwest rear corners, more sites would have been visible. The northwestern corner of camp II at Ardoch is notable, given that from there the tower at Westerton could be seen, as well as Kaims Castle fortlet, whereas from the tower at Black Hill, only the latter site is visible. Woolliscroft did not consider the relevance that camps may have played in the system, nor did he recognise these when he undertook his original analysis, which left some gaps in understanding about why some towers are positioned where they are.

5.2.2. Towers in Southern Scotland

Figure 5.17 shows the intervisibility between the forts and camps at Newstead, and the tower on Eildon Hill North, which was found to be similar in design to the Gask Ridge structures when excavated, and the assumption is that it is Flavian (Steer and Feacham 1952). From the tower, large parts of the surrounding area can be seen, particularly to the north of the Newstead sites, and it may have been possible

Intervisibility

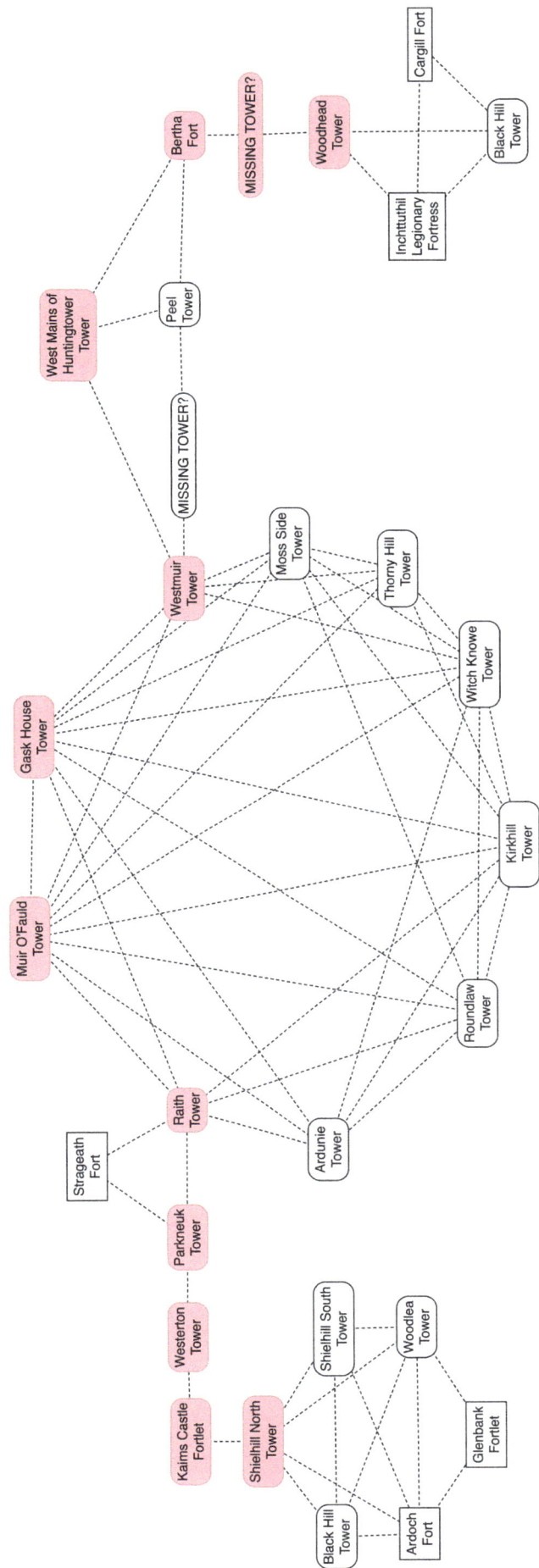

Figure 5.16. Network diagram of signalling between the Gask Ridge fortifications. Red boxes indicate the quickest signalling route.

Facing the Enemy?

Figure 5.17. Line of sight analysis between Newstead fort and Eildon Hill North tower.

to alert those in the fort to advance parties approaching from the south. Figure 5.18 (adapted from the GIS results) shows that the camp at Oakwood would have been able to see the tower on Eildon Hill North, however at around 8km distant, the signal would have been on the edge of daytime visibility, although less of a problem on a clear night.

This hypothesis has only recently been tested by Murphy et al. (2018), who examined this network using binary viewshed analysis in GIS. They argued that a number of sites could be seen from Eildon Hill North tower, including Rubers Law where the tower was first identified by Curle (1905; 1907) from the remnants of dressed stone near the summit, although Curle also speculates the stone may have originated elsewhere and was brought to the site to reinforce an indigenous fort although this seems like a considerable effort. Curle suggests that Rubers Law was a Roman signalling station interlinking to the tower on Eildon Hill North. Rubers Law is undated, although an out of context coin of Vespasian origin was found nearby (Bateson and Holmes 1997:531). Murphy et al also looked at other alleged tower sites including Cross Hill tower and Brownhart Law fortlet, and tested the extent to which other sites may be intervisible with Rubers Law, with results indicating that a wider range of sites could see a signal. Further work on the dating the towers is needed; it is not confirmed if these are Flavian, but it does seem likely that

they form part of a network relaying to and from the sites at Newstead, via Eildon Hill North.

5.3. Summary

My analyses shows, a number of sites beyond those on the Gask Ridge appear to be able to signal to each other, while in the south of Scotland, there appears to be some sort of capacity to signal between a number of towers, but the extent of visibility would have made anything other than rudimentary signals difficult to understand by the receiver, however the case has been made for further analysis of this potential network, including through practical experimentation. Fortifications beyond those on the Gask Ridge, may have had some capacity to signal to each other, although this is difficult to show in the archaeological record. The work of Woolliscroft did not extend to camps, or to sites in Scotland, beyond the Antonine Wall and the Gask Ridge, but there is some possibility that other Flavian fortifications may have been interlinked in this way. It is clear from other frontiers in the Empire, that signalling networks are much more extensive and complex than portrayed by the Gask Ridge, and it certainly seems possible that there could be more sites awaiting discovery in Scotland, and that these networks include various different types of fortification. The other challenge is the dating of various elements of these sites; there is evidence, albeit limited suggesting

Figure 5.18. Line of sight analysis between Oakwood camp and Eildon Hill North tower.

both pre-Agricolan, and post-Flavian activity around the Gask Ridge sites, which add an additional layer of complexity to this area.

The evidence presented in this chapter demonstrates the complexities of signalling networks, and that using variable parameters to Woolliscroft, gives slightly different, but interesting results for interlinking various fortifications; this would be an area worthy of further investigation and practical experimentation. The results also show that intervisibility from one site to another, with some exceptions, does not appear to have been a strong influencing factor in the construction and positioning of Flavian fortification, contrary to Graafstal's (2020) findings regarding fort positioning on the Antonine Wall. The evidence indicates that camps may have a role to play in signalling, and although this needs to be tested archaeologically by looking for signalling structures within encampments, the GIS modelling is indicative of the importance of some sites.

6

Orientation

According to the classical writers 'Pseudo' Hyginus and Vegetius, the orientation or direction which a fortification faces, is an important factor to consider when selecting the location of the site. They write that a fortification should face east, the enemy, or the direction of advance. However, as this chapter will show, most Flavian fortifications in Scotland do not face any of these directions, and instead the orientation – like positioning – appears influenced by the need to control the landscape. The interconnectivity of sites, through the road network is another area which may be key for the army in Flavian Scotland. As noted on other frontiers, the road network is also important; it helps the army to control the landscape, as well as enabling them to move supplies and soldiers efficiently; our knowledge of this in Scotland is limited, and it is difficult to draw too many conclusions because of our fragmented knowledge.

By using a range of sources, I plotted the defences of each fortification in GIS, with various features being used to identify the direction the site is facing. I layered this outline in the DEM of the topographical landscape and binary viewshed of each site, to determine what the fortification is facing. This image combines data on the Roman road network, river crossings, Iron Age and non-Roman sites. The orientation, or direction which a camp or fort faces can be determined if at least one of several key features can be identified: the long/short axis, the gates, the internal roads, and the *principia*. It is the internal positioning of the *principia* and the *aedes* (the central room at the rear of the building) within which best indicates the direction a fortification is facing; the *aedes* should face out of the *principia*, along the *via praetoria*, towards the *porta praetoria*, this being the 'front' entrance of the fortification.

In this chapter, I focus on the orientation of early Roman fortifications in Scotland, beginning with the classical texts which proscribe which way a fort should face and why. I then critically examine some of the previous research which has taken place into fortification orientation, before attempting to discern and summarise the direction which the various military sites face. It then looks at which fortifications were facing east, the enemy, or direction of advance before concluding that this was almost irrelevant to the military. I then summarise what the sites in 1st century Scotland were actually facing, and what can be concluded from this.

6.1. Classical Texts: Orientation

'The Porta Praetoria should always face the enemy.'
'Pseudo' Hyginus, De Munitionibus Castrorum 56

'The gate which is called praetoria should either face east, or the direction which looks towards the enemy, or if on the march it should face the direction in which the army is to proceed.'
Vegetius, Epitoma De Re Militari I.23

'Pseudo' Hyginus and Vegetius state the orientation or direction which a fortification faces should do one of three things; face east, or towards the enemy, or in the direction of advance. To the Roman writers, orientation was a key consideration when locating military structures, but as will be shown, the archaeology tells a different story; that the majority of fortifications are facing water and not as outlined in the classical texts. It is still important to look at fortification orientation in light of the classical texts, partly to prove or disprove these claims, but also because there has never been a large-scale and systematic analysis of this aspect of fortification design. This section begins with an examination of the layout of fortifications, followed by an overview of what the Roman writers claim a fortification should be facing, followed by more recent analysis of the orientation of some sites.

The layout of fortifications has importance in the context of this research because it helps to determine the orientation of a site. Various classical literary texts discuss the layout of camps including Josephus (*Bellum Iudaicum* III.116) and Vegetius (*Epitoma* II.7), but two principal texts, which focus on the layout of camps (by Polybius and Hyginus) are the most relevant and considered here.

Polybius, a cavalry officer in the Roman army, wrote a series of *Histories* about the Second Punic War during the later second century BCE. Within his texts, Polybius recounts construction of a legionary camp, and wrote that once the site had been chosen the position with the clearest view of the site was chosen for the consul's tent (the *praetorium*), with the rest of the camp being constructed around this. Figure 6.1 shows an idealised layout based on the description of a Polybian camp.

The second key text relating to camp layout is attributed to 'Pseudo' Hyginus, and like Polybius, Hyginus details the layout of the ideal Roman camp (Figure 6.2). The layout of forts are believed to follow the guiding principles set out by Polybius and Hyginus, that there is a central area set aside for the commanding officer (the *praetorium*) and administrative purposes (the *principia*), and it is these plans this that the names for the internal features are taken from. While occasionally the shape of fortifications varies, often this is because like camps,

Facing the Enemy?

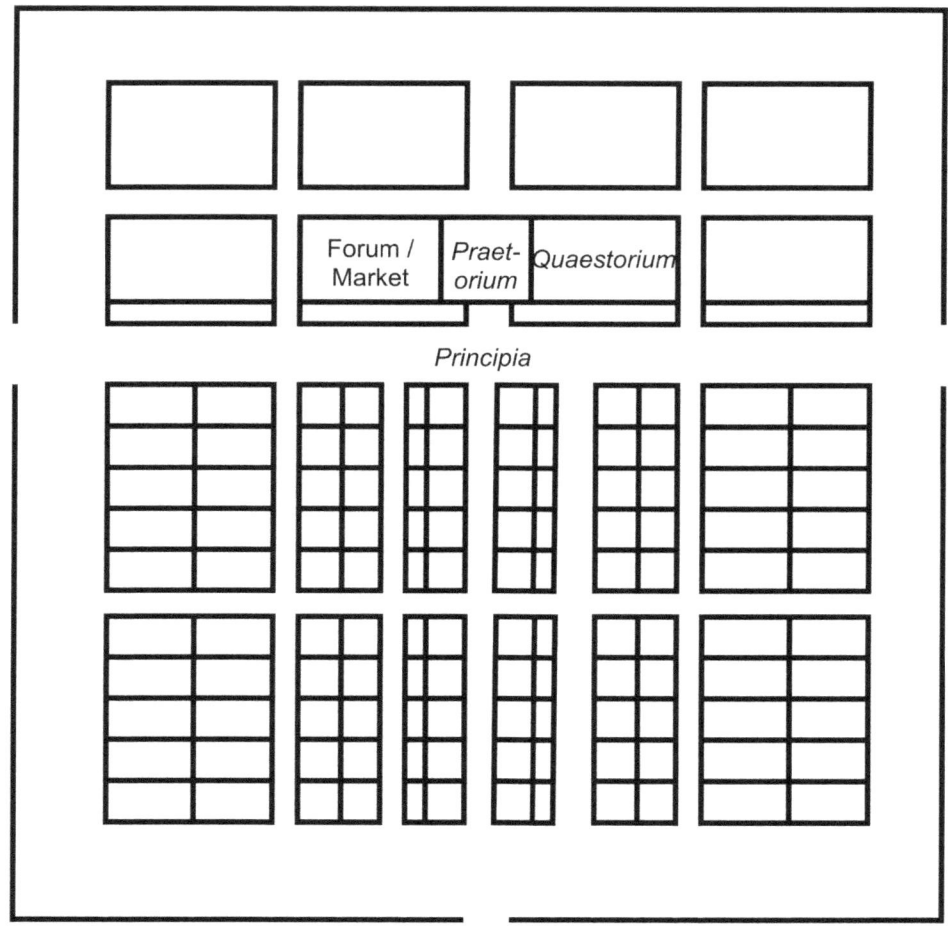

Figure 6.1. Polybian Camp with front entrance at the bottom (After Johnson 1983).

their design makes use of the natural topography. Otherwise, forts are overwhelmingly similar in shape and layout. While it is easier to identify these features in a fort, camps pose a different set of challenges because of their temporary nature, with the former having generally survived better in the archaeological record because of the construction methods and materials used, whereas camps do not have permanent internal structures. Occasionally rows of rubbish pits can be seen in aerial images and are indicative of the positions of the tents, suggesting that camps in Scotland are following these models. Two curious exceptions are the sites at Ward Law and at Dalswinton, Bankhead both of which appear to have the ditch and rampart defences of a fort, but without the internal structures (Hussen, Jones, and Hanson 2009a; 2009b). In her extensive study of Roman camps in Scotland, Jones (2011) illustrates most of the 140+ Scottish camps showing the partial defences of many sites. Many of which have subsequent camps constructed on top of them, so it is challenging to identify which features belong to which site and what period they are from – Ardoch, Castledykes and Lochlands are good examples of this. When only partial defences of a camp are known, it can make identification of the orientation much more difficult, and given the internal layout of such fortifications is rarely know, it is almost impossible to be more specific regarding the direction it faced.

The Roman writers claim that fortifications should face in one of three directions, with Milner (2001:24) attributing the claim by Vegetius that a site should face east, to Christian tradition and suggests that the rising sun would wake those occupying the central area of the camp, but there is no evidence to support this assertion. Although Vegetius was writing in a period where Christian worship was common, few Roman fortifications in Scotland are orientated east, as demonstrated later. If a fortification was on sloping ground, and orientated towards the enemy, then it would be possible for them to see into the interior, and potentially be intimidated by the size of the military force. This is something which Graafstal (2020) has observed with some Antonine sites in Scotland. Possibly, the decision to have the site face the direction of advance was a practical consideration, making it easier for soldiers to leave in the direction they would move, but this seems redundant given the baggage train for the army could be up 10 kilometres (R. H. Jones 2011).

Orientation

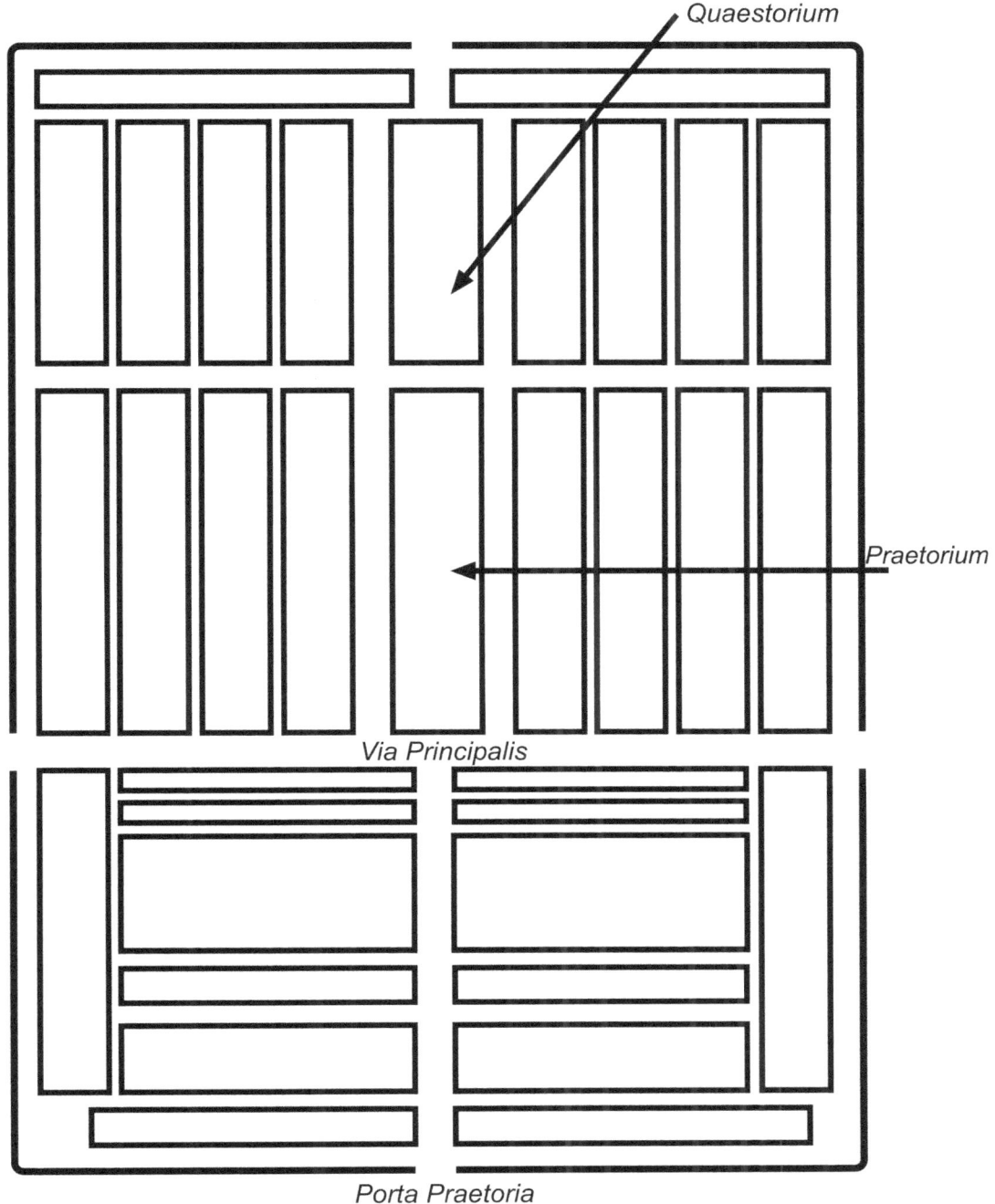

Figure 6.2. Hyginian Camp. The porta decumana is at the top (After Johnson 1983).

'Pseudo' Hyginus and Vegetius wrote that a fortification should overlook the enemy, and it is not clear if there is a symbolic purpose to this. The *aedes*, the central rear room in the *principia,* is where the soldiers kept the *cohort's* standards, and the statues of the Imperial cult. During construction of a camp, the standards are set in position before the rest of the site is laid out (Bishop 2013), and it was believed that by keeping them in the *aedes*, no soldier would dare to desecrate them to steal the monies also kept there. Vegetius discusses the importance of military beliefs and functions, including the importance of the standards and how much military life revolved around these, which is reflected in the *Feriale Duranum* (Rostovtzeff 1934). There is no archaeological or written evidence which shows whether the *aedes* had a role crucial to the orientation of the site, but it may have been symbolic with a line of sight from the Standards in the *aedes*, leading from the *principia*, along the *via praetoria* and out of the *porta praetoria* to overlook the enemy. It is also unclear if there was any importance attached to the *porta praetoria* as the front entrance of a fortification, although there is some evidence that this gate may have been imposing, as at Housesteads (Rushworth 2009:231, 297) and at almost every legionary fortress in the Empire (Bishop 2013:25). For visitors approaching this would have been the first part of the fort which they saw close up. Forts on the Antonine Wall are generally orientated with the *porta praetoria* or the opposite gate, the *porta decumana*, positioned against the Wall, so visitors approaching along the Military Way would have initially encountered the *porta sinistra* and the *porta dextra* rather than the main entrance (Hanson and Maxwell 1986:84).

6.2. Orientation: Recent Studies

The orientation of individual sites is sometimes mentioned in publications about those fortifications, but it is rare that it is discussed in the wider context of frontiers. This seems remiss given that some groupings of fortifications appear to follow a distinct pattern; most of the Stanegate forts face south, as do several forts on the Antonine Wall which face the valleys which eventually open onto the Clyde valley (E. Graafstal 2020:144). Graafstal's analysis does not look at the orientation of the forts, and the modelling appears to use a basic topographical map which does not sure the nuances of the terrain which may have influenced the siting of the fortification. It is more difficult to identify the direction which camps are facing because they do not have permanent structures such as a *principia*. As Welfare and Swan (1995:14) write, it is only possible to guess at the orientation even if the defences are regular, which they seldom are for camp. They also conclude that different sites are orientated in different directions, sometimes facing the enemy, and other times appearing to face the direction of advance. A similar study of the orientation of late Roman forts from the Kharga Oasis in the Western Egyptian desert was undertaken by Rossi and Magli (2019), and who concluded that fortifications are located to take advantage of the natural topography and to encourage the flow of the prevailing wind to ensure that it cools the fortifications by blowing through them, keeping them cool, although it is not clear from their paper how they were able to determine the direction of wind in the Roman period.

Richardson examined the orientation of 67 camps in Britain using published plans, manually recording the orientation of each. He argues that the angle of fort orientation was purely down to decisions by the surveyors who were "laying out right-angled triangles whose non-hypotenuse sides were in whole number rations" (2004:420). Richardson's methodology does not consider the effect of the natural topography on the positioning and layout of a site. Nor does he consider the different phases of construction and goes on to claim that the fort at Croy Hill is Agricolan despite a lack of evidence to support this assertion; Graafstal has recently shown that it appears to be an incomplete Antonine site. Peterson (2007) critiqued Richardson, arguing the original analysis is based on an incorrect statistical interpretation; statistically, there is no significant preference for any angle of orientation. Peterson writes Richardson should, in the future, "seek help when interpreting statistics" (2007:107).

Sparavigna (2016b; 2016a; 2017) has written three papers on fort orientation; one which focuses on Hardknott fort in the Lake District, one on the fort at Caernarfon in Wales, and another on the alignment of Novaesium on the Rhine. Sparavigna claims that the orientation of Roman forts is based on a mixture of astronomical alignment of the summer and winter solstices. The crux of Sparavigna's arguments is a selective quotation from Haverfield (1913) that the "*decumanus* could have been determined to have its direction with the azimuth of the rising sun". Sparavigna claims that this refers to Roman forts, however, Haverfield is referring to a central road in a Roman town. He writes about a road which east-west, casually commenting that "… now and again the latter street seems to point to the spot where the sun rises above the horizon on the dawn of someday important in the history of the town" (1913:77). Haverfield is making a casual observation rather than proposing this as a deliberate act by the town planners or surveyors. Sparavigna claims that Hardknott has a distinctive layout, however, it is no different to most Hadrianic forts in the north of England. She then states that Hardknott is orientated so that the gates are facing towards the summer and winter solstices, with the sunrise and sunset visible through the gates. Sparavigna's approach is flawed in several ways: the website which she uses to calculate sunrise and sunset (sollumis.com) can only calculate this from the year 1900 onwards; astronomical positioning would have been different when the fort was founded, sometime between CE 120 and 138. The next flaw is in her diagrams (from sollumis.com and created in 2014) of positioning of the sunset/sunrise, which shows that the light does not line up with the nearest gate. Sparavigna fails to consider the restrictions caused by the immediate topography; Hardknott is located on an outcrop with bedrock, some of which is visible within the fort walls and restricts the positioning of the site, and the mountains to the south of the site would have limited views of the sun at certain times of the year. As both Richardson and Sparavigna demonstrate, orientation of fortifications is a poorly understood and often mis-interpreted area of fortification design, and it is necessary to not only consider which direction a site faces, but also to consider it in relation to the immediate and wider landscapes.

6.3. Analysis: Fortification Orientation

The orientation and positioning of Roman military fortifications is an area of research which is unexamined in any depth. Analysis of these characteristics will help to develop our knowledge of Roman operations and priorities in frontier zones. Analysis of my dataset of Flavian fortifications, challenges the understanding of the classical writers in relation to the practicalities

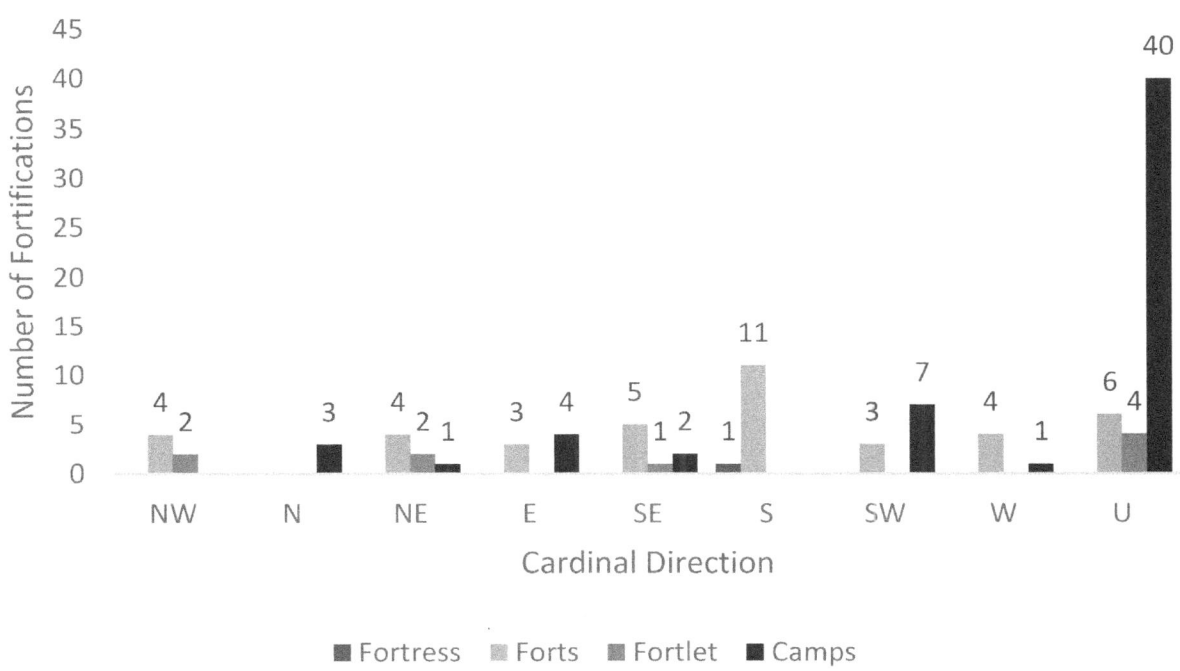

Figure 6.3. Cardinal Direction of Flavian Fortifications.

of military operations on the frontier; Figure 6.3 contains a summary of the orientation of all the Flavian fortification in Scotland. The orientation of several sites is unknown, particularly camps where this can be difficult to identify. The orientation of the remaining fortifications is dispersed across the cardinal directions, although a notably large number of forts are facing south. For comparison, when examining whether or not fortifications are facing east, towards the enemy, or in the direction of advance, I have incorporated the data, extracted from Canmore, from sites dating to the later periods of invasion; there are 22 confirmed Antonine period camps, 53 forts and 20 fortlets; of these, the orientation of 28 is unknown. Of the Severan period fortifications, there are 29 confirmed sites, with the orientation of four being unknown. A summary of the Flavian site data can be found in Appendix Two.

At Inchtuthil legionary fortress, investigations by Richmond (see Pitts and St Joseph 1985), and later Woolliscroft and Hoffmann (2006; 2009b:145; 2009c; 2011:46; and Woolliscroft 2010:136-137) have uncovered the *principia,* indicating that the fortress faced southwest (Figure 3.1).

The orientation of the Flavian forts (Figures 6.4-6.6) are diverse. Bochastle, Newstead and Loudon Hill have unique layouts and defences, and it is not possible with the existing data to discern which way they are facing. Some forts, such as Barochan Hill and possibly Stracathro, face away from their annexes, while Strageath looks into its annexe, implying that this may be a later addition to the fort; we can say the same for Camelon South which is orientated north, and if so, is limited by Camelon North, the implication here being that the north Fort was constructed later than south. Although the analysis of the forts has revealed a slight propensity for orientation to the south, the diversity of findings also illustrates the limits of site-specific analyses, and points to the need for a relational understanding with the wider landscape.

I have taken the outlines of the camp defences in Figures 6.7-6.12 from Jones (2011). Jones used a mixture of excavation and site plans, mapping data and aerial photographs to plot each of the sites, and this technique has informed my approach. As discussed previously, discerning the orientation of camps is challenging, especially when they do not have a discernible long/short axis, such as at Abernethy, Ardoch V, Bankhead II, Dalswinton, Fourmerkland, Glenlochar, and Lochlands. This shows that the army adapted the standard template for the camp on occasions (such as at Raedykes and possibly Woodhead II), because of the local topography, and also because the army varied in size. This is demonstrated at the presumed Severan camp at St Leonard's which is the largest camp in Scotland, and where the armies must have massed before splitting into smaller groups, as the next set of camps from this period were smaller, indicating that they housed fewer soldiers. There are few camps thought to be oriented in a specific direction (such as Cornhill, Dalginross, Eshiels, Glenluce, Glenmailen II, Hillside I, Kirkhouse, Newstead I, and Raeburnfoot) because there is a clear high point to

Facing the Enemy?

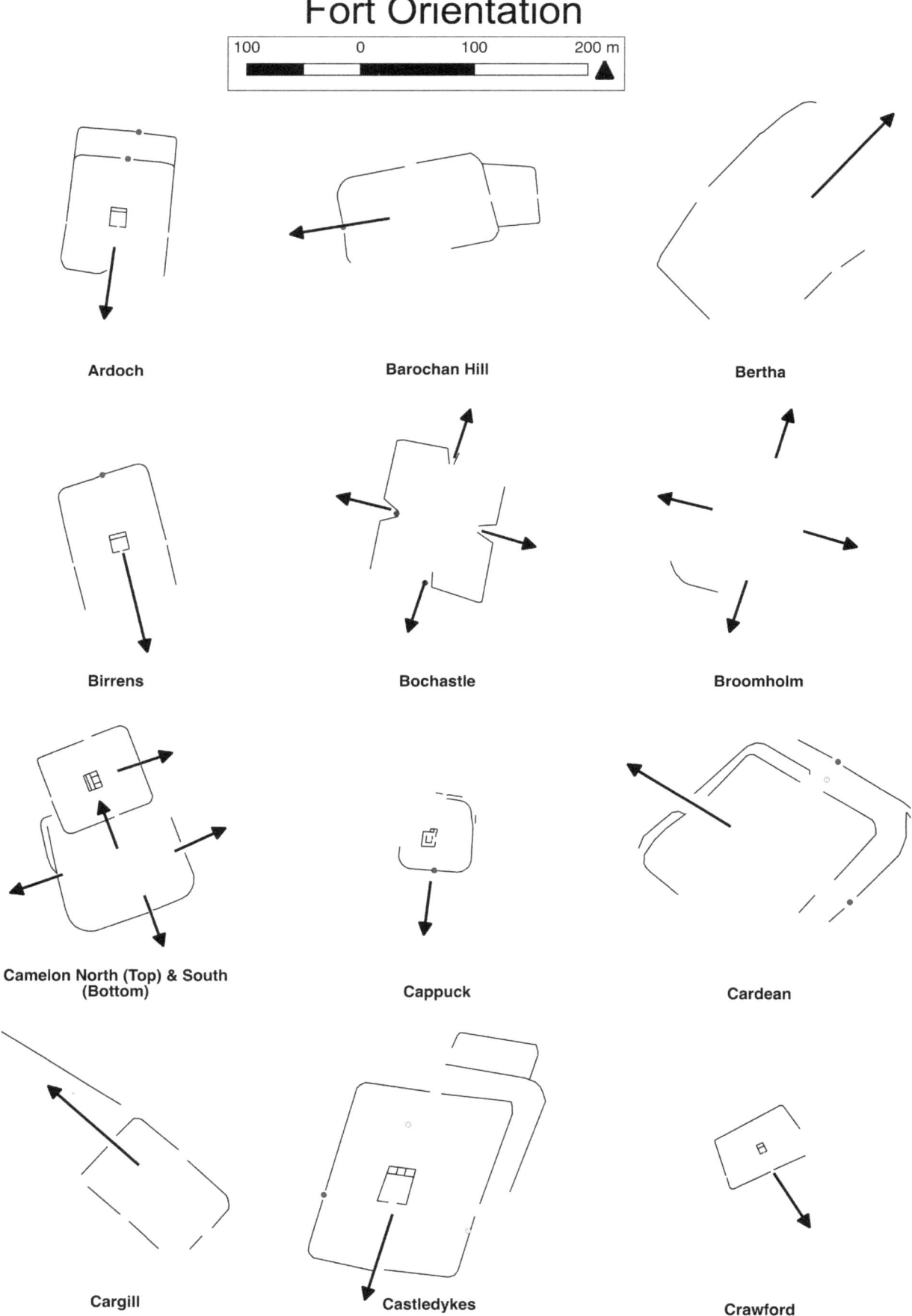

Figure 6.4. Orientation of forts A-C.

Orientation

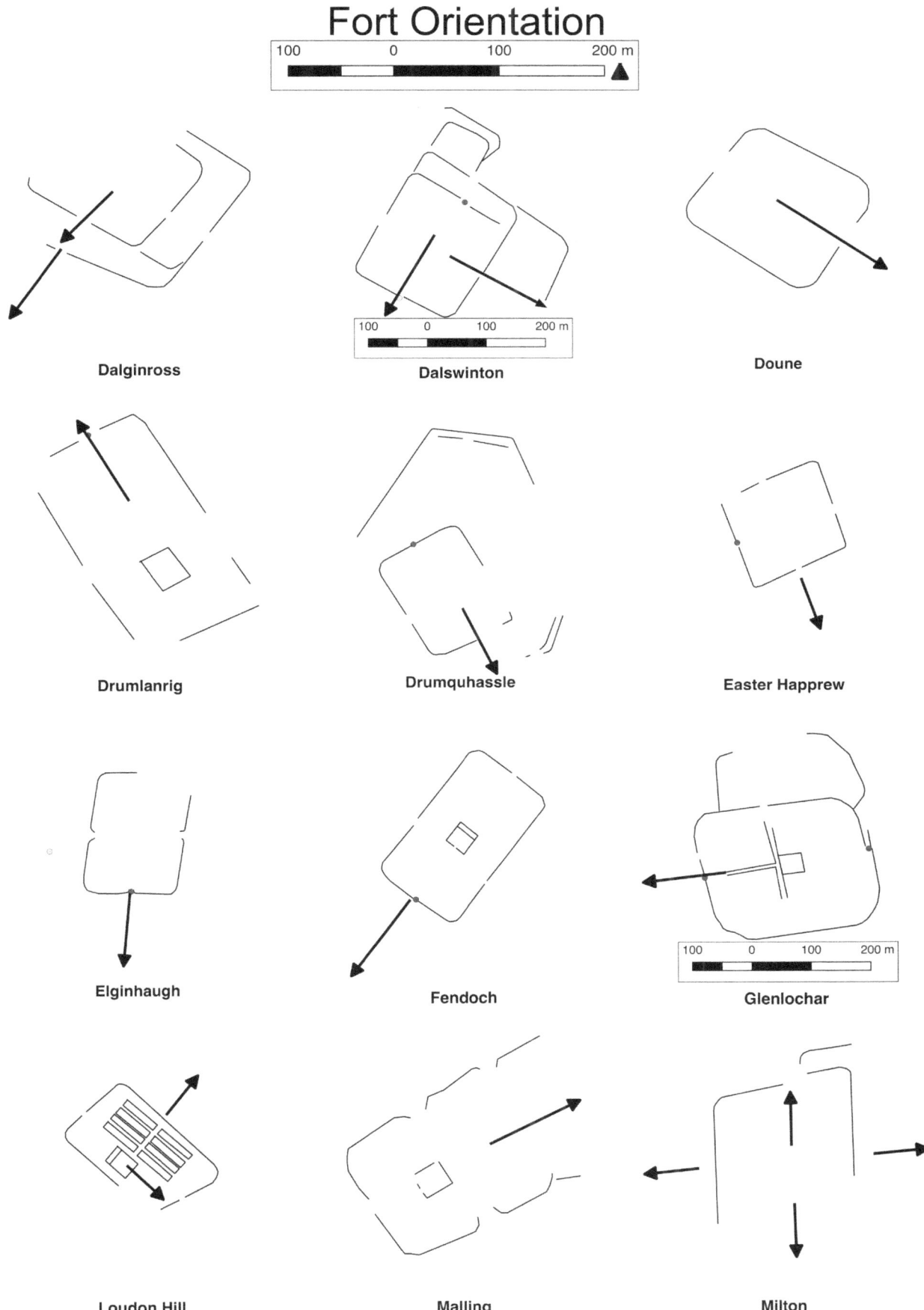

Figure 6.5. Orientation of forts D-M.

Facing the Enemy?

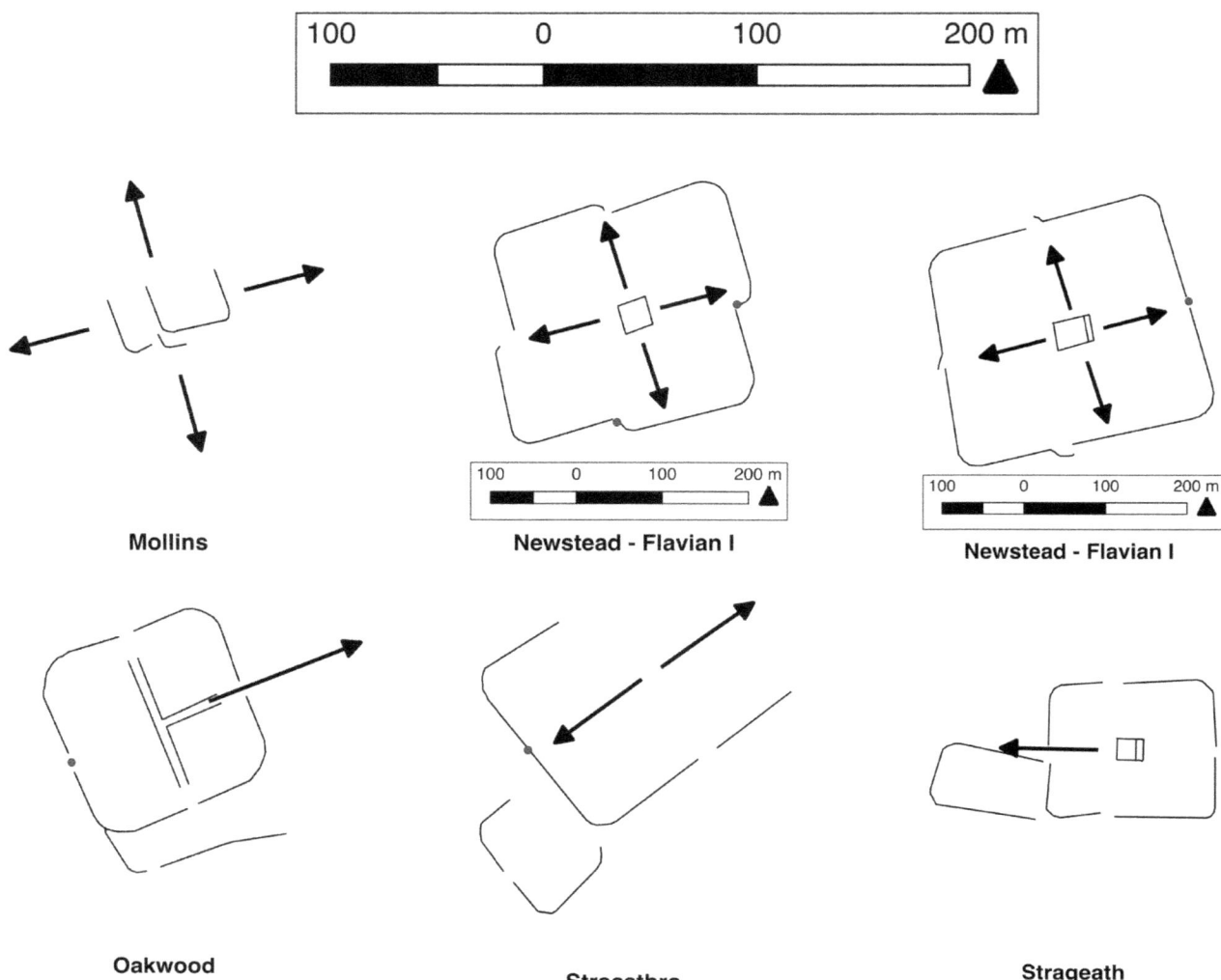

Figure 6.6. Orientation of forts M-S.

the site. Following the classical writers who argued that the *porta decumana* should be at the highest point, it can be hypothesised that the highest point is the back of the camp. But, this assumption needs to be made cautiously as there is no other evidence to support the orientation while, as previously noted, there are various examples where the *porta decumana* is known to not have been located at the highest point. Camp entrances infrequently survive in the archaeological record, and more often than not, the gateway is assumed to be in a particular location because of a gap in the surviving earthworks. If these assumptions are correct, then it is also possible to confirm the orientation of several other camps such as Milton, Ward Law, and Woodhead I.

Arguably, it can be said that fortlets do not have an orientation as they do not have the internal structures (such as a *principia*) which determine the direction the site faces. Instead, this section uses the positioning of the single entrance-way to determine the direction the site is facing. It could be viewed that the entrance is weakest part of the fortification, and that it should not face an advancing threat, and any discussion of the orientation of fortlets should bare this in mind. Out of all the fortlets examined in this study, not enough of remains of Carnwath or Kirkland have been identified to determine the position of the entrances. As Figure 6.13 shows, the fortlet entrances face numerous directions, and while it would be logical to assume that the sites may have a purpose such as guarding a river crossing, the fortlet entrance at Gatehouse of Fleet (Figure 6.14) is orientated northeast with the river to the southwest and the road running south of the site, suggesting the threat may have come from the west. Overall, the lack of consistency in the positioning and orientation of fortifications, points to the multiple roles that Roman these types of fortification had.

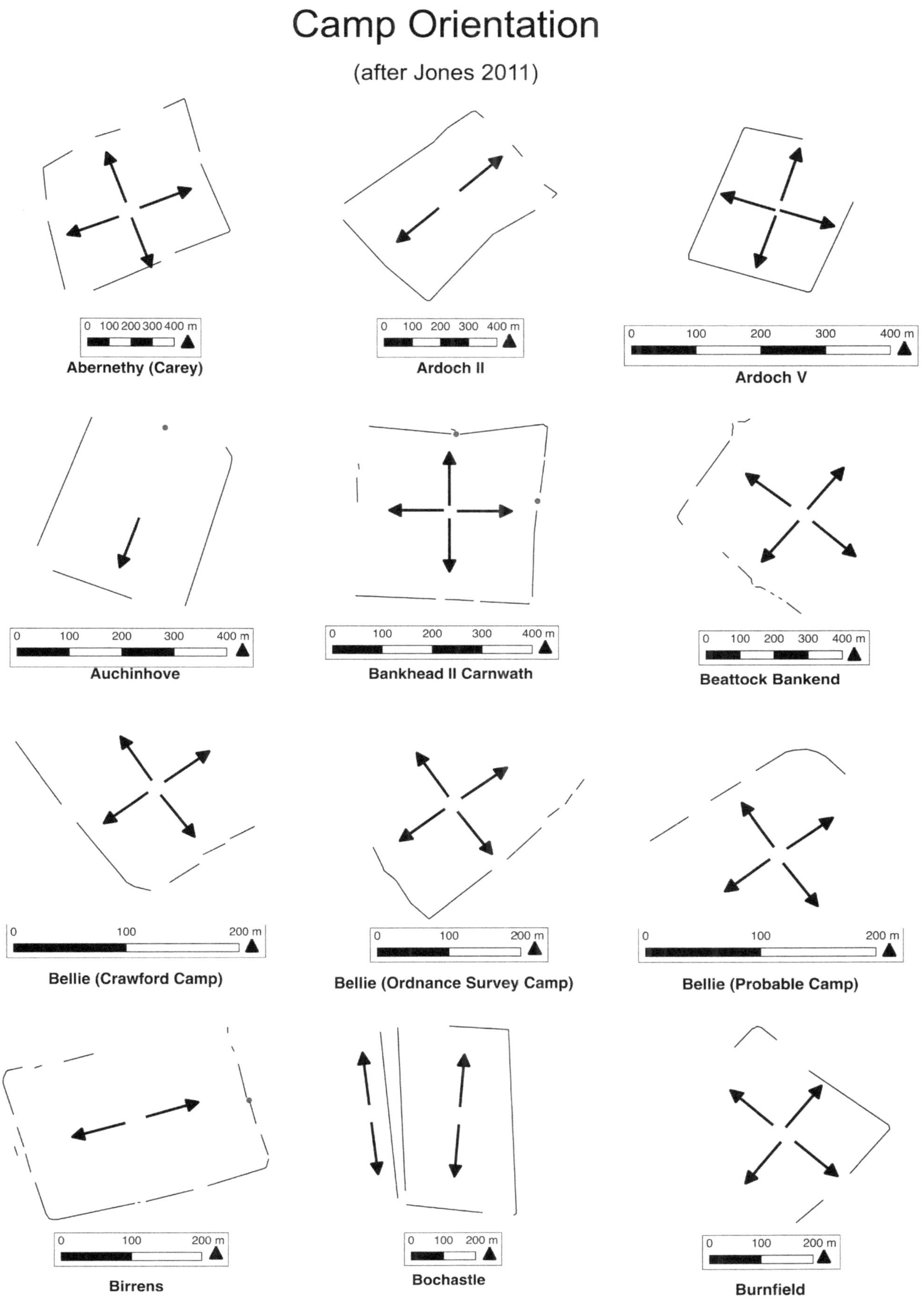
Camp Orientation
(after Jones 2011)
0 100 200 300 400 m
Abernethy (Carey)
0 100 200 300 400 m
Ardoch II
0 100 200 300 400 m
Ardoch V
0 100 200 300 400 m
Auchinhove
0 100 200 300 400 m
Bankhead II Carnwath
0 100 200 300 400 m
Beattock Bankend
0 100 200 m
Bellie (Crawford Camp)
0 100 200 m
Bellie (Ordnance Survey Camp)
0 100 200 m
Bellie (Probable Camp)
0 100 200 m
Birrens
0 100 200 m
Bochastle
0 100 200 m
Burnfield

Figure 6.7. Orientation of camps A-B.

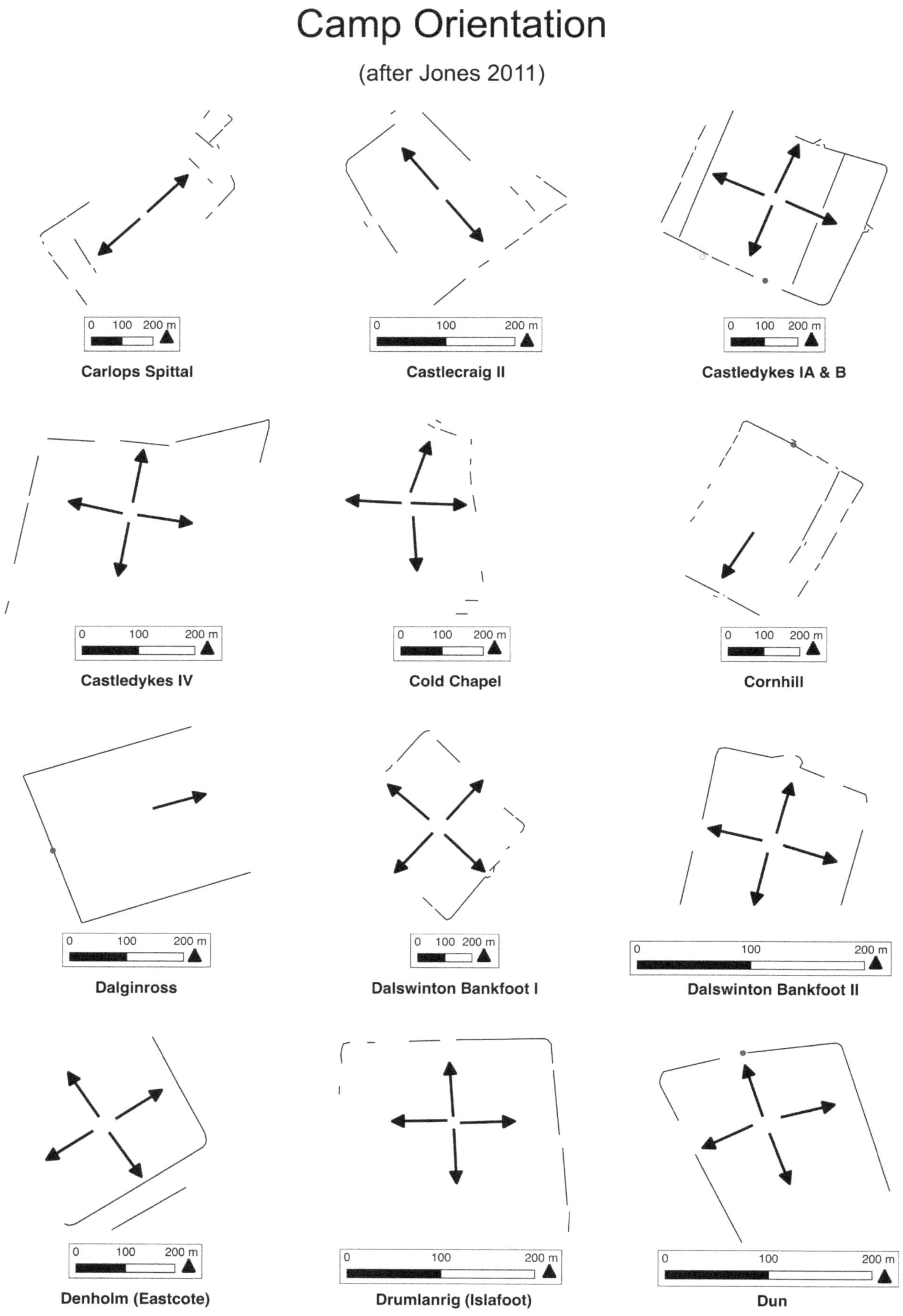

Camp Orientation
(after Jones 2011)
0 100 200 m
Carlops Spittal
0 100 200 m
Castlecraig II
0 100 200 m
Castledykes IA & B
0 100 200 m
Castledykes IV
0 100 200 m
Cold Chapel
0 100 200 m
Cornhill
0 100 200 m
Dalginross
0 100 200 m
Dalswinton Bankfoot I
0 100 200 m
Dalswinton Bankfoot II
0 100 200 m
Denholm (Eastcote)
0 100 200 m
Drumlanrig (Islafoot)
0 100 200 m
Dun

Figure 6.8. Orientation of camps C-D.

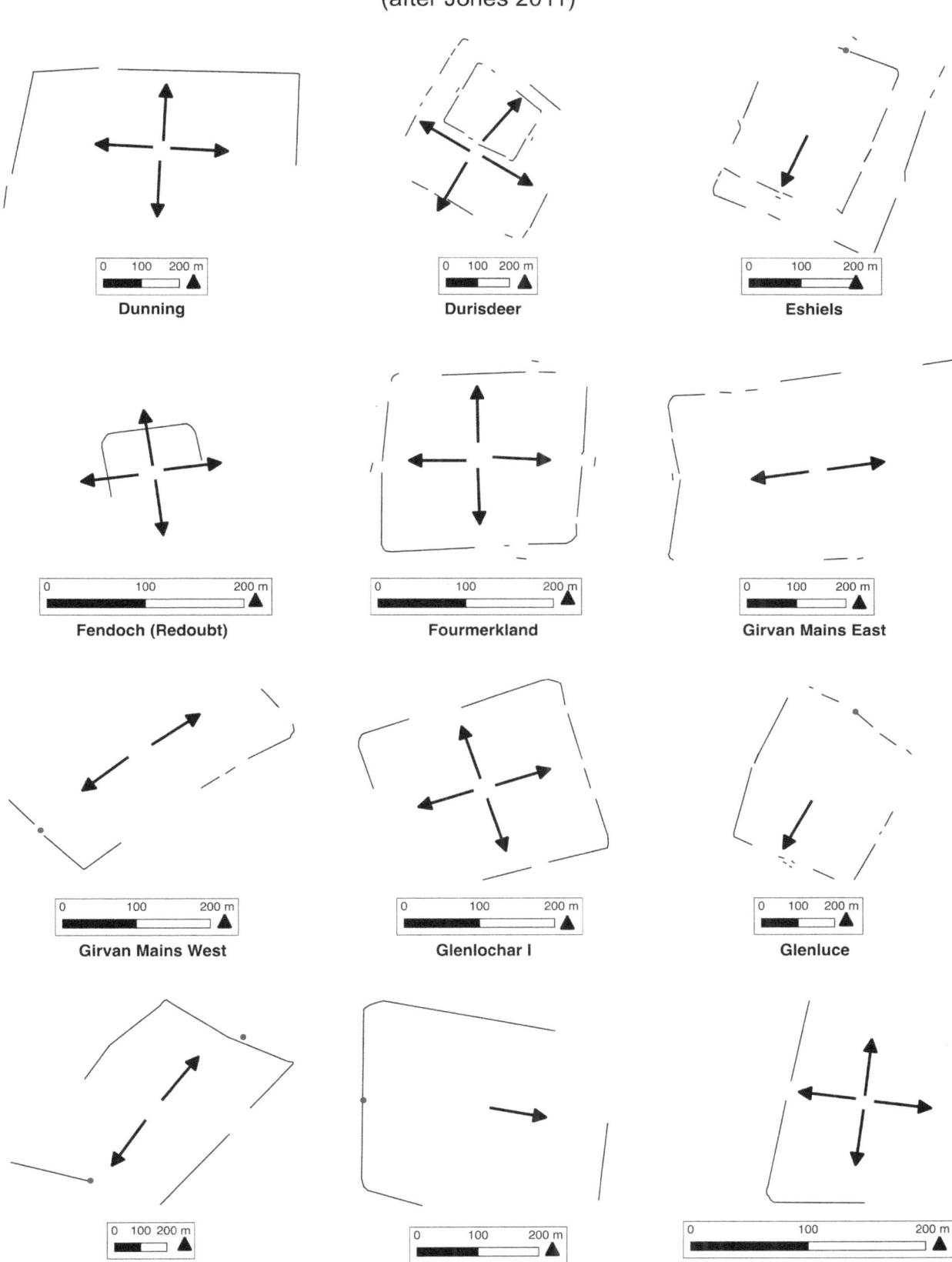

Figure 6.9. Orientation of camps D-G.

Facing the Enemy?

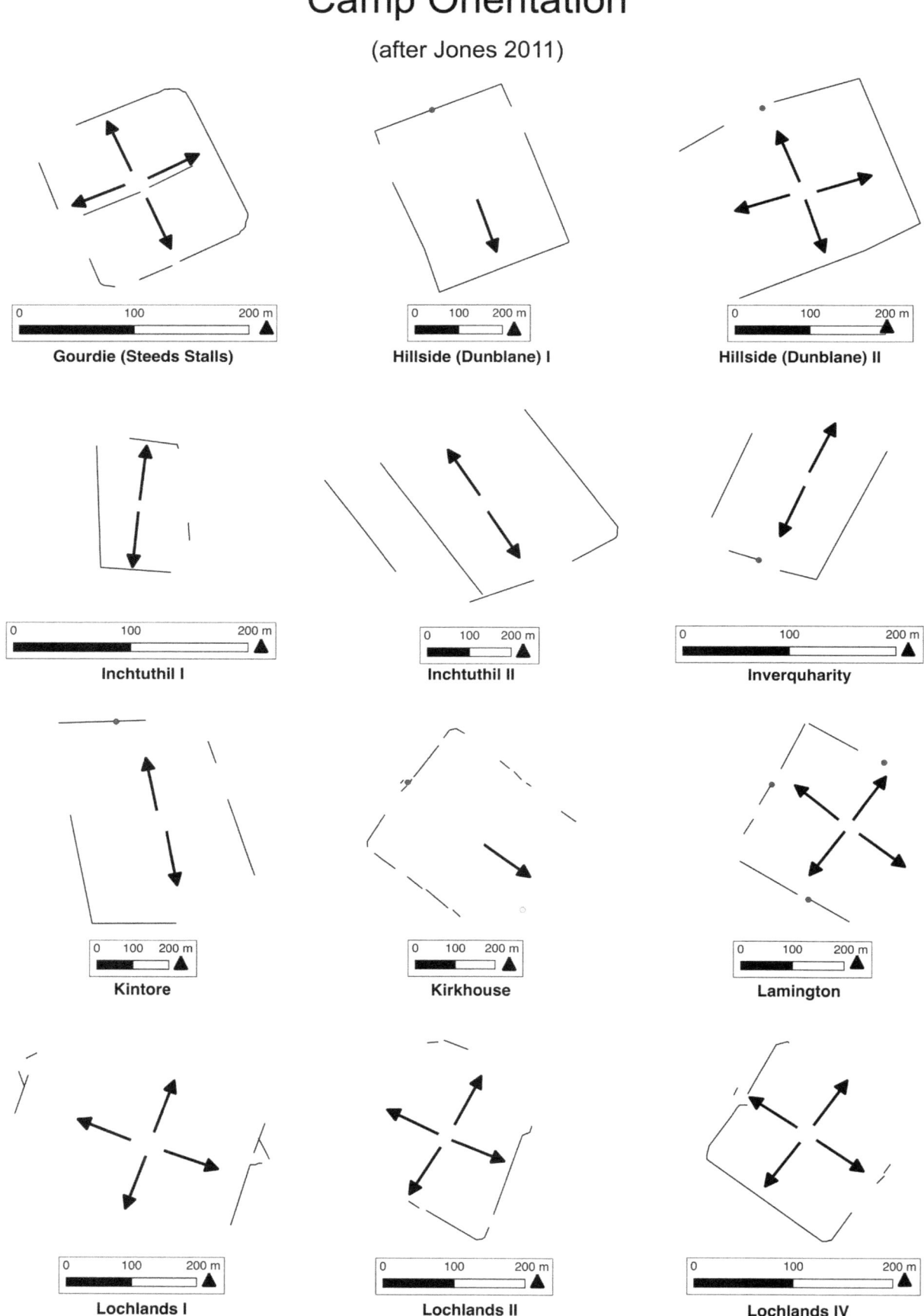

Figure 6.10. Orientation of camps G-L.

Orientation

Camp Orientation
(after Jones 2011)

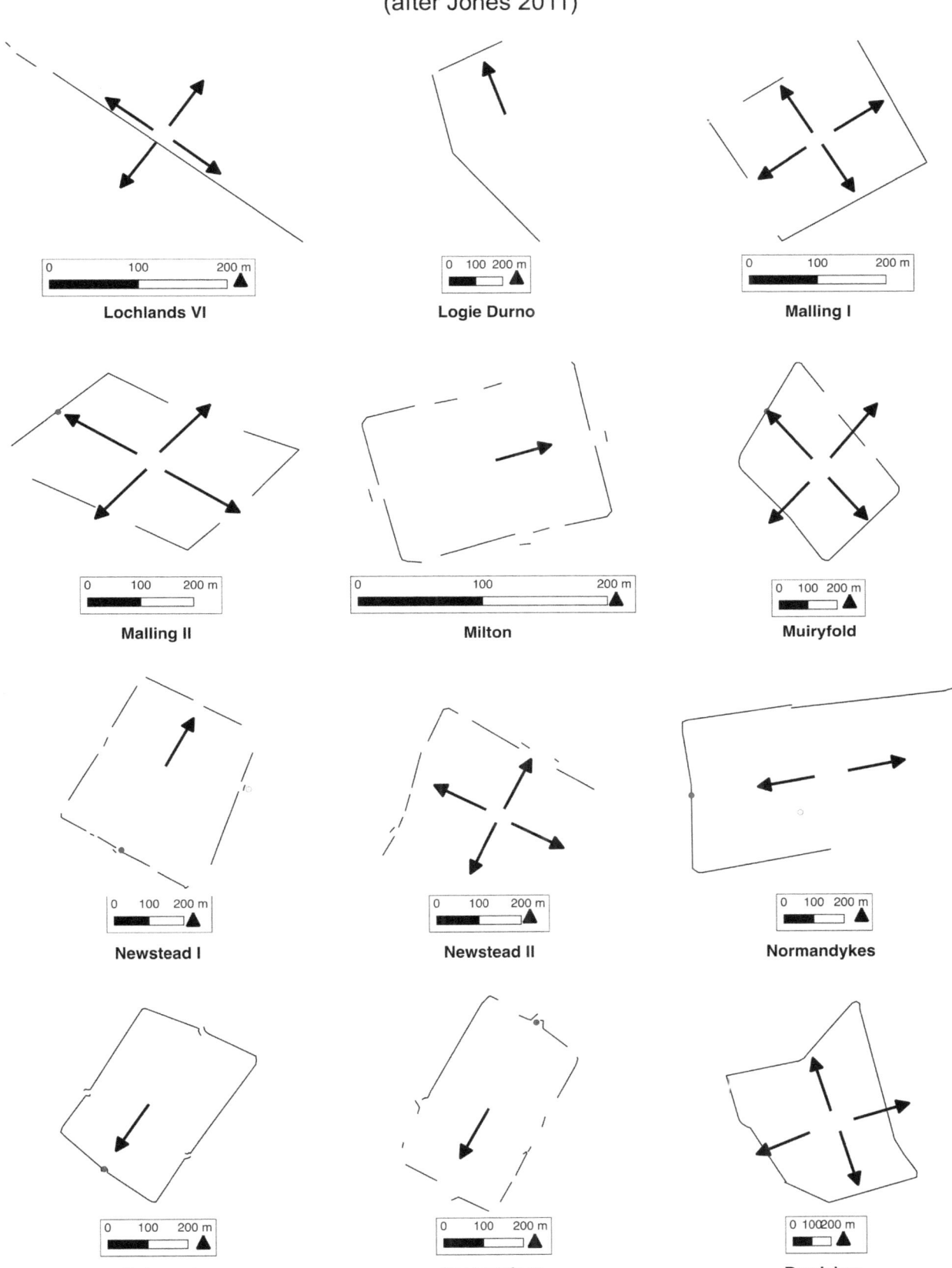

Figure 6.11. Orientation of camps L-R.

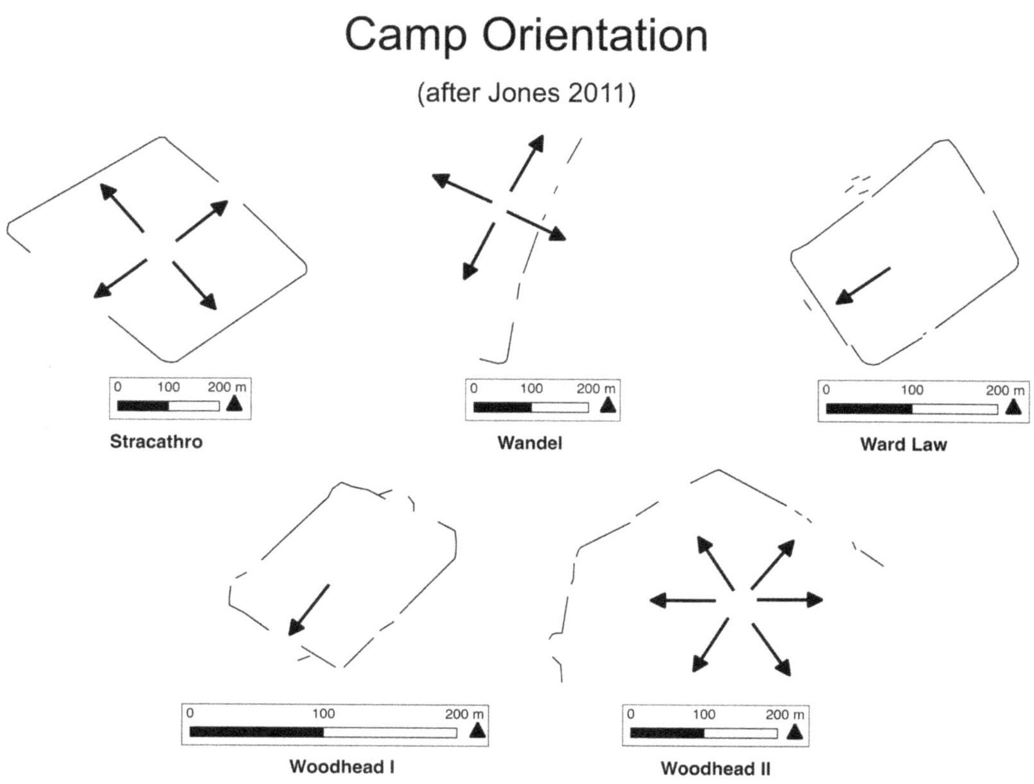

Facing the Enemy?

Camp Orientation
(after Jones 2011)

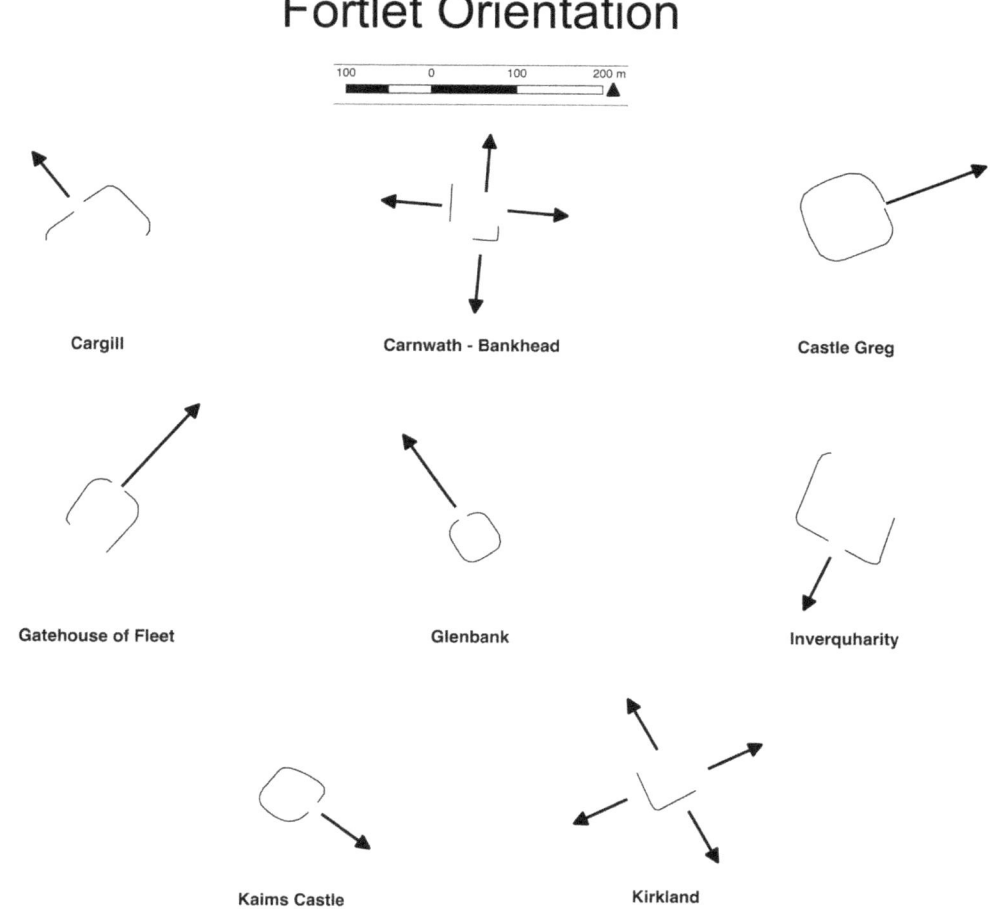

Figure 6.12. Orientation of camps S-W.

Figure 6.13. Orientation of fortlets.

Figure 6.14. Orientation of Gatehouse of Fleet fortlet.

6.4. Analysis: Directions that Fortifications Face

Relatively few Flavian fortifications are facing east (Figure 6.15), and even expanding this definition to include those facing northeast or southeast, the numbers are still low. None of the Antonine camps face directly east, but one (Little Clyde) may face east or west, and six face northeast-southwest (Ardoch I, Balmuildy Cleghorn, Glenlochar II, Torwood, and Wester Carmuirs), while one (Dalginross I) faces southeast, and one southeast-northwest (Pennymuir III). For the forts, three face east (Camelon North, Lyne, Newstead), are on top of Flavian sites, and appear to share the same orientation, seven face northeast (Balmuildy, Bertha, Bothwellhaugh, Crawford I, Crawford II, Duntocher, Mumrills, and Westerwood), three northeast or southwest (Carriden, Raeburnfoot, and Strageath), and one southeast (Castledykes). None of the fortlets face east or almost east.

Nor have any of the Severan camps have been confirmed to face east, although two face east or west (Lintrose, and Innerpeffray East), nine face northeast or southwest (Ardoch I, Ardoch V, Battledykes, Forteviot, Innerpeffray West, Kair House, Kinnell, Longforgan, and Marcus) and eight face southeast or northwest (Auchtermuchty, Craigarnhall, Eassie, Edenwood, Househill, Keithock, Kirkbuddo, and St Leonard's Hill).

As Table 3 shows, out of the Flavian sites examined, 22% face east, northeast or southeast; for the Antonine fortifications, this figure stands at 26%, and 59% for the Severan period sites, however the orientation of many of these, particularly the camps are unknown. There are many factors likely to affect these results, particularly the difficulties of dating sites. Some sites have yielded evidence of multiple phases of occupation, while not enough fieldwork has been undertaken on many sites to conclude with certainty that they date from the period to which they are assigned. The sites north of the Forth-Clyde isthmus generally date to the Flavian period, and were not re-occupied at later dates, while none of those on the Antonine Wall (Figure 6.16) face east, although Camelon North is orientated northeast. Some caution is therefore required when interpreting the dates of later sites and the orientation of earlier ones where the site has been re-occupied later. With only 22% of Flavian sites facing east, northeast or southeast (and only two forts facing due east), the conclusion is that Roman fortifications in Scotland do not generally face the cardinal direction that Vegetius suggests they should.

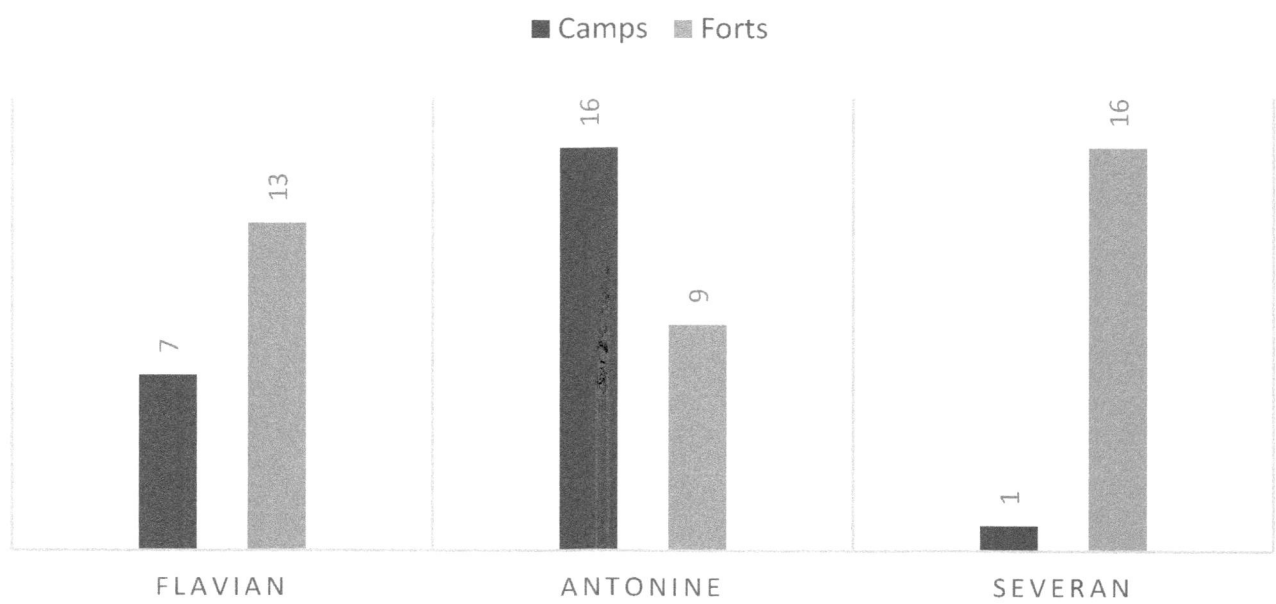

Figure 6.15. Total number of fortifications facing east, northeast or southeast by period.

Table 3. Number of sites facing east, northeast or southeast. Total number of sites examined is in brackets.

	Flavian		Antonine		Severan	
Camps	13 (of 65)	10.5%	9 (of 22)	36%	16 (of 26)	55%
Forts	7 (32)	5.6%	16 (53)	16.8%	1 (3)	3.4%
Fortress	0 (1)	0	N/A	N/A	N/A	N/A
Fortlets	3 (8)	2.4%	0 (20)	0	N/A	N/A
Towers	4 (18)	3.2%	N/A	N/A	N/A	N/A
TOTAL	27 (124)	21.8%	25 (95)	26.3%	17 (29)	58.6%

Extending the analysis to other areas of North Britain which postdate the Flavian period, enable a comparison of the orientation; such an analysis has never previously been undertaken and in this instance asks whether or not the non-Flavian fortifications are following the same patters to the earlier sites. That said, many of these sites are not facing water, probably because of a lack of waterways in the area; the Cumbrian coastal sites being the main exception to this. Out of the Stanegate forts (Figure 6.17) is mixed, with some orientated north and others, south. Kirkbride is the only fort facing west, and this may be because it is on the coast.

The Cumbrian coastal forts Figure 6.18, interpreted as a western extension of Hadrian's Wall (Breeze 2006b), are all facing out to sea, with Beckfoot, Maryport, and Burrow Walls orientated towards the Dumfriesshire coast. Moresby also faces water, but is not orientated to any piece of land. If Ravenglass is facing out to sea, then if it is orientated northwest, it is facing the Dumfriesshire coast, whereas if it is southwest, it is orientated towards the Isle of Man, which would lend credence to the argument by Collingwood (1929) that this was where the army was assembling in advance of an invasion of Ireland.

The majority of fortifications on Hadrian's Wall (Figure 6.19) are orientated north, although there are a small number, Housesteads, Great Chesters, Drumburgh, and Bowness, which are facing east. The natural topography may dictate this; Housesteads is on a natural ridge, and Drumburgh and Bowness are both on the edge of the shorelines of the Solway Firth. Only Carvoran faces south, and this could be because there may be an earlier fort underneath the visible remains which has dictated the later orientation (Breeze 2006b:280).

Orientation

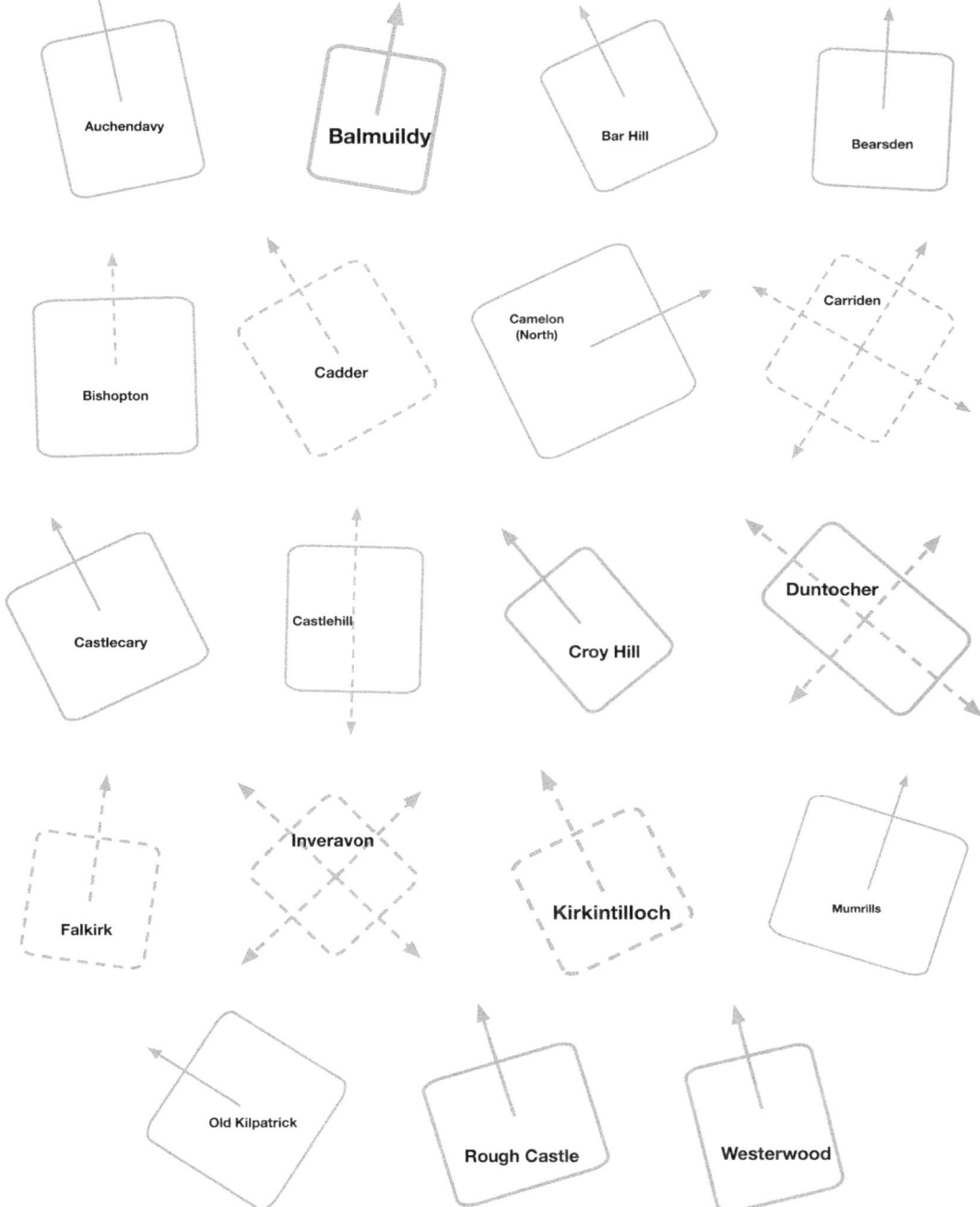

Figure 6.16. Orientation of Antonine Wall forts.

My research demonstrates that most 1st century fortifications do not face east, with only seven Flavian sites facing due east, give or take the 22.5° that I have allowed for, meet the criteria. Even if sites facing northeast and southeast are included (allowing for a 67.5° leeway either side of due east), only 31 fortifications out of 128, meet the east-facing criteria.

If indigenous sites, especially those which are strategic strongholds, are identified in front of a Roman fortification, then perhaps the *agrimensores* were working to the principles later written by Hyginus; that the *porta praetoria* should always face the enemy. The indigenous site has to be dated with some certainty to the LIA, increasing the likelihood that it was occupied at the same time as the Roman fortification. Hyginus does not define what the enemy is; can it be an indigenous settlement, a defensive structure, or does it have a wider meaning such as enemy territory, or lands not under Roman control? Maybe Hyginus meant that fortifications

Facing the Enemy?

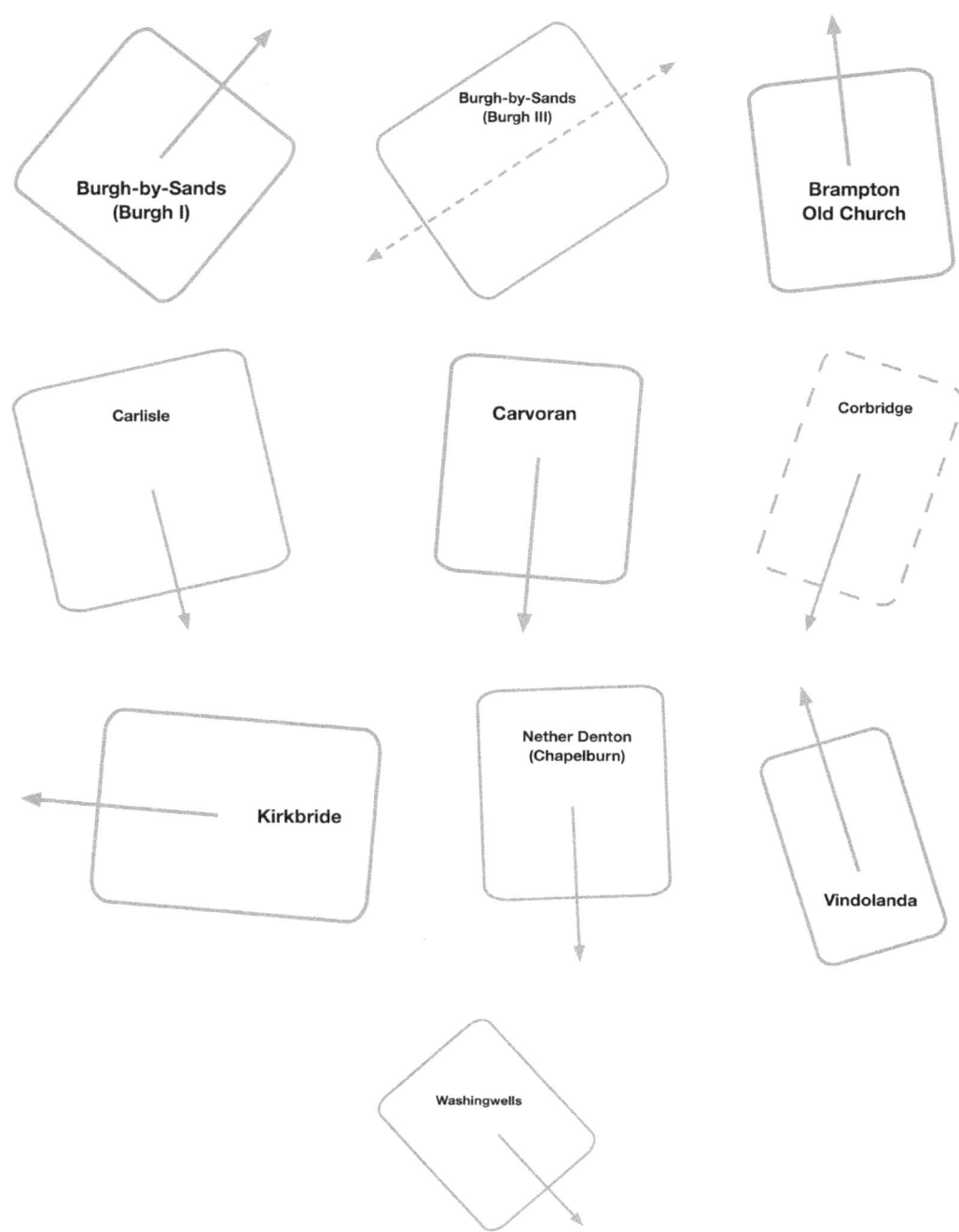

Figure 6.17. Orientation of the Stanegate forts.

should face the general direction which the enemy is thought to be in, so the Roman sites may not have been physically overlooking a specific site, although the archaeological evidence for the Flavian sites suggests otherwise. Harding (2017) has noted that there were few population centres in Late Iron Age North Britain, and Hingley (1992) has argued that society was based around family-style groupings, so it is increasingly difficult discern what, or where the enemy is.

As noted in the *Iron Age Scotland: ScARF Panel Report* (2012a), indigenous fortifications can be sub-divided into different types of forts as well as enclosed settlements. The panel notes that site registers (such as Canmore), classify all

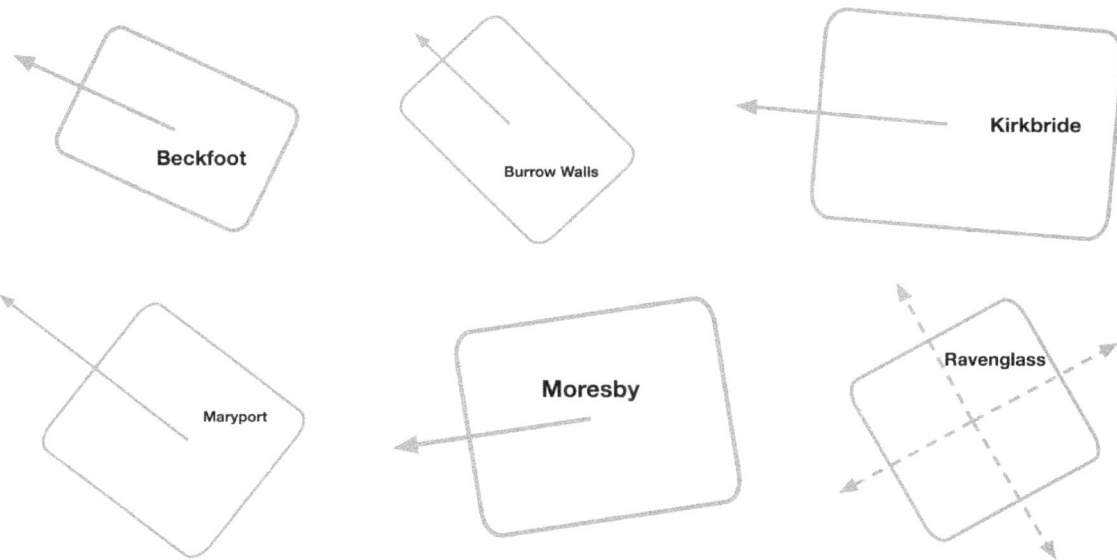

Figure 6.18. Orientation of Cumbrian coastal forts.

sites as an enclosure or hillfort, when there should be more distinctions between the different types. Grouping all sites in this way can lead to wrong assumptions about dating; in reality apparently, similar sites may be thousands of years apart in occupation. Without excavation and recovery of datable artefacts or materials, it is difficult to date the foundation of an indigenous site, something which applies to the hillforts facing the Roman sites covered here. For this research, I will use the term hillfort, and include promontory forts within this categorisation. Scholars of the Late Iron Age debate the function of hillforts, and question whether or not their primary role was defensive or militaristic, particularly given that some indigenous sites are lightly defended, such as some of those in Southern England (Ralston 2006:10; see also Harding 2017). Hillforts are interpreted as practical or symbolic expressions of the power of one or a group of individuals, able to order the construction of these large and complex sites, although some still argue that physical violence and security was a major influence in construction of hillforts (Ralston 2006:10-11). Although their purpose appears to be defensive or military, their relationship with the nearby Roman sites, and whether the occupants were seen as the 'enemy', remains unclear due to a lack of excavation and datable finds.

Only 1% of the total fortifications examined in this research were facing indigenous hillforts. A further 17% may have been facing these, but the orientation of the site was undetermined, and the orientation of a further 4% was unknown. 78% of fortifications are not facing indigenous sites. Four sites face unexplored earthworks (Ardoch fort, Bertha, Cargill fort, and Stracathro camp), while two face cairns (Fendoch, and Logie Durno), two towards cropmarks (Cardean, and Cargill fortlet), and one camp faces a group of souterrains (Inverquharity). Further archaeological investigations of these cropmarks and earthworks may reveal what these sites are, and whether they are related to or are contemporaneous with the Roman fortifications. Although the indigenous sites mentioned here are undated, these types of structures are thought to have been in use long before the Roman invasion of Britain, with evidence from Roman sites such as Kintore and Cramond indicating that the fortifications were themselves constructed on top of earlier indigenous settlements (Alexander 1996; Cook and Dunbar 2008; Cook, Dunbar, and Heawood 2009). As the work at both sites has indicated, there may have been more of an indigenous presence near these than acknowledged, and yet to be discovered. Woolliscroft & Hoffmann have demonstrated the benefits of such landscape surveys, with the latter having undertaken such work in the surroundings of the fort at Cardean, although most of these sites remain undated (2001a; 2001b; 2009). Toolis (2003; 2015; 2021) has undertaken studies of the Iron Age in the southwest of Scotland, and has come to the same, broad conclusion, that there was significantly more activity in this period, than has traditionally been recognised.

Few of the indigenous sites facing Roman fortifications have been excavated, and those which have, do not indicate occupation contemporaneous with the Flavian period. This is not to say that all indigenous forts were unoccupied during this time, as Traprain Law, Burnswark, and Birnie have both revealed evidence of contact or exchange with the Empire (e.g. J. Curle 1932; N. M.

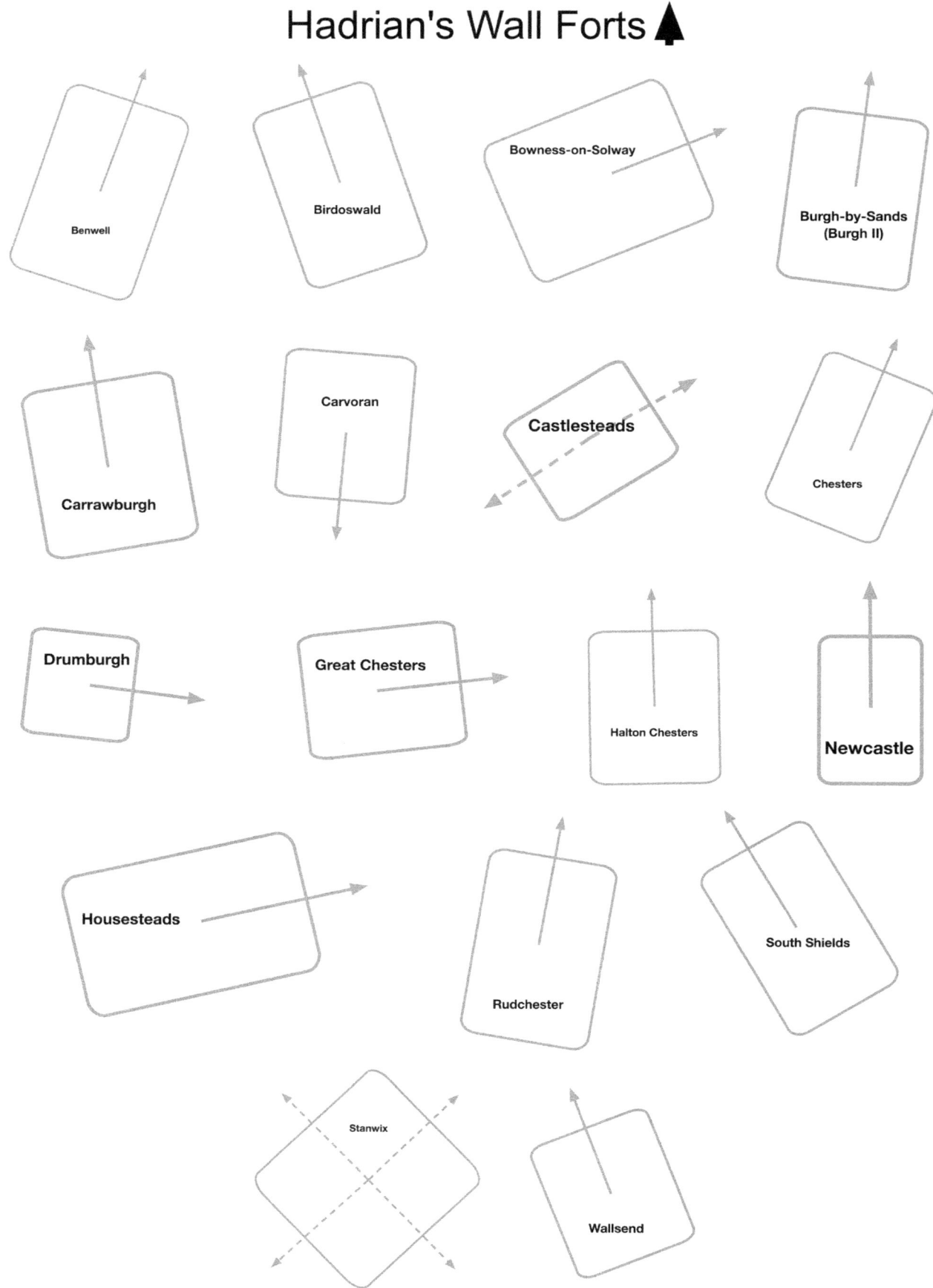

Figure 6.19. Orientation of Hadrian's Wall forts.

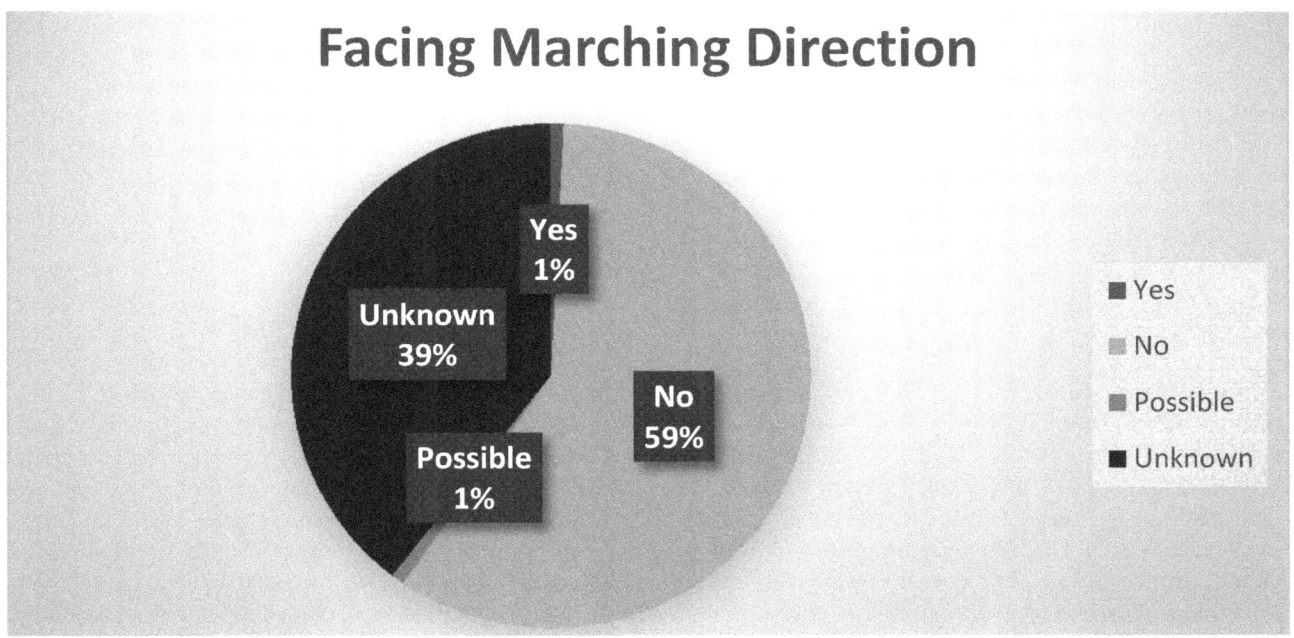

Figure 6.20. Percentage of fortifications facing presumed direction of advance.

M. Holmes 2006a; Hunter and Painter 2013). Curiously, most of the indigenous forts facing the Roman sites are very small, mainly oval, and all less than 0.4ha in size. It remains possible that some of them were occupied and were perceived to pose a threat to the Roman military; only further excavation and recovery of datable artefacts or materials will answer this question. The evidence indicates that the Roman army rarely constructed its fortifications to face indigenous sites and when they did so these seem likely to have been unoccupied, although perhaps the Romans thought the re-occupation of these forts by an indigenous force would pose a security risk, or that they simply indicated the most likely direction of any enemy threat.

The third major criterion for determining fortification orientation, according to the classical writers, was for the Roman site to face the direction of advance. For this research, I assume that the route of an adjacent Roman road would determine this direction, or at least provide a good indication, given that the construction of the fortification may pre-date the road. Out of the 124 Roman sites examined, only two sites, the forts at Bertha and Ardoch are orientated along a Roman road, although the former faces the crossing over the River Tay and the latter faces a short stretch of road before it crosses over the River Knaick and alters direction. Figure 6.20[10] shows the percentage of sites which are orientated in the northerly direction, into which the army may have been advancing. Excluding the towers (all of which are located alongside Roman roads), 33 camps, 20 forts and 6 fortlets were all located within 2km of Roman roads. As Bishop (2014:17) notes, the Romans would not have constructed roads as fast as they advanced, and instead must have used pre-existing routes used by the local populations, later formalising/widened these through construction. Maxwell (1980) also notes that they have constructed some sites to guard routes before they constructed roads, but these fell out of use before they are formalised and metalled.

While there is little evidence that fortifications were orientated in the direction of advance, the importance of controlling movement though a landscape, revealed previously, means it is worth considering a more complex relationship between fortifications, orientation and route networks. Incidentally, as Table 4 shows, numerous fortifications are facing towards the water, and this suggests such positioning was deliberate, with those approaching the fortification, disembarking from a vessel, would approach the *porta praetoria*, which, in some instances may have been elaborately decorated as noted previously.

Table 4. Breakdown of Flavian fortifications which are facing waterways.

Facing Water	No	Possible	Unknown	Yes	Total
Camps	10	22	25	0	57
Fortress	0	0	0	1	1
Forts	10	1	9	17	37
Fortlets	1	0	2	1	4
TOTAL	21	23	36	19	99

---

[10] The sites which are possibly facing marching direction are those where the orientation has been calculated as being in one of two directions. The sites where orientation is not known are the confirmed sites in this chart.

Facing the Enemy?

6.5. Summary

Fortifications are not generally orientated to face east, the enemy, or the direction of advance. In fact, the instances of this do not seem to exceed the statistical chance of them facing these ways, even if no rule was being followed. Few sites face the 'enemy' or indigenous sites, most of which are undated or do not date to the early Roman period, and they would have been too small to pose any sort of threat to the military. If there was a local indigenous threat, it seems likely that fortifications would be more concentrated in certain areas, rather than the widespread of sites which seem to indicate consolidation of the area. Woolliscroft and Hoffmann (2009:98), state that they has identified 'thousands' of Iron Age sites, with 270 alone identified within 10 kilometres of Inchtuthil, however as these are unrecorded on Canmore, and ultimately remain undated, these results are not included here, and there needs to be caution when associating the positioning of the fortress with these indigenous sites. Previously, I set out some of the arguments relating to the dating of Iron Age sites, namely a lack of datable artefacts and a firm chronological framework to fit these into, and the tendency to group Late Iron Age sites together when they may have been occupied at any time in a thousand year period, without firm dating of these sites it is not possible to say if they were occupied at the same time as the Flavian incursion was happening in the north; as the ScARF Iron Age paper has stated, we need a reappraisal of the LIA in Scotland.

The orientation of particular fortifications may have supported the army to control movement through the landscape. Not only is the orientation a powerful symbol of the army, but if the *porta praetoria* was seen as the more significant entrance, then more attention and resources may have been prioritised for this gate. While these entrances in legionary fortresses (and possibly forts) had features of monumentality (Bishop 2014), such as inscriptions and statues, it is unknown if these existed on turf and timber forts as found in Flavian Scotland, or on the camps. If such features did not exist, then the *porta praetoria* would only have been key as the shortest route to the *principia*, but it seems likely that they would have preferred high ranking visitors, and perhaps non-Romans (who would no doubt be impressed and intimidated) to use the main entrance. Hanson and Maxwell (1986:84) comment that the Military Way, on the Antonine Wall, passes through forts using the minor gateways; this is not replicated in Flavian Scotland, with most roads bypassing the fort, such as at Ardoch. However, this could again be a false interpretation based on a lack of evidence. It requires much more research on and knowledge of the road network before we can make assumptions about the relationship between roads and fortifications. This is discussed further in the next chapter.

Figure 6.21. Visibility (shaded area) and orientation from Crawford fort.

In conclusion, fortifications in the Flavian period, and also later periods, in Scotland, are positioned and orientated in directions which help them control the landscape and the movement of people. For example, Crawford (Figure 6.21) is facing southeast, down one valley, but is positioned where another valley, to the east, joins it, and beyond this is a non-Roman fort, demonstrating the control of these valleys, and those moving along them. Fortifications, as a general rule, are not orientated in the direction specified in the classical texts, and are more likely to be positioned to control movement through the landscape. Some fortifications face specific features, particularly river crossings and the road network, but again this is about controlling the wider area by funnelling traffic past or near the fortification to exert control over the indigenous population.

7

Interconnectivity

Marching camps were sited on routes of advance. Not all camps represent the movement of infantry or land-based forces, and perhaps others could have been occupied by marines from the fleet or delineate supply bases in use for particular campaigns at points where land and sea troops would meet...

(R. H. Jones 2011:35)

It is arguable whether or not we know less about either the road network in Roman period Scotland, or the coastal and river networks, but the above quote from Jones helps to understand the likely relationship between fortifications and the coastal and river networks. Using the sea and rivers to navigate by and to facilitate movement (either by following the route of a river, or by sailing along it), may have led to quicker movement of troops and goods than if undertaken using a road network, although the former may have been hazardous and slower in certain conditions and times of the year, while the latter may not have existed in newly occupied territories. Although there is little direct archaeological evidence associated with Roman usage of waterways in Scotland, the circumstantial evidence suggests otherwise; many Flavian period fortifications are located on the coast (usually at the entrance to rivers, upstream of which there are invariably other fortifications), or located on the major river networks and their tributaries, or even at the upper tidal reaches of these. While I am not suggesting that vessels were sailing between these sites, although this would certainly have been possible in some locations, the river valleys could have been used to aid navigation between fortifications. As Evans et al. (2010) suggest, in relation to Wales, the Romans must have made use of the waterways for movement because of the positioning of fortifications on rivers and headlands, something which can also be observed in Scotland.

Most of Scotland was new territory to the Roman army when they began their large-scale invasion in the 1st century, and if the accounts by Tacitus are accurate, *Caledonia* was a hostile land. The army would have aimed to secure new territories quickly and efficiently through the establishment of secure lines for supply and troop movements; transport routes in a new territory would have been basic, and unlikely to have the capacity to transport significant numbers of soldiers, or carts, mules and oxen. The circumstantial evidence for usage of waterways in Scotland includes accounts by Tacitus along with archaeological artefacts such as an anchor and an oar, although the latter are undated; this latter group will be discussed in later chapters. It is important not to discount this information because the evidence from elsewhere in Britain, and on the continent, demonstrates that the army frequently used the coast and waterways for movement and for defence; the evidence from both Wales and the Dutch frontier is that roads follow river valleys, demonstrating that these networks are intertwined.

In this chapter, I begin with separate summaries of what is known about the road and river networks in 1st century Scotland. Focussing on the waterways, I detail the relevant Roman period texts which cover usage of rivers and the Roman navy, before looking at one particular antiquarian text which has relevance for the later analysis of river networks in Scotland. In reappraising the evidence for coastal usage and activity by the Roman army, I also note some of the similarities in arrangements with fortifications from elsewhere in the Empire. This analysis lends weight to the argument that some camps, particularly those on the coast, may have been used by the military as supply bases, or locations where resources could be brought in by sea and moved further inland. While it is challenging to prove that the Romans were using coastal and river sites in this way, by re-assessing the archaeological evidence for individual sites, the role and function of these as both individual fortifications, their contribution to a wider network, may be postulated.

7.1. Road Networks

...published works, usually because of their small scale, depict a universal and oversimplified picture of the road network in Wales.

Silvester 2009 93

Although the above statement was written regarding Roman Wales, it is one which can equally apply to Scotland; knowledge of the overall road network in the north is fragmented and limited. The capacity to interconnect sites may be linked to considerations on where to locate a fortification or the direction to orientate it in. Interconnecting sites through road, as well as coastal and river networks, has been demonstrated on other Roman frontiers, although our limited knowledge of such networks in Scotland makes it difficult to evaluate the extent of interconnectivity between the fortifications, although there is some evidence that some sites were not connected to the road network, limiting the supply to, and functionality of the garrison, and their ability to respond quickly when needed. This section critically assesses our knowledge of this network in Scotland, and compares this with the information from other frontiers, in particular

Wales which was initially occupied prior to Agricola's activities in Scotland.

A good road network would ensure the quick and efficient movement of troops and supplies, getting them to where they need to be. To date, there has been limited modern analysis of the road network in Scotland (Bishop 2014), and analysis which has been undertaken has not used modern technologies or data (such as LiDAR). Elsewhere in Britain, there has been some recent analysis of the road network using LiDAR, such as Gethin and Toller (2014) as well as modelling of movement in the Roman period in England (Franconi and Green 2019), although this has not generally been undertaken in Scotland. Road networks appear to vary in quality, with Silvester (2009) noting a difference in the quality of the roads in upland and lowland Wales, something also seen in Scotland, where Woolliscroft & Hoffmann (2006; Woolliscroft 2007) have identified sections of road which appear to be of a lesser quality than elsewhere. That design differences were commonplace is apparent from a letter by Pliny (Letters 2.17, H. Davies 2002:19) who describes a section of road on the route to Ostia in Italy. Pliny writes that the road has sandy sections, making coach travel on the route difficult, a somewhat different image to the traditional cobbled Roman road, even near Rome itself. Symonds (2018) suggests that this was similar to the situation in Scotland, that many roads were unmetalled and, therefore, difficult to use. Some studies have explored this interconnectivity, particularly those covering forts on the Dutch *limes*, and to a more limited extent on the Antonine Wall. This is another type of analysis which has not been applied to Roman fortifications in the rest of Scotland, and thus presents a good research opportunity for this study, and although there is a lack of accurate data on these routes in Scotland, it is still necessary to summarise our knowledge since roads would have been integral to not only moving the army around, but potentially to moving other traffic through Roman territory on a prescribed route.

There are several classical texts which either refer to the road network, or places they interlinked with; none of these refer to North Britain in any depth, although there are mentions of road maintenance in the Vindolanda tablets which date to immediately after the Flavian period (Bowman and Thomas 1983). Some of these sources, such as the *Ravenna Cosmography* and the *Antonine Itinerary*, relate to later periods, but suggest the existence of an earlier road network. The cartographic source which covers North Britain, and beyond, is *Ptolemy's Geography*, an atlas and treatise on cartography which details parts of the known world, describing local tribes and customs. Britain is covered in Book II, and although there is no map, the cartographic data has subsequently been used to produce plans, including some of *Britannia*, with Scotland turned on its side from later translations; Strang (1997) gives a detailed summary of the work on Ptolemy's *Geography*, particularly those sections covering Scotland, including works by Chalmers (1807), Richmond (1922), Tierney (1959), Rivet and Smith (1981), Breeze (1987), and Mann (1992).

It was not until the 20th century that the first serious attempts to identify and understand the road network in Britain appeared, with Codrington's *Roman Roads in Britain* (1918; 1928) being one of the first. Codrington does not appear to have visited all the sections of road which he writes about, probably because this was a mammoth task. Instead, he relies on the Roman road routes detailed on Ordnance Survey (OS) maps (1928:173). As outlined earlier, many of the OS routes marked as Roman roads in Scotland are an indirect result of the 18th century forgery, *de situ Britanniae* (Bertram 1809), and are therefore not always accurate. Codrington also makes the mistake of assuming the road network in Scotland is simple and that the roads are all part of a main arterial route, Ermine Street, and branches off of this, whereas it is much more complex, and the roads are not all of a single period. Margary (1957; 1967) wrote the most influential publication on the Roman road network in Britain which has been reissued several times. Margary attempted to catalogue all known roads in Britain, creating a numbering system still in use today. Like Codrington, Margary does not cover the road network in Scotland in any depth, dedicating only 50 pages out of 530 in the 1967 edition to these sections. Despite this, the book is still considered to be the foremost authority on roads in Britain and Scotland.

Building on the work of Margary, Davies (2002) contributes significantly to understanding the road network in Britain. Having had a career in surveying and transport networks, Davies brings a fresh approach to the field. At the beginning of his book, he specifies that his aim is not to produce a guide to Roman roads, but to present an analysis from an engineering point of view. Not only does he investigate the design and structure of the roads, but he also examines the ancillary elements of the network, such as river crossings and the overall development of roads, but again, like other writers, there is little coverage beyond Hadrian's Wall.

Silvester and Toller, who examine the road network in Wales have written that "published works, usually because of their small scale, depict a universal and oversimplified picture of the road network in Wales" (2009:93), a statement which can equally apply to Scotland. They write that examination of the road network is a neglected area of research, and acknowledge that little is known about ancillary features, such as milestones and bridges. Unlike in Scotland, several examples of Roman river crossings are identifiable (2009:97), and they conclude that in piecing together as much of the network in Wales as possible, roads frequently follow the river valleys.

Bishop (2014), in *The Secret History of the Roman Roads of Britain*, acknowledges previous work on the planning, surveying, and cataloguing of roads, but instead wants to provide an insight into the origins and destination of roads; where they came from, where they are going to, and why they did this. Bishop's central argument is that many of the roads in new territories existed in some form before the arrival of the Romans, who subsequently adopted and adapted these routes. He argues that these were already going between key locations in the landscape, the same places which the Romans wanted to go, and that they merely straightened and metalled sections of these pre-existing trackways. Bishop details the survival of Roman roads into the medieval period where there are surviving accounts of these routes continuing to be used, something which Haldane (1995; 2011) covers to a lesser extent by charting development of drove roads in Scotland, while Taylor (1996) charts the Scottish military roads, many of which are identified or misidentified as having Roman origins. Bishop writes that there is a lack of modern interpretation of the evidence concerning Roman roads and their pre-Roman origins, despite advances in technology. His book ends with a useful analysis of medieval roads and their relationship to Roman sites in northeast England, and Southeast Scotland (2014:127, 165). This publication is a useful reminder of the complexities of the Roman road network, and how little we understand it, particularly in the post-Roman periods.

To date, there has been limited application of GIS, remote sensing and local archaeological data to the topographical and spatial analysis of Roman frontiers, although it is a growing area of research. Komoroczy and Vlach (2009) surveyed the military invasion of barbarian territories during the Marcomannic Wars, measuring potential routes between legionary sites at *Carnuntum*, *Vindobono* and a fort at Musov-Hradisko, concluding that the Roman road ran along the lower part of the River Morava, showing the likely route of advance into Marcomannic tribal territory. More recently, various studies into road networks on other Roman frontiers has been published in *Finding the Limits of the Limes* (Verhagen, Joyce, and Groenhuijzen 2019), which is a collection of GIS-related studies with an emphasis on the Dutch *limes*. Within this volume are various papers utilising GIS modelling of road networks, including pathways and movement networks. Parcero-Oubiña et al (2019:291) follows this approach, while De Soto (2019:271) applies it to Roman transport and movement on the frontiers. To date, there is only one comparable studies, utilising GIS and various analytical techniques, such as Low Cost Path analysis, for the road network in Scotland (J. Lewis 2020). Further such analysis would provide significant insight into the movement of troops through the landscape and indicate what routes they were taking.

7.2. River Networks

The sea (and to a lesser extent the major rivers) and their potential for transport and supply are fundamental to the understanding of Roman Scotland.
(ScARF 2012a:24)

Previously, I showed that in Scotland, Flavian fortifications are almost always positioned in a location which enables them to exert control of an area, usually through the visible command of valleys. Fortifications located on the coast, not only had oversight their section of the sea, but invariably controlled access to the river networks, along which are usually other Roman military structures. This suggests a close relationship between fortifications, the coast, and waterways; a relationship which has also been observed in Wales (Evans et al. 2010) where there has been a corelation noted, between the rivers, valleys, and the road network (Silvester and Toller 2009). But in Scotland, knowledge of the network of roads is complex, with various undated and fragmentary remains, and often it is not clear if these are Roman or medieval in origin (Bishop 2014).

In the next section, I detail the account by Tacitus which tells us that Agricola made use of the coastal network, and as will be outlined in this chapter, there is some limited archaeological activity of shipping on rivers in Scotland. By re-assessing these pieces of evidence together, along with other historical accounts, we may be able to learn more about the relationship between the 1st century military, and their use of the coastal and river networks. To date, there have been no significant attempts to understand the relationship between Romans and waterways in Scotland, something recognised by the *ScARF: The Roman Presence* (2012a). While there has been little work examining water levels on inland rivers in the Roman period in Scotland, and the research which has been done, has focussed on the sea level on the Firth of Forth (e.g. Hannon 2018), so it is unknown which fortifications in the rest of Scotland could have been reached by using the rivers themselves. We do know that rivers could not have been used as transportation networks for every fortification, but the evidence from Wales (Burnham and Davies 2010), and to a lesser extent Spain (Costa-Garcia 2018), suggests that roads follow the river valleys.

Watercourses have undoubtedly played a significant role in facilitating the expansion of the Roman Empire, something seen on other frontiers, such as the *limes* in Germany (e.g. Sommer 2009) which makes use of rivers including the Donau, Iller, and Rhine. Research into the Dutch river frontier has focussed on shipping (e.g. Jansma and Morel 2007), harbours (e.g. Polak and Wynia 1991; Driessen 2009), as well as interregional transport (Domínguez-Delmás et al. 2014; Groenhuijzen and Verhagen 2015). There is much more opportunity for river transport in the Netherlands due to the wide network of Rhine distributaries, making it even more essential as it is the only way to get around, but there are some similarities between this frontier and the frontier-zone in Scotland. In Scotland, academics researching connectivity have focused on roads and not watercourses, despite comment from Tacitus that coastal routes and rivers were a pivotal part of the Flavian invasion, particularly for supplying the army. Woolliscroft and Hoffman (2006) briefly examine the River Tay in relation to key fortifications on the Gask Ridge, but this is the exception.

The archaeological data and dating classification for the non-Flavian sites, have been extracted from Canmore, and

I have taken data relating to the size of the camps from Jones (2011); those sites which are listed on Canmore as possibly being Roman, but which Jones does not cover in her study, are not included here. The comparative images which are presented in this section, have been compiled using a DEM, with markers for the Roman sites also included. The sites which have been classed as unconfirmed and undated, have either been extracted from Canmore or from Sibbald (1707). The latter details the locations by name, and where these sites have an existing listing in Canmore, I have used those NGR coordinates, otherwise a location matching Sibbald's description is used. For example, if Dunbar is mentioned, a general NGR has been taken from the centre of this urban location; given the vagueness of Sibbald's details, these co-ordinates may not accurately reflect the location he was discussing.

7.3. Classical Texts: Waterways

...[in] his sixth year in post, he enveloped the states situated beyond the Bodotria [Forth]. Because there were fears that all the peoples on the further side might rise and the land routes be threatened by an enemy army, Agricola reconnoitred the harbours with the fleet. It had been brought in by Agricola for the first time to form part of his forces... as it followed along: the war was being pushed forward simultaneously by land and sea...

Tacitus *Agricola* 25

The main source of literary evidence relating to military use of coastal and waterways is the *Agricola*, where Tacitus repeatedly demonstrates the importance of using the sea and Firths to give the military a strategic advantage, even claiming that Agricola was the first to use the fleet to undertake reconnaissance of the enemy.

... long baggage trains were vulnerable to surprise, the sea, he felt, provided a better route. It was easily controlled and inaccessible to enemy intelligence. Besides, arrival by sea would mean an earlier start to the campaign and simultaneous transportation of Roman infantry and supplies. Cavalry and infantry could be taken upriver from the coast and landed intact in mid-Germany.

Tacitus, *Annals* 2:5

Tacitus further demonstrates that the use of the sea and rivers was an effective method of moving troops and supplies on the continent by Germanicus, and it seems reasonable to assume that such an approach was replicated by Agricola in his campaigns in north *Britannia*, particularly if there was a lack of established roads to aid movement on land. As noted previously, water levels would have been higher in 1st century Scotland than they are now, and it is quite possible that sea-going vessels could have reached a number of sites inland. Today, the River Forth is navigable as far inland as Stirling, and Perth is reachable on the River Tay, and flat bottomed vessels could potentially have reached much further inland. For those rivers which were not navigable, it would have been possible to follow the river valley from the mouth far inland where fortifications were located.

7.4. The Antiquarian Account

Many of the antiquarian texts on Scotland detail various sites with visible Roman remains, or which are alleged to have been founded during the period. While some of these have their origins in the forgery, *de situ Britanniae*, other accounts may be based on genuine evidence since lost. These works can offer a genuine insight into Roman activity or fortifications which have subsequently been lost. One such example is by Sir Robert Sibbald's (1707), and whose work contains claims about the Roman origins of various locations on the coast in southern Scotland, most of which do not appear to have been taken from *de situ Britanniae* (Bertram 1809). It is possible that some of his sources may have had knowledge of Roman Scotland which has since been lost, such as the correspondence between Sibbald and Dr Irvine which describes the western terminus of the Antonine Wall, with Irvine claiming to have seen additional forts at Dumbuck Hill and Dumbarton (Sibbald 1707:28), and implying that the Wall may have continued to these sites.

Sibbald describes several sites along the south shore of the Firth of Forth (see Figure 7.3) as well as on the Clyde and Solway coasts, which he thought may be Roman or have been active during the period. He claimed this information was partly based on the remains of buildings and other artefacts, but also based on various Roman sources, particularly the works by Ptolemy (*Table of Albion*) and the *Notitia Dignitatum* (Sibbald 1707:31-35). Although there are a number of coastal sites which are undated and unconfirmed, many of these (along with the locations mentioned by Sibbald) have yielded some evidence of Roman activity, such as at Ayr where Sibbald notes Roman remains which have only recently been rediscovered, and confirmed as a camp (Arabaolaza 2019). Therefore, we should not necessarily dismiss the evidence of Sibbald, or other early antiquarians out of hand. Rather, the findings of my research, along with other archaeological evidence, can facilitate a better-informed reappraisal of these sites, while acknowledging the difficulties in dating them. These findings are detailed in the analysis of Scotland's river networks below.

7.5. Analysis: Fortifications and Roads

A systematic overview of the road network in Scotland, considering all lines claimed as Roman, from aerial and ground survey and excavation evidence, is required. This should also consider the ... study of the post-Roman history and influence on known roads, and of any pre-Roman antecedents. Such an assessment would allow targeted aerial and field survey then to attempt to fill gaps.

ScARF 2012:23

The importance of the connection between fortifications, roads, the coast, and rivers has previously been outlined; use of these ensures both quick and efficient movement of soldiers and supplies, but, as has been observed on other frontiers, can also aid in the control of an area. This research shows that many fortifications were constructed next to roads, but we cannot assume that these were contemporary with each other; the fortification may have been constructed before the road, with the purpose of controlling an indigenous movement route or settlement. Maxwell and Hanson (1986) and further developed by the former (2015), argue that there are some fortifications which were built before roads were constructed, and further argue that these often remained unconstructed because the Roman occupation was so brief. Without a reappraisal of the road network, it is not possible to clarify the relationship between many fortifications and the network, or how many sites were disconnected from this. A summary of the site data can be found in Appendix Two.

65% of the 124 Flavian sites examined for this section of the research were located within 1 Roman mile (or 1,481 metres) of a road. The analysis is skewed by towers which were constructed on either side of the Gask Ridge road, and had a symbiotic relationship with this. Removing the towers from the results indicates that 58% or 62 fortifications, were constructed near a Roman road. These figures can further be broken down into 23 forts, 33 camps and seven fortlets near a road; in contrast, nine forts, 32 camps and one fortlet were not located near the network. This suggests that most camps are not interlinked by roads. While there are many gaps in our knowledge of the road network of Roman Scotland, it does appear that the more permanent structures, especially forts, are connected to these networks (assuming they were occupied long enough). We can say the same for the fortlets, which are normally positioned alongside roads at key strategic locations, such as river crossings and would have needed access to a transport route. Half of the Flavian camps are located next to roads, and these could have functioned as construction bases for the network, and could suggest that these fortifications were not occupied on a short-term basis. North of Inverquharity, and in particular in respect of the camps between Stracathro and Bellie, no roads have been confirmed, possibly indicating that the Romans were not in the area long enough to construct formal routes. In summary, except for Ardoch and Bertha forts, fortifications did not face along a road, although they are frequently located next to them.

The legionary fortress at Inchtuthil is orientated southwards, towards the river (if it flowed to the south of the peninsula in the Roman period); no research has been undertaken into the position of the River Tay in previous years. While we can see some of the road to the southeast, no roads are traceable closer to the fortress, so it is not possible to speculate if there was a relationship between these. While the orientation of the forts do not appear to follow any set pattern, most of the these are located in positions which allow them to control movement along valleys, with some sites possibly having control of river crossings, such as at Cargill and Glenlochar. Whereas the forts at Cappuck, Cargill, Castledykes, Crawford, Dalginross, Drumquhassle, and Easter Happrew, are all facing along river valleys, allowing them to control the landscape and movement along it. Of particular note are the forts at Camelon, which could possibly have been located on the coast if sea levels in the Roman period were higher, as Hannon (2018) postulates. Out of the fortlets, the entrances of Castle Greg, Glenbank, and Kaims Castle, face onto road. Glenbank is the only one of these near a river, although the road does not appear to cross it. The evidence suggests that one of the roles of fortlets (where there are no river crossings) was to control movement along the road, with soldiers presumably monitoring traffic. The views from camps appear to be wider ranging than from forts. Some sites, such as Abernethy, Kirkhouse and Ward Law have almost complete views of the surrounding areas, which suggests that they are positioned in these locations to overlook and control the landscape. For Abernethy this would include the Firth of Tay, and for Ward Law, the Solway Firth. This also suggests that these were not temporary encampments used only for a couple of nights. Views are more restrictive at Dalginross and Oakwood, but both sites are located in valleys which suggest that their purpose may have been to control movement through this landscape.

7.6. Analysis: Coastal and River Networks

95% (or 118) of the 124 Flavian fortifications examined for this section, are located within a Roman mile of water (see Table 5), and these figures includes five additional sites (Drumquhassle, Easter Happrew, and Fendoch forts, as well as Abernethy and Stracathro camps) which are more than one, but less than two Roman miles (under 2.5 kilometres) from a watercourse. All of the Flavian forts and camps in Scotland, were located near water, although occasionally these were next to smaller rivers or large streams (which may have had a larger flow 2,000 years ago), and would have provided a source of freshwater for drinking and food production, and also supplying the rest of the fortification with flushing latrines, industrial workings, and bathhouses for those sites which were occupied long enough to need such support. Six sites (one fortlet and five towers), the remaining 5% and which are located further from water sources were more likely located out of necessity as they are positioned alongside the main road running through Perthshire, between the forts of Ardoch, Strageath and then along the Gask Ridge.

Table 5. Breakdown of Flavian fortifications which are constructed near water.

Near Water	No	Yes	Total
Camps	5	52	57
Fortress	0	1	1
Forts	22	15	37
Fortlets	3	1	4
TOTAL	30	69	99

Facing the Enemy?

Many of the fortifications are located on different stretches of the same river, their tributaries or at the confluences of both, and it appears a watercourse interconnects many of the sites. Therefore, the use of watercourses for transport and navigation cannot be ruled out, given the positioning of most sites alongside major rivers.

7.7. Analysis: River Crossings

Crossing watercourses was both inevitable and essential for the army, particularly during the initial invasion, and it is likely that a formal infrastructure (such as bridges and milestones) were not built until the area was secure. It is therefore challenging to identify crossing points in the archaeological record, which is a key reason why we know little about the road network in Scotland and, in turn, that makes it challenging to estimate the position of other crossing points. In some locations, such as the Clyde valley where the road is known, it is possible to estimate where a road would have crossed streams and rivers, but to date there has been very little attempt to actually identify such crossing points on the road network.

Fords were vital when crossing rivers, especially in the post-Roman – pre-early modern periods before the widespread construction of bridges. An example of this comes from the ford at Drip, near Stirling, and which provided the main crossing point over the Forth-Clyde isthmus, this being the first fordable section of the River Forth, and therefore a key area to control throughout history. As fords were naturally occurring, they require no resources to construct or maintain them, whereas bridges would have been much more resource-intensive to construct and maintain, and are more likely to have been a rarity in Flavian Scotland, because of the limited time that the Roman army was in the north. Hanson (pers. comm.) has suggested that fortifications could be orientated to face crossings. For those sites where the crossing point, road, and orientation are known, fortifications are not facing. As noted previously, the one exception to this is the fort at Bertha which does appear to be facing the crossing over the River Tay, although the caveat here is that the fording point or bridge location, is unconfirmed, and I examine this in more depth later.

7.8. Scotland's River Networks

In this section, I undertake a systematic area-based approach to sites located on the coast, and on the river networks. This includes looking at the positioning of these sites in relation to the immediate area, and in the wider landscape, as well as using GIS to examine the interconnectivity between the fortifications. The river networks will be represented by a simplified diagram, and where there are hypothesised additional sites, such as those proposed by Sibbald, I have added these to the diagrams and analysed the results.

7.8.1. River Tweed

With datable evidence indicating Carlisle was occupied by 72/73 CE (Shotter 2001; Zant 2009:413), there is a possibility that early military activity may have extended into southern Scotland (Hanson 1991:61-64). On the opposite side of the country, beyond Newstead, evidence of early Roman occupation is less certain. Dere Street, the main Roman road through the area is on a general north-south trajectory, with most fortifications located alongside it. Out of these, only the fort and several camps at Newstead, as well as the fortification at Cappuck, have Flavian origins. Instead, the Flavian fortifications are more concentrated on an east-west trajectory, with no known or obvious land route to connect them; this is demonstrated in Figure 7.1. Given the importance of this route (which

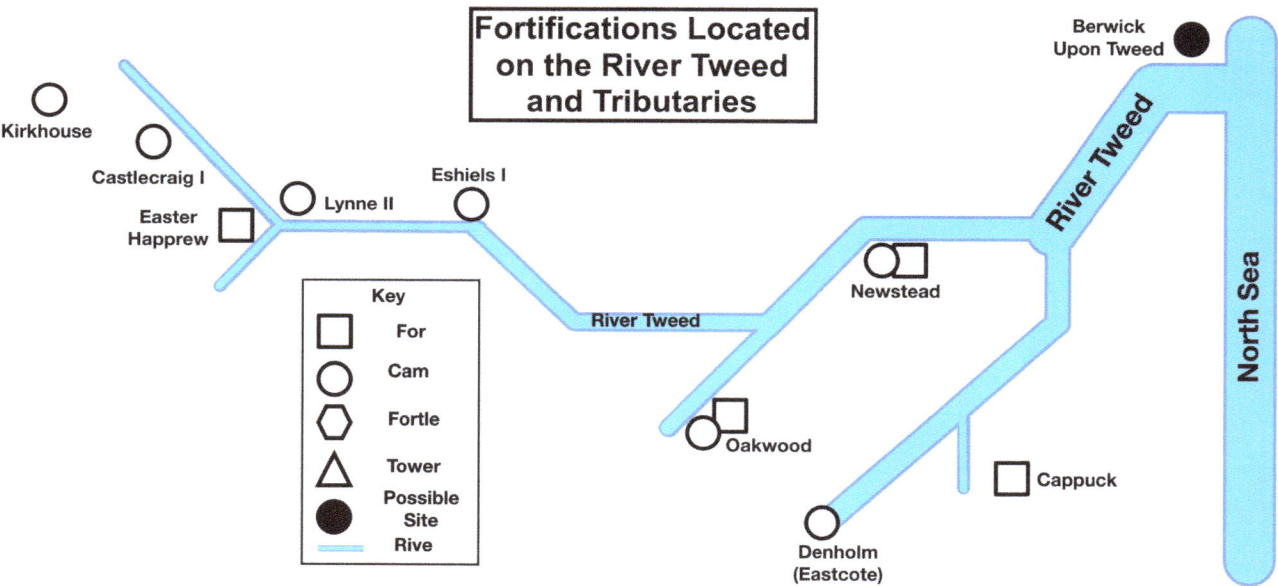

Figure 7.1. Fortifications on the River Tweed.

is essential in the post-Flavian period), it seems likely that some undated sites have Flavian origins. The eastern section of the River Tweed contains few confirmed Roman encampments, while no Roman military installations have been confirmed at Berwick, although the Northumberland Sites and Monuments Record has five potential sites listed which have been identified through cropmarks. These are described as sub-rectangular or curvilinear, which indicates that they are less likely to be Roman. One site (Monument No. 6554), originally identified from the air by St Joseph, has a more complex history.

Located on a rise and overlooking the surrounding area, the site has a double ditch on the east side with rounded corners; St Joseph (1951:56) initially claimed a fragment of excavated pottery to be Antonine, but a decade later revised his opinion, on seeing further cropmarks, describing the ditches as "an irregular circle rather than a rectangle" (St Joseph 1961b:120-121), adding that even though Roman pottery had been uncovered, he suspected the site to be Romano-British. In my reappraisal of the evidence, the aerial photographs are inconclusive, and the site does not show up in LiDAR analysis of the area. The location on the southern side of the River Tweed (like many of the confirmed Roman encampments) would be ideal for a small installation to watch over the surrounding area, although it is a mile from the river itself.

Further east, along the Tweed valley, are several undated fortifications: Norham, East Learmouth, Carham, Wooden Home Farm, and Maxton. The first three are located in England, and are therefore not examined in depth by Jones (R. H. Jones 2011). Table 6 contains a summary of the site details for these fortifications, and until further work is undertaken on those in the eastern section of the Tweed, it is not possible to claim which period these are from. However, Jones (ibid:103) puts forward the suggestion that Wooden Home Farm, given that it is not near other camps of a similar size, may indicate a site used by a large number of troops or to move supplies up the Tweed, potentially from an unidentified fortification near Berwick.

At the western end of the Tweed valley, there is only one camp (Innerleithen) between Newstead and Flavian period Easter Happrew, which is ascribed a tentative Antonine date because of similarities to the camp at Lyne I (R. H. Jones 2011:115). The only other site between the two forts (Newstead and Easter Happrew), is the camp at Eshiels, dated to the Flavian period because of its Stracathro-style gate. It is apparent from the locating of Eshiels, that there was a route east to west through the valley, and that there are either missing camps to the east of Eshiels, or that dating for Innerleithen needs revising. If Innerleithen was a Flavian camp, it may have been a long-term feature in the landscape, but only occupied when soldiers moving between the two forts needed a secure enclosure to stay in overnight.

While a stretch of road runs to the southwest of Newstead, none of the Flavian sites are connected to this (although this may be because the various sections of Road remain unidentified). Some of these sites are isolated and remote from other fortifications as well as the road, but are interconnected through tributaries of the River Tweed, and are around a day's march from one another. Given the positioning of Denholm, it could have been a secure base for overnight stops for moving troops, although where they may have been travelling to is not as clear. This camp could also have a relationship with the apparent Roman site or tower on Rubers Law (Murphy, Gittings, and Crow 2018). Regardless of what period these structures are from,

Table 6. Site details for fortifications on the River Tweed.

Site Name	Notes
Norham	Norham is a site of 0.5 hectares with good views around 800 metres downstream, although these are more limited in the opposite direction (St Joseph 1973:215; Welfare and Swan 1995:118).
East Learmouth	East Learmouth, is 5.5 miles along the river from Norham and is substantially larger at 13.6 hectares (St Joseph 1961b:121; 1973:216; Welfare and Swan 1995:95-96).
Carham	Carham was identified in the early 1960s, but limited cropmarks mean that it is not possible to either estimate the size, or confirm if it is likely to be Roman. Welfare and Swan note a local story of the Scottish army camping in the area in 1296 and suggest Carham is related to this (St. Joseph 1965:78; Welfare and Swan 1995:82).
Wooden Home Farm	Wooden Home Farm is estimated to enclose an area of 16 hectares (Maxwell & D. R. Wilson 1987:32), but reanalysis of aerial photographs by Jones indicate the site could have covered 55.3 hectares (R. H. Jones 2011:319).
Maxton	Maxton has only been photographed once, in 1964 (St Joseph 1965a:78), with Jones subsequently noting a lack of an entrance break in one side, and corners which are too regular, suggesting it may not be Roman (R. H. Jones 2011:337).
St Boswells (Mertoun Bridge)	St Boswells (Mertoun Bridge) where there are two, if not three camps, which are constructed within each other, with II and III using the defences of I to form their ramparts and ditches. The site is ascribed an Antonine date on Canmore, although there have been multiple phases of construction, and no finds to give a conclusive occupation period, so the camps could date to earlier or later periods.

they likely form part of an outer series of defences for the fortifications at Newstead, and further analysis of other sites may indicate whether the towers form part of a wider signalling network as covered earlier in this monograph.

Except for Eshiels (and Innerleithen), the other Flavian fortifications on the Tweed, Lyne and Tarf Waters are on the southern bank of the river which could be coincidental, or for practical reasons. In the eastern section, the fortifications which are undated are also on the southern banks of the various rivers, and this may have been for practical reasons. The aforementioned camps may therefore represent the initial stages of consolidation of the river as a linear barrier or border. It seems more likely that these were temporary bases established as forces moved along the river, occasionally meeting up and requiring a larger site such as at Wooden Home House.

7.8.2. Firth of Forth

This section re-examines the archaeological evidence for the fortifications which are located either directly on the Firth and River Forth, or on one of its tributaries (Figure 7.2). Only two forts, Inveresk and Cramond, are confirmed in the central area, while further west, the Antonine Wall, and there is a complete dearth of Flavian structures in the area to the north of the River Tweed and east of Dere Street. The traditional argument for this, is that they constructed no fortifications in the area because the Romans had a truce with the local tribe, or had bribed them, as evidenced through the Traprain Law hoard (Hunter and Painter 2013).

Elsewhere in Scotland, Flavian fortifications are located on the major rivers and their tributaries, but there are no such watercourses in this area. The largest river is the Tyne that runs from Midlothian northeast through East Lothian, but it much smaller than the Tweed. The Tyne, at Tyninghame, is one location (Figure 7.3) to which Sibbald ascribes a Roman date of origin,

> ...Ancient Sepulchres of stone are found in the neighbourhood, and yet the tyde coming in spreadeth a good way, and at this day, barks come in there.
>
> **(Sibbald 1707:33)**

The evidence which Sibbald puts forward for Tyninghame being Roman, as a series of ancient sepulchres, seems likely to be confused with the remains associated with St Baldred's Church and the earlier monastery (East Lothian Council HER: MEL1605) which is the oldest noted monument in the vicinity, however, no investigations have taken place to see if there is an earlier site underlying these. The Tyne's estuary would have offered a natural harbour for ships, if required, and the camp at Woodhead is located further upriver albeit much further inland. Further west, the evidence is more limited. At Aberlady, described as the port of Haddington, Sibbald matches up

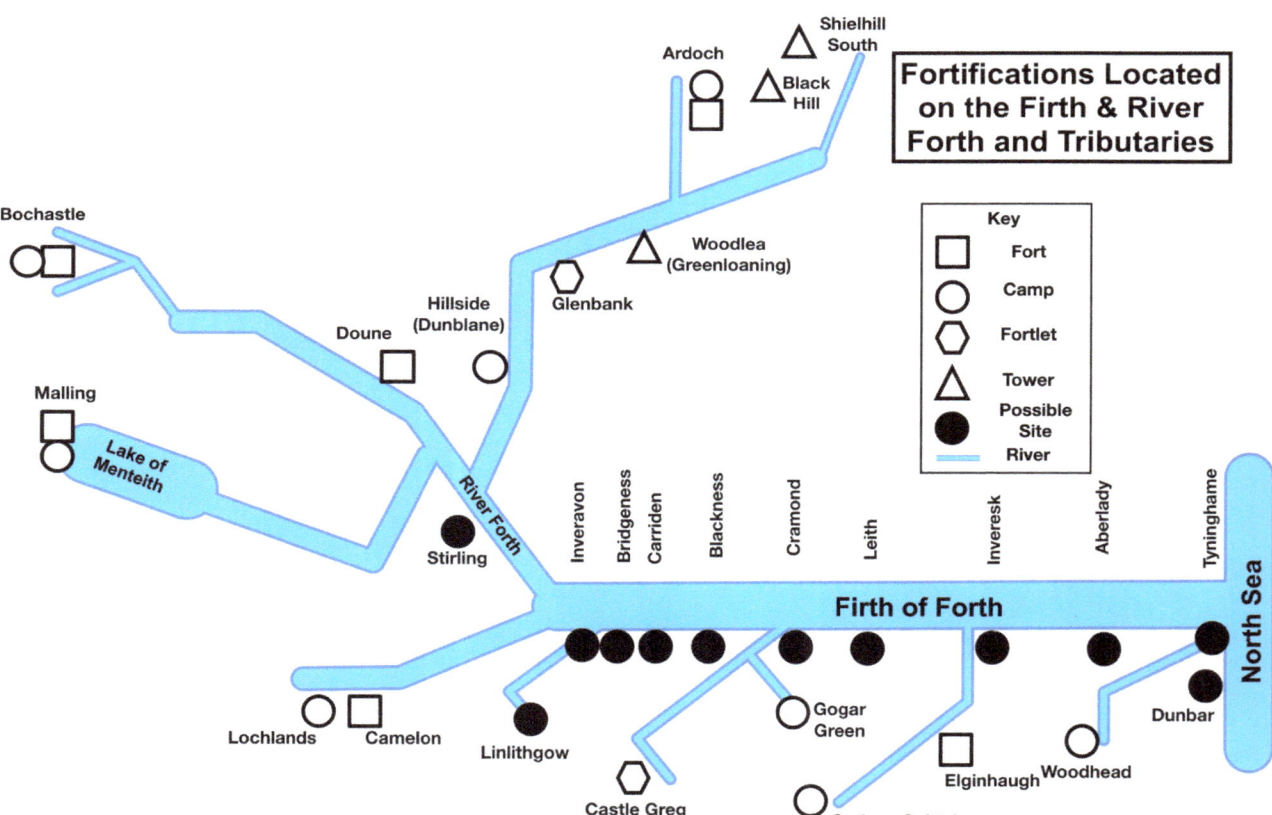

Figure 7.2. Fortifications and possible sites on the Firth, River Forth and tributaries.

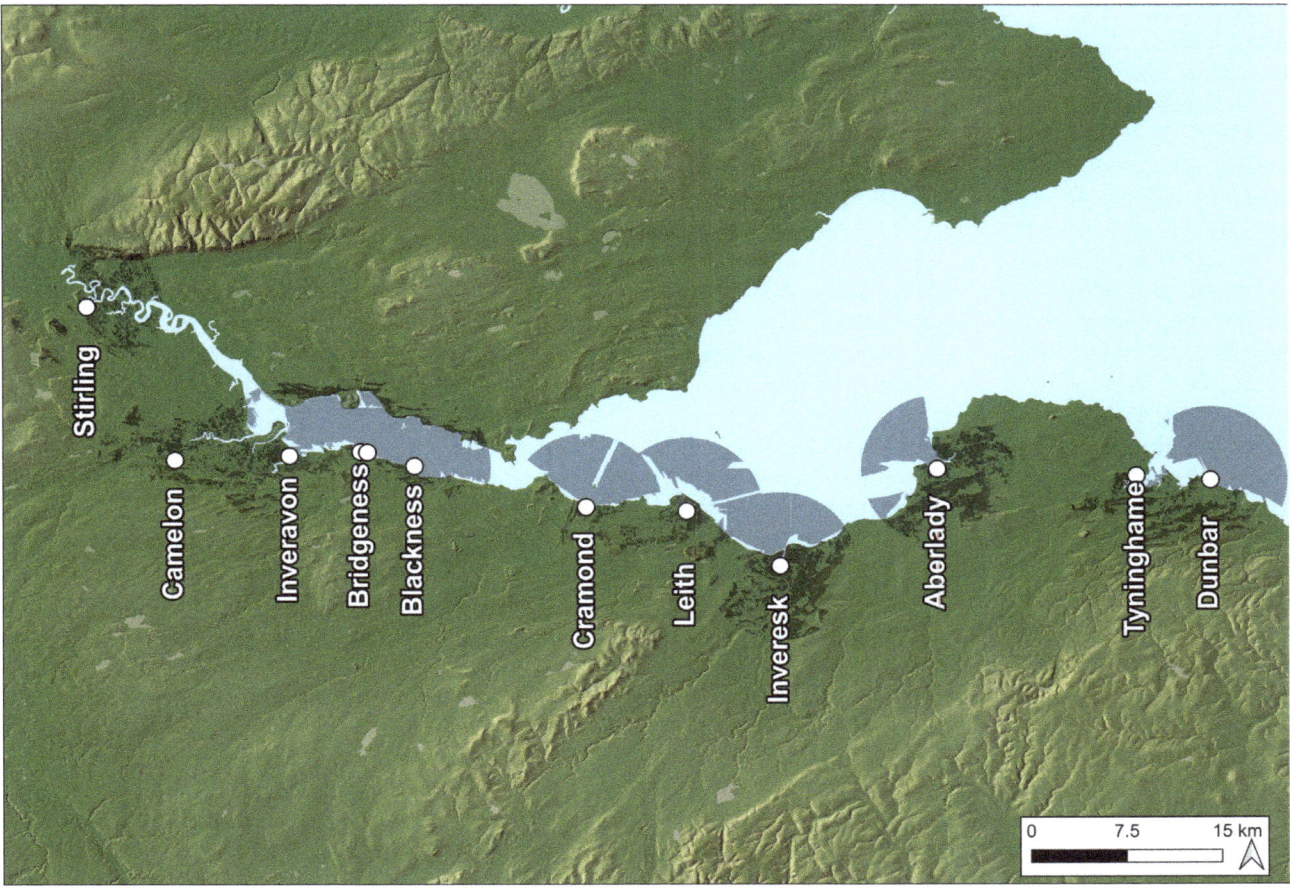

Figure 7.3. Binary viewshed (shaded areas) from the Firth of Forth sites detailed by Sibbald.

the nearby promontory (Gullane Ness) with the *Colonia Promontorium*,

> *It is said there are some ruines of ancient buildings there, and being situate upon the ascent of a hill, with a fertile and well-watered country before it, it is very probable it was a colony placed there by Agricola...*
> **Sibbald 1707:33**

Having searched the literature, and undertaken an examination of archaeological records of the area surrounding both Aberlady or Gullane Ness, I have discovered no evidence for early structures, although a fortification at either location, particularly the latter would have made a good vantage point for visual command over the Forth. Further east, and in the post-Roman period, the mouth of the Esk at Musselburgh has made a good harbour location, and is very close to the fort at Inveresk, where Sibbald predicted a Roman fort which was confirmed in the 1950s; the dating evidence for this fort is strongly post-Flavian (Richmond 1980). Richmond argued a Flavian fort must have been located near to the Antonine fortification, with his argument partly based on a fragment of 1st century *mortarium* recovered through excavation, but there has been little other archaeological evidence uncovered to support this. Hanson (1984) refutes this argument because of the relatively close proximity of Elginhaugh, another Flavian fortification only 3.5 miles away, and also located on the River Esk, making it unlikely that two forts from the same period would be located in close proximity, and although this is a logical conclusion, it does not consider the suitability of Inveresk as a coastal location which could be used as a landing point for supplies and troops. Hanson rejects the dating for the pottery (based on Gillam's assessment in Richmond 1980:302) and notes the recovery of 2nd century coins from the area next to a fragment of hypocaust which Richmond argues is from the 1st century fort (ibid:300). Until archaeological investigations have been undertaken into the area identified by Richmond, it is not possible to completely rule out Flavian activity at Inveresk.

Westwards, there is some evidence of Roman activity in the form of coins recovered from around the Water of Leith, but no remains of buildings have been uncovered. Like the nearby River Esk, the Leith would provide adequate shelter and would have been a suitable candidate for a fortification, with Sibbald suggesting that the river may have been able to accommodate large vessels in the Roman period. There is a local tradition that the Fishwives Causeway, a road running along the shore, from Portobello, near the mouth of the Esk, and Leith, was of Roman origin although this is not proven (Russell 1922), while Maitland (1757:203) also records a section of road uncovered by the pier at Leith. While there are no confirmed sites further upriver of the Water of Leith, the *Old Statistical Account* surmises, from various sources, that the village of Currie was Roman, deriving from the settlement of *Coria* as detailed by in *de situ Britanniae*. On the shore of the Forth, to the west of the mouth of the Leith, the breakwater at Wardie offers a tantalising glimpse of what has been alleged to be a Roman harbour. Boswall (1857) wrote that during an exceptionally low tide, a group of workers were attempting to clear a route through the rocky seabed, but had difficulty cutting through a well-built wall, comprised rocks held together with lime mortar. Boswall concluded that it was a Roman construction because of the mortar, within which he observed pieces of burnt clay and tile, similar to remains found at Inveresk. Maxwell (Graham 1968:281) visited the area and discovered several boulders with some mortar around the low tide mark at Wardie, but found no evidence of a wall. The area, according to Boswall, is only accessible at the lowest of tides, and I have been unable to locate this feature. If confirmed, this would imply a major Roman settlement in this area, something not supported by archaeological finds to date. The evidence from elsewhere in Scotland indicates that most fortifications are located at river mouths, and there is no such arrangement here.

Cramond, another site speculated to be Roman by Sibbald, and subsequently confirmed through pockets of excavation (e.g. Rae and Rae 1955; 1956; 1957; JRS 1962:161, 163; Hassall et al. 1972:304; Goodburn et al. 1976:305-306; Frere, Tomlin, and Hassall 1977:368-369; 1992:264; Burnham et al. 1999:331; 2004:269, 270; N. Holmes 2003; N. Holmes 2006b). Datable artefacts recovered from the site have been reviewed twice, and on both occasions, the conclusion has been that there is no evidence to indicate Flavian occupation. Instead, the evidence indicates the site was occupied during the Antonine and Severan periods (Hartley 1972:8; N. Holmes 2003:153). Wood (1794) records some coins of Claudius, Nero, Galba, Vespasian, and Domitian found out of context in the area, which may indicate early Roman activity nearby. Sibbald postulated that there was a Roman harbour at Cramond,

> *... four miles westward, where now the Village of Nether Cramond stands, there has been a harbour much frequented the time the Romans were here... and upon the east side of the mouth of the River Almond which there runneth in to the Firth of Forth, the foundation of a mole [part of a dock/harbour structure] built upon a rock, doth appear yet very strongly cemented so it seems there has been a dock for small ships there, which dock has advanced some length into the Firth...*
>
> **(Sibbald 1707:33)**

Sibbald's account is reflected by Wood in 1794 who adds,

> *I could not discover any remains of this work; but an intelligent observer who resided on the spot, imagined that he could trace it by the lime and mortar oozing through the sand, and adhering to the shingle or small stones on the beach, for the space of forty yards running east and west parallel to the shore, about 90 feet north of the spade manufactory at Cramond. About a century ago an anchor much corroded with rust was dug up in the garden of Cramond House...*
>
> **(Wood 1794:4)**

Using the measurements in the above accounts, I have calculated that the alleged harbour was adjacent to the river, and on the modern shoreline, although these have both been altered dramatically, mainly due to the construction of water works and war time defences, potentially leading to a loss of any archaeological evidence. Circumstantial evidence of the recovery of the Cramond Lioness, a Roman period statue, from the eastern bank of the River Almond in 1997, may suggest that the object was lost in the mud while being offloaded from a ship (N. Holmes 2003). Further Flavian fortifications (Gogar Green and Castle Greg) can be found upriver from Cramond, via tributaries of the River Almond.

Further fortifications to the west of Cramond, but before Camelon, are alleged by Sibbald, and include Blackness, Carriden and Bridgeness; none of these are located at river mouths. There is no evidence of Roman activity at Blackness, while Carriden is an Antonine fort (Macdonald 1934), and Bridgeness is claimed to be a "small station for ships" (Sibbald 1707:34). Cadell (1870:109-113) writes that originally Bridgeness was a promontory, with the sea flowing around it, which would have created a natural bay, and is the sort of location which is not usually favoured by the Romans. This is where the Bridgeness Distance Slab was discovered, while Macdonald (1937:384) claims men digging a drain uncovered a Romanesque sandstone block from a bathhouse ceiling. Despite all of this, there is no evidence of Flavian activity, and given the proximity of the Antonine Wall, and various finds from that period, it seems more likely that any Roman structures form part of that complex.

At Camelon, there is an antiquarian tradition of a harbour and discoveries of shipping related artefacts, as detailed in Gibson's edition of Camden's *Britannia* (1701:921, 958), Sibbald (1707:34), Maitland (1757:206), and Stuart (1845:177). Sibbald details various finds including a "stone with inscriptions, the vestige of a dock and the ancient sepulchres…" (1707:34). The evidence provides an indication that ships could, in the past, have sailed close to the fortifications at Camelon. This argument is supported by Tatton-Brown (1980) who undertook a study into the accessibility of Camelon to the Forth, and the possibility of it acting as a supply base to the Antonine Wall, and even to the northern forts. Hannon (2018; Hannon, Wilson, and Rohl 2020) has undertaken modelling of the water levels of the Firth of Forth, making a convincing argument that Camelon had direct sea access.

When examined through the river network, the interconnectivity between the fortifications is much clearer, particularly with the Sibbald sites added to the plan of the Forth. If the sites on the Forth were following the patterns set elsewhere in Flavian Scotland, then it would be expected that there should be a fort or camp at the mouth of every river (such as the Water of Leith) and there is little evidence for this, although such sites may be lost under modern development.

Sibbald's work should not be dismissed lightly, particularly as several of his sites have subsequently been proven to have Roman origins, not that all of his predictions have been proven correct. I have undertaken viewshed analysis of these locations (Figure 7.3) to model the visual control which could be exerted from these places. Tacitus has noted that Agricola dispatched the fleet to search for native harbours, possibly indicating a threat in the vicinity of the Firth of Forth, and a system of Roman towers or fortlets would have been a practical security measure; such a system was established later in the Roman period on the Yorkshire coast (e.g. Symonds 2018). Such a network would share some similarities with frontiers from elsewhere in the Empire, such as the Dutch Oude-Rijn and the Gask Ridge, both of which are chains of fortifications overlooking a linear barrier. It seems more likely that if such a chain existed on the Forth, then they may have been part of an eastern outpost extension of the Antonine Wall. This would share similarities with the Cumbrian coastal fortifications which are an extension of Hadrian's Wall.

7.8.3. Firth of Tay

The area around the Firth and River Tay has a number of Flavian fortifications, including the Gask Ridge structures, along with the legionary fortress, would have been the focal point for control in the 1st century. These sites have been extensively researched, and the dating as secure as it can be with the existing evidence. There is only one confirmed Flavian fortification (Dun) on the east coast, located north of the Tay on the Montrose Basin; this is discussed in the next section. Other than the Tay there are no major watercourses which connect with the sea in this area, while in Fife, a lack of large rivers may explain the lack of Flavian fortifications.

In the vicinity of the Firth of Tay, there are several undated Roman sites on the coast with only Abernethy being ascribed a Flavian date. Further up the coast, and beyond the mouth of the Firth are two further sites, Scryne Smithy and Grahamston Cottages, both being the locations for potential camps. Both sites are near the coast, with Scryne having a small, natural harbour (surrounded by rocks) which would offer some shelter, although there is no river here. The Grahamston Cottages site is further inland and on the Elliot Water, which flows into the sea by a sandy beach, which may be an area where boats could have been beached, although this river is considerably smaller than the Tay and its tributaries. Table 7 contains details of the known and suspected fortification on the Firth of Tay and the surrounding area and summarises the evidence for these; without further investigation, it is not possible to confirm the Roman origins of some of the sites, but those such as Scryne and Grahamston Cottages, which do not appear to be typical fortification locations, may represent a form of marching camp for coastal traffic.

With the sites noted in Table 7 on the plan of the Flavian fortifications on the Tay (Figure 7.4), it does not drastically alter understanding, but does show that the sites at St Madoes and Carpow (the latter of which is currently dated to the Severan period), are positioned at a river confluence, something frequently seen elsewhere with Flavian fortifications.

Table 7. Details of the possible sites around the Firth of Tay.

Site Name	Notes
Carpow	Close to where the Firth becomes the River Tay, is the Severan fort at Carpow, adjacent to the shoreline, although this may have an earlier foundation date (Dore and Wilkes 1999).
St Madoes	On the opposite shore of the Tay from Carpow, possibly guarding a crossing point over the Tay, is the small and undated camp at St Madoes (R. H. Jones 2011:301).
Mylnefield	The alleged fort at Mylnefield has with the Firth of Tay on one side and the Invergowrie Burn on the other, the site has the defensive profile of other Flavian Roman forts located near rivers. The site has never been excavated and no dating evidence is available (Mechan 1966).
Invergowrie	Close to Mylnefield is the camp at Invergowrie, identified through aerial photographs, but it has also not yielded datable evidence and remains unconfirmed as a Roman site (R. H. Jones 2011:236-237).
Bullion (Catermilly)	Maitland (1757) describes a possible camp at Bullion which is subsequently dismissed by Crawford (1949). There may be some confusion with the sites at Mylnefield and Invergowrie which are nearby.
Scyrene Smithy (East Haven)	Lies between Arbroath and Carnoustie and identified by Maxwell (1990:122), who suggested could have been a supply base, although it is not clear what or where it would be supplying.
Grahamston Cottages	Jones (2011) notes, is only partially seen as cropmarks, and like Scryne Smithy, needs more investigation before it is confirmed as Roman.

Facing the Enemy?

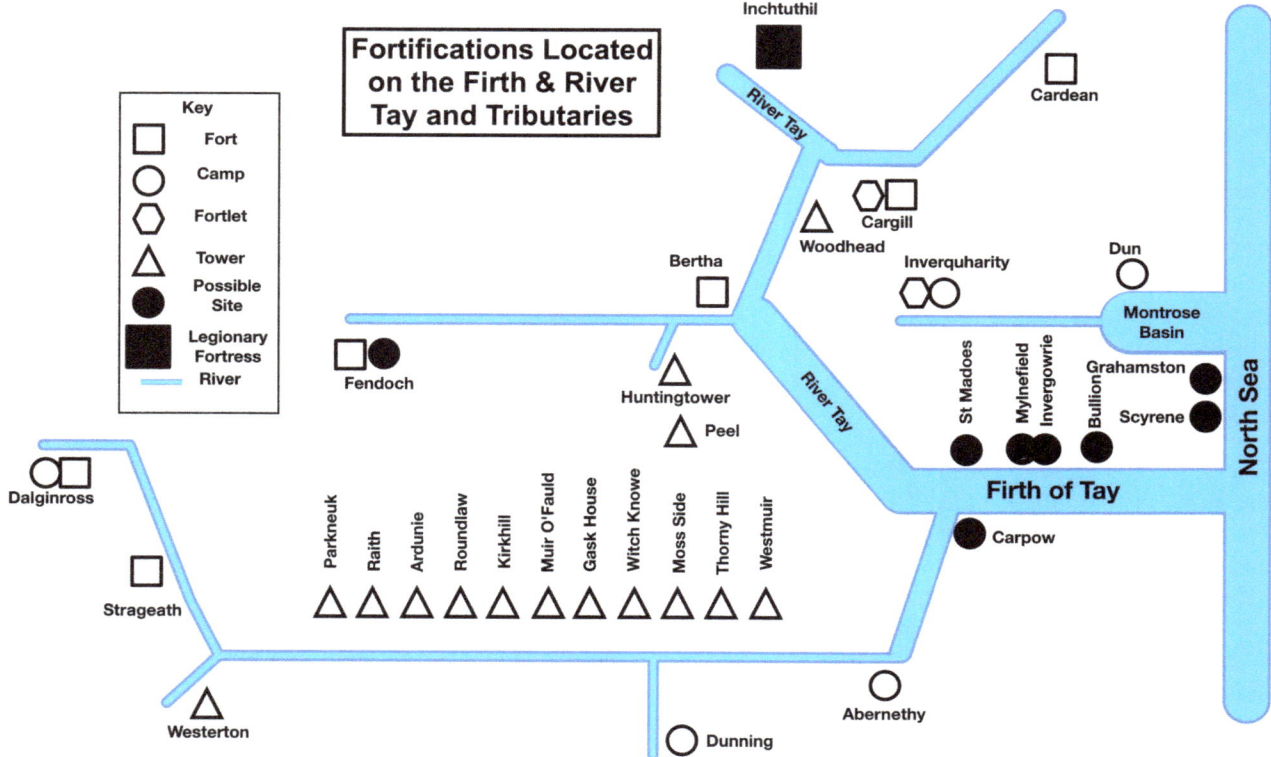

Figure 7.4. Fortifications and possible sites on the Firth, River Tay and tributaries.

Sitting on the southern bank of the River Tay, immediately north of its confluence with the River Almond, the Flavian fort of Bertha is often identified as the Roman crossing point over the River Tay, which is wide at this point, and just beyond the current tidal limit. The earliest mention is by Maitland (1757:198) who describes the route of the Roman road running from Strageath to Innerpeffray, noting that it runs along the northern fort rampart in the direction of the Tay, which was crossed by a bridge. Maitland notes that in the autumn the remains of the bridge can be seen when the river levels are lower, although he gives no further description of where exactly the remains are, or what they look like. Adamson (1774) gives the first detailed account of the remains of the bridge,

> ...the Roman military road, which (according to tradition) leads to a bridge over Tay, about a quarter of a mile above Bertha. The ruins of this bridge are seen at low water in the summer season. Very large and long square oak-planks lie sunk in the river of the spot. Some of them were lately dug up and raised, but one particularly large plank has been attempted in vain... It is a problematical question among Antiquarians, whither this at Bertha, was a wood-bridge erected in stone pillars by the Romans, or by the ancient Caledonian kings...
>
> **(Adamson 1774:27)**

Although wooden planks were retrieved from near the river bank, it is not clear if these came from the bridge or an alternative structure; these planks have subsequently been lost. In 1793, William Roy (1793) drew up a plan of the camp at Grassy Walls, also including the site of the fort at Bertha. He also noted the site of the bridge, although does not describe the remaining structures in the text.

The OSA (15:528) contains a similar account to those noted here; that the foundations of a wooden bridge remain in the form of large oak planks, six to eight inches wide, fastened together by iron clasps. The anonymous author notes that the road continues on the other bank of the Tay. It is not clear from his 1845 account whether Stuart visited Bertha as it is very similar to Adamson's earlier account with some additional detail, recording that adjacent to the ramparts was the crossing known as Derder's Ford, and that 400 yards upstream were the remains of a supposedly Roman bridge, described as follows,

> *The foundations of this bridge consisted of a number of large oak plans, strongly fastened together, and secured by means of iron cramps – some of which planks still remain embedded in the channel. It cannot certainly be proved that they have any decided connection with the Roman road; still it seems improbable that a Roman garrison should have continued for a series of years at Bertha without having some more convenient means of crossing the river than was afforded by the adjacent shallows: it would therefore be unwise wholly to reject the supposition that these oaken timbers belonged to a Roman bridge – a wooden structure, somewhat similar, perhaps, to that which Julius Caesar threw across the Rhine.*
>
> **R. Stuart 1845:204**

Again, Stuart details the probable bridge and describes the remains, but not where these are located (i.e. by the bank or in the middle of the river). Knox (1831:40) records that Agricola used Derder's Ford (NO 10058 26865), located next to the fort, for crossing the River Tay, before going on to further note that this is the first ford above the tidal range of the Tay, making it both important and accessible. Knox notes the continuing importance and later use of the ford in the early medieval period (ibid). They also record the ford in the *Ordnance Survey Name Book for Perthshire* (Survey 1862), which claims there is a local tradition of the Romans using the crossing point, although this 'tradition' may have been taken from Knox. Knox's account is curious, as it does not detail a bridge, instead suggesting the ford was key to crossing the River Tay. J. Graham Callander (1919) summarised the camp at Grassy Walls and the fort at Bertha, and while he does not discuss the bridge in any detail, he places it north of Derder's Ford, but this could be because he is also repeating the earlier accounts. Graham Callander records that the ford had a "gravelly bottom and seems suitable to carts at the present day, except when the river is high" (ibid:145).

In the 1940s, Crawford (1949:60, 61) records his correspondence with a Mr Bradley who found evidence of the crossing, which, on visiting it himself, Crawford noted that this comprised of a small underwater ridge of stones visible from the air, and causing rapids in the river; this is marked as Derder's Ford in Figure 7.5. The ford is the main stony area in the centre of the River Tay. While admitting that the ford could have been used to cross the Tay, Crawford believed it more likely that this was a weir, citing similar examples further downriver at Stanley (ibid:60). The purpose of a weir in this vicinity is unclear given that there are no mills nearby, and no evidence of any such buildings on the old maps of the area. In 1941, Bradley, again according to Crawford, identified another ridge of stones, or potential second crossing, near Derder's Ford which he attempted to use to cross the river, but was "frustrated by his meeting with sudden deeps" (ibid:61). Presumably, this is the second, more northerly set of rocks identified in Figure 7.6; it is clear from this image that the base of the ford is more likely to be rocky rather than gravelly, and potentially impractical as a crossing point. There are substantial anti-tank blocks of concrete to the north of the crossing dating from the Second World War, which originally stretched across the width of the river, so these may have altered the flow of the River Tay, while the effects of the confluence with the River Almond tributary could explain the peculiar 'U' shape of the ford. Alternatively, the ford may be a fish trap. Until more work is done on the crossing, and it is established if the roads end on the banking in this area, it is not possible to confirm if this is a genuine crossing point or some other sort of

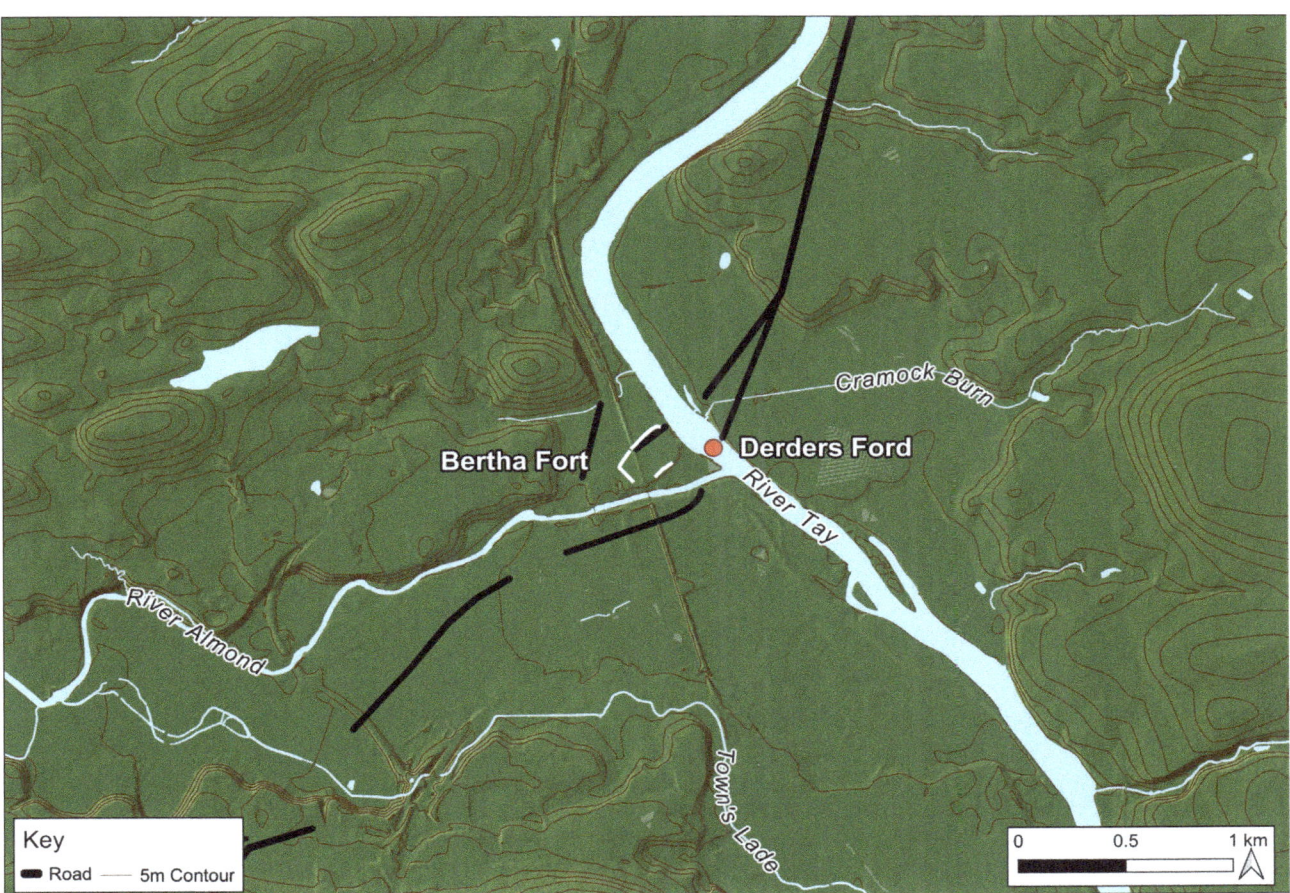

Figure 7.5. Possible ford/crossing point over the River Tay by Bertha fort.

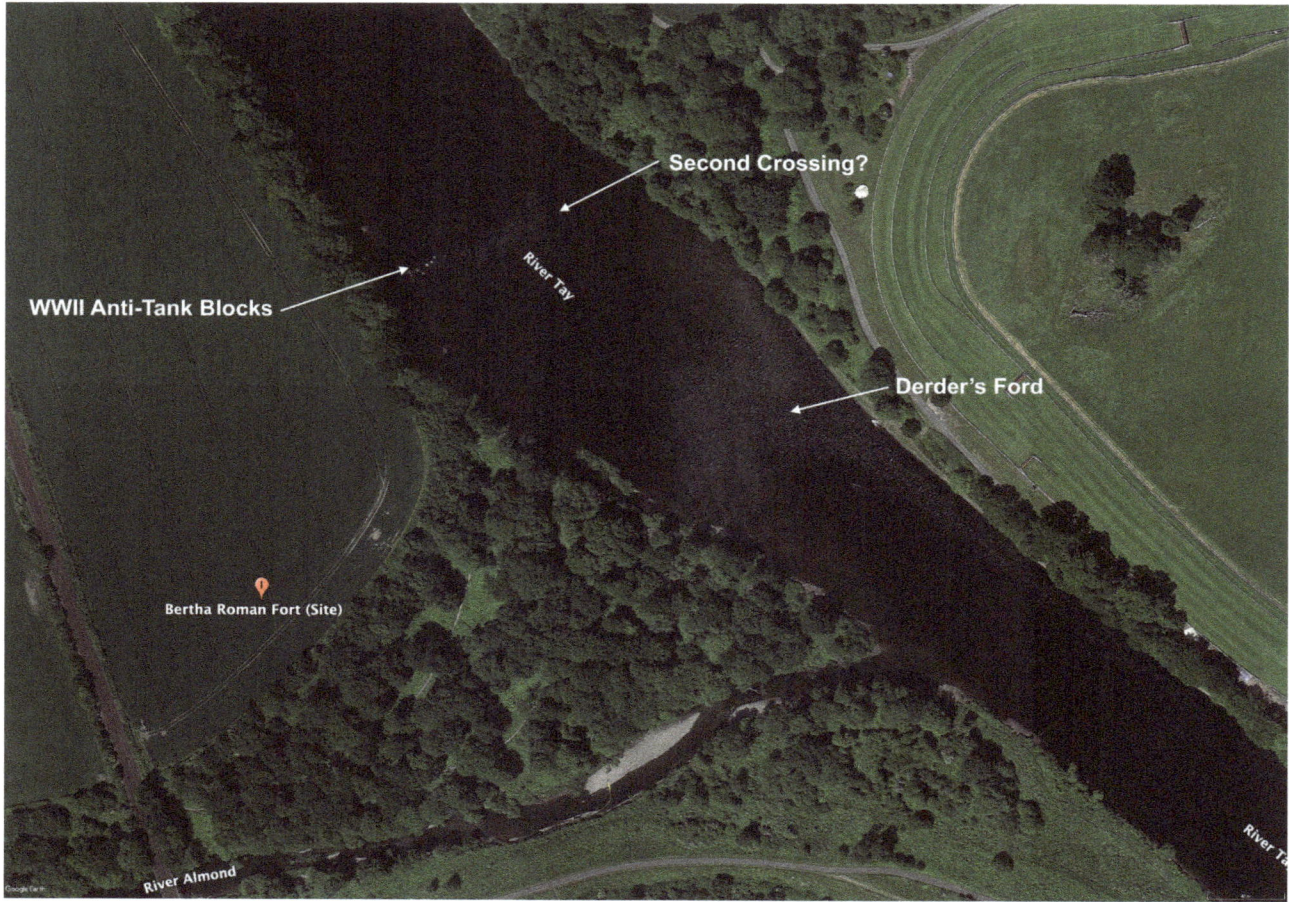

Figure 7.6. Satellite image of Derder's Ford by Bertha fort. (Source: Google Earth June 2018; accessed 10 July 2022).

structure. Woolliscroft and Hoffmann (2006:146) detail the unsuccessful attempt by a local sub-aqua team to identify the bridge foundations underwater. To date, no further work appears to have been undertaken to identify if there was a crossing at this point and what it would have looked like. While the old accounts suggest that the structure was a bridge and may have dated to the Roman period, until it is rediscovered we cannot assume that it was Roman, or even a crossing point as the remains appear to have been found against the bank rather than in the middle of the river. What this demonstrates is that it is difficult to draw conclusions when we have such little information about the coastal and river networks, and how these were used. But despite this, the overall analysis of fortifications in this research, gives us a possible basis on which to postulate about the use of those sites located on these networks.

7.8.4. Northeast and Moray Firth

The majority of fortifications in the North-east area comprise of camps, predominantly Flavian in date, although there are two which are attributed to the Severan campaigns. The only sites which have been scientifically dated are the camps at Kintore and Milltimber, both of which has shown evidence of 1st century occupation, with the possibility of either continuous, or reoccupation into the 3rd century at Kintore. With the exception of the Spey, the area lacks the major rivers which are found further south in Scotland, but the Moray coast is a major estuary.

At the southern end of this section, several sites are located next to rivers which flow into the Montrose Basin. The camp at Dun is located on the northern side of the Montrose Basin, an inland tidal bay which provides shelter from the North Sea. The site is the only confirmed Flavian site on the east coast, and could have been a supply base for the more inland fortifications. The camp is only 2.8 hectares and would not have had the space to store significant amounts of supplies on a long-term basis. While the site has been partially excavated (St Joseph 1973:225; Rogers 1993:286-290), no evidence of specific granary storage has been confirmed. However, there are some cropmarks in the wider area around the camp, indicating there may have been more Roman activity than is confirmed. The coastline to the north of the Montrose Basin is generally rocky, and there are few natural harbours or rivers which would have provided shelter for shipping, or places to offload supplies; both Inverbervie and Catterline, small villages on the coast have rivers which exit to the sea, but neither have yielded evidence of Roman activity either at the river mouths, or further inland.

Stonehaven is another modern settlement, which has two minor rivers exiting into the bay at either end. Both St

Interconnectivity

Joseph (1978:277) and Frere (1980:421-422) agree that Stonehaven seems a probable location for a fort, and the topography fits the profile for fort locations, with a river on one side and the sea on the other, but its capacity as a natural harbour would have been limited in the Roman period as the bay is rocky, with an artificial channel created when rocks were cleared at the southern end in 1825. At the northern end of the bay, near to where the Cowie Water exits into the sea, Fetteresso Glebe (Arduthie) is proposed as a Roman camp, featuring in several early texts including Camden (1722:1257) and Barclay (1792:566). Crawford (1949:104-105) speculates that the suggested area was only wide enough for a small fort, and not a camp, and was more likely to belong to an indigenous site. The site at Fetteresso Glebe now lies under a modern housing estate, and no further investigations of the area have taken place. There has been no evidence for a Roman fortification uncovered at Stonehaven, and it remains a speculative site, although this would seem to be a better location to end the chain of fortifications which run against the Highland Line, beginning at Barochan Hill fort. A lack of fortification in this area would make it easier for the indigenous population to circumvent the main group of forts in the Angus area. The lack of a fortification at Stonehaven suggests that either there was not a substantial indigenous threat in the area, or that the army were not concerned if the local population circumvented the forts; the further the invaders made it into Roman territory, the more likely they would encounter the army or a fortification. More importantly, a lack of a fort here suggests the Flavian army was more concerned with controlling movement in areas around forts, rather than the controlling the wider landscape where there were no fortifications.

The next fortifications to the north, are the Flavian camps at Normandykes and Milltimber, both on the River Dee. To the east of these, still on the Dee, at Nigg, the Aberdeen

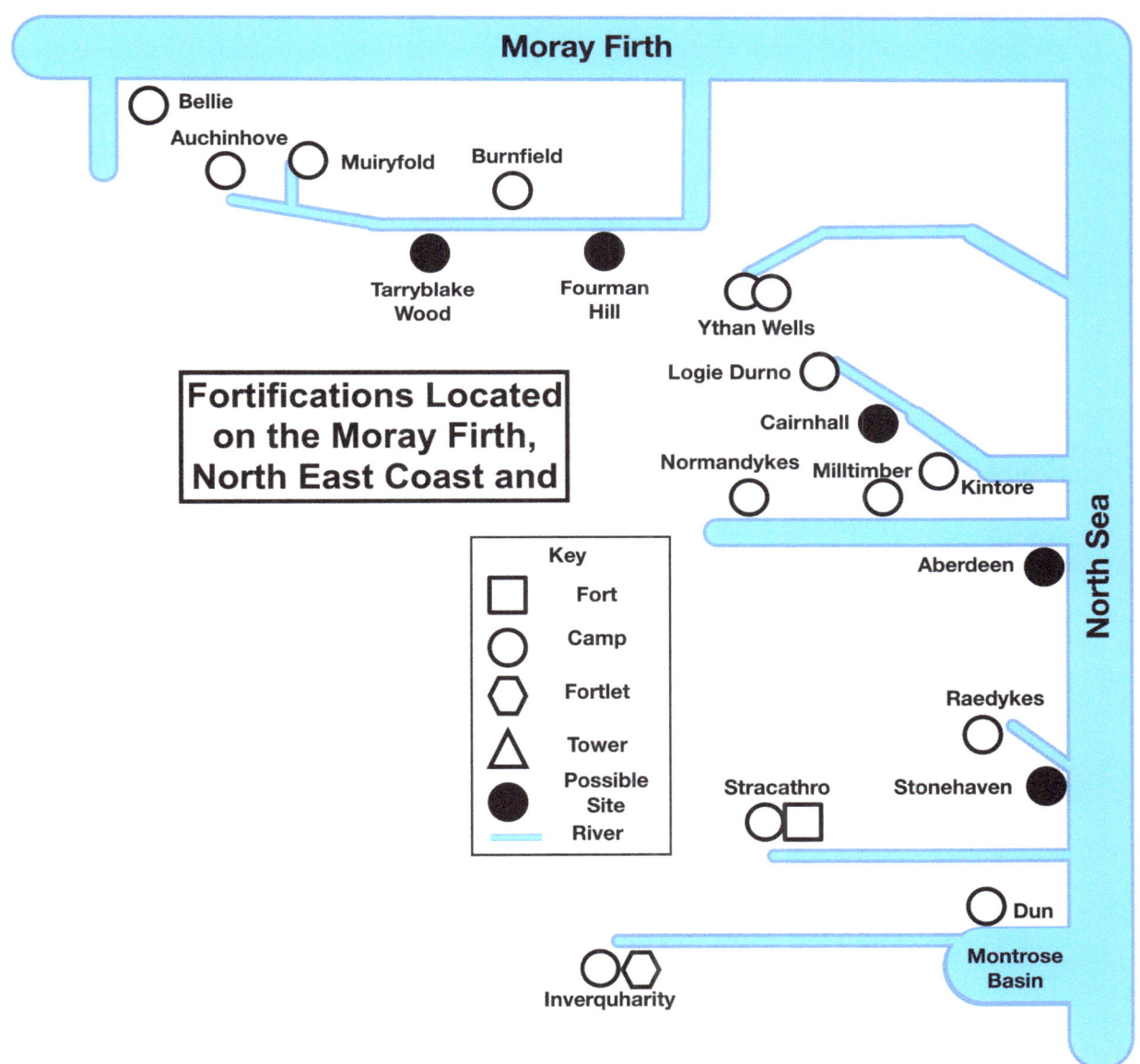

Figure 7.7. Fortifications, possible and unconfirmed sites in the north east, Moray Firth and tributaries.

HER records that in 1969 over 400 fishhooks and pins were recovered from the area and that these are thought to be Roman (Aberdeen HER:NJ90SW0011). Roy (1793) details the discovery of a stone in 1707, from Nigg, which is inscribed R. IM. L. (*Romanii imperii limes*), which he assumed was a marker stone, placed by the fleet to mark the limit of the Empire. However, there are two villages called Nigg in north Scotland, one in Aberdeenshire and another to the north of Cromarty on the Black Isle. Stuart (1822:297) claims that the stone is a "ridiculous fiction" which "does not deserve further notice". The stone has since been lost, and it is not possible to re-evaluate it, but this evidence, along with several coins found in Aberdeen (itself at the mouth of the Dee), suggests there may have been some sort of Roman activity in the area. Don (1896:40-42) details the Roman road which he claims connects Aberdeen and Fochabers, the latter settlement being near the Roman camps of Bellie and Auchinhove, in Moray. The route of this road appears to follow the line of the 18th century military road in the area, which is still in use as the A96. There is no archaeological evidence to support the claim of Roman origin, and it seems likely to be a route which is taken from *de situ Britanniae* (Bertram 1809).

As Figure 7.7 shows, there are a number of fortifications on the river networks, most of which are interconnected, but there are fewer sites on the coast, guarding the entrances to the rivers. This could be because there are few large watercourses in the region. North of Aberdeen, the chain of camps crosses through the hills, cutting off the northeast corner (the Mounth) of Aberdeenshire, before reaching land to the south of the Moray Firth. None of these camps are located on large watercourses, and it is probable that they were following a route through the valleys, possibly ending up at Bellie, on the River Spey which is the largest tributary of the Moray Firth in the eastern sector. Given this chain of sites, and their location in a valley, in positions which are convenient, and do not rely on the natural topography for defence, it would appear that these are marching camps, temporarily sheltering the army as they move through the landscape. A lack of knowledge of these sites, and the general progress of the Romans in this area means that we do not know if Bellie, or one of the other sites nearby was the last fortification constructed by the Romans in this area. The recent discovery of Milltimber camp suggests there are still sites awaiting identification; the proximity of this camp, along its close neighbour at Normandykes, both of which are Flavian and located next to one of the major rivers in the area, could represent the meeting point of soldiers from the army and marines from the fleet, a concept noted previously by Jones (2018). Similar to the Normandykes-Milltimber relationship are the two camps at Kintore and Cairnhall, with Kintore conclusively radiocarbon dated to the 1st century, with some evidence of ongoing or later re-occupation. Cairnhall remains undated, and it may have been occupied at the same time as Kintore. It is not possible to say whether the army was accessing certain sites from the sea, although Milltimber and Normandykes were located on a large river, and not too far from the coast, although the river may not have been navigable as far as the latter site.

7.8.5. *Firth of Clyde*

Fortifications on the River and Firth of Clyde, and tributaries can be split into two periods with Flavian sites in the upper part of the Clyde valley, possibly indicative of a route forward from the south, while to the west is the remote Flavian fort of Loudon Hill, later reoccupied in the Antonine period. In the lower part of the Clyde valley, fortifications, with a couple of exceptions, are dated to the Antonine period. Figure 7.8 shows the Flavian fortifications and this lack of sites in the lower Clyde valley. The Antonine period structures are inevitably associated with the Antonine Wall, although there are several undated encampments along the line of this.

The west coast of Scotland is an area with Roman fortifications from the Flavian and Antonine periods, along with anecdotal evidence of activity at further sites; several of these are put forward by Sibbald, including Dumbarton Rock and Dumbuck Hill. The former became a military stronghold from the early medieval period, taking advantage of the natural volcanic topography. Dumbuck Hill was identified by Dr Irvine as Roman, but there is no evidence to support this (Sibbald 1707:28; R. Stuart 1845:283). The site would be at one end of Dumbuck Ford, which was the first fordable point over the River Clyde before it widens out into the Firth (Riddell 1979:8), with the Antonine fort at Whitemoss located at its southern end. The River Clyde itself has seen much change and development since the Roman period; channelling and industrialisation of the river from at least the early 17th century, has altered the depth and flow of the Clyde, with the ford at Dumbuck being lost around this time (ibid).

Down the coast, at Largs, fragments of Roman tile were uncovered from a garden in the centre of the town in 1820 (Patterson 1852:10), and it was claimed that such discoveries were a common occurrence. One tile was given to John Buchanan in Glasgow, a man who had "much experience in Roman antiquities" (J. E. Reid 1864:23-24) and who confirmed its Roman origins. There have been no formal investigations of the area in recent years, although a newspaper article from 3 July 2019 mentions two Roman jug fragments found on the beach at Largs, in the 1960s, which were recently dated to the 2nd century.

Further south, another potential site has emerged at Brigurd Point. Frank Newall (1966:16) attempted to trace the Roman road which he believed ran from Kilwinning to Hunterston on the coast. Next to Hunterston, where the land forms a small promontory known as Brigurd Point, Newall noted a possible sub-sea structure in aerial photographs, and speculated that the course of the Roman road made its way to the waterside, ending at an area cleared of rock which he interpreted as possible Roman harbour (see Figure 7.9). Newall described the structure,

Interconnectivity

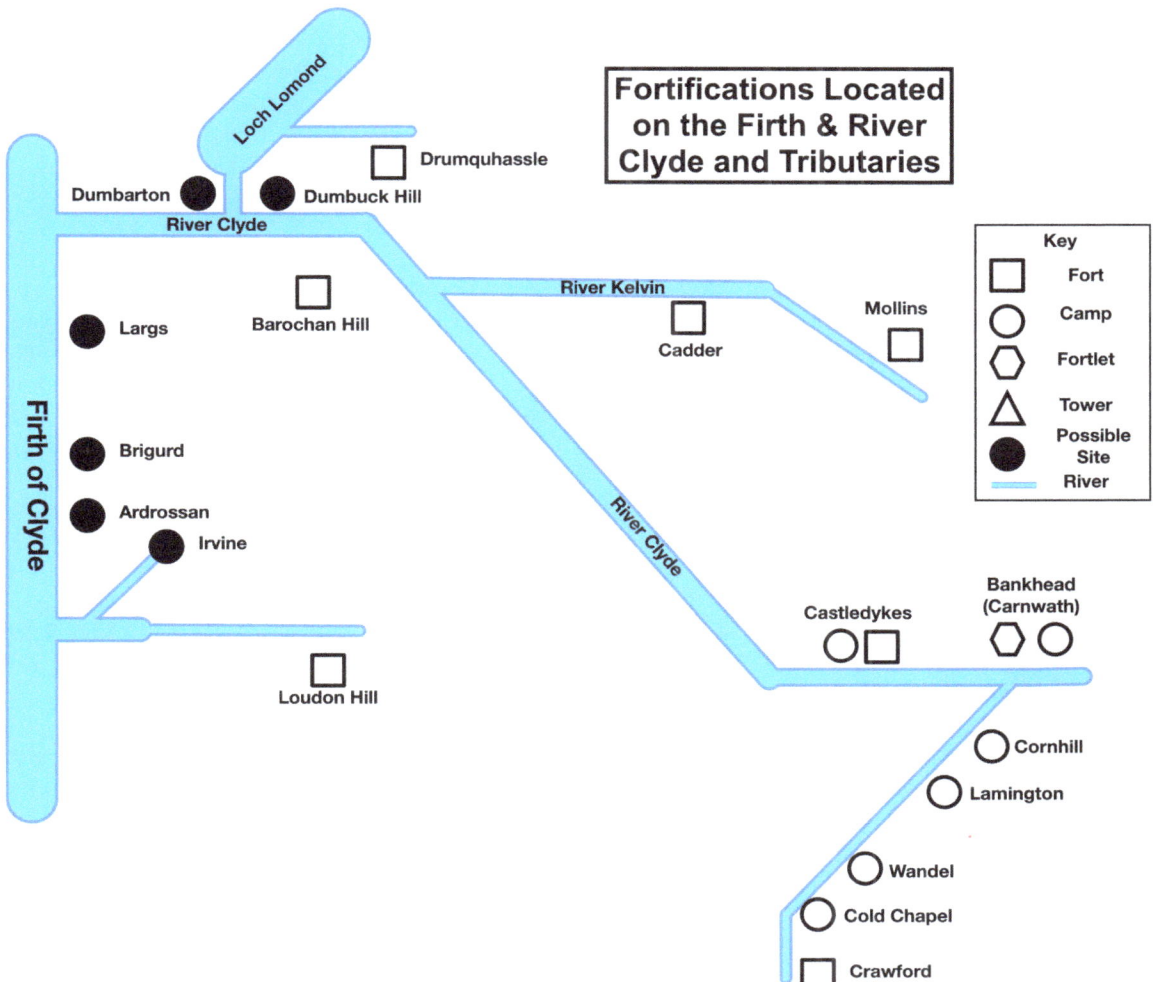

Figure 7.8. Fortifications, possible and unconfirmed sites on the Firth, River Clyde and tributaries.

Figure 7.9. Cleared area (circled) at Brigurd Point, creating an 'n' shape. (Google Earth April 2021; accessed 10 July 2022).

> *On the foreshore extending WNW from the beach head NS182518 a recent fence follows the footings of rough walling 4'-5' wide at the base, but where this, in turn, runs off to N, NS 180519, it can be seen to have overlain the footings of a mile 9' 6"-10" wide, which continues beyond low watermark, curving to the N. This is accompanied along the S side by a cleared way, some 15'-16' wide, curving to the N. This is accompanied along the S side by a cleared way, some 15'-16' wide, curving in the direction of Brigurd Point. Off Brigurd Point, its inner N end showing above water at low tide, is a deep-water berth, some 50' across, the visible end hexagonal and the walls 10' wide and several courses high*
>
> **Newall 1966:16**

Newall suggests it is Roman because of the engineering involved, although he also concedes that it could belong to medieval tide-aligned fishing yairs. Newall (1972) revisited the site, and although he could not provide any further evidence as to the provenance of the site, he argued that it was likely to have been a deep-water harbour, enabling ships to berth there in security and safety. Newall (1976) later speculated that Brigurd would have been much less be vulnerable to blockade than any such site at Dumbarton, where there are topographical restrictions to the waterway. Newall also speculated that Brigurd would be a useful coastal site to land supplies for inland sites, such as the fort at Loudon Hill, as it would be quicker, more efficient, and less vulnerable than if supplies were brought overland from elsewhere in Scotland. Newall speculates that the site could also have been Antonine, supplying the Wall and its outer posts. The site was revisited in 2013 as part of Project SAMPHIRE, looking at coastal sites, with the structural findings of Newall being confirmed, but no evidence for dating, or for Roman activity being attributed to the site (Canmore – Brigurd Point 2019).

The satellite image of the alleged harbour area (Figure 7.9), shows a number of interesting features, with possible walls or tracks visible to the east. A full survey of the cleared area, wider seabed, and surrounding area could strengthen the arguments in support of this site. I have examined old maps and accounts of the area, and can find no indication of any old structures or roads, while LiDAR analysis has also been inconclusive. It should be noted that the site is adjacent to Hunterston Nuclear Power Station, and there is a possibility that some of these features are connected to the construction of this.

Further south, at Ardrossan, there is evidence of Roman activity, with John Smith (1895) noted that Roman baths were found in the neighbourhood of Ardrossan, although he gives no more detail than this. Ardrossan itself is not located at the mouth of a large river, and therefore, is perhaps less likely than some other sites to have Roman origins. But looked at in the wider context of the sites on the Clyde and Solway coasts, perhaps Ardrossan was a natural stop-off point for traffic moving along the coast.

Unlike other parts of Scotland, there are few major rivers in and around the Clyde, and therefore there appear to be fewer fortifications guarding the river network, as per Figure 7.8. Largs, Ayr and Girvan are themselves at the mouths of medium-sized waterways which are, today, limited in their navigability, but would have offered shelter and a stop-off point for vessels.

7.8.6. Southwest and Solway Firth

Southwest Scotland, which for this research covers the Clyde coastal sites at Ayr and Girvan, as well as those on the Solway coast, has a particularly high concentration of Flavian fortifications (Figure 7.10), although relatively few are at the entrances to the river valleys, although the terrain in this area means that some sites, such as Glenluce, could see most of the surrounding area. Besides this, there are numerous undated and unconfirmed sites in the area, which indicates that the distribution of Roman fortifications in the southwest is much more complex than it initially appears. Most of the Flavian and undated sites are located in river valleys, and are accessible from the sea.

Sibbald (1707:36) lists the location of several ports and harbours in this area, which he believed were in use during the Roman period, although he does not necessarily claim they were all founded by the Romans. If these sites have Roman origins or were occupied by them, it suggests that the army may have been attempting to secure the southwest and Solway Firth; perhaps the need to secure this area in response to a particular threat, leads to the construction of the Hadrianic period, Cumbrian coastal sites.

As mentioned previously, a Roman camp without traditional rampart and ditch defences has recently been discovered on the north side of the river in Ayr, at a location that may have been a crossing point over the river itself (Hunter 2017:327; Arabaolaza 2019). Patterson (1852:9) notes the course of a Roman road can be traced on the south side of the river, heading eastwards (away from the newly discovered site), and if this is Roman, it is unclear what site it is heading towards as there are no known sites further upriver from Ayr. The modern A713, which leaves Ayr to the southeast, could follow the route of this Roman road. The modern route follows the valley, cutting off the southwest corner of Scotland, eventually arriving at Glenlochar, in southern Galloway, where there are several Roman fortifications of different periods, and then on to the sites at Ward Law and Lantonside which are discussed shortly.

Sibbald identifies Loch Ryan, a sea loch, with Ptolemy's *Vidogara Aestus*, noting that it is a convenient location for ships on the west side of the Rhins of Galloway. Sibbald may be referring to a site around the modern settlement of Stranraer, which itself is noted as a potential site of Roman origin by Chalmers (1807) and Stuart (1845), but no Roman finds have been recorded from the town. There are traces of Roman road approaching the town (Wilson 1989),

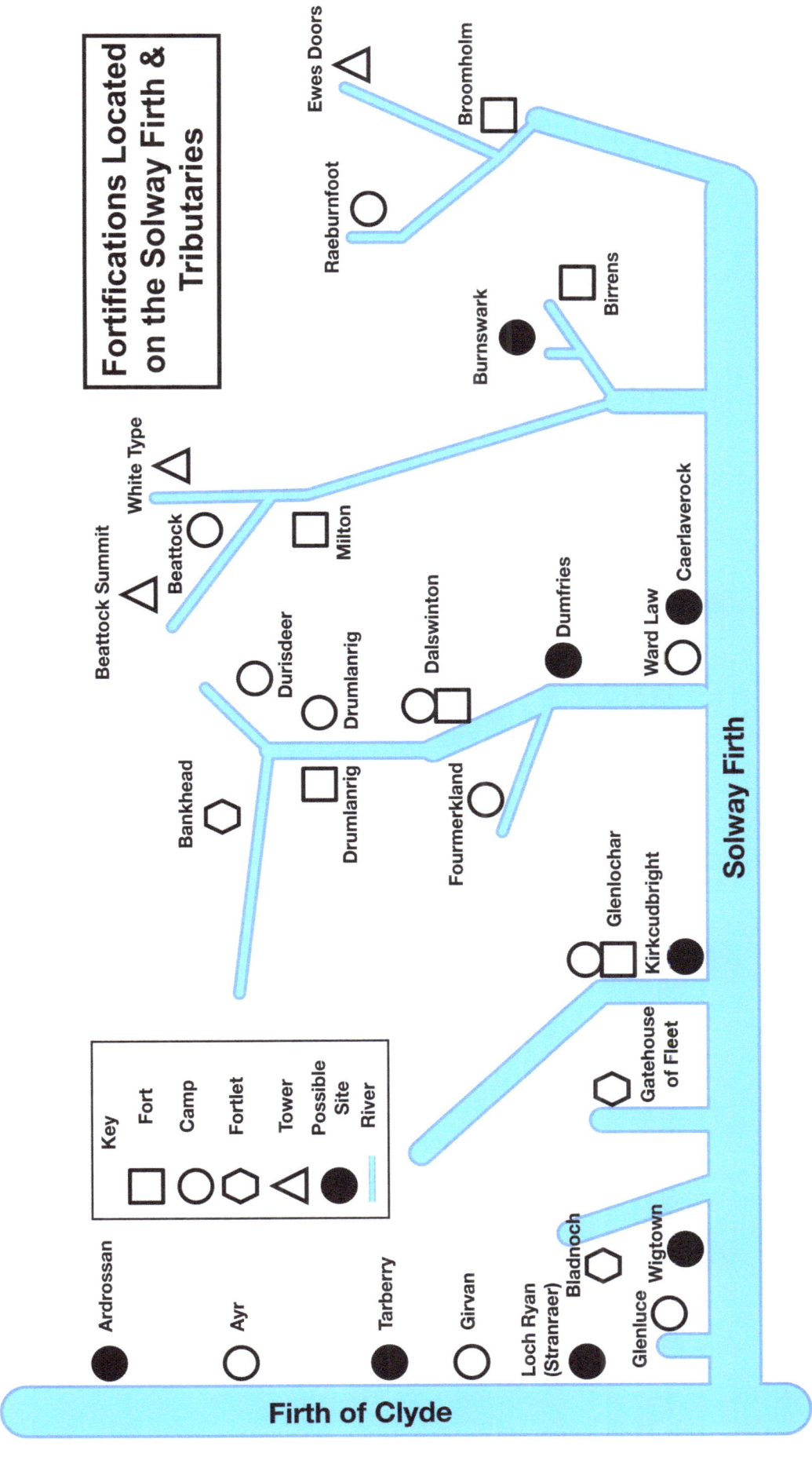

Figure 7.10. Fortifications in the south-west, Solway Firth and tributaries.

with Keppie (Burnham et al. 1993:281) recording its likely route from Glenluce towards the outskirts of Stranraer, and this is a logical place to construct a fortification, particularly as the site is a good, natural harbour and was important for shipping in the modern era until as recently as 2011. Sibbald notes that on the east side of Loch Ryan is *Rerigonium Sunus*, which he identifies with Glenluce, and where a Flavian camp was discovered by Maxwell in 1992 (ibid), and probably dates to the 1st century. Moving eastwards along the Solway coast, the next site mentioned by Sibbald is *Fena Aestuarium*, which he believes is the position occupied by modern Wigtown. The settlement sits at the mouth of the River Bladnoch and maintains a harbour to this day. While there is no evidence for Roman activity at Wigtown, Bladnoch, less than a mile downriver, is the location of a Roman fortlet (Canmore ID:318944) and a possible camp (Canmore ID:361123), both located through cropmarks. The site remains undated, but given the dating of the other fortifications in the area (including the nearby fortlet at Gatehouse of Fleet), then Bladnoch may date to the Flavian period.

Sibbald proposes the site of the medieval castle of Caerlaverock as originating in the Roman period, and although there is no evidence to support this, the Roman camp at Ward Law is less than a mile away, and it may be that Sibbald was confusing the two. Also nearby is the fortlet at Lantonside which Canmore ascribes an Antonine date to, because of similarities in size to the Antonine fortlet at Barburgh Mill (Frere, Hassall, and Tomlin 1985:267; Hussen, Jones, and Hanson 2009b). Ward Law, a site which shares defensive similarities with a fort, but appears to lack any evidence of buildings, giving the appearance of a camp (Hussen, Jones, and Hanson 2009b), is located on the highest hill on this peninsula, overlooking the Solway Firth as well as the River Nith, and appears to be controlling this section of the coast, along with access to the Nith; if the river was not important, then there would be no need to construct either fortification in this location. Travelling along the Nith would take the army into the depths of Galloway, where there are several forts and camps upriver, including Dalswinton and Drumlanrig, and implying that this was a route which needed the security of permanent fortifications. The adjacent, undated fortlet at Lantonside, which has two annexes connected to it, is located next to the shore, although here, the Nith is deep with quicksand at low tide, and crossing the river would only be possible by boat. This suggests the purpose of Lantonside was to control access to the river, which it may have done by working in conjunction with Ward Law, which had better views of the Solway Firth than were visible from the fortlet. Symonds (2018) has reached a broadly conclusion, arguing that the fortlet is too far from the river to control access, unless there was naval capacity based there. Symonds goes on to argue that the fortlet may be Antonine in date, and acted as a supply base for local fortifications and utilising the annexe. It seems likely that if the fortlet is working in conjunction with the fort, then there would have been some shipping capacity at the former, although it is not clear if this was militaristic or not.

A similar symbiotic relationship between fortifications was observed by Hannon (2018), on the Antonine Wall where the fort at Bishopton (Whitemoss), on the River Clyde, along with the fortlet on the hills above at Lurg Moor, could collectively view most of the River Clyde. As can be seen in Figures 7.11 and 7.12, between Ward Law and Lantonside, they have an almost 360° view of the Solway Firth, and can see the entrance to the River Nith. While there is no dating evidence for either site, this analysis indicates that the two sites may have had a symbiotic relationship and have been in operation at the same time. Assuming both fortifications are contemporaneous, a 2nd century date of occupation is possible, but it is also reasonable to assume that Ward Law could be an example of the over-wintering fortifications noted by Tacitus. There is an alternative suggestion based on the location of Ward Law, opposite the western terminus of Hadrian's Wall and the Cumbrian coastal fortifications; that the site is either an outpost for the Wall, or part of an attempt to pacify the sort of indigenous activity which required the construction of the Cumbrian fortifications. All these possible purposes indicate the likelihood of more than short-term occupation.

The fortifications in the southwest of Scotland are extensive and varied, particularly in the east of the region, which may have been influenced by the early Roman occupation of Carlisle, and which may have been when the occupation of the region begins. Understanding of the extent of Roman activity in southwest Scotland is limited, but from the evidence presented here, there is much more to learn about the occupation on both the southwest coast and the Solway Firth. Many sites are unconfirmed and/or undated, and there needs to be a focus on gathering more datable evidence. Given the large number of sites in this area, it is difficult to conclude what the military strategy was here, but it seems likely that most of the fortifications were controlling the landscape, as occurring elsewhere in Scotland. Looking at the undated and unconfirmed sites in Figure 7.10, along with those mentioned by Sibbald, there are many more fortifications which are located at the entrances to the rivers; while upriver of most of these are a number of Flavian fortifications, as can be seen in the figure although for practical reasons I have not included all of the undated sites.

7.9. Summary

The key finding from this chapter, and a piece of research which has not previously been undertaken, is that fortifications were constructed adjacent to, and facing rivers, although not necessarily crossing points. The positioning of some of these fortifications means that the first thing to be seen by an individual approaching via the river or river valley, would have been the *porta praetoria*. While not all waterways would have been navigable, less so the further inland from the sea that the site was, the valley itself may well have been an important route. Securing river crossings would have been strategically significant, and this is clear in some parts of Dumfries and Galloway (such as Glenluce) where the fortifications

Interconnectivity

Figure 7.11. Binary viewshed (shaded area) from Ward Law camp.

Figure 7.12. Binary viewshed (shaded area) from Lantonside fortlet.

are constructed by the rivers, with the road crossing near the site. Again, further research is needed to confirm that the forts and road are contemporary. Evidence from some sites shows that roads and fortifications originated in different periods, such as at Milton camp, where the road passes by the eastern entrance and clips the north-eastern defences which would seem an odd thing to do if they were contemporaneous.

The main aim of this chapter has been to re-examine the evidence for Roman activity on the coast and the main rivers of Scotland, and to argue that the locating of fortifications in these positions was key part of the Roman strategy, as it enabled the military to control these networks, both for their own purposes (supply and movement), but it would also allowed them to control indigenous use of the waterways and coastal waters; control of these networks can be seen in the diagrams in this chapter. Through this analysis, it has become clear that a number of antiquarian texts have indicated Roman origins for various sites, and while it is easy to dismiss these, it cannot be ignored that a number of these places have subsequently yielded evidence of Roman activity. This re-analysis has shown that although the fortifications could have been interconnected through coastal and river networks, the relationship between these is complex; this is not helped by the large proportion of sites which are unconfirmed, undated, or attributed to a period without firm dating evidence. Finally, the analysis has also shown that although there was an overall military strategy focussing on control of the river networks, this varied between the different rivers, essentially creating sub-regional networks.

My research shows that by establishing sites on the coast, usually at river mouths, the army was attempting to control access to coast waters and rivers. What is less clear, is if this strategy is restricted to the Flavian period. The location of the Antonine forts of Cramond and Inveresk, at the entrance to rivers, may suggest that the same strategy is being pursued in the later period. Whereas the lack of coastal fortifications in the Severan period, implies less reliance on the coast and rivers, with Carpow, the only coastal fort, being used a supply base; this would make more sense if the army in the 3rd century is using a road network established in one of the previous invasion periods. An additional observation can be made regarding the sites on the Firth of Clyde and west coast of Scotland. It has not gone unnoticed by Graafstal (2020) and others (e.g. Poulter 2018; Robertson and Keppie 2015; Hannon, Wilson, and Rohl 2020), that there are numerous similarities in the design of the Antonine Wall and Hadrian's Wall, with the former copying elements of the latter. With an Antonine fort (Bishopton Whitemoss) and two fortlets (Lurg Moor and Outerwards) to the west of the Wall, it is apparent that there was a desire to create a system of outposts, controlling the Clyde coast as it turns inland by the Bute peninsula, and potentially acting as an early warning system for the Wall; similar arrangements exist at the western end of Hadrian's Wall, with a series of towers, fortlets and forts spread down the Cumbrian coast (e.g. Breeze and Dobson 2000; and Breeze 2006b). This may also have been replicated along the southern shore of the Firth of Forth, with the Antonine forts at Cramond and Inveresk, forming part of an eastern defensive flank, and although archaeological evidence is lacking, the sites put forward by Sibbald may have formed part of this. If the sites highlighted in this chapter can be confirmed, and dated to the 2nd century, then it can be argued with some certainty, that this was an attempt to further replicate the Hadrian's Wall frontier model in Scotland.

This reappraisal and re-examination of the existing evidence, represents a valuable, new contribution to our understanding of the wider military strategy in the Flavian period. It forces us to rethink the use of coastal movement and river activity in the Flavian period, and demonstrates how the military controlled access to, and movement on these networks. This analysis contributes a new understanding of the relationship between fortifications, suspected and unconfirmed sites, and with the coastal and river networks. I have shown that although our knowledge of these sites is limited, the available archaeological evidence indicates that fortifications on the coast, like those further inland, were maintaining visual control of the immediate landscape, as well as physical control of these routes. In areas where there are no major rivers, there are fewer confirmed or possible Roman fortifications. Therefore, it is plausible that the reason there are no Roman sites in the heart of East Lothian, and only one or two possible (non-Flavian) camps in Fife, is not necessarily because of a *Pax Romana*, but because of the lack of major rivers. If the modelling presented here, regarding the control and usage of waterways and the coast is accurate, it has significant implications for our understanding of the Flavian invasion of Scotland; it was not purely a land based invasion, and that fortifications were not necessarily established based on advancement through the landscape. Rather, my analysis indicates that the river networks played a key role in where the military installations were positioned, with the Tay, Forth, and Clyde being arterial routes, and the fortifications spreading along these, and this would have ensured that the rivers could act as supply routes from coastal traffic. The coastal camps may or may not have been permanently occupied, but can perhaps better be interpreted as supply bases with goods offloaded or transferred to vessels better suited to sailing on rivers. Given that sea-going vessels can reach Perth on the Tay and Stirling on the Forth, this may explain a lack of camps at the entrances to these Firths, although there are a number of unconfirmed sites near the entrance to the former.

Although the overall military strategy during the Flavian period in Scotland was one of controlling movement through key areas, there are some differing arrangements in different parts of the country which enabled the army to achieve their overall goals, and also demonstrating their adaptability to the different regions and challenges which they posed. As I outlined earlier in this research, the relationship with the indigenous population in southwest

Scotland may have been significantly different to those in areas further away from Roman territory and who had had less contact with the military. On the Galloway coast, the military strategy was one which saw the river mouths secured and the establishment of fortifications further up the waterways, while a road network was established across the region. A similar approach is taken on the River Tay and to a lesser extent, the northeast coast, with fortifications at the mouths, and more located on the river and its main tributaries, enabling control of these routes. It is less clear if similar approaches were being taken on the River Tweed, although this is an area with a number of undated sites, and in the lower Clyde valley where it seems likely that there are either more Flavian sites to be discovered, or some have been lost through urban development. The lack of major rivers in parts of the Scottish Borders, East Lothian and Fife may show another regional adaptation of the military strategy in these areas, with fortifications only constructed where necessary; however, the caveat here is that in the latter area there is some unconfirmed evidence of Roman camps and confirmation and dating of these may lead to further reappraisal of the military strategy.

Scholars have often ignored the capacity of the army to use the sea and river networks in 1st century Scotland, partly due to a lack of evidence for harbours and docks, but as this analysis has demonstrated, it should not easily be dismissed because there is clearly a relationship between the location and positioning of fortifications and watercourses. While my findings do not dismiss the importance and necessity of overland incursions, it does suggest that the use of the river and coastal networks was of equal importance at the beginning of the Flavian incursions into Scotland. In the Antonine period, the evidence indicates that a similar strategy was followed, although there may have been attempts to secure more of the Firths of Forth and Clyde, while the evidence for the Severan campaigns indicate that there was less coastal and river-based activity. It is also clear from the coastal and river analysis that the fortifications were not following the instructions set out by the classical writers, other than them being located by water. Nor are these sites adhering to the notion or definition of frontiers, riverine or otherwise. The army is not using the river as a secure linear frontier or barrier, and there are not chains of fortifications in the same arrangements as are seen on other river frontiers on the continent. The exception to this, as noted in this chapter, could be the possible defensive arrangements along the Forth and Clyde in the Antonine period, but there is a lack of evidence to confirm this or not.

8

Discussion

"There has... been no systematic study of the location of forts in terms of their relationship with roads/rivers, orientation, tactical considerations, articulation with other installations, or relations to indigenous settlement patterns or landscape features."

(ScARF 2012a:32-33)

The parameters set out by ScARF, as outlined in more detail at the beginning of this volume, nicely capture the starting point for the investigation undertaken here. I set out to examine the relationship between 1st century Roman forts in Scotland, and the topographical and social landscape, as well as the interrelationships with one another, but I also expanded this to examine not only forts, but also the legionary fortress, camps, fortlets, and towers. As part of this investigation, and in attempt to address the deficiency in our knowledge of these fortifications in their immediate and wider landscapes, I have built a comprehensive and wide-ranging database covering all known, probable, and possible Roman sites in Scotland, refining certain details where possible, to establish a more certain dataset from which to progress this study. Using this, I have demonstrated the benefits of GIS-related spatial analysis, and what this can tell us about the Roman military occupation and strategy in North Britain. It shows the advantages of combining various datasets such as mapping, LiDAR, excavation reports and aerial photographs, processing these in a GIS, and what conclusions these can lead us to regarding Roman activity in an area such as North Britain. From this, and in part using methodologies influenced by Graafstal (2020) and Wooliscroft (2010), I have undertaken extensive analysis of these datasets in the GIS to examine the relationships of fortifications with, and within the landscape. More specifically, I have focused on four key elements; fortification location and positioning, intervisibility, orientation, and interconnectivity. Through this I have been able to generate a range of findings and explanations regarding the military strategy in Flavian Scotland, which may also have relevance and application to the other two main periods of Roman occupation in Scotland, as well as our wider understanding of military activity on Roman frontiers.

The priority of the 1st century army, as demonstrated in this volume, was to construct fortifications in locations and positions which enabled them to control movement through the immediate landscape. The legionary fortress, most of the forts, and some camps, are constructed in such locations, with most being positioned either at the entrance to valleys, or where two or more of these converge, while some are on higher ground to overlook these areas. This strategic positioning suggests an intention to control movement through these valleys, or on specific routes past those fortifications; I discuss this further below. Fortifications took advantage of the natural topography, not only in respect of access to natural resources, but also to provide an additional layer of defensive support; fortifications are often built next to ravines, steep inclines, or with rivers or large streams on one or more side, creating an additional obstacle for attacking enemies to overcome. Very occasionally, fortifications are located on the summit of hills, enabling a much wider view of the landscape over a considerable distance than if they were positioned on lower ground, but the preference is invariably better visibility of the immediate landscape. As has been noted previously, what is perceived to be natural defences at some sites, could have been created or shaped by the army to improve the security of certain locations, although this is a hypothetical suggestion which requires on the ground investigation. A similar suggestion has been made relating to the Roman camp at Rokeby Park in County Durham (Haken 2022). On the eastern side of the camp is the River Greta, and Haken has postulated that the escarpment between the camp and the river has been deliberately 'improved' by the army to increase the security of the camp. While this is an informal suggested which has not been subjected to any invasive investigations on the ground, it is an intriguing idea which should be investigated further, particularly in relation to those fortifications located on sloping sites.

My research findings, in relation to Flavian-period fortifications, can therefore be summarised as follows:

- Most Flavian fortifications were constructed in locations which were usually fertile, and most likely had access to resources necessary for survival and for the construction of the military structures;
- A significant number of fortifications from the Flavian period are located next to bodies of water (rivers and lakes) or on the coast, with a large number of these facing the water;
- The legionary fortress, forts and fortlets, are placed in strategic locations to enable both visual and physical control of the immediate landscape, and more specifically, what appear to be routes of movement for the indigenous population;
- Some camps appear to replicate the role of forts; that they are positioned in strategic locations to enable control of the immediate landscape;

- A number of camps are positioned on the coast, and not only had visual control of the immediate landscape, but appear to be protecting river mouths, and may have been where supplies and troops were offloaded;
- Signalling networks in Scotland may have been more extensive than currently thought and involved camps.

Furthermore,

- Arguments originating from the classical sources on orientation can be dismissed;
- There needs to be caution in using classical and antiquarian sources to interpret the archaeology, and that a similar approach is needed when considering the dating of these sites.

8.1. Roman Control of Scottish Landscapes

Some fortifications had visibility of the wider landscape, but more often than not these views were restrictive, indicating that for the majority of fortifications, their priority was visibility of the immediate area. Locating a fortification in such a prominent position in the landscape, would have enabled the defensive visibility of the site to become a prominent feature, ensuring that the indigenous population or enemy could see the fortification and the power it represented, this itself becoming a form of defence for the site.

While we know very little about Late Iron Age population centres, we do know that there are numerous individual sites located near Roman fortifications, but on the whole, it is less clear how populated these landscapes were, or where the population was moving to and from. Most of the indigenous sites near Roman forts are small, would not have been able to house large numbers of people, and could not have been a significant threat to the army. Of the few LIA population centres which exist, Roman fortifications have only been recorded at Burnswark, with some evidence that these may date to the Antonine period (J. H. Reid and Nicholson 2019), although the site is likely to be more complex than this. Other indigenous centres, such as Traprain Law do not appear to have evidence of nearby Roman military structures or interaction.

It seems unlikely that the army would have had the capacity to secure every valley in Scotland, and instead, they opted to place the forts in a controlling position, usually in locations where the indigenous population had movement routes. This can be with the Highland line forts, positioned at the entrances to glens, and therefore forcing anyone moving from the Highlands to the Lowlands, or vice versa, to move past the forts. Encouraging traffic to move through the landscape using preferred routes is demonstrated at a number of Flavian fortifications, with the clearest example from the fort at Crawford (Figure 6.21) which controls both movement to and from the valley to the east where there is at least one indigenous site, but is also positioned to face oncoming traffic heading northwards from Carlisle.

I have argued that the forts were positioned to exert visual control over the immediate, rather than the wider landscape, partly because the views from many sites are restricted at a greater distance, but also because my analysis shows that some forts could be circumvented, and alternative routes through the landscape could be taken. This could include crossing over hills, or using routes which may not have been 'upgraded' by the army, but inevitably, if another path was taken and which followed a river valley, a Roman fortification would be encountered at some point; there would be little opportunity to escape military scrutiny. Essentially, the primary role of forts is not to control the entirety of the wider landscape; this is a by-product of their presence in a location. Their key role is to restrict and control movement through certain areas, and by making the population pass by fortifications, it would also give the army an opportunity to collect taxes.

Another example of Roman attempts to control traffic movement through the landscape can be seen at Ardoch, one of the few forts not to be located in or near a valley, but at the southern extremity of the road running over the Gask Ridge. One reason for the construction of the fort in this location could be to control access to a pre-existing route, later adopted by the Romans. Bishop (2014) has argued that many Roman roads have their origins in the pre-Roman period. The importance of this route is reflected in the positioning of the fortlets of Kaims Castle and Glenbank, both of which have their entrances facing directly onto the road, which suggests a role in managing this route and movement along it, and could also indicate attempts by the army to tax anyone travelling along this. This is in addition to their probable role as signal relay stations. Another example of this control of movement routes comes from the fortlet at Gatehouse of Fleet, which is next to a Roman road, but also on the River Fleet, and which is orientated eastwards. Although this fortification is near the road, it is not quite next to it, indicating that the fortlet was constructed before the road. As the entrance faces towards the approaching route in the east, it suggests the fortlet was built in anticipation of the road, or that it was constructed next to an earlier, possibly pre-Roman route which was subsequently moved to nearer the river crossing. Either way, the fortlet, like those on the Gask Ridge, appears to have had a role in controlling movement, and possibly taxing traffic wanting to cross the river. As Symonds (2018:216) notes in his analysis of Roman fortlets, early such structures were not just located on roads, but in other parts of the Empire, such as the Rhine, Danube, and Bristol Channel, these were located on the banks or shores of major watercourses.

8.2. Role of 'Temporary Encampments'

I have previously detailed the typologies of camps, focusing on the four categories mentioned in the classical texts, and developed as a concept by archaeologists in recent years. These camps are defined as marching, practice, siege, and construction, although there have been few attempts to assign individual camps to one of these typologies, and where this has happened, it has generally been in relation to camps associated with the construction of the Antonine Wall. It is not straightforward to assign camps to a typology because we do not know what distinguishes one type for another, if such a distinction can be made. From the site profiling undertaken in this research, it can be argued that there are certain features which some encampment sites are lacking, and which indicate that these may have been constructed out of necessity in these locations. This suggests that these camps can be categorised as marching, and potentially occupied briefly, although this is difficult to show in the archaeological record. These missing features include:

- A lack of adequality sized slopes or plains in an area, which leads to the construction of the camp on a hill or steep hillside, these latter locations being positions which most fortifications avoid;
- A lack of natural topographic features in the landscape (such as rivers, steep escarpments, ravines, etc) which can be utilised for the defence of the camp;
- A lack of fertility in the landscape;
- A lack of views from the site, except for those temporary encampments which are located on hills which have a substantial better view of the wider, surrounding landscape.

Any attempt to classify a camp relies on circumstantial evidence; even those camps assumed to be for construction of the Antonine Wall, tend to have unconfirmed or weak dating evidence. Traditionally, Flavian camps are assumed to belong to the marching category, such as those in the northeast beyond Stracathro, because they appear to be part of a chain of fortifications showing the progress of the Flavian army towards the Moray coast. The suggestion by Woolliscroft and Hoffmann (2006) that a small, open-ended, Romano-British style enclosure constructed next to a Roman road near Strageath fort, has a Roman origin is intriguing, and could either represent a construction camp, or a totally new classification. These types of enclosures are prevalent in the Scottish landscape, but we know little about them, and whether or not there is a correlation between the location of such structures and nearby Roman fortifications or the military infrastructure. Further analysis of these sites, using the methodologies developed for this research, could tell us much more about the positioning and location of these enclosures, and if there is a relationship with Roman military fortifications.

Camps are generally much quicker and easier to construct than forts; they require less resources such as timber for buildings, and have simpler defences, usually a single rampart and ditch. As well as the four typologies set out previously, the viewshed analysis indicates that some camps fulfilled a similar role to the forts. Tacitus states that the army over-wintered in fortifications (*Agricola* 22), with the implication being that this was not the standard practice, although it is not clear if this was part of a longer-term strategy, or a last minute decision. This may explain why some camps are placed in the same type of location as forts, positioned in advantageous locations, overlooking, blocking, and/or controlling routes of movement through the landscape. This suggests that these camps may have been occupied on a longer term basis, although how long is not clear in the archaeological record; was it just for one winter season, or several years?

There are a number of camps which appear to fulfil the functions of forts, including Bochastle, Cold Chapel, Cornhill, Glenlochar, and Raeburnfoot. A clear example of the role of such sites in these locations, is demonstrated in respect of Dun camp which appears to supplement the role of the most northerly confirmed fort at Stracathro, and which demonstrates the inability of fortifications to control the whole landscape. Northern or Highland-based invaders could easily avoid Stracathro fort, and travel along the coast by Stonehaven (where there are no confirmed Roman forts), and they would be separated from the army by hills. This example also demonstrates the argument that some camps (including Dun), are replicating the function of forts, so unauthorised movements along the coast would be blocked by that site.

Tacitus makes clear that using the coast and watercourses, was an important tactic deployed by the army, both in Scotland and on the continent, when invading and securing territories. In Flavian Scotland, a number of camps are located in coastal positions, most of which are also at the mouths of rivers; no 1st century forts have been identified in these locations, although there are some examples from the Antonine period. In this research, I have demonstrated the relationship between the Flavian sites, the coast, and rivers, with the majority of fortifications being interconnected by the same waterways, usually with a camp positioned at the entrance to these networks. With fortifications located further upriver, it is plausible that these camps may also have acted as supply bases for those sites, or at the very least, have been a drop-off point for goods and soldiers transported by sea, and then moved inland; a similar argument has been put forward by Evans et al. (2010) in relation to the coastal fortifications in Wales. Although there has been no specific analysis of the river levels in Flavian Scotland, it is more than likely that many of the inland fortifications would have been accessible by river, and that flat-bottomed vessels would have been able to sail to a number of these; as *ScARF: The Roman Presence* (2012) notes, we are yet to find the remains of any such vessels in Scottish waters, and although there is some indication of a waterside infrastructure in some locations, firm archaeological evidence of this remains elusive.

The coastal camps also appear to be replicating the function of the forts, and doing this in two ways; first, they have visual control of the immediate landscape, and second, they control movement through that landscape; for these sites, this manifests itself as guarding access to the river networks. Coastal camps which are fulfilling the role of forts can be found at Ayr, Dun, Girvan Mains, and Ward Law. The latter site, Ward Law, does appear to be slightly different from the other locations as it is not immediately next to the shoreline, but this could be because its location enables it to have near 360° views of the Solway Firth, and surrounding countryside, and suggests that some fortlets may have a similar relationship with other nearby fortifications. This is all in addition to the role of some camps as part of signalling networks as discussed in the next section. Finally, it is important that we begin to think of camps as much more than temporary encampments, as some of the sites clearly had a more significant role. Camps may not have survived as well as other fortifications in the landscape, but this should not result in us being as dismissive of these structures as we have been.

8.3. Intervisibility And Signalling: Testing a Methodology

One of the aims of this investigation was to establish the intervisibility capacity between Roman fortifications, and whether or not sites were constructed in locations which enabled them to signal between each other. In undertaking this element of the site profiling, I wanted to test and develop the signalling methodology established by Woolliscroft (2010), but to also extend the parameters to include camps, and also the capacity and extent of signalling between fortifications. Woolliscroft has already undertaken extensive practical experimentation between various fortifications on different frontiers, including those on the Gask Ridge in 1st century Scotland. Woolliscroft's work was undertaken prior to the capacity to do such modelling in GIS, and his experiments did not include camps. I have recreated his on-the-ground methodology by developing my line-of-sight analysis in a virtual, GIS environment. While his experiments were repeated in relation to the Gask Ridge fortifications, those on the Antonine Wall, and in part, the tower sites in southern Scotland, there has been no previous attempt to apply this methodology to a wide-ranging dataset (130 Flavian sites), as I do here; this also included replicating his signalling experiment, to and from the Gask Ridge fortifications. Unfortunately, there have been no other attempts to replicate Woolliscroft's methodology on the ground at the Gask Ridge sites, and it is therefore not possible to test the validity of his findings through practical methods. As I have shown, the results give a very different perspective on the extent and effectiveness of signalling when the parameters are altered through GIS modelling.

In this investigation, I have not only tested Woolliscroft's methodology, but I have also confirmed his findings from the Gask Ridge sites, that many fortifications on this line were intervisible, and that there was a capability to signal between various sites. Woolliscroft did not model signalling capacity beyond the fort at Bertha, although he did postulate that there were more towers to be discovered. Again, I have expanded on his work and have modelled a possible extension of this signalling network, which demonstrate that signals could reach the legionary fortress, potentially from Doune fort, and that there is the possibility of the network extending north of Inchtuthil. There are some missing tower sites which need to be located to confirm the effectiveness of the communications chain. To the northwest of the Gask Ridge, are the Highland line fortifications, which I have also modelled, undertaking a line-of-sight analysis between the forts and various archaeological features in the landscape (such as earthworks, cropmarks and cairns); all of these features are undated and have not been archaeologically examined, with one exception at the Sma' Glen near Fendoch which has been speculated as a Roman site, but remains unexcavated (Woolliscroft and Hoffmann 2006). Several of the Flavian forts share a line-of-sight with these features in the landscape, raising the possibility of the latter acting as signal relay stations. This also raises the possibility of a signalling network along the Highland line. This analysis also demonstrates the potential importance of camps within such networks, indicating that certain sites may have been integral to these networks.

The results in this research have demonstrated the complexity of signalling chains in Scotland, and this has been emphasised through the network diagram which I have produced for signalling between the Gask Ridge fortifications. This also shows that the network is much more complex than necessary for a simple signalling chain; several towers could be removed from the system, and it would remain effective. This lends some credence to Woolliscroft's hypothesis that the purpose of these sites is to act as an early warning system, and then secondly as a communications chain. The alternative explanation, given that some of the towers were rebuilt at some point in the Roman period, and the lack of datable evidence, is that this is actually two systems, one replacing the other, and which are conflated as one because of a lack of datable material.

8.4. Profiling Fortification Sites

Key to this quantitative investigation has been to profile the sites of Flavian fortifications with the intention of developing our knowledge of individual sites, but also to learn about why the army was opting to construct these in certain locations. To do this, I created a substantial database of archaeological data, and processed this, along with mapping data in a GIS, analysing and modelling the fortifications along with topographical data on their immediate landscapes. For each site, I modelled the defensive topography and elevation of the fortifications, undertook binary viewshed analyses, and projected the line-of-sight from one Roman fortification to another. I also wanted to see if it was possible to establish if there was a common criteria which the army used when selecting a site. Both Vegetius and 'Pseudo' Hyginus set out such a list, although these contained a number of elements which are difficult to prove because of a lack of archaeological evidence, such as the availability of woodland and food sources nearby, but it is likely that most sites would have access to some, or all of the necessary resources, or that the army would have brought additional supplies with them.

This modelling was influenced by Graafstal (2020:174-177) who put forward the concept of sequential stratigraphy in relation for the logical, spatial and structural dependencies of construction of the Antonine Wall fortifications. Graafstal argues that by combining these elements, it is possible to build a sequential profile for the construction of these, including a site profile for each location. From this, Graafstal has concluded that the fortifications on this frontier were built using a criteria, which includes a requirement for the forts to be intervisible with their neighbours, to be located in positions where they can control valleys, constructed on plains (where available), and finally, maintaining the regular spacing along the Wall when possible. Following this logic, Graafstal has theorised which forts are planned first, and those which are later inserted into this ordering. He also concluded that the forts are constructed with a visual line-of-site to the immediate neighbours, and positioned at the entrance to valleys enabling visual control of the landscape. It was not possible to completely replicate Graafstal's approach and calculate which fortifications were constructed before others, partly because his work was focussed on a linear barrier, and while the road along the Gask Ridge could be a proto-linear frontier, most Flavian sites in Scotland are not located in this geographic area, and I wanted to create a set of results which comparable with each other. Instead, as I have outlined earlier in this section, I have adapted parts of Graafstal's methodology, and expanded this, enabling me to develop a site profile for each of fortification locations in the 1st century.

One outcome of site profiling, has been to establish a set of criteria for Flavian fortification sites. This list (Table 8) has been developed from the analytical results taken from

Table 8. Set of criteria for profiling potential fortification sites in Flavian Scotland.

Site Profile	Properties	Explanation
Location And Positioning	Can the natural topography be used for defence?	Most fortifications make use of natural topography such as river valleys, steep escarpments, etc.
	Is the site in fertile of arable land?	Most fortifications are located in areas classed as fertile/arable today, although it is difficult to prove if this was the case in the 1st century.
	Is the site located next to the coast or main river?	Most fortifications are located within 2km of the shoreline or river banks.
	Is the site located near the confluence of two rivers or a river and tributary?	Numerous fortifications are located near the confluence of two rivers.
	Is the site at the entrance to a valley, where two or more valleys converge, or overlooking these?	The legionary fortress, all forts and various camps are located at the entrance to valleys, where these converge or occasionally overlooking them.
	Is the site a plain, slope, or hill?	Most fortifications are located on plains, with slopes the next most common location. A small number of fortifications are located on hills.
	Could the site be subjected to flooding (sites are less likely to be prone to flooding)?	Most fortifications are not in positions which would be prone to flooding. There are a small number or exceptions to this.
Intervisibility	Is the site visible from another same period Roman site? If so, can it be hypothesised to fit in with a signalling network?	Several fortifications are intervisible and could signal to each other, although this does not mean that they were actively signalling or that this was an effective method of communicating.
Orientation	Is the site facing water? If so, what type of watercourse (e.g. coast, river, confluence)?	Where orientation is discernible, most fortifications are facing water, mainly rivers, but in some instances the coast. If partial cropmarks/earthworks are visible, it may be possible to determine orientation.
Interconnectivity: Roads	Is the site near a known/suspected Roman road?	We have limited data confirming which roads have Roman origins, and some fortifications appear not to be connected to the road network, so this factor needs to use considered with caution.
	Is the site located near a potential or likely crossing point over a river?	Many forts and fortlets appear to be located next to crossing points, but often the crossings are not confirmed in the archaeological record.
Interconnectivity: Coastal And Waterways	Is the site located on a river, but near the mouth?	Fortifications on the coast are usually located on the coast at the mouth of a river, or slightly further upriver.
	Are there additional fortifications further up river or on a tributary?	Most fortifications in Scotland are interconnected by being located on the major rivers and their tributaries.

the 130 Flavian fortification sites which I have examined, and contains a list of common properties shared by most of these, although not every site has every element, and some remain unconfirmed, such as the orientation of most camps[11]. Although the profiling was developed from data pertaining to 1st century sites, there are many commonalities with those in the Antonine period in Scotland, which suggests similarities in the military strategy. There are fewer elements in common with Severan fortifications, although as the focus of this work has been on the Flavian sites, I have undertaken limited application of the criteria in relation to post-Flavian, unconfirmed and undated fortifications.

Costa-García (2018:993), Graafstal (2020:143), ScARF (2012a:32-33) and others outlined previously, have all recognised the benefit of examining the landscape surrounding a fortification, and this is something which I have attempted to do here through the profiling of the fortification sites. As I have indicated, there are numerous benefits to this; it shows the use of the natural topography, the defensive capacity of the site, the need for visual control of the landscape, the role and purpose of the fortification in the landscape, the relationship between the military and the indigenous population, and supply and movement of goods and soldiers. Profiling helps us to create a standardised narrative for the location of fortifications, which not only enables us to draw comparisons with fortifications in different locations from the same, and different periods. For those sites which see different fortifications from different periods constructed on top of each other, it could enable us to develop a stratigraphic profile of these locations. This type of profiling could be taken a step further, particularly using a quantitative database, where various datasets such as size, shape, and internal features, could be stored for cross-referencing and comparative purposes; such a system could enable us to better sequence camps, as well as forts.

Not only has site profiling allowed us an insight into the military strategy in Scotland, but there is the potential that it could do the same for fortifications from different periods and locations from across the Empire, particularly in those places where Roman fortifications are suspected or remain unconfirmed. Such profiling would need to be thoroughly tested as the circumstances and strategy may differ in other areas, and would also need to be combined with other data including the topographical and archaeological to build a case. I have already demonstrated the effectiveness of orientation as a profiling tool, and outside of this research have examined the direction which fortifications in northern England are facing. Orientation is only one part of a site profile, telling us what the site is facing, and potentially providing a partial understanding of its purpose. Even better is to combine this with an elevation or defensive topography analysis, as I have done previously, giving much more of an indication of the military strategy in an area. I discuss the profiling of fortifications from other frontiers, and how these compare with the results from Scotland below.

8.5. Roman Military Strategies in Scotland

The findings of this investigation contributes towards our understanding of the Roman military strategies in Scotland not only in the 1st century, but across the three main periods. In the Flavian period, the strategy appears to have been a mixture of campaigning, evidenced through the establishment of marching camps, and attempts to secure the region through the construction of permanent fortifications, and the placing of these in strategic locations. The use of some camps to fulfil the function of forts in visually controlling movement routes, both inland and on the coast, may reflect the need to quickly establish fortifications in certain locations, but the brief nature of the occupation of North Britain meant that these do not appear to have been replaced with permanent fortifications.

In the Antonine period, there appears to have been a similar strategy behind the positioning of the forts; to establish visual control over movement routes, and the immediate landscape surrounding the sites. Like the locating of Flavian camps in coastal positions, a number of permanent fortifications are constructed at the mouths of rivers, particularly on the Firth of Forth at Cramond and Inveresk, and potentially on the Clyde and Solway coasts. The use of forts in the positions shows a distinction between 1st and 2nd century strategic decisions by using permanent fortifications rather than camps, or alternatively, it may suggest that there was more time to upgrade from camps to forts in the Antonine period.

As noted earlier, it has been suggested that the designers of the Antonine Wall may have attempted to replicate many of the facets of Hadrian's Wall. I make two observations in light of this. Firstly, the unconfirmed sites on the Clyde coast (for example, finds have indicated potential Antonine activity at Largs, which is itself close to the same period fortlets of Outerwards, and nearby Lurg Moor) could represent an Antonine attempt to replicate the Hadrianic-period Cumbrian coastal defences, by creating a series of outpost fortifications for the western flank of the Antonine Wall. My second observation, while again acknowledging the limited but circumstantial evidence, relates to the alleged Sibbald sites on the southern shore of the Firth of Forth, which I postulate could represent an eastern outpost extension of the Antonine Wall. Our knowledge of activity to the north of the Wall in the Antonine period is also limited, but there is some artefact evidence that the Flavian forts at Ardoch, Strageath and Bertha were reoccupied, while there is also a possibility of some Antonine activity elsewhere on the Gask Ridge, as well as at Inverquharity. Further investigation of these sites, as well as revising the dating chronology of others, could indicate whether or not the 2nd century strategy was to secure the coast (and protect shipping), and to also occupy additional territory beyond the Wall, or if all of these sites were acting as outposts.

---

[11] A version of this table, which includes a breakdown of the profiling for the Flavian fortifications in Scotland, can be found in Appendix 2.

While we can only hypothesise about the role and purpose of the 2nd century coastal and outpost fortifications, it indicates the need for further research in these areas. A re-evaluation of these sites, combined with modern survey techniques, GIS, re-analysis of any finds, along with my site profiling approach, may support the presence of Antonine activity in these locations.

By the time of the Severan campaigns, the strategy appears to have been quite different, with the predominant fortification being camps; the fortress at Carpow is on the coast, and may have been a supply depot with goods/ troops brought in by sea. The location of the known camps (assuming these date to this period), suggests that these were for advancement through the landscape, rather than having the function of securing indigenous movement routes, as in previous periods. The majority of camps in Scotland remain undated, and it would be a worthwhile exercise to examine these in the context of my site profiling, and to see if there are any discernible patterns which fit with the Flavian, Antonine, or Severan strategies, or even the postulated campaigns which took place before and after the major campaigns.

8.6. Profiling Fortifications Beyond Flavian Scotland

Beyond Scotland there are a number of other frontiers where there have been attempts to understand the role of fortifications in the landscape, primarily in the Netherlands, Judea, Spain, and the Southern Arabian Petraea. While these frontiers have not been subjected to the full extent of site profiling which I have undertaken, they have been examined using GIS modelling. In Spain, Costa-García (2018) undertook an extensive analysis of a wide-range of fortifications dating to different periods, concluding that these were located in positions which enabled the Romans to control mountain passes and hill ranges, which was prioritised over the complete control of the surrounding area, something which has parallels with my findings in Scotland. Costa-García gives a limited impression of the landscape surrounding these sites; were they orientated towards particular features, what resources were available nearby, and probably more significantly in comparison to Scotland, were there waterways nearby? In respect of the last question, while Costa-García (2018:989) produced a high level distribution map of the military sites in northwest Iberia showing a significant number of fortifications located near waterways, he did not investigate the relationship further and it is not clear which sites were contemporary with one another or how significant the waterways were. It would appear that these fortifications would be ideal candidates for site profiling, and could provide comparable material for those in North Britain, although the Spanish sites suffer from a similar lack of datable material as those in Scotland.

Another study which has come to similar conclusions regarding the positioning of fortifications, was undertaken by Castro (2018) in relation to fortifications in the Southern Arabian Petraea. In her study, Castro examined a wide-range of sites, and although these are not contemporary with the Flavian period in Scotland, Castro found that the Roman fortifications were located in positions enabling them to control settlements, as well as water points, wadi, and roads. Similar to the situation in North Britain, these were essentially movement routes through the landscape, and by controlling these, the military would have been able to exert influence and control over the indigenous population.

Pažout (2018) examined the early frontier in the Northern Negev, setting out to examine the intervisibility between military sites, the visual control of the landscape, and the positioning of fortifications in relation to the settlements and roads. Although Pažout's study is not as wide-ranging as the one I have undertaken, he did come to some broad conclusions. For example, some sites (those in the east and south of the study area) are too far to be part of a signalling system, fortifications are located within 3 kilometres of settlements (with most fortifications having a good view of these), and fortifications have visual control of long segments of military roads. Finally, using GIS modelling, Pažout calculated likely routes through the landscape, as most Roman roads remain undetected in his study area. He found that most fortifications are located on the routes of movement which he modelled. Pažout concluded that there were two distinct regions in Judea, with the north being more troublesome, and fortifications there were constructed so close to population centres in order to effectively control them. Although Pažout did not undertake a study of rivers, it is clear that although some fortifications are located on wadi routes, many are not. Undertaking site profiling may give us a better indication of the fortifications in the landscape, and whether or not they are using the natural topography for defence. Such an analysis may give a better indication of the military strategy, and how this compares to other Roman frontiers.

In the Netherlands, the military created secure transport routes, and as Graafstal has noted, there are similarities between this aspect of the Dutch *limes* and the Gask Ridge fortifications, while there are parallels with other sites in the frontier-zone in Scotland (E. Graafstal 2020; see also 2002). It therefore seems likely that the military strategy deployed on the Dutch frontier was replicated, in part, in Scotland, but at the same time adapted for the terrain. It also shows the early emergence of linear frontiers, albeit using the natural topography rather an artificially constructed barriers such as a wall. Although towers have only been located in a few places in Scotland (the Gask Ridge and the Scottish Borders), other frontiers, such as the Lower Rhine, the *limes* Porolissensis, the Middle Danube, and the Southern Arabian Petraea have all recorded evidence of large numbers of towers, and while Scotland was a smaller frontier-zone than these locations, it seems possible that there may be more towers awaiting discovery, and again these hint at the development of a proto-frontier arrangement in Scotland; as suggested previously, there are various archaeological features around the Highland line forts which require further investigation.

8.7. Research Opportunities

By providing a systematic spatial analysis of the positioning, intervisibility, orientation, and interconnectivity of Roman fortifications in Scotland, I have enhanced our understanding of the role and purpose of these sites, their relationship with one another and the wider physical and social landscape, and the overall military strategy that was being employed in North Britain. Inevitably, the research has also raised new questions and revealed some of the limitations of the known archaeological record. The benefits of such research, and widespread use of GIS is perhaps best summed up in *ScARF: The Roman Presence*,

> *Not only can different techniques sometimes bring new information to light, but also future developments in software may necessitate the reprocessing of ... information. Integration of existing spatial data in electronic form, and creation of layers of known Roman features [should be available] for download or display [in an] online GIS. Such a programme would highlight, for example, the poor state of current knowledge of the Roman road network in Scotland.*
>
> **ScARF 2012:67**

My GIS methodologies and some of the more speculative models produced in my research, also have the potential to help better pinpoint the most promising locations for further investigation, as outlined in the previous section. A series of further research priorities therefore emanate from my research findings, and these are set out below.

8.7.1. Fortifications Dating and Sequencing

One of the major challenges in undertaking this analysis has related to the dating of many of the fortifications. There is limited, datable evidence to establish site chronology for Roman fortifications in Scotland, and where sites are dated, this has often relied on a few pottery fragments often recovered from ditches, or from entrance morphology of camps. The latter is made more problematic by albeit limited evidence indicating the use of two different types of entrances on a single encampment, further confusing the chronology, although, this could be a sign that sites were being reoccupied. The last reasonably systematic reappraisal of Roman dating in Scotland, was undertaken by Hartley (1972), although this only involved a small number of sites, and examined one type of evidence. Burnham and Davies (2010) in relation to Roman Wales, and Bidwell and Hodgson (2009) for northern England, have undertaken a reappraisal of the dating evidence, and 50 years on from Hartley, and with new evidence and new technologies and dating techniques available, there needs to be a wider reappraisal of the dating of fortifications in Scotland. A revised dating chronology has implications for the sequencing of camps, which has generally been based on assumptions from the classical texts. These suggest, for example, that the Severan invasion involved a sizeable force and is therefore usually the date of origin assigned to the larger camps, but there is a lack of datable evidence in the archaeological record to support this. This approach to sequencing also does not necessarily consider the reuse of sites by soldiers from different periods, or even constant reuse in one. Some sites are constructed within another or utilise common sections of defences, such as at Dunblane, perhaps suggesting that larger forts were reduced in size at a later date. This, in turn, contributes to the confusion in site chronology caused by reoccupation of the fortification. Another assumption which has been made, is that two sites adjacent to each other were occupied contemporaneously. Where there is a fort and camp next to each other, the latter could be a base for the construction of the former, but, this does not explain why there are two camps and two compounds next to the legionary fortress, or why there are no traces of camps next to the majority of forts. There is also some sign that the principles of camp sequencing might apply to a number of forts which share common features, such as Whitley Castle, Crawford, and Loudon Hill, all of which are trapezoidal in shape, while Bochastle, Newstead, and Oakwood are square in shape. It may be beneficial to explore these sites further as it may indicate the movement of one set of soldiers through the landscape over a period of time. In summary, my investigation has highlighted the deficiencies in the dating and sequencing of fortifications in Scotland, and how this affects the interpretation of the fortifications, their role and purpose in the landscape, and the wider progress of the Flavian army in this period. Limited reappraisal of dating has taken place, and has contributed to a new understanding of our knowledge of the military in North Britain, but, as has been recognised in *ScARF: The Roman Presence* (2012), a more extensive re-examination of the datable evidence could significantly enhance and alter our understanding of the Roman military strategy in the different periods in North Britain and Scotland.

8.7.2. The Indigenous Population

The positioning of fortifications in the Flavian period in Scotland is often less influenced by a sense of there being a major, hostile threat, but appears motivated by a need to control movement in the immediate landscape. Despite there being studies of the Iron Age in Scotland and of the Romans in Scotland, there have been few studies of the relationship between the indigenous population and the Roman army. Mercer's (2018) study of the relationship between the Flavian army and the local population, particularly through the Roman material culture found on the indigenous sites, has shown the opportunity presented by such studies, and it would be helpful to see such work more widely expanded, while also examining the material culture to clarify if there was a trading relationship between the Romans, and local populations in southern Scotland as Mercer proposes. Our knowledge of how the Romans and indigenous populations interacted is growing, but as Hingley (2014) says, we need a reappraisal of artefacts from indigenous sites, as demonstrated through work by Main (1998), Hunter (2001; 2007; 2016), Inglemark (2014), and Reid et al. (2019) which indicates that there were likely to have been both trading and diplomatic relations in some parts of Scotland, such as in Stirlingshire, Birnie in Moray, and later at Traprain Law in East Lothian. Exploring such relationships through the reappraisal of Roman artefacts from indigenous sites from across Scotland may help us better understand the relationship between fortifications and the indigenous landscape, especially as there are known to be a number of roundhouses near Roman forts, an area which remains unexplored. This further ties into the wider ScARF suggestion that there should be examination of an area of 1 kilometre around a fort, which would be a useful project, even through a desk-based assessment (ScARF 2012a).

8.7.3. Signalling

While Woolliscroft's methods have been replicated and developed in this research, and by others (e.g. Murphy, Gittings, and Crow 2018; J. Lewis 2020), and similar outcomes achieved, it is also becoming clear that signalling in Scotland may be more complex than initially argued (e.g. see Chapter 5 and also Woolliscroft 1993; Woolliscroft 2010; Woolliscroft and Hoffmann 2006; Donaldson 1988; Southern 1990). The purpose of the Gask Ridge fortifications is still not clear, although I have put forward the idea that the signalling chain is likely to be more extensive than previously thought, while there is also the possibility of further signalling chains elsewhere in Scotland, such as in the Borders and along the Highland Faultline. The Gask Ridge fortifications do not appear to have been a secure supply line, but the system itself may actually be the product of two different periods of activity which have been conflated as one. My analysis has also revealed a potential role for some camps in signalling, which is not something that has previously been examined, probably because camps have generally been assumed to be temporary whereas a signalling function implies some longevity and the existence of towers. I have identified possible signalling functions through computer modelling of intervisibility rather than the archaeological record, so this needs further work on the ground. If confirmed it would also lend support to the idea that some camps were constructed to be more than a temporary stopover. I am therefore suggesting two areas for further research. First, further computer modelling and practical experimentation of signalling between sites would be helpful; for those fortifications (such as in the Scottish Borders) beyond Woolliscroft's 6 kilometre visibility parameter, need to see signals, or could a simplified form of communications have been adequate? Secondly, there are a number of landscape features which are unexplored, but which the computational modelling has indicated may have been the locations of towers; it is suggested that these sites are investigated on the ground to see if they support this theory.

8.7.4. Road Network

Our fragmentary knowledge of the road network limits the conclusions which can be drawn about interconnectivity and networks of fortifications. There are some sections of road which seem likely to exist, but which remain untraced, such as Dere Street north of the Pentland Hills, while there are also fortifications which appear not to be on the network, which may be because there were not occupied for long enough for the army to get around to building these sections of road. While the influence of *de situ Britanniae* (Bertram 1809) has also affected our interpreting of Roman roads in Scotland. The evidence from literary sources, and in Wales, is that there were different types of road, built to different standards, and there is some indication of this from the Gask Ridge. LiDAR and more advanced analytical techniques mean that it may now be easier to identify some of the missing stretches of road than it once was, although field work is required to confirm their Roman origin.

The history and dating of roads are much more complex than texts such as Codrington (Codrington 1918; 1928) and Margary (Margary 1957; 1967) imply, with the hypothesis that the road network was established in the country's west first, evidenced by early fortifications in the southwest and Clyde valley, whereas there are relatively few Flavian sites along Dere Street, or on the eastern seaboard. Beyond the Forth-Clyde isthmus, the road crosses the River Tay at Bertha and almost reaches Inverquharity, but beyond this, the network is less clear and remains unconfirmed and undated. Did it continue on to other 1st century sites? If the road network was built much later (as possibly evidenced at Innerpeffray), then it raises the prospect that the Antonine invasion was more extensive than previously understood; currently the most northerly evidence of Antonine activity comes from the fort at Bertha, although a number of sites further north potentially date to the 2nd century. As outlined previously, a reappraisal of our existing knowledge and the archaeological evidence for the road network would be welcomed. Using more recent technologies, such as Least Cost Path analyses in a GIS, it may be possible to predict the location of some stretches of previously undiscovered sections of road. More fieldwork is required to identify some sections such as the road on the Gask Ridge and at Kirriemuir. Such an approach has been taken on other frontiers, particularly in the Netherlands, where it has indicated the route of the road along the frontier (Verhagen 2010).

8.7.5. Water Levels

As both Hannon (2018) and Davies (2020) have discussed, changing assumptions about the water levels of the Firth of Forth has led to reinterpretation of the site at Camelon; if water levels were higher relative to the land in the Roman period, as they were in much of Scotland due to isostatic rebound, Camelon could have been on the coast, and would have made an ideal site for a harbour, particularly given the evidence of this having been recovered from the local area (e.g. Sibbald 1707:93). Such modelling would make a significant difference to our knowledge of the river network, not just around the Forth, but for those sites on the River Tay and further north. This might also indicate if shipping could reach the fortress, and if the river flowed to the south of the peninsula; incidentally, Inchtuthil legionary fortress is one of two such sites in the Roman world, which may not have been accessible from a navigable river (Bishop pers. comm.). Modelling of raised water levels could also indicate where we should look for evidence of harbourside structures.

9
Conclusion

The approaches, analysis and conclusions presented here challenges much of what we know about the Flavian invasion of North Britain, and the military strategy behind it. It reminds us that a cautious approach is needed when examining the historical, literary and archaeological evidence, and because these can infrequently be cross-referenced with each other, we cannot take them for granted on their own. My analysis has shown that we need to reconsider the role of camps as part of the invasion and attempts to secure Scotland as part of the Empire. It has also shown that Scotland was part of an emerging frontier-zone, but one which was never fully solidified and absorbed into the Empire. It has also confirmed the role of the so called glen blocking forts, but shown that this is a term which could be applied to all forts, as well as some camps.

It is only now that GIS analysis is being applied to other frontiers, and that archaeologists are beginning to adopt various elements of site profiling, that we can begin to compare different frontiers in any depth. Until the 21st century, such comparisons tended to be surface deep, in that the individual fortification was the primary focus of the research, and the landscape and anything beyond the fort was of less importance and often ignored. But the various quantitative analytical studies of frontiers which I have discussed, demonstrate that fortification landscapes are rarely simple or straightforward, and in order to understand the role of fortifications in Roman military strategy, we need to also understand their relationships both with, and within the wider landscape. But we also need to look at the various different types of fortification, the legionary and vexillation fortresses, the forts, camps, fortlets, towers, the other military structures, as well as the infrastructure, all need to be considered, because they were not built or designed to function on their own, but as an interconnected network. The site profiling and computer modelling employed in this study, along with the variations on this that are beginning to be undertaken elsewhere, are essential tools to help us interpret fortifications in their landscape, and open-up wide-ranging possibilities, not only for the comparison of fortifications and their composite features, but for us to actually be able to interpret the actions, progress, and strategy of the Roman army in different periods, across the frontiers of the Empire. This type of profiling has confirmed that Roman fortifications do not follow most of the instructions set out in the classical texts, and instead are adapted to suit the topography of the landscape enabling oversight of the area, and control of the indigenous population; this even extended to sub-regional control of the river networks.

In summary, by developing and applying quantitative spatial analysis in a Geographic Information System, I conclude that the military strategy in Flavian Scotland was not to restrict all movement through the wider landscape as had previously been implied by the notion of 'glen-blocking forts'. Such a strategy would have been highly resource intensive and challenging in an area with so many glens, valleys, hills, and mountains; it would have been impossible to police them all. In any case, it also seems unlikely that it was necessary to do this. Instead, the aim of the army was to control the main corridors of movement, usually in the vicinity of the fortifications. By doing this, they would exert both visual control and authority over the indigenous population, and negate the need to control the entirety of the landscape in Scotland.

Bibliography

The classical texts are available through two main sources, both of which have been consulted as part of this research; Penguin Classics and Loeb Classical Library (Harvard University Press. Texts from these sources have been used as the standard translation, but where an alternative has been used, this is stated in the main text. Additional translations of specific passages have been sourced from Campbell (1994) or Ireland (1996; 2008).

Ammianus Marcellinus

Bede: *Historia ecclesiastica gentis Anglorum* (Ecclesiastical History of the English People)

Caesar: *de Bello Civili* (The Civil War) | *de Bello Gallico* (The Gallic War)

Cassius Dio: *Epitome*

Feriale Duranam

Gildas: *De Excidio et Conquestu Britanniae* (On the Ruin and Conquest of Britain)

Herodian: History of the Empire

Hyginus ('Pseudo'): *de Munitionibus Castrorum* (The Fortification of the Camp)

Itinerarium Antonini Augusti (Antonine Itinerary)

Imperatoris Antonini Augusti Itinerarium Maritinum (Maritime Itinerary)

Josephus: *Bellum Iudaicum* (The Jewish War)

Libanus Oration

Nennius, 2000. *Nennius: History Of The Britons (Historia Brittonum)* J. A. Giles, ed., Cambridge, Ontario: In parentheses Publications.

New Statistical Account of Scotland or The Report Of The Committee Of The Society For The Sons And Daughters Of The Clergy Superintending The New Statistical Account Of Scotland, To The General Assembly Of The Church Of Scotland (NSA)

Notitia Dignitatum

Old Statistical Account of Scotland Drawn from the Communications of the Ministers of the Different Parishes (OSA)

Panegyrici Latini Vetares (Pan. Lat. Vet.)

Nemesianus: *Cynegetica*

Pliny the Younger: Letters

Pliny the Elder: Natural History

Pomponius Mela: *De Chorographia*

Ptolemy: Geographia

Ravenna Cosmography

Strabo: Geographica

Suetonius: *Julius*

Tacitus: *Agricola* (Birley 2009; Woodman & Kraus 2014) | *Annals* | *Historiae* (Histories)

Vegetius: *Epitoma De Re Militari* (Epitome of Military Science) (Milner 2001)

Main Bibliographic Sources

Abercromby, John. 1902. "Account of the Excavation of the Roman Station at Inchtuthil, Perthshire Undertaken by the Society of Antiquaries in Scotland in 1901." Proceedings of the Society of Antiquaries of Scotland 36: 182–203.

Adamson, Henry. 1774. *The Muses Threnodie, or, Mirthfull Mournings, on the Death of Master Gall Containing Varietie of Pleasant Poëticall Descriptions, Morall Instructions, Historicall Narrations, and Divine Observations, with the Most Remarkable Antiquities of Scotland, Especially at Perth.* George Anderson.

Alexander, D. 1996. "A96 Kintore Bypass (Kintore Parish), Early Prehistoric Pits, Roman Camp, Later Prehistoric and Early Historic Structures." *Discovery Excavation in Scotland*, 8–9.

Arabaolaza, Iraia. 2019. "A Roman Marching Camp in Ayr." *Britannia* 50 (November): 330–349. doi:10.1017/s0068113x19000059.

Armit, I, and I Ralston. 2003. "The Iron Age." In *Scotland After the Ice Age: Environment, Archaeology and History, 8000 BCE - CE 1000*, edited by Kevin J Edwards and I Ralston, 169–193. Edinburgh University Press.

Bachagha, Nabil. Lei Luo, Xinyuan Wang, Nicola Masini, Tababi Moussa, Houcine Khatteli, and Rosa Lasaponara. 2020. "Mapping the Roman Water Supply System of the Wadi El Melah Valley in Gafsa, Tunisia, Using Remote Sensing." *Sustainability* 12 (2): 567. doi:10.3390/su12020567.

Bachagha, Nabil, Xinyuan Wang, Lei Luo, Li Li, Houcine Khatteli, and Rosa Lasaponara. 2020. "Remote Sensing and GIS Techniques for Reconstructing the Military Fort System on the Roman Boundary (Tunisian Section) and Identifying Archaeological Sites." *Remote Sensing of Environment* 236: 111418. doi:10.1016/j.rse.2019.111418.

Barclay, Robert. 1792. "On Agricola's Engagement with the Caledonians, Under Their Leader Galgacus." *Archaeologia Scotica* 1: 565–569.

Bateson, J D, and N M McQ Holmes. 1997. "Roman and Medieval Coins Found in Scotland, 1988-95." *Proceedings of the Society of Antiquaries of Scotland* 127: 527–561.

Bertram, Charles. 1809. *The Description of Britain, Translated From Richard of Cirencester: With the Original Treatise De Situ Britanniae and Commentary on the Itinerary*. J. White & Co.

Bidwell, Paul. 2013. *Roman Forts in Britain*. Stroud: The History Press.

Bidwell, Paul, and Nick Hodgson. 2009. *The Roman Army in Northern England*. Arbeia Society.

Birley, A R. 2010. "The Agricola." In *The Cambridge Companion to Tacitus*, edited by A J Woodman, 47–58. Cambridge: Cambridge University Press. doi:10.1017/ccol9780521874601.005.

Bishop, M C. 2004. *Inveresk Gate: Excavations in the Roman Civil Settlement at Inveresk, East Lothian, 1996-2000*. Scottish Trust for Archaeological Research.

Bishop, M C. 2013. *Handbook to Roman Legionary Fortresses*. Pen & Sword Military.

Bishop, M C. 2014. *The Secret History of the Roman Roads of Britain*. Barnsley: Pen & Sword Books.

Blanco, Andrés Menéndez, Jesús García Sánchez, José Manuel Costa-García, João Fonte, David González-Álvarez, and Víctor Vicente García. 2020. "Following the Roman Army between the Southern Foothills of the Cantabrian Mountains and the Northern Plains of Castile and León (North of Spain): Archaeological Applications of Remote Sensing and Geospatial Tools." *Geosciences* 10 (12): 485. doi:10.3390/geosciences10120485.

Boece, Hector. 1527. *Scotorum Historiae a Prima Gentis Origine (the History and Chronicles of Scotland)*.

Boswall, Donaldson. 1857. "Notice of an Ancient Bulwark Discovered on the Sea-Shore of the Lands of Wardie, Near Edinburgh." *Archaeologia Scotica* 4: 302–304.

Bowman, A K. 1994. *Life and Letters on the Roman Frontier*. British Museum Press.

Bowman, A K, and J D Thomas. 1983. *Vindolanda: The Latin Writing-Tablets*. Society for the Promotion of Roman Studies. Society for the Promotion of Roman Studies.

Boyd, W E. 1988. "Cereals in Scottish Antiquity." *Circaea* 5 (2): 101–110.

Breeze, David J. 1970. "Excavations at Ardoch 1970." *Proceedings of the Society of Antiquaries of Scotland* 102: 122–128.

Breeze, David J. 1987. "Ptolemy, Tacitus and the Tribes of North Britain." *Proceedings of the Society of Antiquaries of Scotland* 117: 85–91.

Breeze, David J. 1993. *The Northern Frontiers of Roman Britain*. London: Batsford Academic & Educational.

Breeze, David J. 2006a. *The Antonine Wall*. John Donald Publishers.

Breeze, David J. 2006b. *J. Collingwood Bruce's Handbook to the Roman Wall*. Society of Antiquaries of Newcastle upon Tyne.

Breeze, David J. 2008. *Edge of Empire: Scotland's Roman Frontier*. Edinburgh: Birlinn.

Breeze, David J. 2009. "Introduction." In *First Contact: Rome and Northern Britain*, edited by David J Breeze, Lisbeth M Thoms, and Derek W Hall, 1–8. Tayside and Fife Archaeological Committee.

Breeze, David J. 2011. *Frontiers of Imperial Rome*. Barnsley: Pen & Sword Military.

Breeze, David J. 2015. *The Antonine Wall*. Birlinn.

Breeze, David J. 2016. *Bearsden: A Roman Fort on the Antonine Wall*. Edited by David J Breeze. Society of Antiquaries of Scotland. doi:10.9750/9781908332189.

Breeze, David J. 2017. "The Placing of the Forts on Hadrian's Wall." *Archaeologia Aeliana* 46: 21–39.

Breeze, David J. 2018. "The Value of Studying Roman Frontiers." *Theoretical Roman Archaeology Journal* 1 (1): 1–17. doi:10.16995/traj.212.

Breeze, David J, and Brian Dobson. 2000. *Hadrian's Wall*. London: Penguin.

Breeze, David J, Lisbeth M Thoms, and Derek W Hall, eds. 2009. *First Contact: Rome and Northern Britain*. Vol. Monograph 7. Perth: Tayside and Fife Archaeological Committee.

Brughmans, Tom, and Ulrik Brandes. 2017. "Visibility Network Patterns and Methods for Studying Visual Relational Phenomena in Archaeology." *Frontiers in Digital Humanities* 4: 17. doi:10.3389/fdigh.2017.00017.

Burnham, Barry C, A S Esmonde Cleary, M W C Hassall, Lawrence Keppie, and R S O Tomlin. 1993. "Roman Britain in 1992." *Britannia* 24: 277–284. doi:10.2307/526740.

Burnham, Barry C, and Jeffrey L Davies, eds. 2010. *Roman Frontiers in Wales and the Marches*. Cardiff: Royal Commission on the Ancient and Historical Monuments of Wales.

Burnham, Barry C, Fraser Hunter, A P Fitzpatrick, S Worrell, M W C Hassall, and R S O Tomlin. 2004. "Roman Britain in 2003." *Britannia* 35: 253–349.

Burnham, Barry C, Lawrence Keppie, A S Esmonde Cleary, M W C Hassall, and R S O Tomlin. 1999. "Roman Britain in 1998." *Britannia* 30: 319–386.

Burrough, Peter A, Rachael A McDonnell, and Christopher D Lloyd. 2015. *Principles of Geographical Information Systems*. Oxford University Press. Oxford University Press.

Bushe-Fox, J. P. 1913. "The Use of Sam Ian Pottery in Dating the Early Roman Occupation of the North of Britain." *Archaeologia* 64: 295–314.

Cadell, Henry. 1870. "Notice on a Sculptured Roman Slab." *Proceedings of the Society of Antiquaries of Scotland* 8: 109–113.

Callander, J G. 1919. "Roman Remains at Grassy Walls and Bertha." *Proceedings of the Society of Antiquaries of Scotland* 53: 137–152.

Camden, William. 1701. *Camden's Britannia Abridged*. Vol. I. Joseph Wild.

Camden, William. 1722. *Britannia: Or a Chorographical Description of Great Britain and Ireland*. Second Edition. Vol. II. Awnsham Churchill.

Campbell, B. 1994. *The Roman Army, 31 BCE - CE 337: A Sourcebook*. Routledge.

Campbell, Duncan B. 2009. "A Camp in Search of a Campaign." *Ancient Warfare Magazine* III (3): 46–49.

Carter, Stephen, Fraser Hunter, and Andrea Smith. 2010. "5th Century BCE Iron Age Chariot Burial From Newbridge." *Proceedings of the Prehistoric Society* 76: 31–74.

Casson, Lionel. 1971. *Ships and Seamanship in the Ancient World*. Princeton University Press.

Castro, Mariana. 2018. *The Function of the Roman Army in Southern Arabia Petraea*. Archaeopress Roman Archaeology 48. Oxford: Archaeopress.

Chalmers, George. 1807. *Caledonia, or an Account, Historical and Topographical of North Britain*. Vol. I. T. Cadell & W. Davies.

Chapman, Henry. 2006. *Landscape Archaeology and GIS*. The History Press.

Christison, D. 1901. "Account of the Excavation of the Roman Station of Camelon, Near Falkirk, Stirlingshire, Undertaken by the Society in 1900. I. History and General Description." *Proceedings of the Society of Antiquaries of Scotland* 35: 329–350.

Clarke, John. 1947. "Report on Excavation at Tassieholm (Milton), Beattock, During 1946." *Transactions of the Dumfriesshire and Galloway Natural History and Antiquarian Society* 24 (3rd series): 100–110.

Clarke, John. 1948. "The Forts at Milton, Near Beattock (Tassieholm)." *Transactions of the Dumfriesshire and Galloway Natural History and Antiquarian Society* 25 (3rd series): 10–26.

Clarke, John. 1949. "Excavations at Milton." *Transactions of the Dumfriesshire and Galloway Natural History and Antiquarian Society* 26 (3rd series): 133–149.

Clarke, John. 1950. "The Roman Forts at Milton (Tassieholm) Near Beattock, Dumfriesshire." *Transactions of the Dumfriesshire and Galloway Natural History and Antiquarian Society* 27 (3rd series): 197–201.

Clarke, John. 1951. "Excavations at Milton (Tassieholm) in the Season 1950." *Transactions of the Dumfriesshire and Galloway Natural History and Antiquarian Society* 28 (3rd series): 199–221.

Clarke, John. 1952. "Milton (Tassieholm)." In , edited by S N Miller, 104–110. The Roman Occupation of South Western Scotland. Glasgow University Publications.

Codrington, Thomas. 1918. *Roman Roads in Britain*. London: Society for Promoting Christian Knowledge.

Codrington, Thomas. 1928. *Roman Roads in Britain*. The Sheldon Press.

Collingwood, R G. 1929. *Roman Eskdale*. The Whitehaven News.

Conolly, James. 2006. *Geographical Information Systems in Archaeology*. Vol. Cambridge Manuals in Archaeology. Cambridge University Press.

Cook, Murray. 2010. "New Light on Oblong Forts: Excavations at Dunnideer, Aberdeenshire." *Proceedings of the Society of Antiquaries of Scotland* 140: 79–91.

Cook, Murray, and L Dunbar. 2008. *Rituals, Roundhouses and Romans. Excavations at Kintore, Aberdeenshire 2000-2006. Volume 1: Forest Road*. Vol. 1. Loanhead: Scottish Trust for Archaeological Research.

Cook, Murray, L Dunbar, and R Heawood. 2009. *Rituals, Roundhouses and Romans. Excavations at Kintore, Aberdeenshire 2000-2006. Volume 2: Other Sites*. Vol. 2. Loanhead: Scottish Trust for Archaeological Research.

Cook, Murray. Letter to Andrew Tibbs. 2018. "Dating of Kintore Roman Camp."

Costa-Garcia, Jose Manuel. 2018. "Roman Camp and Fort Design in Hispania: An Approach to the Distribution, Morphology and Settlement Pattern of Roman Military Sites During the Early Empire." In *LIMES XXIII. Proceedings of the 23rd International Congress of Roman Frontier Studies Ingolstadt 2015*, edited by C Sebastian Sommer and S Matešić, 986–993. Mainz: Nünnerich-Asmus Verlag.

Crawford, O G S. 1949. *Topography of Roman Scotland North of the Antonine Wall*. Cambridge: Cambridge University Press.

Curle, Alexander. 1905. "Description of the Fortifications on Ruberslaw, Roxburghshire, and Notices of Roman Remains Found There." *Proceedings of the Society of Antiquaries of Scotland* 39: 219–232.

Curle, Alexander. 1907. "Note of Excavations on Ruberslaw, Roxburghshire, Supplementary to the Description of the Fortifications Thereon." *Proceedings of the Society of Antiquaries of Scotland* 41: 451–453.

Curle, James. 1911. *A Roman Frontier Post and Its People: The Fort of Newstead in the Parish of Melrose*. James Maclehose and Sons.

Curle, James. 1932. "An Inventory of Objects of Roman and Provincial Roman Origin Found on Sites in Scotland Not Definitely Associated with Roman Constructions." *Proceedings of the Society of Antiquaries of Scotland*, 1–125.

Dark, Ken, and Petra Dark. 1998. *The Landscape of Roman Britain*. Sutton Publishing.

Davies, Hugh. 2002. *Roads in Roman Britain*. Tempus.

Davies, Mairi H. 2020. "The Landscape at the Time of the Construction of the Antonine Wall." In *The Antonine Wall: Papers in Honour of Professor Lawrence Keppie*, edited by David J Breeze and William S Hanson, 37–46. Archaeopress.

Dickson, Camilla, and James H Dickson. 2016. "Plant Remains." In *Bearsden: A Roman Fort on the Antonine Wall*, edited by David J Breeze, 223–280. Society of Antiquaries of Scotland.

Dilke, O A W. 1971. *The Roman Land Surveyors: An Introduction to the Agrimensores*. David & Charles.

Dingwall, Kirsty, and John Shepherd. 2018. *Highway Through History: An Archaeological Journey on the Aberdeen Western Peripheral Route*. Edited by Christopher Lowe and Luke Craddock-Bennett. Edinburgh: Headland Archaeology (UK) Ltd.

Dobat, Erik. 2009. "The Gask 'System' in Perthshire: The First Artificial Frontier Line of the Roman Empire." In *First Contact: Rome and Northern Britain*, edited by David J Breeze, Lisbeth M Thoms, and Derek W Hall, 39–48. Tayside and Fife Archaeological Committee.

Domínguez-Delmás, Marta, Mark Driessen, Ignacio García-González, Niels van Helmond, Ronald Visser, and Esther Jansma. 2014. "Long-Distance Oak Supply in Mid-2nd Century CE Revealed: The Case of a Roman Harbour (Voorburg-Arentsburg) in the Netherlands." *Journal of Archaeological Science* 41: 642–654. doi:10.1016/j.jas.2013.09.009.

Don, William Gerard. 1896. *Archaeological Notes on Early Scotland*. D. H. Edwards.

Donaldson, G H. 1988. "Signalling Communications and the Roman Imperial Army." *Britannia* 19: 349–356.

Dore, J N, and J J Wilkes. 1999. "Excavations Directed by JD Leach and JJ Wilkes on the Site of a Roman Fortress at Carpow, Perthshire, 1964-79." *Proceedings of the Society of Antiquaries of Scotland* 129: 481–575.

Driessen, M J. 2009. "Voorburg-Arentsburg: A Roman Harbour with a British Connection in the Hinterland of the Limes." In *Roman Frontier Studies 2009: Proceedings of the XXI International Congress of Roman Frontier Studies (Limes Congress) Held at Newcastle upon Tyne in August 2009*, edited by Nick Hodgson, Paul Bidwell, and Judith Schachtmann, 579–585. Archaeopress.

Dyčka, Michal. 2017. "To See and to Be Seen – the Antonine Wall in the Context of Spatial Analysis." *Studia Hercynea* XX (2): 40–66 & 165–169.

Dyčka, Michal. 2018. "The Modus Operandi Of the Antonine Wall. Implications of the Viewshed Analysis to the Way How Roman Frontiers Could Actually Work." In *LIMES XXIII. Proceedings of the 23rd International Congress of Roman Frontier Studies Ingolstadt 2015*, edited by C Sebastian Sommer and S Matešić, 315–322. Nünnerich-Asmus Verlag.

Evans, E M, D Hopewell, D J P Mason, K Murphy, O T P Roberts, and R J Silvester. 2010. "The Communications System: (B) Shipping." In *Roman Frontiers in Wales and the Marches*, edited by Barry C Burnham and Jeffrey L Davies, 98–102. Cardiff: Royal Commission on the Ancient and Historical Monuments of Wales.

Foglia, Alberto Bello. 2014. "Turrets as Watchtowers on Hadrian's Wall: A GIS and Source-Based Analysis of Appearance and Surveillance Capabilities." *Archaeologia Aeliana* 43: 27–46.

Franconi, Tyler, and Chris Green. 2019. "Broad and Coarse: Modelling Demography, Subsistence and Transportation in Roman England." In *Finding the Limits of the Limes: Modelling Demography, Economy and Transport on the Edge of the Roman Empire*, edited by Philip Verhagen, Jamie Joyce, and Mark R Groenhuijzen, 61–76. Springer.

Frere, S S. 1980. "Naming Roman Britain: The Place-Names of Roman Britain by ALF Rivet and Colin Smith." *Britannia* 11: 419–423. doi:10.2307/525700.

Frere, S S, M W C Hassall, and R S O Tomlin. 1985. "Roman Britain in 1984." *Britannia* 16: 251–332. doi:10.2307/526410.

Frere, S S, M W C Hassall, and R S O Tomlin. 1992. "Roman Britain in 1991." *Britannia* 23: 255–308.

Frere, S S, R S O Tomlin, and M W C Hassall. 1977. "Roman Britain in 1976." *Britannia* 8: 355–449.

Frere, S S, R S O Tomlin, and M W C Hassall. 1984. "Roman Britain in 1983." *Britannia* 15: 273–276. doi:10.2307/526612.

Frere, S S, R S O Tomlin, and M W C Hassall. 1990. "Roman Britain in 1989." *Britannia*, 310–314.

Frere, S S, and J J Wilkes. 1989. *Strageath: Excavations Within the Roman Fort 1973-1986*. Vol. Britannia Monograph Series No. 9. Society for the Promotion of Roman Studies. London: Society for the Promotion of Roman Studies.

Gehrels, W Roland. 2010. "Late Holocene Land- and Sea-Level Changes in the British Isles: Implications for Future Sea-Level Predictions." *Quaternary Science Reviews* 29 (13–14): 1648–1660. doi:10.1016/j.quascirev.2009.09.015.

Gethin, B, and H Toller. 2014. "The Roman Marching Camp and Road at Loups Fell, Tebay." *Britannia* 45: 1–10.

Gillings, Mark. 2012. "Landscape Phenomenology, GIS and the Role of Affordance." *Journal of Archaeological Method and Theory* 19 (4): 601–611. doi:10.1007/s10816-012-9137-4.

Goodburn, R, R P Wright, M W C Hassall, and R S O Tomlin. 1976. "Roman Britain in 1975." *Britannia* 7: 290–392.

Graafstal, Erik. 2002. *Logistiek, Communicatie En Watermanagement : Over De Uitrusting Van De Romeinse Rijksgrens in Nederland.* Vol. 51.

Graafstal, Erik. 2020. "Wing-Walls and Waterworks. On the Planning and Purpose of the Antonine Wall." In *The Antonine Wall: Papers in Honour of Professor Lawrence Keppie*, edited by David J Breeze and William S Hanson. Vol. 142–185. Oxford: Archaeopress.

Graafstal, Erik, David J Breeze, Rebecca H. Jones, and Matthew Symonds. 2015. "Sacred Cows in the Landscape: Rethinking the Planning of the Antonine Wall." In *Understanding Roman Frontiers: A Celebration for Professor Bill Hanson*, edited by David J Breeze, Rebecca H. Jones, and Ioana A Oltean, 54–69. John Donald.

Graafstal, Erik P. 2021. "The Original Plan for Hadrian's Wall: A New Purpose for Pons Aelius?" *Archaeological Journal* 178 (1): 107–145. doi:10.1080/00665983.2020.1863670.

Graham, Angus. 1968. "Archaeological Notes on Some Harbours in Eastern Scotland." *Proceedings of the Society of Antiquaries of Scotland* 101: 200–285.

Green, K. 1986. *The Archaeology of the Roman Economy.* Batsford.

Groenhuijzen, Mark R, and Philip Verhagen. 2015. "Exploring the Dynamics of Transport in the Dutch Limes." Edited by Weibke Bebermeier, Daniel Knitter, and Oliver Nakoinz, 25–47.

Gwilt, A, and C Haselgrove, eds. 1997. *Reconstructing Iron Age Societies: New Approaches to the British Iron Age.* Oxbow.

Haken, Mike. 2022. "The Stainmore Road, Its Unique Roman Camps, And Venutius' War." May 26. https://www.youtube.com/watch?v=Adp0FlB0Z8E.

Haldane, A R B. 1995. *New Ways Through the Glens.* House of Lochar.

Haldane, A R B. 2011. *The Drove Roads of Scotland.* Birlinn.

Hall, M A. 2002. "A Pair of Silver Denarii From Findo Gask, Strathearn, Perthshire." In *The Roman Frontier on the Gask Ridge, Perth and Kinross: An Interim Report on the Roman Gask Project 1995-2000*, edited by David Woolliscroft, 82–83. Oxford: British Archaeological Reports.

Hamilton, D., and C. Haselgrove. 2009. "Absolute Dating." In *The Traprain Law Environs Project: Fieldwork and Excavations, 2000-2004*, edited by C> Haselgrove, 187–204. Edinburgh: Society of Antiquaries of Scotland.

Hamilton, J, and C McGill. 1997. "A96 Kintore Bypass (Kintore; Kinellar; Dyce Parishes); Early Prehistoric Pits and Later Prehistoric Features." *Discovery Excavation in Scotland*, 10.

Hannon, Nick. 2018. "The Hidden Landscape of a Roman Frontier: A LiDAR Survey of the Antonine Wall, World Heritage Site."

Hannon, Nick, Lyn Wilson, and Darrell J Rohl. 2020. "Planning the Antonine Wall: An Archaeometric Reassessment of Installation Spacing." In *The Antonine Wall: Papers in Honour of Professor Lawrence Keppie*, edited by David J Breeze and William S Hanson, 67–85. Archaeopress.

Hanson, William S. 1984. "Inveresk Roman Fort: Trial Trenching." *Proceedings of the Society of Antiquaries of Scotland* 114: 251–259.

Hanson, William S. 1991. *Agricola and the Conquest of the North.* London: BT Batsford.

Hanson, William S. 1996. "Forest Clearance and the Roman Army." *Britannia* 27: 354–358.

Hanson, William S. 2007a. *A Roman Frontier Fort in Scotland: Elginhaugh.* Stroud: Tempus.

Hanson, William S. 2007b. *Elginhaugh: A Flavian Fort and Its Annexe.* Vol. 2. Society for the Promotion of Roman Studies. London: Society for the Promotion of Roman Studies.

Hanson, William S. 2009. "The Fort at Elginhaugh and Its Implications for Agricola's Role in the Conquest of Scotland." In *First Contact: Rome and Northern Britain*, edited by David J Breeze, Lisbeth M Thoms, and Derek W Hall, 49–58. Tayside and Fife Archaeological Committee.

Hanson, William S. 2015. "Newstead and Roman Scotland: The Flavian to Antonine Periods." In *A Roman Frontier Post and Its People: Newstead 1911-2011*, edited by Fraser Hunter, 63–76. NMSE Publishing.

Hanson, William S, and J G P Friell. 1995. "Westerton: A Roman Watchtower on the Gask Frontier." *Proceedings of the Society of Antiquaries of Scotland* 125: 499–519.

Hanson, William S, and L Macinnes. 1980. "Forests, Forts and Fields: A Discussion." In *Agricola's Campaigns in Scotland*, edited by James Kenworthy, 98–113. Edinburgh University Press.

Hanson, William S, and G S Maxwell. 1980. "An Agricolan Praesidium on the Forth-Clyde Isthmus

(Mollins, Strathclyde)." *Britannia* 11: 43–49. doi:10.2307/525670.

Hanson, William S, and G S Maxwell. 1986. *Rome's North-West Frontier: The Antonine Wall*. Edinburgh University Press.

Harding, Dennis W. 2012. *Iron Age Hillforts in Britain and Beyond*. Oxford University Press.

Harding, Dennis W. 2017. *The Iron Age in Northern Britain: Britons and Romans, Natives and Settlers*. Second Edition. London: Routledge.

Hartley, B R. 1972. "The Roman Occupations of Scotland: The Evidence of Samian Ware." *Britannia* 3: 1–55. doi:10.2307/526021.

Hassall, M W C, D R Wilson, R P Wright, and J Rea. 1972. "Roman Britain in 1971." *Britannia* 3: 298–367.

Haverfield, F. 1913. *Ancient Town-Planning*. Clarendon Press.

Himmler, Florian. 2009. "Ultro Citroque Discurrere - Operational Patterns and Tactics of Late Roman Frontier Fleets on Rivers." In *Roman Frontier Studies 2009: Proceedings of the XXI International Congress of Roman Frontier Studies (Limes Congress) Held at Newcastle upon Tyne in August 2009*, edited by Nick Hodgson, Paul Bidwell, and Judith Schachtmann, 674–678. Archaeopress.

Hind, J G F. 2013. "Summers and Winters in Tacitus' Account of Agricola's Campaigns in Britain." *Northern History* 21 (1): 1–18. doi:10.1179/007817285790176165.

Hingley, Richard. 1992. "Society in Scotland From 700 BCE to CE 200." *Proceedings of the Society of Antiquaries of Scotland* 122: 7–53.

Hingley, Richard. 2014. "The Iron Age on the Northumberland Coastal Plain: Excavations in Advance of Development 2002-2010 by N. Hodgson, J. McKelvey and W. Muncaster."

Hobley, Andrew S. 1989. "The Numismatic Evidence for the Post-Agricolan Abandonment of the Roman Frontier in Northern Scotland." *Britannia* 20: 69–74.

Hodgson, Nick. 1995. "Were There Two Antonine Occupations of Scotland?" *Britannia* 26: 29–49.

Hodgson, Nick. 2009. "Review Article: Elginhaugh: The Most Complete Fort Plan in the Roman Empire." *Britannia* 40: 365–398.

Hoffmann, Birgitta. 2001a. "Cardean Roman Fort, Angus (Airlie Parish)." *Discovery Excavation in Scotland*, 14–15.

Hoffmann, Birgitta. 2001b. "Cardean 2001: Geophysical Survey. the Results of the Survey at the Roman Fort of Cardean, August 2001." http://www.theromangaskproject.org/?page_id=148.

Hoffmann, Birgitta. 2009. "Cardean: The Changing Face of a Flavian Fort in Scotland." In *First Contact: Rome and Northern Britain*, edited by David J Breeze, Lisbeth M Thoms, and Derek W Hall, 29–32. Tayside and Fife Archaeological Committee.

Hoffmann, Birgitta. 2013. *The Roman Invasion of Britain: Archaeology Versus History*. Pen & Sword Archaeology.

Holmes, N M McQ. 2006a. "Two Denarius Hoards From Birnie, Moray." *The British Numismatic Journal* 76: 1–46.

Holmes, N M McQ. 2006b. "Cramond Roman Military and Civilian Sites." *Discovery Excavation in Scotland*, 13–14.

Holmes, Nicholas. 2003. *Excavation of Roman Sites at Cramond, Edinburgh*. Edited by Mark Collard and John A Lawson. Vol. Monograph 23. Society of Antiquaries of Scotland Monograph 3. Edinburgh: Society of Antiquaries of Scotland.

Hunter, Fraser. 2001. "Roman and Native in Scotland: New Approaches." *Journal of Roman Archaeology* 14: 289–309.

Hunter, Fraser. 2007. *Beyond the Edge of the Empire*. Rosemarkie: Groam House Museum.

Hunter, Fraser, ed. 2015. *A Roman Frontier Post and Its People: Newstead 1911-2011*. NMSE Publishing.

Hunter, Fraser. 2016. "Beyond Hadrian's Wall." In *Handbook of Roman Britain*, edited by M. Millett, L. Revell, and A. Moore. Oxford: Oxford University Press.

Hunter, Fraser. 2017. "Roman Britain in 2016. Sites Explored 2. Scotland." *Britannia* 48: 322–327.

Hunter, Fraser. 2018. "Roman Britain in 2017: Sites Explored 2. Scotland." *Britannia* 49 (September): 335–339. doi:10.1017/s0068113x18000302.

Hunter, Fraser, and K S Painter, eds. 2013. *Late Roman Silver: The Traprain Treasure in Context*. Society of Antiquaries of Scotland. Society of Antiquaries of Scotland.

Hussen, C-M R, Rebecca H. Jones, and William S Hanson. 2009a. "Geophysical Survey on Roman Camps in Scotland - Dalswinton Bankhead, Dumfries and Galloway (Kirkmahoe Parish), Geophysical Survey." *Discovery Excavation in Scotland*, 59.

Hussen, C-M R, Rebecca H. Jones, and William S Hanson. 2009b. "Geophysical Survey on Roman Camps in Scotland - Ward Law, Dumfries and Galloway (Caerlaverock Parish)." *Discovery Excavation in Scotland*, 53.

Ingemark, D. 2014. *Glass, Alcohol & Power in Roman Iron Age Scotland*. Edinburgh: National Museums of Scotland.

Ireland, S. 1996. *Roman Britain: A Sourcebook*. Routledge.

Ireland, Stanley. 2008. *Roman Britain: A Sourcebook*. 3rd ed. London: Routledge. doi:10.4324/9780203886694.

Issac, Benjamin. 1988. "The Meaning of 'Limes' and 'Limitanei' in Ancient Sources." *Journal of Roman Studies* 78: 125–147.

Jansma, E, and J M A W Morel. 2007. *Een Romeinse Rijnaak, Gevonden in Utrecht-De Meern. Resultaten Van Het Onderzoek Naar De Platbondem "De Meern I."* Vol. Rapportage Archeologische Monumentenzorg 144. Rijksdienst voor Archeologie, Cultuurlandschap en Monumenten.

Jobey, George. 1966. "Burnswark, Hill-Fort and Roman Works." *Discovery Excavation in Scotland*, 21–22.

Johnson, Anne. 1983. *Roman Forts of the 1st and 2nd Centuries CE in Britain and the German Provinces*. London: A & C Black.

Jones, Rebecca H. 2009a. "Chasing the Army: The Problems of Dating Camps." In *First Contact: Rome and Northern Britain*, edited by David J Breeze, Lisbeth M Thoms, and Derek W Hall, 21–27. Tayside and Fife Archaeological Committee.

Jones, Rebecca H. 2009b. "Troop Movements in Scotland: The Evidence From Marching Camps." In *Limes XX: Estudios Sobre La Frontera Romana (Roman Frontier Studies)*, edited by Angel Morillo, Norbert Hanel, and Esperanza Martín, 867–878. CSIC.

Jones, Rebecca H. 2011. *Roman Camps in Scotland*. Society of Antiquaries of Scotland. Edinburgh: Society of Antiquaries of Scotland.

Jones, Rebecca H. 2012. *Roman Camps in Britain*. Stroud: Amberley.

Jones, Rebecca H. 2018. "Soldiers and Sailors in the Conquest of Scotland." In *LIMES XXIII. Proceedings of the 23rd International Congress of Roman Frontier Studies Ingolstadt 2015*, edited by C Sebastian Sommer and S Matešić, 781–787. Nünnerich-Asmus Verlag.

Jones, Rebecca H. 2020. "The Curious Incident of the Structure at Bar Hill and Its Implications." In *The Antonine Wall: Papers in Honour of Professor Lawrence Keppie*, edited by David J Breeze and William S Hanson, 86–95. Archaeopress.

Jones, Richard, and Alan F Leslie. 2015. "The Contribution of Geophysical Surveys to the Understanding of Roman Frontiers." In *Understanding Roman Frontiers: A Celebration for Professor Bill Hanson*, edited by David J Breeze, Rebecca H. Jones, and Ioana A Oltean, 22:313–327. John Donald.

JRS. 1958. "Roman Britain in 1957." *Journal of Roman Studies* 48: 130–142.

JRS. 1962. "Roman Britain in 1961." *Journal of Roman Studies* 51: 160–199.

Kemp, Andrew C., Benjamin P. Horton, Jeffrey P. Donnelly, Michael E. Mann, Martin Vermeer, and Stefan Rahmstorf. 2011. "Climate Related Sea-Level Variations Over the Past Two Millennia." *Proceedings of the National Academy of Sciences of the United States of America* 108 (27): 11017–11022.

Keppie, Lawrence. 1998. *Scotland's Roman Remains*. John Donald Publishers.

Keppie, Lawrence. 2012. *The Antiquarian Rediscovery of the Antonine Wall*. The Society of Antiquaries of Scotland. The Society of Antiquaries of Scotland.

Knox, James. 1831. *The Topography of the Basin of the Tay*. Andrew Shortreed.

Komoróczy, Balázs, and Marek Vlach. 2009. "GIS Application in Roman Military Invasion Survey Within Barbarian Territories During the Marcomannic Wars - Introduction Into Problems and Perspectives." In *Roman Frontier Studies 2009: Proceedings of the XXI International Congress of Roman Frontier Studies (Limes Congress) Held at Newcastle upon Tyne in August 2009*, edited by Nick Hodgson, Paul Bidwell, and Judith Schachtmann, 545–551. Archaeopress.

Kooistra, Laura I, Pauline van Rijn, and Silke Lange. 2018. "Supply Networks of the Roman Army in the Rhine Delta During the Pre-Flavian Period." In *LIMES XXIII. Proceedings of the 23rd International Congress of Roman Frontier Studies Ingolstadt 2015*, edited by C Sebastian Sommer and S Matešić, 1001–1006. Nünnerich-Asmus Verlag.

Lake, M, S Mithen, and P Woodman. 1998. "Tailoring GIS Software for Archaeological Applications: An Example Concerning Viewshed Analysis." *Journal of Archaeological Science* 25: 27–38.

Lasaponara, Rosa, Rosa Coluzzi, Fabrizio T Gizzi, and Nicola Masini. 2010. "On the LiDAR Contribution for the Archaeological and Geomorphological Study of a Deserted Medieval Village in Southern Italy." *Journal of Geophysics and Engineering* 7 (2): 155–163. doi:doi:10.1088/1742-2132/7/2/S01.

Lepper, F, and S S Frere. 1988. *Trajan's Column*. Stroud: Alan Sutton.

Leslie, Alan F. 1995. "Roman Temporary Camps in Britain."

Leussen, M. van. 1999. "Viewshed and Cost Surface Analysis Using GIS (Cartographic Modelling in a Cell-Based GIS II)." In *New Techniques for Old Times. CAA98. Computer Applications and Quantitative Methods in Archaeology. Proceedings of the 26th Conference, Barcelona, March 1998*, edited by J.A. Barceló, I. Briz, and A. Vila, 215–224. International Series 757. Oxford: BAR Publishing.

Lewis, Joseph. 2020. "Visibility of the Gask Ridge Road from Simulated Watchtowers: A Monte Carlo Testing Approach." *Journal of Archaeological Science: Reports* 33 (October): 102482–2. doi:10.1016/j.jasrep.2020.102482.

Lewis, W V, and W G V Balchin. 1940. "Past Sea-Levels at Dungeness." *The Geographical Journal* 96 (4): 258–277. doi:10.2307/1787581.

Lock, G, and T Harris. 1997. "Analysing Change Through Time Within a Cultural Landscape: Conceptual and Functional Limitations of a GIS Approach." In *Urban Origins in Eastern Africa*, edited by P Sinclair. Vol. One World series. World Archaeological Congress.

Lock, G. R., and Ian Ralston. 2022. *Atlas of the Hillforts of Britain and Ireland*. Edinburgh: Edinburgh University Press.

Luttwack, Edward. 1976. *The Grand Strategy of the Roman Empire*. Baltimore: The John Hopkins University Press.

MacDonald, George. 1918. "The Highlands and Western Isles of Scotland, in Letters to Sir Walter Scott." *Proceedings of the Society of Antiquaries of Scotland* 52: 203–276.

Macdonald, George. 1934. *The Roman Wall in Scotland*. The Clarendon Press.

Macdonald, George. 1937. "Miscellanea Romano-Caledonica I." *Proceedings of the Society of Antiquaries of Scotland* 71: 373–387.

Macdonald, George, and Alexander Park. 1906. *The Roman Forts on the Bar Hill, Dunbartonshire*. James Maclehose and Sons.

Main, Lorna. 1998. "Excavations of a Timber Roundhouse & Broch at the Fairy Knowe, Buchlyvie, Stirlingshire." *Proceedings of the Society of Antiquaries of Scotland* 128: 293–417.

Maitland, William. 1757. *The History and Antiquities of Scotland, from the Earliest Account of Time to the Death of James the First, Anno 1437*. London: A. Millar.

Mann, J C. 1992. "Ravenna's and the Antonine Wall." *Proceedings of the Society of Antiquaries of Scotland* 122: 189–195..

Manning, W H. 1975. "Economic Influences on Land Use in the Military Areas of the Highland Zone During the Roman Period." In *The Effect of Man on the Landscape: The Highland Zone*, edited by Jeremy Evans, Susan Limbrey, and Henry Cleere. Vol. 112–116. The Council for British Archaeology.

Marcu, Felix, George Cupcea, Radu Zăgreanu, and Horațiu Cociș. 2018. "Recent Developments in Understanding the Limes Porolissensis." In *LIMES XXIII. Proceedings of the 23rd International Congress of Roman Frontier Studies Ingolstadt 2015*, edited by C Sebastian Sommer and S Matešić, 772–780. Nünnerich-Asmus Verlag.

Margary, I D. 1957. *Roman Roads in Britain: North of the Foss Way - Bristol Channel (Including Wales and Scotland)*. Vol. 2. Phoenix House.

Margary, I D. 1967. *Roman Roads in Britain*. John Baker.

Marsden, Peter. 1994. *Ships of the Port of London: First to Eleventh Centuries CE*. English Heritage.

Martin, Colin. 1992. "Water Transport and the Roman Occupation of North Britain." In *Scotland and the Sea*, edited by T C Smout, 1–34. John Donald Publishers.

Masini, Nicola, Fabrizio Terenzio Gizzi, Marilisa Biscione, Vincenzo Fundone, Michele Sedile, Maria Sileo, Antonio Pecci, Biagio Lacovara, and Rosa Lasaponara. 2018. "Medieval Archaeology Under the Canopy with LiDAR. The (Re)Discovery of a Medieval Fortified Settlement in Southern Italy." *Remote Sensing* 10 (10): 1598. doi:10.3390/rs10101598.

Mason, David J P. 2003. *Roman Britain and the Roman Navy*. Stroud: Tempus.

Máté, Ian D, and Sjoerd Bohncke. 2016. "Soils." In *Bearsden: A Roman Fort on the Antonine Wall*, 77–80. Society of Antiquaries of Scotland.

Maxwell, G S. 1976. "A Roman Timber Tower at Beattock Summit, Lanarkshire." *Britannia* 7: 33–38.

Maxwell, G S. 1980. "Agricola's Campaigns: The Evidence of the Temporary Camps." In *Agricola's Campaigns in Scotland*, edited by James Kenworthy, 25–54. Edinburgh: Edinburgh University Press.

Maxwell, G S. 1983. "Recent Aerial Discoveries in Roman Scotland: Drumquhassle, Elginhaugh and Woodhead." *Britannia* 14: 167–181. doi:10.2307/526347.

Maxwell, G S. 1989. *The Romans in Scotland*. Edinburgh: James Thin. The Mercat Press.

Maxwell, G S. 1990. *A Battle Lost: Romans and Caledonians at Mons Graupius*. Edinburgh University Press. Edinburgh: Edinburgh University Press.

Maxwell, G S. 2015. "The Road Still Not Taken..." In *Understanding Roman Frontiers: A Celebration for Professor Bill Hanson*, edited by David J Breeze, Rebecca H. Jones, and Ioana A Oltean. John Donald.

Maxwell, G S, and D R Wilson. 1987. "Air Reconnaissance in Roman Britain 1977-84." *Journal of Roman Studies* 18: 1–48. doi:10.2307/526438.

M'Call, Hardy Bertram. 1894. *The History and Antiquities of the Parish of Mid-Calder with Some Account of the Religious House of Torphichen, Founded Upon Record*. Richard Cameron.

McGrail, Sean. 1987. *Ancient Boats in N. W. Europe: The Archaeology of Water Transport to CE 1500*. Longman.

Mechan, G W H. 1966. "Catermilly: A Lost Roman Fort Near Invergowrie, with Notes on Two Recent Finds of Roman Coins." In *Aspects of Antiquity: A Miscellany by Members of the Archaeological Section of the Abertay Historical Society*, edited by Elise M Wilson, 32–40. Abertay Historical Society.

Mercer, Roger. 2018. *Native and Roman on the Northern Frontier: Excavations and Survey in a Later Prehistoric*

Landscape in Upper Eskdale, Dumfriesshire. Society of Antiquaries of Scotland.

Miller, S N. 1922. *The Roman Fort at Balmuildy (Summerston, Near Glasgow) on the Antonine Wall*. Maclehose, Jackson and Co.

Miller, S N, ed. 1952. *The Roman Occupation of South Western Scotland*. Glasgow: Glasgow University Publications.

Milner, N P. 2001. *Vegetius: Epitome of Military Science (Epitoma De Re Militari)*. 3rd ed. Liverpool University Press.

Moir, D M. 1860. *The Roman Antiquities of Inveresk*.

Mowat, Robert J C. 1996. *The Logboats of Scotland: With Notes on Related Artefact Types*. Vol. Oxbow Monograph Series 68. Oxbow.

Murphy, Kathryn M, Bruce Gittings, and Jim Crow. 2018. "Visibility Analysis of the Roman Communication Network in Southern Scotland." *Journal of Archaeological Science: Reports* 17 (February): 111–124. doi:10.1016/j.jasrep.2017.10.047.

Nayling, N, D Maynard, and Sean McGrail. 1994. "Barlands Farm, Magor, Gwent: A Romano-Celtic Boat." *Antiquity* 68: 596–603.

Nayling, Nigel, and Seán McGrail. 2004. *The Barland's Farm Romano-Celtic Boat*. CBA Research Report 138. Council for British Archaeology.

Nennius. 2000. *Nennius: History Of The Britons (Historia Brittonum)*. Edited and translated by J A Giles. Vol. Medieval Latin Series. In Parentheses Publications.

Newall, F. 1966. "Kilwinning - Hunterston, the Avondale Roman Road." *Discovery Excavation in Scotland*, 15–17.

Newall, F. 1976. "The Roman Signal Fortlet at Outerwards, Ayrshire." *Glasgow Archaeological Journal* 4 (1): 111–123.

Newall, F, and W Lonie. 1972. "Brigurd Harbour." *Discovery Excavation in Scotland*, 14.

Nicasie, M J. 1997. "The Borders of the Roman Empire in the Fourth Century." In *Roman Frontier Studies 1995 : Proceedings of the XVIth International Congress of Roman Frontier Studies*, edited by W Groenman-van Waateringe, B L van Beek, W J H Willems, and S L Wynia, 455–460. Oxbow.

Noble, Gordon, and Cathy MacIver. 2016. "Dunnicaer." *Discovery and Excavation in Scotland* 17.

Noble, Gordon, and Cathy MacIver. 2017. "Dunnicaer." *Discovery and Excavation in Scotland* 18.

Noble, Gordon, Cathy MacIver, James O'Driscoll, and Edouard Masson-Maclean. 2018. "Tap O' Noth." *Discovery and Excavation in Scotland* 19.

Noble, Gordon, Cathy MacIver, James O'Driscoll, and Edouard Masson-Maclean. 2019. "Tap O' Noth." *Discovery and Excavation in Scotland* 20.

Ogilvie, R. M., and I. A. Richmond, eds. 1967. *Cornelii Taciti de Vita Agricolae*. Oxford: The Clarendon Press.

Parcero-Oubiña, Cesar, Alejandro Guimil-Farina, Joao Fonte Guimil-Farina, and Jose Manuel Costa-Garcia. 2019. "Footprints and Cartwheels in a Pixel Road: On the Applicability of GIS for the Modelling of Ancient (Roman) Routes." In *Finding the Limits of the Limes: Modelling Demography, Economy and Transport on the Edge of the Roman Empire*, edited by Philip Verhagen, Jamie Joyce, and Mark R Groenhuijzen, 291–312. Springer.

Patterson, J. 1852. *History of the Counties of Ayr and Wigton*. J. Ainslie & W. Faden: Edinburgh.

Pažout, Adam. 2018. "Early Roman Fortifications in the Northern Negev - A Spatial Analysis." In *LIMES XXIII. Proceedings of the 23rd International Congress of Roman Frontier Studies Ingolstadt 2015*, edited by C Sebastian Sommer and S Matešić, 174–182. Nünnerich-Asmus Verlag.

Pennant, T. 1790. *A Tour in Scotland, 1769*. Vol. 2. B. White.

Peterson, J W M. 2007. "Random Orientation of Roman Camps." *Oxford Journal of Archaeology* 26 (1): 103–108. doi:10.1111/j.1468-0092.2007.00275.x.

Pirazzoli, Paolo A. 1976. "Sea Level Variations in the Northwest Mediterranean During Roman Times." *Science* 194 (New Series): 519–521. doi:10.2307/1742473.

Pitts, Lynne F, and J K St Joseph. 1985. *Inchtuthil: The Roman Legionary Fortress*. Vol. 6. Society for the Promotion of Roman Studies. London: Society for the Promotion of Roman Studies.

Polak, M, and S J Wynia. 1991. "The Roman Forts at Vechten. A Survey of the Excavations 1829-1989." *Oudheidkundige Mededelingen van Het Rijksmuseum van Oudheden Te Leiden*, no. 71: 125–156.

Polla, Silvia, and Philip Verhagen, eds. 2014. *Computational Approaches to the Study of Movement in Archaeology: Theory, Practice and Interpretation of Factors and Effects of Long Term Landscape Formation and Transformation*. Topoi: Berlin Studies of the Ancient World 23. Berlin/Boston: Walter de Gruyter GmbH.

Poulter, John. 2018. "New Discoveries Relating to the Planning of the Antonine Wall in Scotland." *Britannia* 49: 113–146. doi:10.1017/s0068113x18000284.

Rae, A, and V Rae. 1955. "Cramond (Roman Fort)." *Discovery Excavation in Scotland*, 20.

Rae, A, and V Rae. 1956. "Cramond." *Discovery Excavation in Scotland*, 17.

Rae, A, and V Rae. 1957. "Cramond." *Discovery Excavation in Scotland*, 20.

Ralston, I. 2006. *Celtic Fortifications*. Tempus.

Rankov, Boris. 2005. "Do Rivers Make Good Frontiers?" In *Limes XIX: Proceedings of the XIXth International Congress of Roman Frontier Studies Held in Pécs, Hungary, September 2003*, edited by Zsolt Visy, 175–181. University of Pécs.

Rankov, Boris. 2009. "The Frontier Fleets: What Were They and What Did They Do?" In *Roman Frontier Studies 2009: Proceedings of the XXI International Congress of Roman Frontier Studies (Limes Congress) Held at Newcastle upon Tyne in August 2009*, edited by Nick Hodgson, Paul Bidwell, and Judith Schachtmann, 687–690. Archaeopress.

RCAHMS. 1994. *The Royal Commission on the Ancient and Historical Monuments of Scotland. South-East Perth: An Archaeological Landscape*. RCAHMS.

Reid, John Eaton. 1864. *History of the County of Bute and Families Connected Therewith*. T. Murray & Son.

Reid, John H., and Andrew Nicholson. 2019. "Burnswark Hill: The Opening Shot of the Antonine Reconquest of Scotland?" *Journal of Roman Archaeology* 32: 459–477. doi:10.1017/s1047759419000230.

Richardson, Alan. 2004. *Theoretical Aspects of Roman Camp and Fort Design*. Vol. BAR International Series 1321. British Archaeological Reports (BAR) 1321. Oxford: British Archaeological Reports (BAR).

Richmond, Ian A. 1922. "Ptolemaic Scotland: Some New Suggestions Based on Recent Research and on the Work of Glazenbrook Rylands." *Proceedings of the Society of Antiquaries of Scotland* 56: 288–301.

Richmond, Ian A. 1952. "Perthshire." *Discovery Excavation in Scotland*, 10–11.

Richmond, Ian A. 1955. "Roman Britain and Roman Military Antiquities. Albert Reckitt Archaeological Lecture." *Proceedings of the British Academy* 41: 297–315.

Richmond, Ian A. 1980. "A Roman Fort at Inveresk, Midlothian." Edited by William S Hanson. *Proceedings of the Society of Antiquaries of Scotland*, 286–304.

Riddell, John F. 1979. *Clyde Navigation: A History of the Development and Deepening of the River Clyde*. John Donald Publishers.

Rivet, A L F, and Colin Smith. 1981. *The Place-Names of Roman Britain*. Book Club Associates.

Robertson, Anne S. 1964. "Birrens 1962-63." *Transactions of the Dumfriesshire and Galloway Natural History and Antiquarian Society* Series III. Vol. 41: 135–155.

Robertson, Anne S. 1975. *Birrens (Blatobulgium)*. Glasgow: T. & A. Constable.

Robertson, Anne S, and Lawrence Keppie. 2015. *The Antonine Wall: A Handbook to Scotland's Roman Frontier*. Glasgow Archaeological Society. Glasgow Archaeological Society.

Rogers, I M. 1993. "Dalginross and Dun: Excavations at Two Roman Camps." *Proceedings of the Society of Antiquaries of Scotland* 123: 277–290.

Rossi, C, and G Magli. 2019. "Wind, Sand and Water. The Orientation of the Late Roman Forts in the Kharga Oasis (Egyptian Western Desert)." In *Archaeoastronomy in the Roman World*, edited by G Magli, A González-García, J Belmonte Aviles, and E Antonello, 153–166. Springer.

Rossi, Lino. 1971. *Trajan's Column and the Dacian Wars*. Thames and Hudson.

Rostovtzeff, M. I., ed. 1934. *The Excavations at Dura-Europos Conducted by Yale University and the French Academy of Inscriptions and Letters. Preliminary Report of Fifth Season of Work, October 1931 – March 1932*. Yale: Yale University Press. doi:10.1017/s0003581500051313.

Roy, William. 1793. *Military Antiquities of the Romans in North Britain*. W. Bulmer & Co.

Rule, Margaret, and Jason Monaghan. 1993. *A Gallo-Roman Trading Vessel From Guernsey: The Excavation and Recovery of a Third Century Shipwreck*. Guernsey Museums and Galleries.

Rummel, Christoph. 2009. "The Northern Fleets in the Principate." In *Roman Frontier Studies 2009: Proceedings of the XXI International Congress of Roman Frontier Studies (Limes Congress) Held at Newcastle upon Tyne in August 2009*, edited by Nick Hodgson, Paul Bidwell, and Judith Schachtmann, 691–695. Archaeopress.

Rushworth, Alan. 2009. *Housesteads Roman Fort – the Grandest Station: Excavation and Survey at Housesteads, 1954–95, by Charles Daniels, John Gillam, James Crow and Others*. Vol. 1 Structural Report and Discussion. English Heritage.

Russell, John. 1922. *The Story of Leith*. T. Nelson & Sons.

ScARF. 2012a. *Scotland: The Roman Presence: ScARF Panel Report*. Scottish Archaeological Research Framework. Edinburgh: Society of Antiquaries of Scotland.

ScARF. 2012b. *Iron Age Scotland: ScARF Panel Report*. Edited by Fraser Hunter and Martin Carruthers. Society of Antiquaries of Scotland. Society of Antiquaries of Scotland.

Scotland, Historic. 2013. *The Antonine Wall Management Plan 2014-19*.

Shennan, Ian, Sarah L Bradley, and Robin Edwards. 2018. "Relative Sea-Level Changes and Crustal Movements in Britain and Ireland Since the Last Glacial Maximum." *Quaternary Science Reviews* 188 (May): 143–159. doi:10.1016/j.quascirev.2018.03.031.

Shennan, Ian, Ben Horton, Jim Innes, W Roland Gehrels, Jerry Lloyd, Jenny McArthur, and Mairead Rutherford. 2000. "Late Quaternary Sea-level Changes, Crustal Movements and Coastal Evolution in Northumberland, UK." *Journal of Quaternary Science* 15 (3): 215–237. doi:10.1002/(sici)1099-1417(200003)15:3

Shirley, Elizabeth. 1996. "The Building of the Legionary Fortress at Inchtuthil." *Britannia* 27: 111–128.

Shirley, Elizabeth. 2001. *Building a Roman Legionary Fortress*. Stroud: Tempus.

Shotter, David. 1996. *The Roman Frontier in Britain*. Preston: Carnegie Publishing.

Shotter, David. 2001. "Petillius Cerialis in Carlisle: A Numismatic Contribution." *Transactions of the Cumberland and Westmorland Antiquarian and Archaeological Society* 1 (3rd series): 21–30.

Shotter, David. 2004. *Roman Britain*. Routledge.

Shotter, David. 2009. "When Did the Romans Invade Scotland?" In *First Contact: Rome and Northern Britain*, edited by David J Breeze, Lisbeth M Thoms, and Derek W Hall, 15–20. Perth: Tayside and Fife Archaeological Committee.

Sibbald, Sir Robert. 1707. *Historical Inquiries, Concerning the Roman Monuments and Antiquities in the North-Part of Britain Called Scotland*. J. Watson.

Silvester, R J, and H. Toller. 2009. "Roman Roads in Wales." In *Roman Frontier Studies 2009: Proceedings of the XXI International Congress of Roman Frontier Studies (Limes Congress) Held at Newcastle upon Tyne in August 2009*, edited by Nick Hodgson, Paul Bidwell, and Judith Schachtmann, 93–98. Archaeopress.

Small, Andrew. 1823. *Interesting Roman Antiquities Recently Discovered in Fife*. Andrew Small.

Smith, D E, Mairi H. Davies, C L Brooks, T M Mighall, S Dawson, B R Read, J T Jordan, and L K Holloway. 2010. "Holocene Relative Sea Levels and Related Prehistoric Activity in the Forth Lowland, Scotland." *Quaternary Science Reviews* 29: 2382–2410.

Smith, J. 1895. *Prehistoric Man in Ayrshire*. E. Stock.

Sommer, C. Sebastian. 2009. "Why There? The Positioning of Forts along the Riverine Frontiers of the Roman Empire." In *The Army and Frontiers of Rome. Papers Offered to David J. Breeze*, edited by William Hanson, 103–114. Journal of Roman Archaeology Supplementary Series 74. Portsmouth, Rhode Island: JRA.

Soto, Pau de. 2019. "Network Analysis to Model and Analyse Roman Transport and Mobility." In *Finding the Limits of the Limes: Modelling Demography, Economy and Transport on the Edge of the Roman Empire*, edited by Philip Verhagen, Jamie Joyce, and Mark R Groenhuijzen, 271–290. Springer.

Southern, Pat. 1990. "Signals Versus Illumination on Roman Frontiers." *Britannia* 21: 233–242.

Sparavigna, Amelia Carolina. 2016a. "Solstices at the Hardknott Roman Fort." *SSRN Electronic Journal*, March, 1–8.

Sparavigna, Amelia Carolina. 2016b. "On the Orientation of the Roman Grumentum." *SSRN Electronic Journal*, June, 1–4.

Sparavigna, Amelia Carolina. 2017. "The Solstices and the Orientation of the Roman Fort of Segontium." *SSRN Electronic Journal*, 1–7. doi:10.2139/ssrn.2990995.

Starek, Michael J., Tianxing Chu, Helena Mitasova, and Russell S. Harmon. 2020. "Viewshed Simulation and Optimization for Digital Terrain Modelling with Terrestrial Laser Scanning." *International Journal of Remote Sensing* 41 (16): 6409–6426. doi:https://doi.org/10.1080/01431161.2020.1752952.

Steer, K A. 1964. "Ardoch Fort." *Archaeological Journal* 121: 196.

Steer, K A, and R W Feacham. 1952. "A Roman Signal-Station on Eildon Hill North, Roxburghshire." *Proceedings of the Society of Antiquaries of Scotland* 86: 202–205.

St Joseph, J K. 1951. "Air Reconnaissance of North Britain." *Journal of Roman Studies* 41 (1–2): 52–65. doi:10.2307/298069.

St Joseph, J K. 1960. "Gatehouse of Fleet." *Discovery Excavation in Scotland*, 29.

St Joseph, J K. 1961a. "Gatehouse of Fleet." *Discovery Excavation in Scotland*, 35.

St Joseph, J K. 1961b. "Air Reconnaissance in Britain, 1958–1960." *Journal of Roman Studies* 51 (1–2): 119–135. doi:10.2307/298845.

St Joseph, J K. 1965. "Cargill Roman Fortlet." *Discovery Excavation in Scotland*, 30.

St. Joseph, J. K. 1965. "Air Reconnaissance in Britain, 1961–64." *Journal of Roman Studies* 55: 74–89. doi:10.2307/297432.

St Joseph, J. K. 1973. "Air Reconnaissance in Britain, 1969–72." *Journal of Roman Studies* 63: 214–246. doi:10.2307/299178.

St Joseph, J K. 1978. "A Roman Camp Near Girvan, Ayrshire." *Britannia* 9 (1–2): 397–401. doi:10.2307/525960.

Strang, A. 1997. "Explaining Ptolemy's Roman Britain." *Britannia* 28: 1–30.

Stuart, John. 1822. "Observations Upon the Various Accounts of the Progress of the Roman Arms in Scotland." *Archaeologia Scotica* II. Part II: 289–313.

Stuart, Robert. 1845. *Caledonia Romana: A Descriptive Account of the Roman Antiquities of Scotland*. William Eadie & Co.

Stukeley, William. 1720. *An Account of a Roman Temple and Other Antiquities, near Graham's Dike in Scotland*.

Stukeley, William. 1756. *An Account of Richard of Cirencester, Monk of Westminster, and of His Works: With His Ancient Map of Roman Britain; and the Itinerary Therof*. R. Hett.

Survey, Ordnance. 1862. *Perthshire Ordnance Survey Name Books, 1859-1862*. Vol. 75. Ordnance Survey.

Symonds, Matthew. 2018. *Protecting the Empire: Fortlets, Frontiers and the Quest for Post-Conquest Security*. Cambridge: Cambridge University Press.

Symonds, Matthew. 2020. "Fords and the Frontier: Waging Counter-Mobility on Hadrian's Wall." *Antiquity* 94 (373): 92–109. doi:10.15184/aqy.2019.216.

Tagg, Harry F. 1911. "Vegetable Remains." In *A Roman Frontier Post and Its People: The Fort of Newstead in the Parish of Melrose*, edited by James Curle, 353–361. James Maclehose and Sons.

Tatton-Brown, T W T. 1980. "Camelon, Arthur's O'on and the Main Supply Base for the Antonine Wall." *Britannia* 11: 340–343.

Taylor, David J A. 2000. "The Forts on Hadrian's Wall: A Comparative Analysis of the Form and Construction of Some Buildings." *British Archaeological Reports* BAR British Series 305.

Taylor, Joan du Plat, and Henry Cleere, eds. 1978. *Roman Shipping and Trade: Britain and the Rhine Provinces*. Vol. CBA Research Report 24. Council for British Archaeology. Council for British Archaeology.

Taylor, William. 1996. *The Military Roads in Scotland*. House of Lochar.

Teodor, Eugen S. 2018. "Watching and Warning Along the Limes Transalutanus. the Search for Watchtowers Along Its Southern Sector." In *LIMES XXIII. Proceedings of the 23rd International Congress of Roman Frontier Studies Ingolstadt 2015*, edited by C Sebastian Sommer and S Matešić, 331–342. Nünnerich-Asmus Verlag.

Thorne, J. 2007. "Battle, Tactics, and the Emergence of the Limites in the West." In *A Companion to the Roman Army*, edited by P Erdkamp, 218–234. Blackwell.

Tibbs, Andrew. 2019. *Beyond the Empire: A Guide to Scotland's Roman Remains*. Marlborough: Robert Hale.

Tierney, James T. 1959. "Ptolemy's Map of Scotland." *The Journal for Hellenic Studies* 79: 132–148.

Tipping, Richard. 1997a. "Vegetational History of Southern Scotland." *Botanical Journal of Scotland* 49 (2): 151–162.

Tipping, Richard. 1997b. "Pollen Analysis and the Impact of Rome on Native Agriculture Around Hadrian's Wall." In *Reconstructing Iron Age Societies: New Approaches to the British Iron Age*, edited by A Gwilt and C Haselgrove, 239–247. Oxbow.

Tipping, Richard, and Eileen Tisdall. 2005. "The Landscape Context of the Antonine Wall: A Review of the Literature." *Proceedings of the Society of Antiquaries of Scotland* 135: 443–469.

Toolis, Ronan. 2003. "A Survey of the Promontory Forts of the North Solway Coast." *Transactions of the Dumfriesshire and Galloway Natural History and Antiquarian Society* 77: 37–78.

Toolis, Ronan. 2015. "Iron Age Settlement Patterns in Galloway." *Transactions of the Dumfriesshire and Galloway Natural History and Antiquarian Society* 89: 17–34.

Toolis, Ronan. 2021. "Shifting Perspectives on 1st-Millennia Scotland." *Proceedings of the Society of Antiquaries of Scotland* 150: 247–278.

Veen, M van der. 1992. *Crop Husbandry Regimes: An Archaeobotanical Study of Farming in Northern England 1000 BCE - CE 500*. Vol. Sheffield Archaeological Monographs 3. J. R. Collis Publications.

Verhagen, Philip. 2010. "On the Road to Nowhere? Least Cost Paths, Accessibility and the Predictive Modelling Perspective." In *Fusion of Cultures. Proceedings of the 38th Annual Conference on Computer Applications and Quantitative Methods in Archaeology, Granada, Spain. April 2010*, edited by Francisco Contreras, Mercedes Farjas, and Francisco Javier Melero, 383–390. Archaeopress.

Verhagen, Philip, Tom Brughmans, Laure Nuninger, and Frederique Bertoncello. 2012. "The Long and Winding Road: Combining Least Cost Paths and Network Analysis Techniques for Settlement Location Analysis and Predictive Modelling." In *CAA Proceedings of the Conference in Computer Applications and Quantitative Methods in Archaeology*, edited by Graeme Earl, Tim Sly, Angeliki Chrysanthi, Patricia Murrieta-Flores, Constantinos Papadopoulos, Iza Romanowska, and David Wheatley, 1–10.

Verhagen, Philip, and Karen Jeneson. 2012. "A Roman Puzzle. Trying to Find the Via Belgica with GIS." In *Thinking Beyond the Tool. Archaeological Computing and the Interpretive Process*, by A. Chrysanthi, P. Murrieta Flores, and C. Papadopoulus, 123–130. Oxford: Archaeopress.

Verhagen, Philip, Jamie Joyce, and Mark R Groenhuijzen. 2019. *Finding the Limits of the Limes: Modelling Demography, Economy and Transport on the Edge of the Roman Empire*. Edited by Philip Verhagen, Jamie Joyce, and Mark R Groenhuijzen. Springer. Springer.

Visy, Zsolt. 2015. "The River Line Frontiers of the Roman Empire." In *Understanding Roman Frontiers: A Celebration for Professor Bill Hanson*, edited by David J Breeze, Rebecca H. Jones, and Ioana A Oltean, 27–36. John Donald.

Waddelove, A C, and E Waddelove. 1990. "Archaeology and Research Into Sea-Level During the Roman Era: Towards a Methodology Based on Highest Astronomical Tide." *Britannia* 21: 253–266.

Warry, P. 2006. *Tegulae Manufacture, Typology and Use in Roman Britain*. British Series 417. Oxford: BAR Publishing.

Webster, Graham. 1985. *The Roman Imperial Army of the First and Second Centuries A.D.* A & C Black.

Welfare, Humphrey, and Vivien Swan. 1995. *Roman Camps in England: The Field Archaeology*. London: HMSO.

Wells, C M. 1972. *The German Policy of Augustus*. Clarendon Press.

Wex, Friedrich Karl. 1846. *Ueber Ricardus Corinensis*. Rheinisches Museum fur Philologie.

Wheatley, David. 1995. "Cumulative Viewshed Analysis: A GIS-Based Method for Investigating Intervisibility and Its Archaeological Application." In *Archaeology and Geographical Information Systems: A European Perspective*, 171–185. Taylor & Francis.

Wheatley, David. 1996. "The Use of GIS to Understand Regional Variation in Earlier Neolithic Wessex." In *New Methods, Old Problems: Geographic Information Systems in Modern Archaeological Research*, edited by Herbert D G Maschner, 75–103. Southern Illinois University.

Wheatley, David, and Mark Gillings. 2002. *Spatial Technology and Archaeology: The Archaeological Application of GIS*. Taylor and Francis.

Whittaker, C. R. 1997. *Frontiers of the Roman Empire: A Social and Economic Study*. Baltimore: The Johns Hopkins University Press.

Wilson, Allan. 1989. "Roman Penetration in West Dumfries & Galloway: A Field Survey." *Transactions of the Dumfriesshire and Galloway Natural History and Antiquarian Society* 64: 7–21.

Witcher, Robert. 2000. "GIS and Landscapes of Perception." In *Geographical Information Systems and Landscape Archaeology*, edited by Mark Gillings, David Mattingly, and Jan van Dalen, 13–22. Oxbow Books.

Wood, John Philp. 1794. *The Ancient and Modern State of the Parish of Cramond*. John Paterson.

Woodman, A. J., and C. S. Kraus, eds. 2014. *Tacitus: Agricola*. Cambridge: Cambridge University Press.

Woolliscroft, David. 1989. "Signalling and the Design of Hadrian's Wall." *Archaeologia Aeliana* 17: 5–20.

Woolliscroft, David. 1993. "Signalling and the Design of the Gask Ridge System." *Proceedings of the Society of Antiquaries of Scotland* 123: 291–313.

Woolliscroft, David. 1994. "Signalling and the Design of the Cumberland Coast System." *Transactions of the Cumberland & Westmorland Antiquarian & Archaeological Society* 94: 55–64.

Woolliscroft, David. 1996. "Signalling and the Design of the Antonine Wall." *Britannia* 27: 153–177. doi:10.2307/527043.

Woolliscroft, David, ed. 2002. *The Roman Frontier on the Gask Ridge, Perth and Kinross: An Interim Report on the Roman Gask Project 1995-2000*. Vol. British Series 255. British Archaeological Reports. British Archaeological Reports.

Woolliscroft, David. 2007. "Innerpeffray West Temporary Camp, Perth and Kinross (Crieff Parish), Excavation." *Discovery Excavation in Scotland*, 152.

Woolliscroft, David. 2009. "Roman Towers." In *Roman Frontier Studies 2009: Proceedings of the XXI International Congress of Roman Frontier Studies (Limes Congress) Held at Newcastle upon Tyne in August 2009*, edited by Nick Hodgson, Paul Bidwell, and Judith Schachtmann, 213–220. Archaeopress.

Woolliscroft, David. 2010. *Roman Military Signalling*. Stroud: The History Press.

Woolliscroft, David, and Birgitta Hoffmann. 2003. "Cargill." *Discovery Excavation in Scotland*, 103.

Woolliscroft, David, and Birgitta Hoffmann. 2006. *Rome's First Frontier: The Flavian Occupation of Northern Scotland*. Stroud: Tempus.

Woolliscroft, David, and Birgitta Hoffmann. 2009a. "The Roman Gask System Fortlet of Glenbank, Perthshire." *Proceedings of the Society of Antiquaries of Scotland* 139: 167–193.

Woolliscroft, David, and Birgitta Hoffmann. 2009b. "The Roman Gask Project." In *Roman Scotland: A Handbook to Accompany the Post-Congress Excursion to Scotland, 24-26 August 2009*, edited by Nick Hodgson, 85–94. Tyne & Wear Archives & Museums.

Woolliscroft, David, and Birgitta Hoffmann. 2009c. "Inchtuthil, Perth and Kinross (Caputh Parish), Geophysical Survey." *Discovery Excavation in Scotland* 10: 145.

Woolliscroft, David, and Birgitta Hoffmann. 2011. "Inchtuthil Roman Fortress, Perth and Kinross (Caputh Parish), Geophysical Survey." *Discovery Excavation in Scotland* 12: 46.

Woolliscroft, David, A J Hughes, and N J Lockett. 2002. "Six Suspected Small Roman Temporary Camps." In *The Roman Frontier on the Gask Ridge, Perth and*

Kinross: An Interim Report on the Roman Gask Project 1995-2000, 29–39. British Archaeological Reports.

Woolliscroft, David, S A M Swain, and N J Lockett. 1992. "Barcombe B, A Second Roman 'Signal' Tower on Barcombe Hill." *Archaeologia Aeliana* 20: 57–62.

Zant, J. 2009. *The Carlisle Millennium Project: Excavations in Carlisle 1998-2001*. Vol. 1. Lancaster Imprints.

Appendix One:
Flavian Sites

Table 9. Details of the Flavian Fortress in Scotland.

Name	Local Authority Area	Type	National Grid Reference	X	Y	Canmore Record
Inchtuthil	Perth & Kinross	Legionary Fortress	NO 1251 3971	312510	739710	https://canmore.org.uk/site/28592/Inchtuthil

Table 10. Details of Flavian Forts in Scotland.

Name	Local Authority Area	Type	National Grid Reference	X	Y	Canmore Record
Ardoch	Perth & Kinross	Fort	NN 8390 0990	283900	709900	https://canmore.org.uk/site/25227/ardoch
Barochan Hill	Renfrewshire	Fort	NS 4148 6906	241480	669060	https://canmore.org.uk/site/43107/barochan-hill
Bertha	Perth & Kinross	Fort	NO 0974 2680	309740	726800	https://canmore.org.uk/site/26734/bertha
Birrens	Dumfries & Galloway	Fort	NY 2190 7518	321900	575180	https://canmore.org.uk/site/67099/Birrens
Bochastle	Stirling	Fort	NN 6142 0790	261420	707900	https://canmore.org.uk/site/24337/Bochastle
Broomholm	Dumfries & Galloway	Fort	NY 3786 8145	337860	581450	https://canmore.org.uk/site/67709/Broomholm
Camelon North	Falkirk	Fort	NS 8630 8097	286300	680970	https://canmore.org.uk/site/46920/falkirk-camelon
Camelon South	Falkirk	Fort	NS 8630 8097	286300	680970	https://canmore.org.uk/site/46920/falkirk-camelon
Cappuck	Scottish Borders	Fort	NT 6950 2123	369500	621230	https://canmore.org.uk/site/57050/Cappuck
Cardean	Angus	Fort	NO 2890 4600	328900	746000	https://canmore.org.uk/site/30689/Cardean
Cargill	Perth & Kinross	Fort	NO 1661 3790	316610	737900	https://canmore.org.uk/site/28493/Cargill
Castledykes	South Lanarkshire	Fort	NS 9286 4425	292860	644250	https://canmore.org.uk/site/47721/Castledykes
Crawford	South Lanarkshire	Fort	NS 9538 2143	295380	621430	https://canmore.org.uk/site/47396/Crawford
Dalginross	Perth & Kinross	Fort	NN 7732 2104	277320	721040	https://canmore.org.uk/site/24832/Dalginross
Dalswinton, Bankfoot	Dumfries & Galloway	Fort	NX 9331 8485	293310	584850	https://canmore.org.uk/site/65893/dalswinton-bankhead
Dalswinton Bankhead II	Dumfries & Galloway	Fort	NX 9331 8485	293310	584850	https://canmore.org.uk/site/65893/dalswinton-bankhead
Doune	Stirling	Fort	NN 7273 0130	272730	701300	https://canmore.org.uk/site/24767/Doune-roman-fort-and-annexe
Drumlanrig	Dumfries & Galloway	Fort	NX 8542 9890	285420	598900	https://canmore.org.uk/site/65200/Drumlanrig-roman-fort
Drumquhassle	Stirling	Fort	NS 4843 8744	248430	687440	https://canmore.org.uk/site/43408/Drumquhassle
Easter Happrew	Scottish Borders	Fort	NT 1946 4011	319460	640110	https://canmore.org.uk/site/50032/easter-happrew
Elginhaugh	Midlothian	Fort	NT 3213 6734	332130	667340	https://canmore.org.uk/site/53492/Elginhaugh
Fendoch	Perth & Kinross	Fort	NN 9196 2830	291960	728300	https://canmore.org.uk/site/26132/Fendoch
Glenlochar	Dumfries & Galloway	Fort	NX 7350 6452	273500	564520	https://canmore.org.uk/site/64687/Glenlochar
Loudoun Hill	East Ayrshire	Fort	NS 6059 3712	260590	637120	https://canmore.org.uk/site/44771/loudoun-hill
Malling	Stirling	Fort	NN 5640 0006	256400	700060	https://canmore.org.uk/site/24065/Malling
Milton	Dumfries & Galloway	Fort	NT 0923 0141	309230	601410	https://canmore.org.uk/site/48383/Milton
Mollins	North Lanarkshire	Fort	NS 7139 7189	271390	671890	https://canmore.org.uk/site/45931/mollins

Name	Local Authority Area	Type	National Grid Reference	X	Y	Canmore Record
Newstead Flavian I	Scottish Borders	Fort	NT 5698 3441	356980	634410	https://canmore.org.uk/site/55621/Newstead
Newstead Flavian II	Scottish Borders	Fort	NT 5698 3441	356980	634410	https://canmore.org.uk/site/55621/Newstead
Oakwood	Scottish Borders	Fort	NT 4250 2491	342500	624910	https://canmore.org.uk/site/54330/Oakwood
Stracathro	Angus	Fort	NO 6170 6575	361700	765750	https://canmore.org.uk/site/35945/Stracathro
Strageath	Perth & Kinross	Fort	NN 8980 1800	289800	718000	https://canmore.org.uk/site/25296/Strageath

Table 11. Details of Flavian Camps in Scotland.

Name	Local Authority Area	Type	National Grid Reference	X	Y	Canmore Record
Abernethy (Carey)	Perth & Kinross	Camp	NO 17319 16458	317319	716458	http://canmore.org.uk/site/27933
Ardoch II	Perth & Kinross	Camp	NN 8390 1090	283900	710900	http://canmore.org.uk/site/25388
Ardoch V	Perth & Kinross	Camp	NN 84046 10229	284046	710229	http://canmore.org.uk/site/25392
Auchinhove	Moray	Camp	NJ 46185 51705	346185	851705	http://canmore.org.uk/site/17349
Bankhead II (Carnwath)	South Lanarkshire	Camp	NS 98238 44925	298238	644925	http://canmore.org.uk/site/47656
Beattock, Bankend	Dumfries & Galloway	Camp	NT 08488 02049	308488	602049	http://canmore.org.uk/site/48398
Bellie (from Crawford)	Moray	Camp	NJ 3573 6170	335730	861700	https://canmore.org.uk/site/16947
Bellie (Ordnance Survey)	Moray	Camp	NJ 3551 6103	335510	861030	https://canmore.org.uk/site/16947
Birrens	Dumfries & Galloway	Camp	NY 22462 75028	322462	575028	https://canmore.org.uk/site/67103/birrens
Bochastle	Stirling	Camp	NN 6117 0772	261170	707720	http://canmore.org.uk/site/24351
Burnfield	Aberdeenshire	Camp	NJ 540 476	354000	847600	http://canmore.org.uk/site/17841
Carlops, Spittal	Midlothian	Camp	NT 1715 5725	317150	657250	http://canmore.org.uk/site/50170
Castlecraig II	Scottish Borders	Camp	NT 1256 4455	312560	644550	http://canmore.org.uk/site/50117
Castledykes IA & B	South Lanarkshire	Camp	NS 92726 44497	292726	644497	http://canmore.org.uk/site/79355
Castledykes IV	South Lanarkshire	Camp	NS 92850 44590	292850	644590	http://canmore.org.uk/site/47691
Cold Chapel	South Lanarkshire	Camp	NS 9352 2490	293520	624900	http://canmore.org.uk/site/47447
Cornhill	South Lanarkshire	Camp	NT 0215 3574	302150	635740	http://canmore.org.uk/site/48667
Dalginross I	Perth & Kinross	Camp	NN 7742 2078	277420	720780	http://canmore.org.uk/site/24821
Dalswinton Bankfoot I	Dumfries & Galloway	Camp	NX 93440 84081	293440	584081	http://canmore.org.uk/site/65895
Dalswinton Bankfoot II	Dumfries & Galloway	Camp	NX 93678 83837	293678	583837	http://canmore.org.uk/site/65942
Denholm (Eastcote)	Dumfries & Galloway	Camp	NX 85721 98841	285721	598841	http://canmore.org.uk/site/65205
Drumlanrig Islafoot	Dumfries & Galloway	Camp	NX 85721 98841	285721	598841	http://canmore.org.uk/site/65205
Dun	Angus	Camp	NO 6890 5959	368900	759590	http://canmore.org.uk/site/35673
Dunning	Perth & Kinross	Camp	NO 02508 15025	302508	715025	http://canmore.org.uk/site/26662
Durisdeer	Dumfries & Galloway	Camp	NS 89138 03092	289138	603092	http://canmore.org.uk/site/46377
Eshiels	Scottish Borders	Camp	NT 28150 39530	328150	639530	http://canmore.org.uk/site/51256
Fourmerkland	Dumfries & Galloway	Camp	NX 91502 80052	291502	580052	https://canmore.org.uk/site/65936/fourmerkland
Girvan Mains East	South Ayrshire	Camp	NX 1870 9900	218700	599000	http://canmore.org.uk/site/71541
Girvan Mains West	South Ayrshire	Camp	NX 19000 99106	219000	599106	http://canmore.org.uk/site/62049
Glenlochar I	Dumfries & Galloway	Camp	NX 73707 65189	273707	565189	http://canmore.org.uk/site/64610
Glenluce	Dumfries & Galloway	Camp	NX 19805 56603	219805	556603	http://canmore.org.uk/site/79047
Glenmailen (Ythan Wells) I	Aberdeenshire	Camp	NJ 655 381	365500	838100	http://canmore.org.uk/site/18225
Glenmailen (Ythan Wells) II	Aberdeenshire	Camp	NJ 6603 3847	366030	838470	http://canmore.org.uk/site/80931

Appendix One

Name	Local Authority Area	Type	National Grid Reference	X	Y	Canmore Record
Gogar Green	Edinburgh	Camp	NT 1765 7175	317650	671750	http://canmore.org.uk/site/50664
Gourdie (Steeds Stalls)	Perth & Kinross	Camp	NO 1151 4271	311510	742710	https://canmore.org.uk/site/28932
Hillside (Dunblane) I	Stirling	Camp	NN 775 005	277500	700500	http://canmore.org.uk/site/24668
Hillside (Dunblane) II	Stirling	Camp	NN 775 005	277500	700500	http://canmore.org.uk/site/24668
Inchtuthil I	Perth & Kinross	Camp	NO 1165 3934	311650	739340	https://canmore.org.uk/site/28594/inchtuthil
Inchtuthil II	Perth & Kinross	Camp	NO 1197 3945	311650	739340	https://canmore.org.uk/site/28593/inchtuthil
Inverquharity	Angus	Camp	NO 40660 58000	340660	758000	http://canmore.org.uk/site/33728
Kintore	Aberdeenshire	Camp	NJ 78739 16232	378739	816232	http://canmore.org.uk/site/18584
Kirkhouse	South Lanarkshire	Camp	NT 0980 4620	309800	646200	http://canmore.org.uk/site/48851
Lamington	South Lanarkshire	Camp	NS 977 307	297700	630700	http://canmore.org.uk/site/72377
Lochlands I	Falkirk	Camp	NS 8530 8160	285300	681600	http://canmore.org.uk/site/46968
Lochlands II	Falkirk	Camp	NS 8540 8183	285400	681830	http://canmore.org.uk/site/47001
Lochlands IV	Falkirk	Camp	NS 8560 8150	285600	681500	http://canmore.org.uk/site/46972
Lochlands VI	Falkirk	Camp	NS 8534 8148	285340	681480	http://canmore.org.uk/site/46973
Logie Durno	Aberdeenshire	Camp	NJ 6985 2718	369850	827180	http://canmore.org.uk/site/18107
Malling I	Stirling	Camp	NN 56070 00080	256070	700080	http://canmore.org.uk/site/24038
Malling II	Stirling	Camp	NS 56560 99810	256560	699810	http://canmore.org.uk/site/44615
Milton	Dumfries & Galloway	Camp	NT 09233 01419	309233	601419	https://canmore.org.uk/site/48383/milton
Muiryfold	Moray	Camp	NJ 48900 52080	348900	852080	http://canmore.org.uk/site/17346
Newstead I	Scottish Borders	Camp	NT 57000 34400	357000	634400	http://canmore.org.uk/site/55620
Newstead II	Scottish Borders	Camp	NT 57400 34100	357400	634100	http://canmore.org.uk/site/55625
Normandykes	Aberdeen	Camp	NO 82970 99380	382970	799380	http://canmore.org.uk/site/37075
Oakwood	Scottish Borders	Camp	NT 4248 2544	342480	625440	http://canmore.org.uk/site/54276
Raeburnfoot	Dumfries & Galloway	Camp	NY 25000 99598	325000	599598	http://canmore.org.uk/site/274593
Raedykes	Aberdeenshire	Camp	NO 841 902	384100	790200	http://canmore.org.uk/site/37153
Stracathro	Angus	Camp	NO 61370 65610	361370	765610	http://canmore.org.uk/site/35940
Wandel	South Lanarkshire	Camp	NS 944 267	294400	626700	http://canmore.org.uk/site/47371
Ward Law	Dumfries & Galloway	Camp	NY 02400 66870	302400	566870	http://canmore.org.uk/site/66098
Woodhead I	Midlothian	Camp	NT 38411 63867	338411	663867	http://canmore.org.uk/site/53546
Woodhead II	Midlothian	Camp	NT 38411 63867	338411	663867	http://canmore.org.uk/site/53546

Table 12. Details of Flavian Fortlets in Scotland.

Name	Local Authority Area	Type	National Grid Reference	X	Y	Canmore Record
Cargill	Perth & Kinross	Fortlet	NO 16347 37665	316347	737665	http://canmore.org.uk/site/28492
Bankhead (Carnwath)	South Lanarkshire	Fortlet	NS 971 449	297100	644900	http://canmore.org.uk/site/47670
Castle Greg	West Lothian	Fortlet	NT 05020 59250	305020	659250	http://canmore.org.uk/site/48988
Gatehouse of Fleet	Dumfries & Galloway	Fortlet	NX 59550 57373	259550	557373	https://canmore.org.uk/site/63631/gatehouse-of-fleet
Glenbank	Perth & Kinross	Fortlet	NN 8121 0570	281210	705700	http://canmore.org.uk/site/25236
Inverquharity	Angus	Fortlet	NO 40510 58144	340510	758144	http://canmore.org.uk/site/33713
Kaims Castle	Perth & Kinross	Fortlet	NN 8608 1295	286080	712950	http://canmore.org.uk/site/25365
Kirkland	Dumfries & Galloway	Fortlet	NX 80413 90113	280413	590113	https://canmore.org.uk/site/70823/kirkland?u=

Table 13. Details of Flavian (Gask Ridge) Towers in Scotland.

Name	Local Authority Area	Type	National Grid Reference	X	Y	Canmore Record
Ardoch	Perth & Kinross	Tower	NN 8390 0990	283900	709900	https://canmore.org.uk/site/25227/ardoch
Ardunie	Perth & Kinross	Tower	NN 9469 1876	294690	718760	http://canmore.org.uk/site/26019
Gask House	Perth & Kinross	Tower	NN 9903 1919	299030	719190	http://canmore.org.uk/site/25977
Kirkhill	Perth & Kinross	Tower	NN 9676 1883	296760	718830	http://canmore.org.uk/site/25988
Moss Side	Perth & Kinross	Tower	NO 00782 19924	300782	719924	http://canmore.org.uk/site/26613
Muir O' Fauld	Perth & Kinross	Tower	NN 9821 1897	298210	718970	http://canmore.org.uk/site/25990
Parkneuk	Perth & Kinross	Tower	NN 9167 1846	291670	718460	http://canmore.org.uk/site/26042
Peel	Perth & Kinross	Tower	NO 0604 2322	306040	723220	http://canmore.org.uk/site/26888
Raith	Perth & Kinross	Tower	NN 9319 1852	293190	718520	http://canmore.org.uk/site/26008
Roundlaw	Perth & Kinross	Tower	NN 9580 1889	295800	718890	http://canmore.org.uk/site/25966
Shielhill North	Perth & Kinross	Tower	NN 8559 1219	285590	712190	http://canmore.org.uk/site/25378
Shielhill South	Perth & Kinross	Tower	NN 8499 1150	284990	711500	http://canmore.org.uk/site/25404
Thorny Hill	Perth & Kinross	Tower	NO 0206 2043	302060	720430	http://canmore.org.uk/site/26952
Westerton	Perth & Kinross	Tower	NN 8731 1457	287310	714570	http://canmore.org.uk/site/25377
Westmuir	Perth & Kinross	Tower	NO 0287 2078	302870	720780	http://canmore.org.uk/site/26954
Witch Knowe	Perth & Kinross	Tower	NN 9976 1953	299760	719530	http://canmore.org.uk/site/25991
Woodhead	Perth & Kinross	Tower	NO 1438 3465	314380	734650	http://canmore.org.uk/site/28635
Woodlea	Perth & Kinross	Tower	NN 8304 0716	283040	707160	http://canmore.org.uk/site/25257

Appendix Two: Site Data

Notes: U = Unknown | Slope defined as being a difference greater than 10 metres in height across a site.

Table 14. Summary of site data for the Flavian fortress.

Inchtuthil Legionary Fortress													
Site Dating: Entrances (E); Finds (F); Morphology (M); Proximity (P); Radio Carbon dating (RC)	Fort Plateau Type: Hill (H); Slope (S); Plain (P)	Altitude of fortification (in metres)	Fortification plateau partially protected by edge of plateau/valley/river	Near entrance to valley or where valleys converge	Orientation - Cardinal Direction	Orientation - Degrees	Located near road	Located next to ford	Fortification within 2km of river (not streams)	Side of nearest river fortification is located	Fortification facing water?	Fortification near confluence of rivers
F	P	50			S	207	U			N		

Table 15. Summary of site data for the Flavian forts A-D.

	Forts																		
	Ardoch	Barochan Hill	Bertha	Birrens	Bochastle	Broomholm	Camelon North	Camelon South	Cappuck	Cardean	Cargill	Castledykes	Crawford	Dalginross	Dalswinton Bankfoot	Dalswinton Bankhead I	Dalswinton Bankhead II	Doune	Drumlanrig	Drumquhassle
Site Dating: Entrances (E); Finds (F); Morphology (M); Proximity (P); Radio carbon dating (RC)	F	F	F	F	F	F	F	F	F	F	F	F	F	F	P	F	F	E F	E	E F
Fort Plateau Type: Hill (H); Slope (S); Plain (P)	P	H	P	P	P	H	P	P	P	P	P	H	P	P	H	H	H	P	P	H
Altitude of fortification (in metres)	125	70	10	60	75	125	25	25	100	50	35	210	255	65	20	45	45	35	75	60
Fortification plateau partially protected by edge of plateau/valley/river																				
Near entrance to valley or where valleys converge																				
Orientation - Cardinal Direction	S	W	NE	S	N?	U	NE	U	S	NW	NW	S	SE	SW	U	SW	SE	SE	NW	SE
Orientation - Degrees	193	263	44	167			67	67?	192	303	311	192	144	233		212	126	124	332	154
Located near road		U			U	U						U					U			U
Located next to ford																				
Fortification within 2km of river (not streams)																				
Side of nearest river fortification is located	E	N/S	W	N	N/S	E	S	S	E	N/S	S	N/S	N	E/S	E	E	E	N	E	N
Fortification facing water?					U	U		U					U	U						
Fortification near confluence of rivers																				

Table 16. Summary of site data for the Flavian forts E-S.

	Forts											
	Easter Happrew	Elginhaugh	Fendoch	Glenlochar	Loudoun Hill	Malling	Milton	Mollins	Newstead I & II	Oakwood	Stracathro	Strageath
Site Dating: Entrances (E); Finds (F); Morphology (M); Proximity (P); Radio Carbon dating (RC)	F	F	F	F	F	P	F	F	F	F	E F	F
Fort Plateau Type: Hill (H); Slope (S); Plain (P)	S	P	H	P	S	P	S	P	S	H	P	P
Altitude of fortification (in metres)	215	70	210	50	190	20	105	65	120	250	45	35
Fortification plateau partially protected by edge of plateau/valley/river												
Near entrance to valley or where valleys converge												
Orientation - Cardinal Direction	SE	S	SW	W	NE	NE	U	U	W	E	U	W
Orientation - Degrees	140	186	219	263	40	67			253	70		270
Located near road			U	U		U		U		U		
Located next to ford												
Fortification within 2km of river (not streams)												
Side of nearest river fortification is located	N/S	N	SW	E		W	W	S	S	S	S	S/W
Fortification facing water?						U	U			U		
Fortification near confluence of rivers												

Table 17. Summary of site data for the Flavian fortlets.

	Fortlets								
	Bankhead (Carnwath)	Beattock Barnhill	Cargill	Castle Greg	Gatehouse of Fleet	Glenbank	Inverquharity	Kaims Castle	Kirkland
Site Dating: Entrances (E); Finds (F); Morphology (M); Proximity (P); Radio carbon dating (RC)	M	P	F	E F	F	P	M P	M P	M
Fort Plateau Type: Hill (H); Slope (S); Plain (P)	P	P	H	H	P	S	H	S	H
Altitude of fortification (in metres)	200	95	40	285	15	120	115	200	100
Fortification plateau partially protected by edge of plateau/valley/river									
Near entrance to valley or where valleys converge									
Orientation - Cardinal Direction	U	U	NW	NE	NE	NW	U	SE	U
Orientation - Degrees			325	66	42	325		121	
Located near road									U
Located next to ford									
Fortification within 2km of river (not streams)									
Side of nearest river fortification is located	N	N	S	W	E	S	S		S
Fortification facing water?	U	U							U
Fortification near confluence of rivers									

Table 18. Summary of site data for the Flavian camps A-C.

	Camps															
	Abernethy (Carey)	Ardoch II	Ardoch V	Auchinhove	Bankhead II (Carnwath)	Beattock, Bankend	Bellie (all sites)	Birrens	Bochastle I	Burnfield	Carlops Spittal	Castlecraig II	Castledykes IA & B	Castledykes IV	Cold Chapel	Cornhill
Site Dating: Entrances (E); Finds (F); Morphology (M); Proximity (P); Radio carbon dating (RC)	F M	M	M	E	E	E	P	E P	E F	M P	M	P	P	P	M	M
Fort Plateau Type: Hill (H); Slope (S); Plain (P)	P	S	P		P	P	P	P	P	S	H	H	P	S	P	S
Altitude of fortification (in metres)	10	150	130	105	215	100	25	70	75	90	34	260	210	200	230	235
Fortification plateau partially protected by edge of plateau/valley/river																
Near entrance to valley or where valleys converge																
Orientation - Cardinal Direction	U	U	U	SW	U	U	U	W	U	U	U	U	U	U	U	SW
Orientation - Degrees				207				255								214
Located near road	U			U		U		U	U							
Located next to ford																
Fortification within 2km of river (no streams)																
Side of nearest river fortification is located	S	E	E	N	E	W	E	S	N/S	S	N	N	N/S	N/S	E	E
Fortification facing water?	U	U	U		U	U	U	U		U	U	U	U	U	U	
Fortification near confluence of rivers																

Table 19. Summary of site data for the Flavian camps D-G.

	Camps																	
	Dalginross I	Dalswinton Bankfoot I	Dalswinton Bankfoot II	Denholm (Eastcote)	Drumlanrig Islafoot	Dun	Dunning	Durisdeer	Eshiels	Fendoch	Fourmerkland	Girvan Mains East	Girvan Mains West	Glenlochar I	Glenluce	Glenmailen (Ythan Wells) I	Glenmailen (Ythan Wells) II	Gogar Green
Site Dating: Entrances (E); Finds (F); Morphology (M); Proximity (P); Radio carbon dating (RC)	E P	E P	E P	M	P	E F	M	M	E	P	M	F P	F P	P	P	E P	E P	P
Fort Plateau Type: Hill (H); Slope (S); Plain (P)	P	P	P	P	P	P	H	S	P	P	P	P	S	P	H	H	H	P
Altitude of fortification (in metres)	65	20	20	80	60	10	65	165	155	76	30	15	20	55	45	250	175	50
Fortification plateau partially protected by edge of plateau/ valley/river																		
Near entrance to valley or where valleys converge																		
Orientation - Cardinal Direction	E	U	U	U	U	U	U	U	SW	U	E	U	U	U	SW	U	N	U
Orientation - Degrees	73								204		92				207		99	
Located near road	U			U		U	U		U	U	U	U	U	U		U	U	U
Located next to ford																		
Fortification within 2km of river (no streams)																		
Side of nearest river fortification is located	E	E	E	E/S	W	N	S	E	N	S	N	N	N	E	E	E	E	E
Fortification facing water?	U	U	U	U	U	U	U	U		U	U	U	U	U			U	U
Fortification near confluence of rivers																		

Appendix Two

Table 20. Summary of site data for the Flavian camps G-M.

	Camps												
	Gourdie (Steeds Stalls)	Dunblane (Hillside) I	Dunblane (Hillside) II	Inchtuthil I	Inchtuthil II	Inverquharity	Kintore	Kirkhouse	Lamington	Lochlands II, IV, VI	Logie Durno	Malling I	Malling II
Site Dating: Entrances (E); Finds (F); Morphology (M); Proximity (P); Radio carbon dating (RC)	P	E	E	M P	M P	E	RC	P	M	F	M	E P	E P
Fort Plateau Type: Hill (H); Slope (S); Plain (P)	S	H	H	P	P	F	S	s	p	P	H	P	P
Altitude of fortification (in metres)	125	115	115	50	50	120	60	270	215	25	125	20	20
Fortification plateau partially protected by edge of plateau/valley/river													
Near entrance to valley or where valleys converge													
Orientation - Cardinal Direction	U	SE	SE	U	U	N	U	SE	U	U	N	U	U
Orientation - Degrees		156	156	330	330	22		125			342		
Located near road	U			U	U		U				U	U	U
Located next to ford													
Fortification within 2km of river (no streams)													
Side of nearest river fortification is located		W	W	N	N	S	W		E	S	E	W	W
Fortification facing water?	U	U	U	U	U		U	U	U	U	U	U	U
Fortification near confluence of rivers													

Table 21. Summary of site data for the Flavian camps M-W.

	Camps												
	Milton	Muiryfold	Newstead I	Newstead II	Normandykes	Oakwood	Raeburnfoot	Raedykes	Stracathro	Wandel	Ward Law	Woodhead I	Woodhead II
Site Dating: Entrances (E); Finds (F); Morphology (M); Proximity (P); Radio carbon dating (RC)	P	E P	P	P	P	P	E	E	E P	P	P	E	E
Fort Plateau Type: Hill (H); Slope (S); Plain (P)	H	S	H	H	H	S	S	H	P	P	H	P	S
Altitude of fortification (in metres)	105	140	120	120	70	245	225	200	45	235	85	145	150
Fortification plateau partially protected by edge of plateau/valley/river													
Near entrance to valley or where valleys converge													
Orientation - Cardinal Direction	E	U	NE	U	E	SW	SW	U	U	U	U	SW	U
Orientation - Degrees	76		24		80	210	209					214	
Located near road		U			U			U	U		U		
Located next to ford													
Fortification within 2km of river (no streams)													
Side of nearest river fortification is located	W	N	S	S	N	S	E		S	E	W	W	W
Fortification facing water?	U	U		U		U		U	U	U	U	U	U
Fortification near confluence of rivers													

Index of Main Sites

Aberdeen, 117
Abernethy (Carey) (Camp), 7, 23, 28, 32, 59, 60, 83, 87, 107, 113, 114
Aberlady, 23, 110, 111
Antonine Wall, 1, 2, 3, 4, 11, 14, 19, 23, 34, 35, 36, 39, 40, 41, 51, 53, 56, 63, 64, 65, 75, 76, 77, 93, 95, 100, 104, 106, 110, 112, 113, 118, 122, 124, 129, 130, 131, 132
Ardoch (Fort, Camps II, V), 3, 7, 20, 21, 30, 33, 44, 55, 57, 58, 61, 70, 74, 80, 83, 84, 87, 93, 97, 99, 100, 107, 110, 128, 132
Ardunie (Tower), 7, 70, 72, 75, 114
Auchendavy (Fort), 95
Auchinhove (Camp), 2, 35, 53, 55, 66, 67, 87, 117, 118
Ayr (Camp), 7, 9, 17, 23, 33, 37, 43, 44, 59, 61, 106, 120, 121, 129, 139

Balmuildy (Fort), 93, 95
Bankhead (Carnwath) (Camp II, Fortlet), 5, 7, 20, 30, 55, 59, 66, 68, 83, 87, 92, 119, 121
Bar Hill (Fort), 5, 18, 30, 56, 65, 95
Barochan Hill (Fort), 7, 20, 44, 56, 57, 83, 84, 117, 119
Bearsden (Fort), 9, 33, 34, 51, 95
Beattock Summit (Tower), 7, 56, 57, 121
Beattock: Barnhill (Fortlet), 7, 21, 121
Beattock: Bankend (Camp), 7, 56, 87, 121
Beckfoot (Fort), 94, 97
Bellie (Camp), 5, 7, 27, 43, 87, 107, 117, 118
Benwell (Fort), 98
Bertha (Fort), 3, 7, 15, 21, 23, 26, 39, 55, 57, 61, 67, 71, 72, 73, 74, 75, 84, 93, 97, 99, 107, 108, 114, 115, 116, 130, 132, 135
Berwick Upon Tweet, 28, 108, 109
Birdoswald (Fort), 98
Birrens (Fort, Camp), 3, 7, 9, 17, 18, 34, 36, 55, 57, 61, 84, 87, 121
Bishopton (Whitemoss) (Fort), 23, 65, 95, 122, 124
Black Hill (By Ardoch) (Tower), 7, 70, 74, 75, 110
Black Hill (Tower), 7, 72, 73, 75
Blackness, 111
Bladnoch (Fortlet), 121
Bochastle (Fort, Camps), 7, 35, 43, 53, 55, 57, 74, 83, 84, 87, 110, 129, 134
Bowness-on-Solway (Fort), 94, 98
Brampton Old Church (Fort), 96
Bridgeness, 110, 111
Brigurd (Possible Harbour), 18, 23, 26, 118, 119, 120
Broomholm (Fort), 7, 44, 56, 84, 121
Burgh-by-Sands (Fort I, II, III), 96, 98
Burnfield (Camp), 7, 33, 35, 59, 87, 117
Burnswark, 16, 17, 19, 31, 97, 121, 128,
Burrow Walls (Fort), 94, 95

Cadder (Fort), 95, 119
Camelon North & South (Forts), 7, 12, 20, 21, 23, 55, 83, 84, 93, 95, 107, 110, 111, 112, 135,
Cappuck (Fort, Camp), 7, 28, 31, 84, 107, 108
Cardean (Fort), 7, 15, 55, 74, 84, 97, 114
Cargill (Fort, Fortlet), 7, 15, 20, 33, 56, 57, 59, 61, 72, 73, 74, 75, 84, 92, 97, 107, 114
Carham (Camp), 109
Carlisle (Fort), 12, 17, 36, 96, 108, 122, 128
Carlops Spittal (Camp), 7, 33, 53, 54, 59, 88, 110
Carnwath (*See* Bankhead)
Carpow (Vexillation Fortress), 18, 23, 28, 30, 113, 114, 124, 133
Carrawburgh (Fort), 98
Carriden (Fort), 23, 93, 95, 110, 112
Carvoran (Fort), 94, 98
Castlecary (Fort), 95
Castlecraig II (Camp), 88, 108
Castledykes (Fort, Camp IA & B, IV), 84, 88, 119
Castle Greg (Fortlet) 92
Castlesteads (Fort), 98
Castlehill (Fort), 95
Carvoran (Fort), 96
Castle Greg (Fortlet), 110
Castlecraig (Camp), 7, 33
Castledykes (Fort, Camps), 7, 12, 30, 43, 56, 66, 68, 80, 93, 107
Chapelburn (Fort) (*See* Nether Denton)
Chesters (Fort), 94, 98
Cold Chapel (Camp), 7, 33, 55, 88, 119, 129
Corbridge (Fort), 96
Cornhill (Camp), 7, 56, 83, 88, 119, 129
Cramond (Fort), 5, 12, 18, 23, 26, 97, 110, 111, 112, 124, 132
Crawford (Fort), 7, 23, 28, 30, 32, 33, 57, 73, 84, 93, 100, 101, 107, 113, 115, 117, 119, 128, 134
Croy Hill (Fort), 82, 95
Cumbrian Coast, 17, 94, 97, 113, 120, 122, 124, 132

Dalginross (Fort, Camp), 7, 30, 32, 33, 39, 44, 57, 74, 83, 85, 88, 93, 107, 114
Dalswinton: Bankhead (Fort), Bankfoot (Fort, Camp I, II) 7, 19, 31, 32, 36, 44, 56, 57, 66, 69, 80, 83, 85, 88, 121, 122
Denholm (Eastcote) (Camp), 7, 55, 88, 108, 109
Derder's Ford, 114-116
Dere Street, 33, 108, 110, 135
Doune (Fort), 7, 55, 57, 73 74, 85, 110, 130
Drumburgh (Fort), 94, 98
Drumlanrig (Fort), Islafoot (Camp), 7, 31, 32, 55, 85, 88, 121, 122
Drumquhassle (Fort), 7, 32, 56, 57, 85, 107, 119
Dumbarton, 23, 30, 106, 118, 119, 120

Facing the Enemy?

Dumbuck Hill, 23, 27, 30, 106, 118, 119
Dun (Camp), 7, 21, 23, 25, 37, 55, 59, 61, 88, 113, 114, 116, 117, 129
Dunbar, 106, 110, 111
Dunblane (*See* Hillside)
Dunning (Camp), 7, 28, 59, 65, 66, 74, 89, 114
Duntocher (Fort), 93, 95
Durisdeer (Camps), 7, 33, 56, 89, 121

Eastcote (*See* Denholm)
Easter Happrew (Fort), 7, 32, 33, 57, 85, 107, 108, 109
East Learmouth (Camp), 109
Eildon Hill North (Tower), 7, 57, 74, 76, 77
Elginhaugh (Fort), 7, 9, 12, 13, 32, 33, 85, 110, 111
Eshiels (Camp I), 7, 83, 89, 108, 109, 110
Ewes Doors (Tower), 31, 57, 121

Falkirk (Fort), 30, 95
Fendoch (Fort, Camp Redoubt), 7, 30, 42, 56, 57, 74, 85, 89, 107, 114, 130
Firths: Clyde, Forth, Moray, Tay, Solway (*See* Rivers)
Fourmerkland (Camp), 7, 31, 66, 69, 83, 89, 121

Gask House (Tower), 7, 30, 72, 74, 75, 114
Gask Ridge (*See also* individual fortifications),
Gatehouse of Fleet (Fortlet), 7, 20, 24, 59, 86, 92, 93, 121, 122, 128
Girvan Mains East & West (Camps), 7, 23, 33, 37, 59, 61, 89, 120, 121, 129
Glenbank (Fortlet), 7, 20, 55, 59, 63, 70, 74, 75, 92, 107, 110, 128
Glenlochar (Fort, Camp I), 7, 31, 57, 58, 59, 61, 83, 85, 89, 93, 107, 120, 121, 129
Glenluce (Camp), 7, 23, 33, 59, 83, 89, 120, 121, 122
Glenmailen (Ythan Wells) (Camp I, II), 5, 7, 83, 89, 117
Gogar Green (Camp), 7, 55, 89, 110, 112
Gourdie, Steeds Stalls (Camp), 7, 18, 90
Grassy Walls (Camp), 23, 67, 72, 73, 114, 115
Great Chesters (Fort), 94, 98
Greenloaning (*See* Woodlea)

Hadrian's Wall, 98
Halton Chesters (Fort), 98
Hillside, Dunblane (Camp I, II), 7, 73, 90, 110, 134
Hiltonshill (Camp), 7
Housesteads (Fort), 44, 65, 82, 94, 98
Huntingtower (*See* West Mains of Huntingtower)

Inchtuthil (Fortress, Camp I, II), 2, 7, 9, 12, 14, 18, 19, 21, 30, 35, 36, 39, 42, 44, 45, 46, 47, 48, 54, 57, 61, 67, 73, 74, 75, 83, 90, 100, 107, 114, 120, 136
Inveravon (Fort), 23, 95, 110, 111
Inveresk (Fort), 9, 23, 33, 34, 39, 110, 111, 112, 124, 132
Inverquharity (Camp, Fortlet), 7, 20, 23, 28, 35, 56, 59, 74, 90, 92, 97, 107, 114, 117, 132, 135

Kaims Castle (Fortlet), 7, 21, 55, 59, 63, 70, 74, 75, 92, 107, 128
Kintore (Camp), 3, 7, 9, 19, 31, 33, 34, 90, 97, 116, 117, 118

Kirkbride (Fort), 94, 96, 97
Kirkhill (Tower), 7, 72, 75, 114
Kirkhouse (Camp), 7, 33, 56, 83, 90, 107, 108
Kirkintilloch (Fort), 51, 95
Kirkland (Fortlet), 7, 20, 56, 59, 86, 92

Lamington (Camp), 7, 30, 90, 119
Lantonside (Fortlet), 23, 65, 120, 122, 123
Largs, 23, 118, 119, 120, 132
Leith, 23, 109, 110, 111, 112, 113
Lochlands (Camp I, II, IV, VI), 5, 7, 19, 20, 30, 33, 80, 83, 90, 91, 110
Logie Durno (Camp), 7, 91, 97, 117
Loudon Hill (Fort), 28, 55, 57, 67, 83, 85, 118, 119, 120, 134
Loudoun Hill (*See* Loudon Hill),
Lurg Moor (Fortlet), 65, 122, 124, 132
Lyne (Fortlet, Camp II), 30, 93, 108, 109, 110

Malling (Fort, Camp I, II), 7, 55, 57, 85, 91, 110
Maryport (Fort), 94, 97
Maxton (Camp), 30, 109
Mertoun Bridge (*See* St Boswalls)
Milltimber (Camp), 3, 7, 9, 17, 33, 43, 44, 116, 117, 118
Milton (Fort, Camp), 7, 16, 20, 33, 44, 55, 57, 85, 86, 91, 121, 124
Mollins (Fort), 20, 28, 32, 44, 55, 86, 119
Montrose Bay (*See* Rivers)
Moresby (Fort), 94, 97
Moss Side (Tower), 7, 23, 72, 74, 75, 114, 118, 122, 124
Muir O' Fauld (Tower), 7, 72, 74, 75, 114
Muiryfold (Camp), 7, 35, 55, 66, 67, 91, 117
Mumrills (Fort), 93, 95

Nether Denton (Chapelburn) (Fort), 96
Newcastle Upon Tyne (Fort), 98
Newstead (Fort I, II, Camp I, II), 3, 7, 9, 12, 21, 26, 27, 30, 33, 34, 55, 57, 63, 74, 76, 83, 86, 91, 93, 108, 109, 110, 134
Nigg, 117, 118
Norham (Camp), 109
Normandykes (Camp), 7, 33, 59, 60, 91, 117, 118

Oakwood (Fort, Camp), 7, 32, 56, 57, 65, 76, 77, 86, 91, 107, 108, 134
Old Kilpatrick (Fort), 23, 95
Outerwards (Fortlet), 124, 132

Parkneuk (Tower), 7, 72, 114
Peel (Tower), 7, 67, 71, 75, 114

Raeburnfoot (Camp), 7, 56, 59, 83, 91, 93, 121, 129
Raedykes (Camp), 7, 17, 31, 56, 66, 83, 91, 117
Raith (Tower), 7, 70, 72, 75, 114
Ravenglass (Fort), 94, 97
Rivers & Waterways (Including Firths):
    Caron, 20, 39
    Clyde, 1, 2, 10, 11, 12, 13, 14, 20, 23, 27, 28, 33, 35, 40, 55, 65, 82, 93, 106, 108, 118, 119, 120, 122, 124, 125, 132, 135

Dee, 117, 118
   Forth, 1, 2, 10, 11, 12, 13, 14, 20, 23, 28, 35, 40, 47,
      55, 93, 105, 106, 108, 110, 111, 112, 113, 124,
      125, 132, 135
   Isla, 57
   Montrose Bay, 21, 25, 113, 116, 117
   Moray Firth, 3, 11, 12, 35, 49, 53, 66, 116, 117, 118,
      129, 135,
   Nith, 122
   Solway Firth, 2, 11, 12, 13, 17, 65, 94, 106, 107, 120,
      121, 122, 130, 132
   Spey, 11, 116, 118
   Tay, 13, 18, 21, 23, 26, 35, 43, 52, 55, 57, 59, 99,
      105, 106, 107, 108, 109, 113, 114, 115, 124, 125,
      135
   Teith, 55, 73
   Tweed, 2, 27, 108, 109, 110, 125
Rough Castle (Fort), 95
Roundlaw (Tower), 7, 72, 75, 114
Rubers Law, 30, 76, 109
Rudchester (Fort), 98

Scone Park (Camp), 23, 67, 72
Shielhill North (Tower), 7, 70, 75, 156
Shielhill South (Tower), 7, 70, 75, 110, 156
South Shields (Fort), 98
Stanegate, 2, 3, 11, 12, 17, 63, 82, 94, 96
Stanwix (Fort), 98
St Boswalls (Mertoun Bridge) (Camp), 109
Stirling, 23, 106, 108, 110, 111, 124, 135
Stonehaven, 20, 23, 30, 116, 117, 129
Stracathro (Fort, Camp), 7, 12, 20, 23, 31, 32, 35, 55, 57,
   83, 86, 92, 97, 107, 109, 117, 129
Strageath (Fort), 3, 7, 9, 12, 18, 21, 30, 33, 67, 70, 73, 74,
   75, 83, 86, 93, 107, 114, 129, 132

Thorny Hill (Tower), 7, 72, 75, 114
Tyninghame, 23, 110, 111

Vindolanda (Fort, Tablets), 14, 96, 104

Wallsend (Fort), 98
Wandel (Camp), 7, 33, 55, 92, 119
Ward Law (Fort), 7, 23, 31, 59, 61, 65, 86, 92, 107, 120,
   121, 122, 123, 129
West Mains of Huntingtower (Tower), 7, 75, 114
Westerton (Tower), 7, 70, 74, 75, 114
Westerwood (Fort), 93, 95
Westmuir (Tower), 7, 30, 67, 72, 75, 114
Whitemoss (*See* Bishopton)
White Type (Tower), 30, 121
Witch Knowe (Tower), 7, 72, 74, 75, 114
Wooden Home Farm (Camp), 31, 109
Woodhead (Camp I, II), 7, 83, 86, 92, 110
Woodhead (Tower), 7, 30, 67, 73, 75, 110, 114
Woodlea (Greenloaning) (Tower), 7, 70, 75, 110

Ythan Wells (Camps) (*See* Glenmailen)

Lightning Source UK Ltd.
Milton Keynes UK
UKHW051218041122
411566UK00008B/53